Stories and Their Limits

Reflective Bioethics
Edited by Hilde Lindemann Nelson & James Lindemann Nelson

Also published in the series:

Do We Still Need Doctors?
John D. Lantos, M.D.

The Patient in the Family: An Ethics of Medicine and Families
Hilde Lindemann Nelson & James Lindemann Nelson

Stories and Their Limits

Narrative Approaches to Bioethics

Edited and with an Introduction by
Hilde Lindemann Nelson

ROUTLEDGE
New York *and* London

This book is for Jim, who plots with me.

Published in 1997 by
Routledge
29 West 35th Street
New York, NY   10001

Published in Great Britain by
Routledge
11 New Fetter Lane
London EC4P   4EE

Copyright © 1997 by Routledge
Printed in the United States of America on acid-free paper.
Book design by Charles B. Hames

Library of Congress Cataloging-in-Publication Data
Stories and their limits : narrative approaches to bioethics / edited and
with an introduction by Hilde Lindemann Nelson.
       p.   cm.
   Includes bibliographical references and index.
   ISBN 0-415-91909-6 (hb.)   ISBN 0-415-91910-X (pbk.)
    1. Medical ethics—Methodology.   2. Narration (Rhetoric)—Moral
and ethical aspects.   3. Storytelling—Moral and ethical aspects.
4. Medicine in literature.   I. Nelson, Hilde Lindemann.
   R725.5.S76   1997
   174'.2—dc21
                                                  97-36487
                                                  CIP

Contents

III. Literary Criticism in the Clinic

IV. Narratives Invoked

Introduction

How to Do Things with Stories

Hilde Lindemann Nelson

Tom Brown, who is recovering from a long illness, lies in his hospital bed, bored, restless, and at a loose end. His friend John Smith comes in once again, this time with a book that Brown has been wanting to read. On his many previous visits, the faithful Smith, a colleague of Brown's in the philosophy department, has always brought something—a rose from his garden, a crossword puzzle, fruit to tempt a fretful appetite. Brown thinks to himself, and not for the first time, what a good and true friend Smith has proved to be. He thanks him profusely, grateful for the kindness that brings Smith all the way across town to cheer him up. So effusive is he that Smith protests he's always tried to do his duty, to do what he judges best. At first Brown thinks Smith is engaging in self-deprecation out of a sense of politeness or concern to keep Brown from feeling beholden to him. But as the two men talk, it dawns on Brown that Smith means exactly what he says: he's not been visiting because he likes Brown, not because he and Brown are friends, but because he thought it his duty as a colleague and knows of no one more in need of cheering up. When he understands this, Brown feels flat, even ill-used. He can't help thinking there's something missing from Smith's view of the moral life.[1]

Depending on whom you ask, the moral life is mainly a matter of various trainings, right reason, virtuous habits, rules that tell you when you go right and when you go wrong, taking others' interests seriously, freedom of agency, benevolence and other moral emotions, previously established interpersonal practices of responsibility, a reasonably just society, or any combination of the above. Some of these elements have received considerably more theoretical scrutiny than others. In the twentieth century, for example, moral philosophers (among them, Brown's friend Smith) have largely been preoccupied with duties derived from right reason—the part of morality that involves making and justifying decisions about what should be done. Even those who put a premium on abstract, propositional reasoning, however, are generally willing to acknowledge that it is not the whole of morality.

Recently there has been an upsurge of philosophical attention to the question of whether, either in conjunction with or instead of some of the aforementioned elements, *narratives* might not play a central role in the moral life. Do bedtime stories mold character? Do movies and plays install or shift a society's ethical norms? Do our practices of accountability provide the plots for the stories we enact as we live out our lives? Do the tales we swap with friends or coworkers offer guidance about what is the best thing to do? And, if narratives do inform the moral life in any of these ways, *ought* they so to inform it?

Who Uses Narrative Approaches?

Philosophers in England and the U.S. began to develop their current interest in narrative approaches to ethics more than a decade ago. Bernard Williams, Michael Stocker, Lawrence Blum, Jeffrey Blustein, Annette Baier, Margaret Urban Walker,[2] and others gave moral theory a "personal turn" by challenging the orthodox assumption that ethics has primarily to do with right conduct among strangers, is universalizable, and favors no one. The motivation for the personal turn was perhaps expressed most trenchantly in Williams's well-known observation that the theoretically unlimited demands of impartialist systems of morality elbow out much that gives meaning to life, including anything that could inspire us to take any moral goal seriously.

Stocker raised a rather different, but related, point. Because impartialist systems are impersonal, they cannot capture what is morally significant about such interpersonal relationships as friendship, love, or community. As Stocker put it, "The defect of these theories in regard to love, to take one case, is not that they do not value love (which often they do not) but that they do not value the beloved."[3] What drops out of account, as my opening story about Brown and Smith is intended to reveal, are the *persons* who must be valued if friendship or love are to have any moral significance at all.

The task for those who were troubled by impartialist ethical theories, then, became one of constructing an ethics that honors the personal and the particular, but does so in a nonarbitrary way. Because narratives permit philosophers to work "up close"—to put faces on faceless generalizations, to take the particulars of a given situation carefully into account—they have become an important tool for this kind of construction. Narrative approaches to ethics have in general been based on two interrelated propositions. The first is that moral principles are not lawlike, universal, and unyielding, but modifiable in light of the particulars of a given experience or situation. The second is that these particulars either naturally take a narrative form or must be given a narrative structure if they are to have moral meaning.

It's not only personalist moral philosophers who have conjoined narrative and ethics, however. Religious studies scholars have done so as well. In their landmark 1977 criticism of contemporary ethical theory's overreliance on abstract reason, David Burrell and Stanley Hauerwas[4] argued that when we separate moral reasoning from the narrative contexts in which it goes on (and they had in mind the tradition of Judeo-Christian narratives in particular), we produce impoverished and distorted accounts of our experience as moral agents. Their claim was that ethical principles alone cannot adequately guide deliberation about any particular state of affairs—a claim that was to receive a great deal of attention in religious studies in the following decade. Indeed, their insight extends beyond moral deliberation. For Jews, Christians, and Moslems, God acts in and through history, so that when something happens, where it happens, and with whom God is interacting just then are of crucial importance. Moreover, many of the classical religious teachers—in other traditions as well as Western—use parables rather than principles to teach religious truths. When asked, "Who is my neighbor?" Jesus doesn't supply a classificatory scheme; he says, "A certain man went down from Jerusalem to Jericho. . . ."

Perhaps the most significant ethical turn in literary criticism has been the emergence of the subfield of narratology, which developed out of structuralist linguistics. Structuralism offered formal, scientific accounts of the grammar and deep structure of language, based on differences in sound production that could be marked, mapped, and classified. Entertaining the possibility that narratives too might have a grammar and deep structure, Vladimir Propp, Tzvetan Todorov, Claude Lévi-Strauss, Roland Barthes, and others applied structuralist methodology to folktales, films, and other narrative forms. In the 1960s Jacques Derrida[5] and others challenged the French structuralists' "lab coat" approach to literature, arguing that a purely formal system of linguistic differences can refer to nothing outside itself and so is incapable of anchoring meaning—whether moral, social, or aesthetic. The earlier work of Mikhail M. Bakhtin[6] now helped linguistic structuralism refocus on narrative's social dynamics: he and Fredric Jameson[7] offered powerful demonstrations of how the analysis of form could be used to critique social ideologies.

Since then, narratologists such as Hayden White, Paul Ricoeur, Girard Genette, Gerald Prince, and Seymour Chatman have continued to develop the theoretical basis for the social critique that now dominates narratology. Their work raises a number of questions. How does meaning enter into narrative systems, given that their logic arises (as White claims) not from any inherent logic of events in the world, but from the purely human activity that shapes and orders these events? What connects the reality of the text with social realities such that the critiques of gender, empire, and other ideologies that now form the bulk of narratology are relevant to both? And from what do these critiques draw their moral force? These and similar questions continue to dog narrative approaches to ethics, whether within narratology or outside it.

Five Things to Do with Stories

It seems to me that the various narrative approaches to ethics fall into roughly five categories, each of which works with stories in a different way. The first approach is to read stories (or listen to them, or view them). Here the idea is to attend carefully to the nuances and complexities of great literature, films, or plays as a means of sharpening one's moral sensibilities. Martha Nussbaum[8] is perhaps best known for her exploration of the role of literature in developing the moral emotions. By reading serious fiction, she argues, one can make of oneself a person "on whom nothing is lost." One does this by allowing the author of the work to direct one's attention to the rich and subtle particulars of the narrative—the moral, intellectual, emotional, and social nuances. When the author has set these out with skill and imagination, overlooking no meaningful detail, the reader can see what is morally at issue in the narrative: she becomes "finely aware and richly responsible."

Political reasoning, too, can benefit from the emotions evoked by the literary imagination. As Nussbaum observes in the preface to *Poetic Justice*, "the ability to imagine the concrete ways in which people different from oneself grapple with disadvantage" can have great public and practical value, given the vast amounts of racism, homophobia, ethnic animosity, sexism, and other invidious hatreds that run rampant in the world. Nussbaum is quick to point out that the literary imagination will not always prevail against deep prejudices, but the proper response to this failure, she argues, is not to repudiate the imagination but to cultivate it more consistently and humanely.

A second approach is that of *telling* stories. In this approach, one makes moral sense of something by choosing particulars from the array of experience and looking at them in the light of relevant moral ideas. One example of this sort of storytelling is the narrative activity that Margaret Urban Walker calls "strong moral self-definition."[9] Walker describes how a morally developed person can turn to her own personal history to help her make a decision in the present moment that best reflects who she is and wants to be. As she looks back over her life, she can either ratify a course of action on which she has already embarked, or repudiate it and set a new course. Either way, by what she does now she installs precedents for herself that commit her to future courses of action. These precedents, Walker argues, are also morally self-defining. As Walker acknowledges, the ongoing stories have their own inertia, entailing commitments the agent didn't intend and imposing burdens the agent didn't want. Nor are such stories entirely of the agent's own making: the stories others tell about us can strongly define us as well.

My own work[10] has recently been devoted to the stories that dominant members of a community tell about marginalized and oppressed others to keep them in their place. I have been exploring the conditions under which counter-stories—stories of resistance and insubordination told or enacted by the oppressed or on their behalf—exert pressure against these stories of domination, allowing the oppressed to decline the identities their oppressors have constructed for them, and so to gain access to more of the good things their community has to offer.

A third approach is to *compare*, rather than read or tell, stories. Albert Jonsen and Stephen Toulmin[11] are among the most vocal advocates of a revival, particularly for use in bioethics, of the medieval Christian practice of comparing cases of conscience to provide moral guidance in specific, concrete situations. In its current form, the case-based approach works like this: a particular case is analyzed in terms of formal topics (for example, in clinical ethics the topics might be medical indications, patient preferences, quality of life, and context of care) that permit one to note its similarities to a paradigm case. The paradigm case is the one that displays most visibly the moral maxims and principles that guide action in "cases of this sort." Analogous cases are those in which particular circumstances justify qualifications of the principles or exceptions to the general maxim. By clustering cases around a paradigm case in which one already knows what to do, one can reason by analogy about what to do in the case at hand.

A fourth approach to ethics is that of *literary analysis*. Here one applies the tools of textual criticism either to stories that are explicit narratives or to a social practice that one treats as a literary text. An illness narrative, promotion and tenure policies within the academy, a corporation's mission statement, federal guidelines for the disposal of biohazardous wastes could in principle all be explained, challenged, or otherwise interpreted by using a hermeneutics grounded in some form of literary criticism.

Some literary critics have explicitly taken themselves to be "doing" ethics. Others, including several contributors to this volume, do not think of themselves as ethicists; rather, they would say they use their knowledge of literature to illuminate social practice. But what are they illuminating? When, for example, they bring literary criticism to bear on medicine, they are uncovering moral meanings of health and illness, identifying what counts as a virtuous practice of medicine, noting how ethical responsibilities are assigned within this practice, explaining what condemns or excuses people in the context of the clinic, describing how such identities as "noncompliant patient," "negligent practitioner," or "compassionate medical student" come into existence, or attending to a host of other matters that bear directly on the moral values operating within medicine. If "doing ethics" means developing and defending formal ethical systems, then they are not doing ethics. But if it means reflecting on the moral aspects of particular encounters within a powerful social institution where what is said and done reveals a great deal about who we are and what matters in our lives, then they are indeed ethicists, in at least a loose sense of that word.

Somewhere in the neighborhood of these four categories is a fifth thing to do with stories: *invoke* them. We invoke a story when, for instance, we employ it to make or illustrate a moral point; fables, parables, and funny or telling anecdotes are generally used in this way. Cautionary tales are often invoked as well: "Little Red Riding Hood" is used to warn little girls (and big ones too) of the dangers of speaking to strangers. Bioethics case studies are often invoked to validate a particular ethical perspective; their sketchiness tends to drive a specific conclusion even when they masquerade as a genuinely neutral telling of the story for purposes of moral exploration. That legal cases can be invoked is perhaps their greatest strength, as invocation is the means by which they set precedents and build up the body of the law. And like bioethics cases, some legal cases become oft-invoked myths: think of *Brown v. Board of Education*, for example, or, more negatively, *Bowers v. Hardwick*. Stories, it seems, serve many moral purposes, whether they are read, told, compared, analyzed, or invoked.

Criticisms of Narrative Approaches to Ethics

Although many people have enthusiastically adopted one or more of these narrative approaches to ethics, others have been more skeptical, arguing that when it comes to ethical analysis, stories have their limits. It does seem that the approaches could go wrong unless care is taken to keep the narrative particulars firmly anchored to the moral resources at hand. I can think of two ways in which they might come apart.

The first way is if the moral ideas should fail to guide the instant case. This, I think, is likely to happen when the moral terms are conceived as lawlike principles that float above the particular story instead of interacting with its details. Narrative approaches above all others must avoid this pitfall, as the narrative turn in ethics arose largely out of the perception that Kantian and utilitarian systems of morality go wrong in just this way.

Narrative approaches that successfully resolve the "floating" problem are arguably those in which the principles are just as subject to reexamination in light of the particulars of the situation as the other way around. For example, instead of retaining a fixed notion of justice as an impartial principle for distributing benefits and burdens without respect of person, one might allow the history of interactions among bonded siblings looking after a frail elderly parent to point to a rather different understanding of justice when the context is one of intimacy. Justice in this context might be reconceived as apportioning time, energy, and resources differently on different occasions, depending on who needs what, while at the same time ensuring that all members of the family are valued and respected. Here the particulars of the family's history point to a new understanding of a principle, which may, in turn, show up the relevance of other particulars, which may lead us to revise our view of other principles, and so on, until particulars and principles are in an equilibrium that points to a specific understanding of the instant state of affairs. To put this point in a slightly different way, just as a narrative's selection and ordering of the particulars of experience must be guided by relevant principles and values if it is to do the work of ethics, so too must our understanding of what exactly the principle entails be guided by the narrative if the principle is to have any practical force.

The second way in which narrative approaches to ethics could go wrong is if a narrative were illicitly to feature too narrow a preferred subset of the relevant moral ideas. If we are deliberating together, for example, about the wisdom of legalizing physician-assisted suicide, *my* fine-grained Nussbaumian perception may show me a person who courageously seeks to end her life with dignity, while *your* fine-grained perception shows you that same person engaged in a selfish act of cowardly escape. My moral imagination inclines me to favor one set of ethical understandings; yours champions another. So how does reading great literature provide us with a basis for agreement about what it is best to do?

My own (tentative) answer is that stories aren't much help in settling these differences because they cannot exhaust the work of moral justification any more than principles can, although their usefulness for moral discovery, their role in revising moral understandings, and their ability to help us make moral sense of our lives do contribute significantly to this work. A good story of the kind Nussbaum has in mind is one that broadens our imaginations, showing us the significance of things we had previously overlooked as we attempt to assess a particular practice. A good story will also give us a clearer idea of what we mean by such moral concepts as honesty, kindness, respect for another's dignity, and so on. But it is bound to privilege certain of these concepts over others, to take some but not all possible ethical stances. It is, after all, in the nature of narrative to be selective, to foreground certain moral motifs, to keep others hovering discreetly at a distance, and to hide still others altogether from view. Indeed, we are often drawn to particular narratives because they enrich our understanding of the moral ideas to which we are already firmly committed.

If, then, we find our imaginations gripped by a story whose moral resources are lopsided or too narrowly confined to one ethical point of view, we will get from it relatively little guidance. When several very different stories can be told about the same request for physician-assisted suicide, to cleave to our earlier example, then we need to go to work to see if they all square equally well with all the available information, whether the characters portrayed by the various stories are plausible in light of what we know about people in general and these people in particular, whether the principles, virtues, and values in play are intelligible in terms of the details of the stories, and so on. Then we need to try to harmonize or mesh or sort out the differences among the several stories told about this request. And if the stories obstinately refuse to mesh, then either we don't know enough of the particulars of the situation or else we don't have shared moral understandings at all, but conflicting understandings that do not—cannot—themselves specify how they apply to this situation. When there is ethical disagreement about a course of action, we are forced to fall back on the reasons we can give for taking the moral positions we do. It's these reasons that allow us, if anything does, to choose between my perception and yours.

But this is only my own response to one set of difficulties concerning the uses of narrative for ethics. There are other problems and other attempts to solve them, and all of this has begun to make up a growing debate about how useful narrative approaches to ethics actually are. Even among those who find them very useful indeed, there are perplexities about which bits of the moral life are most fruitfully examined when approached through narratives, and just how far such an approach can take us.

Narrative Approaches to Bioethics

This collection engages that debate not as it has to do with ethics generally, but as it has been conducted in one of ethics' subfields. Narratives have played a prominent role in the new and rapidly growing interdisciplinary field of bioethics ever since it was first created some quarter of a century ago. All bioethicists work with cases, whether the court cases that have shaped health policy about such matters as withholding or withdrawing life-sustaining treatment, bioethics cases that permeate the literature and are a staple of any ethics committee's diet, or medical charts, such as those recently used in the well-publicized SUPPORT study that examined how Americans die in hospitals. Some bioethicists have also told their own stories as a means of getting at bioethical nuances of various kinds. Others have conducted thoughtful metaethical discussions of the sorts of tasks (if any at all) narratives are fitted for within bioethics. And because the practice of medicine has often been the subject matter for exalted works of literary fiction as well as attracting more humble forms of storytelling, theorists within the medical humanities have been very interested in bringing great literature to bear on medical practice.

These essays, representing both the scholars who use narratives to do ethical work of one kind or another and those who reflect on the nature and limits of such work, grew out of the 1996 spring meeting of the Society for Health and Human Values, which was hosted by the University of Tennessee's Center for Applied and Professional Ethics. Leading figures in bioethics and the medical humanities were invited to meet in Knoxville to air their differences over narrative approaches and to seek common ground. Younger voices also joined the fray, and one result is the seventeen essays that form this collection. The essays represent a wide range of interests, trainings, and points of view. They were written by physicians, literary critics, religious studies scholars, philosophers, sociologists, a comparatist. Some have newly entered bioethics; others helped to found the field. Here, then, is an overview of the collection.

I. Telling the Patient's Story

THOMAS H. MURRAY wants to know what we mean by "narrative ethics." He sketches four uses of the concept: narrative as moral education, narrative as moral methodology, narrative as an appropriate form of moral discourse, and narrative in moral justification. The first of these he finds relatively uncontroversial: most people learn most of what they know about morality from narratives of one kind or another. The second is more problematic, and Murray concludes that case-based methodologies do not tell us everything. But he does think that much moral discourse is embedded within, conditioned by, and conducted through narratives. Finally, he believes that the narratives by which we understand ourselves and those around us are crucial raw materials for making and justifying moral judgments.

HOWARD BRODY, in reflecting on Arthur Frank's *The Wounded Storyteller,* asks: Who gets to tell the story? He is sympathetic to Frank's postmodern argument that the practice of medicine is a political practice, and that this has implications for physicians' modernist claims to objective knowledge about their patients. If, Brody argues, physicians take refuge behind objectivity and so remain detached from their patient's suffering, then they hinder rather than help with the construction of the patient's story, the patient's suffering remains without meaning, and healing is rendered impossible. Brody examines Frank's insights critically, asking what challenges they pose not only to the medical profession, but to bioethics as well.

ARTHUR W. FRANK considers stories by patients that are neither told nor written, but enacted. He borrows Louis Althusser's idea that an ideology "hails" people and so imposes an identity on them. People can, he considers, be strongly hailed by the ideology of medicine and end up with a new identity: that of patient-with-a-diagnosis. At the same time as patients embrace what medicine has to offer them, however, they may resist full identification with the persona that medicine requires them to be. This resistance can take the form of narrative enactments, where patients, when outside the medical gaze, behave in ways that say: I am not what you have tried to make me be. Frank concludes by explaining the value of telling stories and attending to the stories of others.

JOHN HARDWIG, like Brody, is interested in who gets to tell the patient's story. He argues that patient autobiographies are epistemically suspect, and that exclusive trust in them weakens the practice of medicine. Because ignorance, innocent mistakes, self-deception, and lies can make autobiography particularly unreliable, caregivers who take these stories at face value may be deceived in their belief that they know the patient's interests and wishes. Moreover, insisting on the primacy of autobiography can harm those most closely connected to the patient, for they come to matter only as minor characters in the patient's story. Hardwig calls for bioethicists and clinicians to become biographers, weaving the patient's story together with others that bear on it in the clinical encounter.

JOHN D. ARRAS poses the "so what?" question: It's a nice story, but so what? He first considers the idea that narrative is a supplement to principlist ethics and agrees that it is indeed a powerful corrective to the abstractness of principle-driven approaches. Next he inspects the view that narrative is the very ground of all moral justification, a view that, he thinks, risks falling back into principlism or sinking into a relativistic slough of incommensurable narratives. Finally he canvasses the place of narrative within postmodern ethics, where it appears to substitute for ethical justification. This view he rejects altogether, arguing that postmodern approaches to ethics risk mistaking the authenticity of the narrator for ethical truth and often ignore the larger social picture.

II. Reading Narratives of Illness

RITA CHARON offers a close and attentive reading of Henry James's *The Wings of the Dove* to show how its two leading characters undergo journeys of moral development. She argues that the dying Milly Theale and the unscrupulous Merton Densher, who marries Milly for her money so that after her death he may lay his new-found wealth at the feet of the woman he loves, both struggle toward the right way to live, searching for goodness and ultimately attaining it. Examining the novel's structure, points of view, and narrative voices, Charon explains how considerations of James's method merge into considerations of the reader's experience of the book: the reader is called on to see Milly through her ordeal with an attention that is morally redemptive.

CHARLES WEIJER notes that film has received little attention from bioethicists, either as a source of stories or as an alternative medium for storytelling. He examines several narrative devices employed in Akira Kurosawa's 1952 film, *Ikiru* ("To Live"). The film tells the story of the last five months in the life of a bureaucrat, Kanji Watanabe, who is dying of stomach cancer. Weijer describes and critiques, from *Ikiru*'s decidedly postmodern perspective, current views of life-narrative in bioethics, including what he calls the "self-authored life-narrative" and the "jointly authored life-narrative." He notes that a postmodern understanding of life-narrative implies the need for a new approach to collecting information about patients' lives.

TOM TOMLINSON is perplexed about narrative ethics—particularly, about what role literary narratives might play in moral justification. He argues that anything a narrative can do to help us understand and sympathize with others can be done more directly by other means. Similarly, he does not see how narratives bridge the gap between abstract principles and the concrete circumstances of real cases; they cannot, he thinks, resolve interpretive conflicts. And he also rejects the idea that the unity of an ongoing life-narrative can serve as a standard for judging the moral worth of decisions made within it, as that unity can offer only coherence and not moral warrant. However, he believes a close look at a genuine narrative could show how ethical principle is mediated by special narrative competencies.

MARK KUCZEWSKI parts company with Tomlinson, arguing not only that narrative approaches are useful, but that there is a strong consensus among bioethicists regarding the importance of narrative for bioethical methodology. He summarizes seven points of consensus about method, all of which are constructed around a double center: a conception of narrative ethics and a corresponding agent of a certain character, judgment, or virtue who is essential to the narrative conception. After a look at criticisms that the agreed-upon methodology is too inflexible to deal with other cultures or so pliable that it fails to provide guidance, he argues that these criticisms are far less of a problem than is the inability to convince dissenters that they should become a part of the consensus-building process.

III. Literary Criticism in the Clinic

ANNE HUNSAKER HAWKINS uses James Joyce's concept of the "epiphany"—a sudden revelation of profound meaning—to describe an element in the way physicians perceive and resolve ethical issues. Epiphanic knowing is not arrived at through discursive reasoning, but is experienced as abrupt and all of a piece: the penny drops. Noting that the epiphanies of literary narratives can help us to understand what is morally meaningful about even the most trivial events, she claims that physicians who are aware of the epiphanic dimensions of their ordinary interactions with patients will be better able to recognize the ethical issues embedded in a patient's narrative, and this will have a powerful impact on the way they practice medicine. She concludes with two narratives of physicians' epiphanic knowing.

TOD CHAMBERS uses the tools of narratology to theorize the bioethics case as literary text. He contends that the features of reportability, action, tempo, and closure are part of the defining characteristics of the bioethics case as a distinct genre, and that these characteristics raise certain expectations in readers as to what is morally relevant about the case. The expectations raised by the genre in turn condition the type of information included for—and excluded from—consideration. Because cases are based on plot rather than character, for example, the virtue ethicist's concern with moral development seems beside the point. Understanding what the genre excludes thus permits bioethicists to resist the potential tyranny of this highly stylized form of narrative.

MARTHA MONTELLO argues that the same literary skills that critical readers use to interpret a story allow clinicians to respond to the moral realities embedded in people's lives. Narrative competence, then, is a necessary element of moral competence. But of what does it consist? How is it acquired? And how does it enhance physicians' capacities for moral reasoning? Montello explains how three processes within the reader—departure, performance, and change—are set into motion by reading, and shows how similar processes enhance physicians' moral response to patients. Narrative competence can help physicians negotiate a balance between involvement and detachment, alter their perspectives regarding patients, and change themselves through the experience of another's suffering.

JAN MARTA employs the critical theory of Paul Ricoeur to challenge the dominant model of informed consent. She contends that a narrative hermeneutic approach to informed consent can increase sensitivity to individual, relational, and cultural factors by reformulating the consent process as an experiential, expressive, and interpretive act. On this approach, physician and patient structure the stories of the patient's illness and the physician's medical interventions as interconnected persons, alternately narrator and listener, and in interconnected roles, informer and consenter. Seen as a performative speech act, informed consent twins patient and physician within individual and collective narratives that are continually reinterpreted and refigured.

IV. Narratives Invoked

KATHRYN MONTGOMERY HUNTER conceives of the practical reasoning of the physician as a patchwork of diagnostic and therapeutic plots, summarized and expressed in the aphorisms, old saws, and rules of thumb that are invoked in clinical education and the care of patients. Calling them clinical medicine's operational rules, Hunter examines maxims concerned with history-taking, the physical examination, diagnostic reasoning, and therapeutic choice. While aphorisms are often contradictory, Hunter sees that as a strength, as their paradoxes preserve genuine tensions and conflicting goals in medical practice. Always contextual and interpretive, aphorisms are a reminder to physicians that the practice of medicine is a balancing act.

RONALD A. CARSON invokes James Dickey's poem, "The Celebration," to illustrate his contention that David Burrell and Stanley Hauerwas had the better of the exchange with Edmund Pellegrino several decades ago. Hauerwas and Burrell famously argued that narrative is a form of rationality better suited to ethics than is reasoning by abstract moral principles. Pellegrino objected, pointing out that stories cannot uncover moral truth. Carson now replies that they do something better: they presuppose faith in the followability of experience, not only in the connectedness of events but in how these connections disclose to us something about ourselves or about the human condition that we need to know. His exegesis of Dickey's poem shows what such disclosure can be.

LOIS LACIVITA NIXON invokes literature, art, poetry, and film to show medical students what it means to be human. Poetry and the other arts, she argues, serve as a corrective to the rigidity, hierarchy, and authoritarianism that pervade medical culture. She sees her function as similar to that of I. M. Pei's "Pyramide" in the courtyard of the Louvre—an installation that disrupts the received culture while simultaneously inviting new ways of seeing. The role of the humanities in medical schools, Nixon believes, is to allow students to gain practice in experiencing unsettling ideas so that, when they become doctors, they can better respond to life's complexities. They may be trained in square rooms, she concludes, but (to invoke Wallace Stevens) they face a world of "rhomboids, cones, waving lines."

JAMES F. CHILDRESS is given the last word. He argues that the debate about norms versus narratives in ethics is largely misplaced. Not only do many different positions fall under each category, but proponents of each share more with the other than they recognize. He focuses first on the dispute between casuists and principlists, maintaining that principles needn't be considered invariant and eternal, and that the relationship between them and particular case judgments is best seen as dialectical. Then he turns to the role of narratives of different kinds in explicating requirements of the principle of respect for persons, using the cases of Dax Cowart to move his argument forward. Finally he examines the claim of moral authority for particular experiences, concluding that there is value in the distance expressed in general moral norms that are embedded in a community's narratives.

. . .

In assembling this collection I've had invaluable help from a number of people. My deepest debt of gratitude is owed to Maureen MacGrogan, who has been for me, as for many Routledge authors, a highly skillful editor, an insightful collaborator, and a dear friend. Her departure is a serious loss to Routledge. Warm thanks are also owed to Allen Dunn, John Hardwig, Anne Hunsaker Hawkins, Jan Marta, James Lindemann Nelson, Elise L. E. Robinson, and Margaret Urban Walker, who helped me get clearer about the ethical things one can do with stories. And finally, many thanks to the members of the Department of Philosophy at the University of Tennessee, Knoxville, for urging me to organize the conference that made this book possible and for their unswerving support of my work.

Notes

1. This story is retold, with many liberties, from Michael Stocker, "The Schizophrenia of Modern Ethical Theories," in *The Virtues: Contemporary Essays on Moral Character,* ed. Robert B. Kruschwitz and Robert C. Roberts (Belmont, CA: Wadsworth, 1987), p. 42.

2. Bernard Williams, "Persons, Character, and Morality," in *Moral Luck* (New York: Cambridge University Press, 1981); Michael Stocker, "Schizophrenia of Modern Ethical Theories"; Lawrence A. Blum, *Friendship, Altruism and Morality* (London: Routledge and Kegan Paul, 1980); Jeffrey Blustein, *Parents and Children: The Ethics of the Family* (New York: Oxford, 1982); Annette Baier, "The Need for More Than Justice," in *Science, Morality, and Feminist Theory,* ed. Marsha Hansen and Kai Neilsen, Supplement, *Canadian Journal of Philosophy* 13 (1987):41ff.; Margaret Urban Walker, "Moral Particularity," *Metaphilosophy* 18, no. 3/4 (1987):171–185, and *Moral Understandings: A Feminist Study in Ethics* (New York: Routledge, forthcoming 1998).

3. Stocker, "Schizophrenia of Modern Ethical Theories," p. 40.

4. See David Burrell and Stanley Hauerwas, "From System to Story: An Alternative Pattern for Rationality in Ethics," in *The Foundations of Ethics and Its Relationship to Science: Knowledge, Value, and Belief,* vol. 2, ed. H. Tristram Engelhardt, Jr., and Daniel Callahan (Hastings-on-Hudson, NY: Hastings Center, 1977).

5. Jacques Derrida, "Structure, Sign and Play in the Discourse of the Human Sciences," in *The Languages of Criticism and the Sciences of Man: The Structuralist Controversy,* ed. Richard Macksey and Eugenio Donato (Baltimore: Johns Hopkins Press, 1970).

6. Mikhail M. Bakhtin, "Discourse in the Novel," in *The Dialogic Imagination,* ed. Michael Holquist, trans. Caryl Emerson and Michael Holquist (essays written in the 1930s; Austin: University of Texas Press, 1981).

7. Fredric Jameson, *The Prison-House of Language: A Critical Account of Structuralism and Russian Formalism* (Princeton, NJ: Princeton University Press, 1974).

8. Martha C. Nussbaum, *The Fragility of Goodness* (New York: Cambridge University Press, 1986); *Love's Knowledge* (New York: Oxford University Press, 1992); *Poetic Justice: The Literary Imagination and Public Life* (Boston: Beacon Press, 1995).

9. Walker, "Moral Particularity."

10. Hilde Lindemann Nelson, "Resistance and Insubordination," *Hypatia* 10, no. 2 (Spring 1995): 23–40; and "Sophie Doesn't," *Hypatia* 11, no. 1 (Winter 1996):91–104.

11. Albert Jonsen and Stephen Toulmin, *The Abuse of Casuistry* (Berkeley and Los Angeles: University of California Press, 1988).

ONE

Telling the Patient's Story

1

What Do We Mean by "Narrative Ethics"?

Thomas H. Murray

I remember the event with remarkable clarity. It was a warm and humid spring day on the campus of New College in Sarasota, Florida. There I was, on my very first interview for a faculty position. I had on my only respectable-looking jacket, more suited to the winters of Princeton, New Jersey, than the humid springs of Florida's Gulf Coast. The selection committee had led me through the cafeteria line to a table outside, where I sat facing the sun, contemplating the meal I had chosen, which oozed unidentifiable liquids. Then came the very first question, from a large person with a deep, authoritative voice: "Why are you here? I mean, how do you defend your existence?"

I have been asking myself that same question about writing a paper for this volume on the relationship between literature and philosophy. I have no formal degree in either discipline, and though my work has been in ethics for nearly twenty years, it would not surprise me to learn that some philosophers may complain that I was never properly socialized—housebroken?—into the proper ways of thinking taught to those whose principal training is in moral philosophy. Those complaints have some merit: what was obviously true and beyond question to the properly socialized was to me often mysterious, sometimes wonderful, occasionally arbitrary or dubious. In particular, I increasingly found myself asking why a question was being framed in this way, by these persons, with that sort of response regarded as the right kind of answer.

My title to expertise in literature is much shakier still. My main memory about the formal study of literature is of my freshman English composition course. The instructor, whom I remember as being less than thrilled to be saddled with this cross section of Philadelphia's population, was fond of repeating, "If it's not in the poem, it's not in the poem!" Aside from that, I have occasionally tried to read literary criticism, but I have too often found it either unintelligible or else preoccupied with issues for which I could muster no enthusiasm.

So why am I here? The obvious answer is that one of the Nelsons announced the conference from which this paper comes at a meeting of the Society for Health and Human Values, including a list of speakers—which included me. As I was sitting next to the other Nelson, I asked, somewhat startled, whether I had agreed to give such a talk. I was assured that I most certainly had.

But there was another reason as well. I have become increasingly curious about the role played by narratives in moral reasoning, perception, action, and theory. This conference offered a splendid opportunity to learn more about narrative and ethics, and to try to organize my own hitherto scattered reflections about the significance of narrative in ethics. Those reflections are, in a way, efforts to answer the questions asked by the interrogator (who later became my friend): Why am I here? How do I defend my existence? Or to give the question a more explicitly Aristotelian form, how should a human being live?

There is considerable disagreement about whether narratives offer any help in answering the question of how we human beings should live. Part of the disagreement, I believe, is because people use the concept "narrative ethics" to mean a variety of different things. Thus the title of this paper, What Do We Mean by "Narrative Ethics?" I will sketch four more or less distinct uses of the concept. But a more important part of the disagreement goes to the heart of morality: How do we do sound moral reasoning? What role do narratives play in moral discourse? Are narratives sources of reliable moral knowledge?

The problem begins with the ambivalent relationship of twentieth-century moral philosophy to narratives. On the one hand, philosophers with an analytic bent are apt to have suspicion or contempt for the claim that narratives are important for morality. They are inclined to view narrative as woolly, soft, a second cousin to, perhaps the progenitor of, moral relativism. On the other hand, many of those same philosophers use narratives in their own arguments, albeit narratives in two particular genres. There is an undeniable intellectual tension, as well as a political struggle, between those who insist on the importance of narrative in morality and those who want to focus on the defensibility of propositions as the core of moral thought. This conflict is also, I suspect, a reflection of differences in sensibility and personal history.

One way of drawing the contrast is between any approach that gives narratives a significant place in the content of morality versus an understanding of ethics as a set of propositions expressed as sentences. On this latter view, the content of morality is the set of propositions shown to be true and all valid inferences drawn from this—possibly very small—set of propositions. Martha Nussbaum describes the prose style typical of modern Anglo-American philosophy: "correct, scientific, abstract, hygienically pallid, a style that seemed to be regarded as a kind of all-purpose solvent in which philosophical issues of any kind at all could be efficiently disentangled, any and all conclusions neatly disengaged" (Nussbaum 1990, p. 19). It is a style perfectly suited to a conception of moral philosophy as a collection of isolable propositions. In her book, *Love's Knowledge*, Nussbaum argues that style is not so readily disengaged from substance, that we can express important matters in certain literary forms much better than in others, including matters at the heart of morality.

Is narrative ethics any real threat to the conception of ethics as a set of propositions? The remainder of this paper is an effort to answer that question, so I will give only a brief preview here: one of the four possible meanings of narrative ethics is not necessarily inconsistent with the propositional conception of ethics; the other three meanings offer a more serious challenge.

What happens when we confront a profound narrative—a great novel, for instance? We are inclined to say that such a narrative helps us to gain moral insight. What could we mean by such a claim? The evidence of copious experience shows that great narratives, such as great novels, affect us, change us in unmistakable ways. Although it can be very difficult to specify what sort of change this is, it does not seem to be reducible to learning some new propositions about morality or grasping the truth of some proposition we had heard earlier but whose proof had eluded us. Is it that we previously lacked the ability to identify and articulate those propositions that constitute the exhaustive entirety of whatever moral insights we gain from attentive reading of great narratives? Or is it rather that those insights are not wholly reducible to propositions? Are there morally substantive things to be derived from narratives that go beyond propositional moral logic?

If my question is: What do we mean by "narrative ethics?" I suppose I should first say what I mean by narrative. For my purpose in this essay, I want to take a broad, inclusive view of narrative. Nussbaum contrasts the rich narratives one finds in great novels with "[s]chematic philosophers' examples [that] almost always lack the particularity, the emotive appeal, the absorbing plottedness, the variety and indeterminacy, of good fiction; they lack, too, good fiction's way of making the reader a participant and a friend" (Nussbaum 1990, p. 46). I certainly do not want to claim that Dickens's *David Copperfield* and James's *The Golden*

Bowl are indistinguishable from what Dena Davis calls "stick figure" stories, the hypotheticals that philosophers—and others—use on occasion to make a point. But I do want to admit both of them as narratives, albeit of vastly different genres. Kathryn Montgomery Hunter's working definition fits my aims here. Hunter writes: "In using the word 'narrative' somewhat interchangeably with 'story' I mean to designate a more or less coherent written, spoken, or (by extension) enacted account of occurrences, whether historical or fictional" (Hunter 1996, p. 306). The differences among the genres are at least as interesting as the similarities. But one important thing that they share is their implicit or explicit contrast to the view that the substance of morality consists of the set of true propositions.

With this working definition of narrative, we can turn to four possible answers to the question in this chapter's title: What do we mean by "narrative ethics?" They are:

1. Narrative as moral education;
2. Narrative as moral methodology;
3. Narrative as an appropriate form of moral discourse; and
4. Narrative in moral justification.

Narrative as Moral Education

We learn through stories as children. Whether what we learn can be reduced to the propositionlike maxims that are given to children as the "moral" of the story is another issue. Martha Nussbaum argues energetically and persuasively against such a narrow, blinkered view of the significance of narrative in the development of our moral capacities. In *Love's Knowledge*, Nussbaum links the significance of literary texts in moral education to an Aristotelian perspective: "A large part of learning takes place in the experience of the concrete. This experiential learning, in turn, requires the cultivation of perception and responsiveness; the ability to read a situation, singling out what is relevant for thought and action. This active task is not a technique; one learns it by guidance rather than by a formula" (Nussbaum 1990, p. 44).

Even the most committed devotee of analytical rigor must admit that most people, most of the time, learn most of what they know about morality from narratives of one kind or another, from the fairy tales of childhood to the life-stories we tell one another, to the narratives that permeate our culture, both high and low. To say that narrative contributes to ethics in the sense of moral education is not, I think, a particularly controversial claim, but a very important one nonetheless. It is powerful enough to keep literary scholars employed as educators of health professionals, certainly. But it does not say very much of significance about the relation of narrative to the substance of morality.

Defenders of the ethics-as-propositions conception could argue that people are simply too dense to grasp, remember, or learn how to use propositions as such, so we must fall back on stories as heuristic devices. Narratives, on this view, are second-best instruments for representing the content of morality in a vivid, memorable way. But they are not themselves that content. Indeed, proponents of that view may believe that the style and detail of a narrative is a distraction from the important, substantive content.

Narrative and the Substance of Morality

"The ancient quarrel between the poets and the philosophers" described in Plato's *Republic* "could be called a quarrel only because it was about a single subject. The subject was human life and how to live it" (Nussbaum 1990, p. 15). Nussbaum argues for an answer to Aristotle's question of how we should live our life

> that requires, for its adequate and complete investigation and statement, forms and structures such as those we find in . . . novels. Thus if the enterprise of moral philosophy is understood as we have understood it, as a pursuit of truth in all its forms, requiring a deep and sympathetic investigation of all major ethical alternatives and the comparison of each with our active sense of life, then moral philosophy requires such literary texts, and the experience of loving and attentive novel-reading, for its own completion. (Nussbaum 1990, p. 26)

Does narrative have, as Nussbaum claims, a place at the heart of ethics? Not merely as a tool in moral education, but as an essential element in moral understanding itself? I will look critically but sympathetically at three possible answers to the title question that would give narrative an important substantive role in ethics.

Narrative in Moral Methodology

It is impossible to do bioethics, at least any form of bioethics that involves talking about real issues or real cases, without using a particular kind of narrative—the case. The "case" in bioethics is actually a collection of several different genres, from the telegraphically terse hypothetical used to illustrate a particular philosophical point, through the patient-case—thick on numbers and thin on nuance—of the medical chart, to rich and complex narratives that weave together clinical facts with observations about human motivations, perceptions, and relationships.

A method of case-centered moral reasoning with roots in antiquity has experienced a recent resurgence of interest. Blaise Pascal's brutal and brilliant assault on its abuses in his *Provincial Letters* made casuistry a term of dishonor. Nonetheless, as ethicists struggled with real cases, the case-centered approach typical of casuistry was often employed on a variety of moral problems, including those in bioethics. Albert Jonsen and Stephen Toulmin began the restoration of casuistry as an intellectually respectable method of moral reasoning (Jonsen and Toulmin 1988). Because other authors—including authors in this volume—have examined casuistry in considerable depth, my discussion here will be very brief.

There can be no doubt that narratives, in the form of case stories, play an important role in moral reasoning. But what sort of role, and of how much importance? Philosophers such as K. Danner Clouser are perfectly willing to grant that competent bioethics requires attentiveness to the relevant details of the case. He acknowledges that "narrative ethics is one method of eliciting rich and important detailed facts that are crucial for making appropriate moral decisions" (Clouser 1996, p. 339). Ethicists who fail to pay attention to those details perform their tasks poorly, whatever their purported methodological predilections. Casuistry in this sense poses no fundamental challenge to the methods or theories of moral philosophy.

Beyond the immersion in the particulars of cases that casuistry commends, it also makes a claim about the nature of ethics—as practical reasoning or *phronesis*—along with an assertion about the sources of reliable moral knowledge—what Jonsen and Toulmin refer to as the "locus of moral certitude." In this second sense, casuistry rejects the primacy of propositional moral logic. It declares that the case is at least as important; the principle we draw from it is an interpretation of that case, open to revision. What we know is the rightness or wrongness embodied in the case. The moral content, that is, resides in the case; the propositions we draw from it are interpretations of that content. Kathryn Hunter presents a form of this argument that draws a parallel with medicine's relationship with science:

> While principles remain essential to bioethics and biological science must always inform good clinical practice, the tendency to collapse morality into principles and medicine into science impoverishes the two practices. In both instances such a reduction takes science as a model for what cannot be purely scientific. It is an attempt to know generally and abstractly what cannot be known except through the particular case—and to be best understood the case must be richly understood. (Hunter 1996, p. 316)

Before leaving casuistry, it is worth pondering yet another reason for thinking that narratives may be more important than as merely useful tools for filling in the blanks of previously composed moral syllogisms. Jonsen and Toulmin wrote:

> The heart of moral experience does not lie in a mastery of general rules and theoretical principles, however sound and well reasoned those principles may appear. It is located, rather, in the wisdom that comes from seeing how the ideas behind those rules work out in the course of people's lives: in particular, seeing more exactly what is involved in insisting on (or waiving) this or that rule in one or another set of circumstances. Only experience of this kind will give individual agents the practical priorities that they need in weighing moral considerations of different kinds and resolving conflicts between those different considerations. (Jonsen and Toulmin 1988, p. 314)

Casuistry tells us important details of the positive role of narrative in moral reasoning, but it does not tell us everything.

Narrative as an Appropriate Form of Moral Discourse

Moral philosophers and others writing about ethics do not behave as geometricians in their moral discourse, even in their writings about moral theory. They do not, that is, simply put forth axioms, definitions, and theorems. They typically tell stories, at least two different genres of stories.

First is the "philosopher's hypothetical" that is meant to make a particular point, usually about the plausibility or implausibility of some assertion about ethics. Judith Jarvis Thomson's violinist (Thomson 1971) and Bernard Williams's traveler in South America who stumbles upon a mass execution (Williams 1973) are well-known examples of the genre. What is going on when philosophers tell such stories? They are used frequently to establish the moral plausibility or implausibility of some philosophical point. If it's not obviously wicked for a woman who wakes up and finds herself attached to a violinist to want to disconnect the tubes that are keeping him alive, then neither is it obviously wicked for a woman who finds herself pregnant to want to cease supporting the fetus growing inside of her. Or so Thomson's story is meant to suggest.

Narratives such as these philosophers' hypotheticals occupy an interesting place in ethics. If one insisted that the content of ethics was the set of true propositions, then such stories could be taken only as suggestive, and only then if they somehow illuminated the truth of propositions that would have to be established on other grounds. Yet these stories often seem to constitute a much stronger test than such a conception of ethics appears to presuppose. Our grasp of the rightness or wrongness of the stories can be more secure than our faith in some proposition about ethics. Indeed, the stories function either to reinforce our confidence in the proposition in question, or to show its defects. To me, at least, this looks remarkably like the claim made by proponents of casuistry about the independent moral significance of cases. Is the narrative persuasive because it embodies a valid moral proposition, or is the proposition's validity buttressed by the narrative?

The second genre of narrative is less often noted. This is the narrative intended to set up, motivate, show the necessity of the approach taken by the theorist. These are foundation stories such as MacIntyre's opening to *After Virtue* (MacIntyre 1981), in which he describes contemporary morality as a collection of incompatible shards of earlier moralities that were more coherent, or H. Tristram Engelhardt's opening to *Foundations of Bioethics* (Engelhardt 1986), where he depicts a world in which differing conceptions of the good lead inexorably to tyranny and violence when one group attempts to impose its conception on another. These large projects in moral philosophy are born in narrative and motivated by narrative—by stories about who we are, what we are like, and how we came to be in our current situation. Much, if not all, moral discourse, including moral theory, is embedded within, conditioned by, and conducted in narratives. This is true, I suspect, even for certain works in bioethics that claim to be completely above the fray, claim merely to explicate what is given to us by unaided reason, such as Engelhardt's *The Foundations of Bioethics*.

The first edition of Engelhardt's important book begins with Martin Luther nailing his ninety-five theses on the church door in Wittenberg, and "the crumbling of the presumed possibility of a uniformity of moral viewpoint" along with any hope of living "in a society that could aspire to a single moral viewpoint governed by a supreme moral authority" (Englehardt 1986, p. 3). The reader is reminded of the violence of the Thirty Years' War and of the Copernican Revolution, which helped to create a world "devoid of a sense of absolute or final perspective: man was to cease to be the center of the cosmos, and the established Christian view of the cosmos was to be overturned" (Englehardt 1986, p. 3). The Enlightenment, for all of its hopes, proved unable to "fill the void left by the collapse of the hegemony of Christian thought in the West" (Englehardt 1986, p. 4). Engelhardt's quest, then, is to find an ethic for "peaceable secular pluralist societies," one that "can speak with rational authority across the great diversity of moral viewpoints." Lest anyone doubt how nasty the alternatives might be, we are given examples of "imposed orthodoxy," such as the Soviet Union and Iran.[1]

I do not believe that this particular narrative—about Western civilization, moral authority, war, the centrality of reason, and the evils of "imposed orthodoxy"—is merely an incidental adornment to what its author insists is a strictly philosophical argument. The plot is not hard to follow: moral pluralism is now an undeniable reality, and efforts to suppress or deny it are oppressive and likely to lead to political violence. But the author of this particular narrative wants to tell the rest of the story. There has emerged, he tells the reader, "a special secular tradition that attempts to frame answers in terms of no particular tradition, but rather in ways open to rational individuals as such" (Englehardt 1986, p. 5). Bioethics, he assures us, "draws on a tradition of the West that in fact attempts to step outside the constraints of particular cultures, including Western culture itself, by giving reasons and arguments anyone should accept" (Englehardt 1986, p. 6). This foundation narrative is an effort to explain why we should find the author's particular philosophical approach necessary and why we should fear other approaches.

It is certainly not the only plausible narrative to address the history of moral disagreement—and agreement—in the West. It is not the only story one could tell about the sources of moral authority. And it is certainly not the only narrative one could construct about the role of "rational individuals as such" in moral reasoning. But Engelhardt's version serves his purposes well, and provides a grounding for the mostly libertarian version of ethics and public policy he will go on to elaborate.

Engelhardt's book also illustrates the different ways we can retell others' stories. As an example of moral diversity he uses Colin Turnbull's study of the Ik, who, at the time Turnbull was studying them, would take food from their starving fellow Ik (Turnbull 1972). What Engelhardt leaves out of his discussion is the fact that the Ik's culture had been radically disordered by a forced relocation from their traditional homes to mountains from which they were unable to wrest enough food to support themselves. The Ik are less an example of moral diversity than of moral disintegration, and of the crucial importance of social structures robust enough to support a moral community.

Alasdair MacIntyre's *After Virtue* begins with a fable. He asks the reader to imagine that the natural sciences, as we know them, have been destroyed by a public that blames them for environmental catastrophes. After that catastrophe, people try to revive science. But there is a problem:

> [A]ll that they possess are fragments: a knowledge of experiments detached from any knowledge of the theoretical context which gave them significance; parts of theories unrelated to the other bits and pieces of theory which they possess or to experiment; instruments whose use has been forgotten; half-chapters from books, single pages from articles, not always fully legible because torn and charred. . . . Children learn by heart the surviving portions of the periodic table and recite as incantations some of the theorems of Euclid. Nobody, or almost nobody, realizes

that what they are doing is not natural science in any proper sense at all. For everything that they do and say conforms to certain canons of consistency and coherence and those contexts which would be needed to make sense of what they are
doing have been lost, perhaps irretrievably. (MacIntyre 1981, p. 1)

MacIntyre asks us also to imagine whether philosophy, in its many flavors,
would be able to detect this disorder in science; he believes it would not. Then
he gives the lesson his fable is meant to teach:

The hypothesis which I wish to advance is that in the actual world which we
inhabit the language of morality is in the same state of grave disorder as the
language of natural science in the imaginary world which I described. What we
possess, if this view is true, are the fragments of a conceptual scheme, parts which
now lack those contexts from which their significance derived. We possess indeed
simulacra of morality, we continue to use many of the key expressions. But we
have—very largely, if not entirely—lost our comprehension, both theoretical and
practical, of morality. (MacIntyre 1981, p. 2)

The fable MacIntyre tells is self-consciously a narrative in three stages: first,
a stage in which the enterprise—natural history in the fable, morality in
MacIntyre's argument—flourished; a catastrophic second stage; and finally, a
stage of partial restoration, but "in damaged and disordered form." He asks us
to notice that this history, far from being a "neutral chronicle . . . presuppose[s]
standards of achievement and failure, of order and disorder" (MacIntyre 1981,
p. 3). It is not just any story, but a narrative of rise and fall. Those of us who
came after the fall are left to pick through the shards of what once were vibrant,
meaningful practices. We may put some of the pieces together, but we cannot
appreciate what they meant to people who experienced them in their full,
vigorous context.

MacIntyre's narrative is a powerful one. It establishes his method—a sort of
philosophical history or historically situated philosophy. It suggests that other
ways of doing moral philosophy—analytic, phenomenological, or existential—
are incapable of even noticing what MacIntyre takes to be the central problem
in contemporary morality. And it provides a foundational story—a kind of
"just-so" story—about our current situation that captures enough features of
modern moral life to be provocative.

I believe that MacIntyre's foundational narrative is successful. It is vivid and
compelling, and forces attentive readers to think in novel ways about morality,
past and present. I also agree with critics of MacIntyre that his narrative over-
states the moral homogeneity of the past and understates the resources for

resolving moral disagreement currently available to us (Stout 1988). But the important point in the context of this essay is that, like Engelhardt's story of moral disagreement and political violence, MacIntyre's narrative is more than merely a clever story; it is the narrative foundation on which MacIntyre will build his argument.

Some commentators could maintain that such narratives are mere rhetorical devices to engage the reader. I disagree. I suspect that these narratives are meant as justifications, as explanations for the necessity of the author's project. Because different people have different conceptions of the good for persons, and because those differences can and have erupted into violence and oppression, Engelhardt argues that we must abandon all efforts at imposing any particular conception of the good on anyone who does not accept it voluntarily. Because the moral world is broken to pieces, because our current morality is made up of incompatible fragments of irreconcilable moral traditions, MacIntyre insists that we must recover an intelligible, internally coherent, moral tradition. Just how much of moral philosophy is similarly embedded in narrative, I cannot be certain. But I would guess that it is a good deal more than one might think, especially if we include those in which the narratives are not nearly so skillfully integrated into the text as these two.

It may also be worth noting that these two authors take rather different stances toward narrative. MacIntyre, on one view, uses his story to help persuade us that we must, in the end, accept some coherent narrative. In contrast, Engelhardt's use of narrative is ironic; he tells us a story in order to convince us not to trust other stories—narratives of any richness and depth about good and bad lives. Narratives, as philosophers' hypotheticals and as foundation stories, are ubiquitous in moral philosophy. And they do not function as mere adornments or pedagogical devices. They seem, in fact, to give philosophy some of its persuasive power.

Martha Nussbaum offers another view of the role of narrative in moral discourse. Writing about the novels of Henry James, Nussbaum says: "Moral knowledge . . . is not simply intellectual grasp of propositions; it is not even simply intellectual grasp of particular facts; it is perception. It is seeing a complex, concrete reality in a highly lucid and richly responsive way; it is taking in what is there, with imagination and feeling" (Nussbaum 1990, p. 152). Great narratives, that is, sharpen our perceptions and enrich our moral discourse. But do they do any more? Do narratives ever tell us about the substance of morality?

Narrative in Moral Justification

What gives us confidence in our moral judgments? What do we know about ethics, and how can we justify our convictions, our actions, our judgments, our way of life? What can we do when we encounter moral disagreement? How can I know what I ought to do or what I am permitted to do? Here I take the purpose of moral justification to be assessing the confidence with which we make moral judgments, ranging from judgments about whether it is reasonable to support some general moral theory to judgments in particular moral circumstances. Judgments such as these turn on a number of considerations, including, for theories, internal consistency, and, for practical judgments, the facts of the case. But all such judgments rely also on what we know about morality; not merely on a catalogue of propositions about morality, but on a nuanced and complex assessment of how confidently we know certain things to be good or bad, right or wrong, certain ways of living a life as admirable or disgraceful. What are the sources of confident knowledge about morality? What role do narratives play in that knowledge?

I will not rehearse the arguments for and against foundationalism, antifoundationalism, or similar positions. Instead, I want to describe briefly a pair of metaphors that I found helpful in understanding what I attempted to do in my book, *The Worth of a Child* (Murray 1996). I used the metaphor of a *tapestry* to suggest why images rich in particulars and redolent with context are necessary to an account of the moral significance of children—in themselves as morally considerable beings, and in the lives of the adults whose own lives shape and are shaped by the children they raise. I used the metaphor of a *web* to suggest what justification in practical moral reasoning looks like. Webs may be weak and flimsy, consisting of only a few strands badly put together. They can be narrow, with a strong central thread but weak on either side. They can be very irregular with many holes. Or they can be strong and symmetrical, composed of many strong strands woven together harmoniously. The threads making up such webs are borrowed from the tapestry, the collection of images we rely upon to understand the worth of children in the flourishing of adults.

The metaphors of tapestry and web must be stretched a bit to encompass the role of narratives. But not much. Tapestries typically depict many images that, taken together, tell stories. The stories, images, and tapestries I am concerned with, the ones I believe are central to morality, are those that depict good lives and bad lives, human flourishing and its contrary. Tapestries tell stories; the images on the tapestry portray key scenes from those crucial stories. In that way they are intimately related.

At least some of our most reliable moral knowledge, I am suggesting, comes in the form of images or stories recorded on the tapestry. Some are stories of cruelty; these we know to be bad. Some are stories of steadfast caring, of parents loving and sacrificing for their children; of grown children caring for their failing parents. These we know to be good. Moral justification often consists of tracing the threads that tie the case now under scrutiny back to the images or narratives on the tapestry that we know well and confidently. It is figuring out what sort of web supports the judgment in this case or on this principle.

Take as an example the image of a two-year-old child torn away from the only parents the child has known. The parents are in tears, the child is reaching out to them in desperation, sobbing while being carried away. The parents, in this story, are adoptive parents; the child is being removed from their home by an officer of the court to be brought to its biological father. (This is part of the stories known to the American public as Baby Richard and Baby Jessica.) On the other side is a picture of a woman wailing in remorse over having given up her infant for adoption.

I want to argue that these images are connected to even deeper narratives— stories and images of good, fulfilling, meaningful lives for women, men, and children. These narratives tell us about the relative significance of biological and rearing parents. Some give primacy to the attachments that grow from the soil of sustained and committed love, from the daily little acts of caring; others highlight the connections of biology, much as the ancient Greeks and Romans told their stories of anagnorisis—of the reuniting of biological parents and children. Some stories are of parental love of fathers as well as mothers; other stories portray a sharp division into male and female spheres. (I believe that such a division, and the different stories told thereby about women's flourishing in particular, are at the heart of our differences over abortion.)

The tapestry metaphor also alerts us to look for worn and ugly threads that originate in images we would like to remove from the tapestry. In *The Worth of a Child*, I argued that the current primacy given by American law to the rights of biological parents in adoption disputes, especially biological fathers, is in part a remnant of old images in Anglo-American law and culture—of patriarchy and of the child as property. This is not to say that biological parents, fathers included, ought to have no legally protectable interest in their offspring. But we need to give nurturing its due as well. The twin metaphors of tapestry and web allow us to understand how strands such as the child-as-paternal-property support particular legal practices. Following the thread back to the images from which it arose permits us to criticize it more effectively or, at least, to raise suspicions about its fit with other images that we have come to value.

Understanding moral reasoning as embedded in tapestries also enriches our understanding of why particular views tend to be shared by people who share other characteristics. Kristin Luker's work on pro-life and pro-choice advocates reveals remarkably rich tapestries that weave together education, social position, and views of human flourishing for women and men, with metaphysical convictions about the moral status of fetuses (Luker 1984). Seeing how these moral views are woven into the most intimate and important details of lives also helps explain the passion behind the public debate over abortion.

We may be able to offer new, possibly more tractable ways to interpret particular moral disputes and invite dialogue where it was not possible before. Abortion is one example. We know that disagreements over the ethics of abortion and the moral status of fetuses are not isolated disputes, but tend to be entwined with other disagreements, especially over the importance in women's lives of what is described alternatively as openness to procreation, or uncontrolled fertility. These views represent two very different images on the tapestry, two conflicting narratives about women's flourishing. The differences are no less deep or passionate than the difference over the moral status of fetuses. But where the latter metaphysical dispute seems to offer no territory for compromise— fetuses either are or are not persons, taking the life of a fetus either is or is not killing a person who has done no injustice to anyone—the former provides some possibility of common ground, dialogue, and perhaps even accommodation.

When Luker did her original research, most pro-life activists were raising their children at home, not competing in the labor market. Many more women with children are working today, including perhaps more pro-life advocates. How are such women accommodating their images on the tapestry, which emphasized women's special suitability for the sphere of the home rather than the roughness of the workplace? How to cope with the demands of work without sacrificing what is valued about home and family is a problem that faces pro-choice and pro-life activists alike. It is a tremendously important practical problem about what kind of life to lead but, unlike the moral status of fetuses, it invites practical rather than metaphysical solutions. Encouraging public engagement on what images on the tapestry and what narratives we should celebrate and strive for, holds out hope for genuine dialogue. We have not seen such dialogue on the metaphysics of fetal personhood, nor is there any reason to think we might in the foreseeable future.

My emphasis has been on the content of the images on the tapestry, on the stories by which we understand ourselves and our relationships with those among whom we live our lives. Martha Nussbaum calls for a further step—for taking the form and style of the narrative seriously, as well as its content *per se:*

> [L]iterary theory can improve the self-understanding of ethical theory by confronting it with a distinctive conception or conceptions of various aspects of human ethical life, realized in a form that is the most appropriate one for their expression. Insofar as great literature has moved and engaged the hearts and minds of its readers, it has established already its claim to be taken seriously when we work through the alternative conceptions. (Nussbaum 1990, p. 191)

It is essential to grasp the implications of what it means to be meaning-making creatures. The meanings we look for and seek to construct in our lives are not collections of propositions. (Nussbaum refers disparagingly to ethical theory "that simply mines the [literary] work for a set of propositional claims" [Nussbaum 1990, p. 191].) Meanings are better understood and conveyed as narratives. The "tapestries" that I suggest play such an important role in our moral lives could perhaps just as well be described as narratives. Images on those tapestries are like excerpts from narratives: they vibrantly capture centrally important scenes from human lives. Those images and excerpts are crucial raw materials for making and justifying moral judgments. They are intimately tied to the central project of morality—the effort to understand and to live a good, fully human life.

Note

1. In the second edition (1996) the sentiment and many of the words remain the same. Some new material is interposed. More attention is given to the explicitly religious nature of the moral authority dominant in the sixteenth and seventeenth centuries. And the references to the Soviet Union and Iran are displaced by Stalin and Hitler, Pol Pot and the Gang of Four, all of which are described as "attempts by force to make states single moral communities" (p. 10).

References

Clouser, K.D. (1996) "Philosophy, Literature, and Ethics: Let the Engagement Begin." *Journal of Medicine and Philosophy,* 21:321–340.

Engelhardt, H.T. Jr. (1986) *The Foundations of Bioethics.* New York: Oxford University Press.

Hunter, K.M. (1996) "Narrative, Literature, and the Clinical Exercise of Practical Reason." *Journal of Medicine and Philosophy,* 21:303–320.

Jonsen, A.R., and Toulmin. T.S. (1988) *The Abuse of Casuistry: A History of Moral Reasoning.* Berkeley, CA: University of California Press.

Luker, K. (1984) *Abortion and the Politics of Motherhood.* Berkeley, CA: University of California Press.

MacIntyre, A. (1981) *After Virtue.* Notre Dame, IN: University of Notre Dame Press.

Murray, T. H. (1996) *The Worth of a Child.* Berkeley, CA: University of California Press.

Nussbaum, M.C. (1990) *Love's Knowledge: Essays on Philosophy and Literature.* New York: Oxford University Press.

Pascal, B. (1967) *The Provincial Letters.* Trans. A. J. Krailsheimer. New York: Penguin.

Stout, J. (1988). *Ethics after Babel: The Languages of Morals and Their Discontents.* Boston: Beacon Press.

Thomson, J.J. (1971) "A Defense of Abortion." *Philosophy and Public Affairs,* 1(1):67–95.

Turnbull, C.M. (1972) *The Mountain People.* New York: Simon and Schuster.

Williams, B. (1973) "A Critique of Utilitarianism." In J.J.C. Smart and Bernard Williams (eds.), *Utilitarianism: For and Against.* New York: Cambridge University Press.

2

Who Gets to Tell the Story?
Narrative in Postmodern Bioethics

Howard Brody

In what way is today's bioethics in need of reform? And what role might a narrative approach play in such a reform? One way to look at these questions is to begin by examining one sort of critique of bioethics, which has been labeled "postmodern." I will begin with an analysis of some aspects of a book by a Canadian sociologist, Arthur Frank, *The Wounded Storyteller.*[1] As the title implies, this work adopts an approach in which narrative is central to an understanding of illness and of healing; it grows out of Frank's own confrontation with two life-threatening diseases in middle age. After spending some time discussing Frank's ideas, I will then review some important aspects of postmodern criticism generally and, finally, develop some suggestions for reform in bioethics.

I will address in this discussion two variants of postmodern criticism—the one referred to by Frank in his book (to be defined below), and the other based on my understanding of certain critics of standard U.S. bioethics who have adopted "postmodern" as a label for their views. I have not surveyed in depth the literature on postmodernism, apart from the writings of Richard Rorty, and so my comments below may be irrelevant to many, or even most, varieties of postmodern thinking.[2] To borrow a phrase from Steve Miles, I might refer to what I am engaged in below as "drive-by postmodernism.

Frank on Postmodern Healing
I find Frank's book rich and complex. My comments here follow merely one thread, and do not constitute an overall review or summary of his work.

One difficulty for today's bioethicist in engaging fruitfully in an inquiry or debate that involves a postmodern critique of bioethics is to find a definition of "postmodern" that is reasonably understandable and free of jargon. Frank's definition, in this regard, is a model of clarity. Frank describes modern medicine as the attempt to control or cure disease by subjecting it to the attentions of scientific experts:

> Folks no longer go to bed and die, cared for by family members and neighbors who have a talent for healing. Folks now go to paid professionals who reinterpret their pains as symptoms, using a specialized language that is unfamiliar and overwhelming. As patients, these folk accumulate entries on medical charts which in most instances they are neither able nor allowed to read; the chart becomes the official story of the illness. . . . The story told by the physician becomes the one against which [other narratives] are ultimately judged true or false, useful or not. . . . I understand this obligation [described by Talcott Parsons] of seeking medical care as a *narrative surrender* and mark it as the central moment in modernist illness experience. (pp. 5–6)

> What is distinct in postmodern times is people feeling a need for a voice they can recognize as their own. This sense of need for a personal voice depends on the availability of the means—the rhetorical tools and cultural legitimacy—for expressing this voice. *Postmodern times are when the capacity for telling one's own story is reclaimed.* Modernist medicine hardly goes away: the postmodern claim to one's own voice is halting, self-doubting, and often inarticulate, but such claims have enough currency for illness to take on a different feel. (p. 7)

Frank goes on to describe this new sort of experience with illness as "post-colonial":

> Those who work to express this voice are not only postmodern but, more specif-ically, *post-colonial* in their construction of self. Just as political and economic colonialism took over geographic areas, modernist medicine claimed the body of its patient as its territory, at least for the duration of the treatment. . . . The ill person who plays out Parsons's sick role accepts having the particularity of his individual suffering reduced to medicine's general view. Modernity did not ques-tion this reduction because its benefits were immediate and its cost was not yet apparent. The colonialization of experience was judged worth the cure, or the attempted cure. But illnesses have shifted from the acute to the chronic, and self-awareness has shifted. The post-colonial ill person, living with illness for the long term, wants her own suffering recognized in its individual particularity; "reclaiming" is the relevant postmodern phrase. (pp. 10–11)

> [T]he new feel of [post-colonial] stories begins in how often medicine and physicians do *not* enter the stories. Postmodern illness stories are told so that

> people can place themselves outside the "unifying general view." For people to
> move their stories outside the professional purview involves a profound assump-
> tion of personal responsibility. In Parsons's sick role the ill person as patient was
> responsible only for getting well; . . . the post-colonial ill person takes responsi-
> bility for what illness means in his life. (p. 13)

Frank's conception of the postmodern world thus is tied to this notion of
individual responsibility and is, at its core, a moral conception. The responsibility, moreover, is communal as well as individual:

> Storytelling is *for* an other just as much as it is for oneself. In the reciprocity that
> is storytelling, the teller offers herself as a guide to the other's self-formation. The
> other's receipt of that guidance not only recognizes but *values* the teller. The
> moral genius of storytelling is that each, teller and listener, enters the space of the
> story *for* the other. Telling stories in postmodern times, and perhaps in all times,
> attempts to change one's own life by affecting the lives of others. (pp. 17–18)

An ethic that understands the communal responsibility of storytelling must also
understand storytelling as a special way of knowing. On this aspect of illness
narrative Frank is less clear, and seems to be trying to use words to point toward
or hint at a reality that cannot ultimately be expressed in words. The two critical
ideas here are what it means to think *with* stories instead of merely to think *of or
about* stories; and that of the "communicative body," which tells its own story
through its own suffering, as opposed to a nonbodily, mental "self" telling the
story of the illness *about* the body conceived as object.

As Frank elaborates further, "thinking with stories" means:

1. While the modernist professional sees a patient's story as something to carry a
   message away from, the patient cannot ultimately escape from his own story; and
   so both the patient and the would-be healer must ultimately learn how not to
   move on, but rather to stay with the story, really live in it, so that one can reflect
   upon whom one is becoming by living in the story and finally modifying the
   story accordingly.

2. The "same" story, retold on different occasions over a span of time, will be heard
   differently. The self actually engages in change and reformulation by retelling the
   "same" story. Thinking with stories thus demands that we attend carefully to how
   a story is *used* when it is told, how different meanings or shades of meaning are
   assigned to the story as a result.

3. "Thinking with stories means that narrative ethics cannot offer people clear
   guidelines or principles for making decisions. Instead, what is offered is permis-

sion to *allow the story to lead in certain directions*" (p. 160). For Frank, the ethical professional may be the one who feels permitted in this way to discern "how the present illness fits into the pattern of [the patient's and her loved ones'] lives, and where both the physicians and the patients . . . see their pattern leading" (p. 160), so that in the end a decision may be based more on a sense of narrative fitness or coherence than on a deduction from principles. Indeed, the would-be caregiver (lay or professional) is invited by the narrative not merely to make certain decisions but to change how one lives one's life: "the story invites *becoming the sort of person* who could act within the story in ways that [the sick person] would appreciate" (p. 163).

The notion of the communicative body is tied closely with that of *testimony*, a point to which Frank frequently returns. Testimony of suffering is the communal (as well as the individual) moral duty of the ill person. To describe this process in the more usual way, we imagine that the sick person "thinks about" his own suffering, eventually finds words to describe it, and tells those words to another. The other, through some process of "empathy," then imagines what it must be like to suffer in that way. But this is far too dualistic and mediated an account. Frank argues that we will fail to grasp the importance and the power of testimony unless we understand this experience in a much more direct way. We must see the story of the sick person as the suffering body *itself* giving the testimony of its suffering; and the listener to the story is necessarily present, not as a taker-in of information, but as herself a potentially suffering body that receives the testimony of suffering in a much more immediate, body-to-body fashion.

The moral duty of testimony starts from one psychological truth—that others may not wish to hear stories of suffering, and yet we may still be morally obliged to tell them. But it arrives at a deeper psychological truth. In a culture that prizes autonomy and independence, we may fondly imagine that most people are whole and intact, unlike those who suffer from disease. We resist the critical deeper insight that all of us have abundances and all of us have lacks, and that we must participate in a reciprocal network in which one's abundances supply another's lacks and vice versa. Charity toward the sick ultimately seeks domination, and assumes that I have all the abundance and you have all the lack. But "if we would be communicative bodies—then empathy would no longer be spoken of as something one person 'has for' another. Instead, empathy is what a person 'is with' another: a relationship in which each understands herself as requiring completion by the other" (p. 150). Charity tends to assume that I start off whole and remain whole while I offer aid to the suffering. Empathy and testimony require a full awareness of my own vulnerability and radical incompleteness; to be with the suffering as a cohuman presence will require that I change, and that I take advantage (ironically) of the other's abundance of suffering to make up some of my own lacks.

This network is mutual and reciprocal at multiple levels. Today I listen to the testimony of someone's suffering; tomorrow that person (or someone else) will be listening to my testimony of my own. Today I help to heal the sufferer by listening to and validating her story; tomorrow that sufferer will have helped to heal me, as her testimony becomes a model I can use to better make sense of and deal with my own suffering. As I tell my story to my listener, I too am listening to my own story; hearing myself tell it changes me just as it changes him. To be healed of my suffering, I must tell my story, and use my story to attach meaning to my illness within my life; and so as I tell my own story and listen to my own story, I become simultaneously the sufferer and the healer.

Postmodern Critiques of Bioethics

Postmodern critiques of bioethics have occurred around the fringes of the "movement" for many years, and have gained a more central place recently with renewed calls for standardization of bioethics education and certification of bioethics practitioners.[3] The first target of postmodern criticism is, of course, modernist medicine; and bioethics comes in for its share of criticism as it is shown to have become an integral part of the modernist medical enterprise and not, as it may have proudly and naively assumed during its recent renaissance, a critical attack upon and corrective of that medical system.

Philosophically, the postmodern divide is crossed when one sees the distinction between objective knowledge and privileged interpretation. On the other side of the divide, the power wielded by the physician over the patient is natural, understandable, and therefore immune from critical scrutiny, simply because the physician knows things the patient doesn't, and those things are objectively true. As soon as one crosses the divide, one sees that what it means for something to be "objectively true" is itself puzzling and requires analysis; but in any event, the exercise of power is a social and political act, and no theory of scientific objectivity, however well grounded, automatically grants the sort of privilege that medicine has traditionally claimed for itself as a social enterprise. One realizes that practicing medicine is a political act; developing a theory of scientific objectivity to justify what medicine does is a political act; and political acts must be justified, or not, on their own terms and not as an extension of some unarticulated and unexamined natural law or divine right. This divide is a true paradigm shift in the Kuhnian sense; once it is crossed, one can never go back to the unquestioning stance previously held.

In extremely compressed form, the postmodern critique of bioethics views that activity as a sort of fraud and coverup. Modernist medicine cannot at its core take patient autonomy seriously.[4] It cannot simultaneously accept the patient as the physician's moral equal and privilege the professional, expert account of illness as the only "true" narrative. It can pretend to take autonomy seriously only by carefully chopping off bits of activity, paying attention to the patient's will and the patient's story in some selected and ritualized settings ("getting informed consent," for instance, or "getting a pastoral care consult"), so long as those are carefully barricaded off from the main sphere of medical business. This being so, bioethics had to make a radical choice. It could demand a return of power to the patient, or it could acquiesce in the monopoly of medical power. To do the former would require that bioethics somehow become a grass-roots political movement, neither welcome within, nor seeking to be welcomed by, the hospital and the academic medical center. This obviously had clear implications for both the social status and the income of the bioethicist. And so bioethics chose the second route, went to bed with medicine, and reaped the rewards of helping medicine to justify its power monopoly—ironically, by engaging in just enough criticism of just enough aspects of medical practice so that no one (except the postmodernist critics) would notice that the main edifice remained immune from challenge.

To return to Frank's initial analysis, when the sick person is trying to find her own voice while being subjected to medical treatment, it is not at all clear that bioethics does any better than modern medicine in helping rather than hindering that process, "respect for autonomy" to the contrary. The dominant, principlist approach to bioethics says that the voice worth listening to is the one that expresses itself in terms of certain abstract ethical concepts. The patient's life experience has to be translated somehow into autonomy, beneficence, nonmaleficence, and justice before we can draw any moral conclusions—and it is hard to imagine the average patient being able to carry out that translation unaided by us experts. Just as modern medicine has developed many ploys for dismissing stories it would rather not hear ("the patient is uninformed; the patient is depressed"), bioethics has developed quite an extensive list of its own ploys ("the patient lacks decisional capacity; the decision, while rationally deliberated, is inauthentic; the surrogate's evidence is not clear and convincing").

Indeed, just as modern medicine has become proficient in laying out its "truths" in such a way that any controversial presuppositions remain well hidden, modern bioethics may be less than candid in addressing the "facts" of the "case." Tod Chambers has recently shown how the way a bioethicist tells the narrative of a case study may presuppose some key methodological assumptions, yielding in the end a case study that can be satisfactorily "resolved" only if one employs that bioethicist's own pet method.[5] On the one hand, these bioethicists are hardly shy about describing and defending their favorite methods, and so no concealment seems intended. But on the other hand, the average reader will all too readily accept that the case "simply happened that way," and miss the active role the bioethicist has played in constructing the case narrative in one fashion rather than in another.

All well and good, up to this point. But having come this far, there are now many opportunities for the postmodern criticism of bioethics to get offtrack. The most obvious way, which nevertheless poses a constant trap for the unwary, is for postmodernism to commit the logical inconsistency of aspiring to modernism and claiming some privileged status for postmodern criticism. In this way it could directly undermine its democratic pretensions, portraying postmodern critics of bioethics as whiners who would like to grab some power for themselves and are ticked off because the bioethicists who are in bed with modern medicine won't give them any. If one is looking for a reason to dismiss a sick person's story, one can just as well do so because the story isn't postmodern enough. Frank very carefully dances around the edges of this pitfall when he discusses one form of illness narrative, the restitution narrative—I will be a good Parsonian patient; medical technology will cure me; and all will be well with my life again. Frank is obviously aware of the logical fallacy were he simply to discount this narrative template as a way in which a patient could honestly and reflectively make sense of an experience of chronic illness. He is careful to point out how, for periods of time and at certain stages, this narrative can be helpful and adaptive. But he still wants to express his firm value judgment that this is generally a defective story of a *chronic* illness and will ultimately set up the individual for greater suffering if not replaced later by a "better" narrative. (Indeed, Frank is commendably aware that he is to some extent betraying his postmodern convictions by his sociological efforts to offer *any sorts of generalizations at all* about sick persons' illness narratives, instead of simply recounting a series of individual narratives.)

The next danger is to "Americanize" and thus, inevitably, to Balkanize the postmodern call for democracy. Try telling an American two things—first, that each person needs to find her own voice to tell her own story; and second, that we are all incomplete and mutually dependent, and that our only possible route to human wholeness lies in full participation in a network of mutual, reciprocal relationships. The American cultural experience virtually guarantees that the first message will be heard loud and clear, while the second will be garbled if not missed entirely. It is easy to hear the first part of the message as: powerful forces outside of my control are trying to force me to live in a community that would be a real community only if I truly attend to a very wide range of stories; I am fearful that in this free-for-all my own story won't be listened to or valued; so I will feel good about myself, and fully participate in "community," only if I can withdraw into an enclave of those who share so many of my values that I can be assured of hearing only stories very similar to mine. It is very American of us to desire to have all the benefits of community while denying the need for reciprocity and the personal vulnerability that are, at root, what make us communal creatures.

Finally, postmodern criticism can render itself irrelevant and even silly through an intellectual narcissism that falls in love with its own cleverness at seeing through the modernist presumptions that have seduced so many of one's fellow creatures, including nearly all physicians and so many prominent bioethicists. In this narcissistic mode, one starts to have grand fun describing the new world we will all live in as soon as modernism looks at itself in the mirror, becomes suitably embarrassed, and leaves. Here the postmodern critic completely misses the obvious and yet critical point Frank builds into his account at the outset: "Modernist medicine hardly goes away" (p. 7). The edifice of modernism generally, and modernist medicine in particular, is not going to crumble simply because postmodern criticism has appeared; and indeed sick persons—and postmodern critics get sick too—will not want it to disappear. The challenge for the postmodern critic who wishes to matter is that the postmodern world is in important ways still the modern world. Once having passed through the Kuhnian paradigm shift, the critic can no longer see the world in the old way, but that insight does not change the world's practices or its power relationships. As more and more people see the world in the new way, and start to see choices where the old worldview saw only inevitability, then change will come, but the change will not amount to the wholesale dismantling of what we are calling modernism. Some practices and some power relationships will persist, because there is a good reason for them to persist, or because alternative arrangements turn out to have even more problems.

Toward a Postmodern but Humble Narrative Bioethics

How should we be modifying the enterprise of bioethics so as to take full advantage of the postmodern criticism? A useful warning at the start is that some postmodern critics end up sounding rather arrogant. Their excuse, that bioethics itself is quite arrogant and that they are simply struggling to be heard in that arena, is not without some merit. But if the postmodern criticism has value, we should all be aspiring to a posture of greater humility instead. In this regard I find Frank's work encouraging; while carefully avoiding almost all of the pitfalls of postmodern criticism listed above, his discussion seems also refreshingly free of arrogance.

If the besetting sin of modernity is first assuming one has a clear window into objective reality, and then concluding from that that one has a right to claim special power and privileges over others, a narrative turn will serve as a useful antidote to both modernist medicine and modernist bioethics. Frank, like others before him, has stressed the democratic and communal nature of narrative. Once we establish that the patient's story is necessarily the starting point of medical inquiry (one cannot, after all, order an MRI scan or a battery of blood tests without taking at least *some* history), virtually any sort of narrative analysis will cast doubt on medicine's presumption to be better able than the patient to tell that story. One need not pursue a narrative line of inquiry very far before the hierarchy of modern medicine is turned on its head. Where once the patient's own story of her own experience was relegated to the back corridors, the medical narrative and the medical chart are now highly suspect. They are privileged in a hypothetical and methodological way for purposes of performing various specific tasks, but they constantly demand cross-checking and critical reinterpretation.

We must pause here to note an important point. Narrative inquiry gets its foothold in medicine with the primacy of the patient's story of the illness.[6] Who, so far, has claimed this primacy? Contrary to what has been implied by some postmodernists, the criticism of modernist medicine that dismisses and devalues the patient's story has arisen inside as well as outside medicine. Some medical scientists have for some time now been calling attention to the inadequacies of the modernist model of objective, value-free truth, mind-body dualism, and reliance on general laws to explain particulars.[7] Others have complained about modernist medicine's exclusive focus on the individual patient to the detriment of community and population approaches.[8] The thrust of their criticism, often ignored both by physicians and by critics outside medicine, is that the more dogmatically medicine tries to cling to modernity, the more unscientific it becomes. It is medical science every bit as much as (if not more than) medical humanism that prompts these physicians and investigators to call for renewed interest in the patient's narrative of the illness.

The importance of this point is for those who would be change agents when no wholesale dismantling of the modernist medical enterprise is possible (even if desirable). It is critically important to see that to establish a pivotal role for the patient's narrative, one need not do battle with all of medicine, medical science, or medical academe. One may form selective alliances within the medical enterprise in the name of narrative reform.

Frank's rich account holds many lessons for medicine and for clinical ethics, nearly all of which Frank himself consciously ignores. He is much more concerned to establish the responsibility of patients individually, and the community of patients jointly, for telling their stories and hence assigning meaning to their suffering. He knows that each diversion into offering advice for professionals is one more distraction that could undermine his message of the responsibility of the sick for their own fate. It is therefore up to us to elaborate upon some of the lessons from his thinking.

First, we need to address what Frank means by "thinking with stories." In medicine, narrative ethics and narrative epistemology need to be developed together. We need to understand what stories tell us, and how we come to know those things, before we can understand how that knowledge gives us ethical guidance.

An important starting point is that just as we must resist the privileged knowledge claimed for scientific medicine by modernity, we must resist the inappropriate privileging of the patient's story of his own experience. Without doubt, the patient's self-story will, under most circumstances, be the best account we are likely to get about that experience, at least at the start of the inquiry. But all of us have, at one time or another, told a narrative about our experience that we would admit, upon later reflection, was seriously defective or misleading. For narratives to be of any use in bioethics, they must be seen as corrigible.

As Wayne Booth has emphasized, we come to discover the deficiencies in one narrative (including its ethical deficiencies) not by rejecting narrative or by moving outside of narrative, but rather by telling a *better* narrative.[9] Sometimes the scientifically grounded medical narrative will be "better" in the relevant sense than the narrative the patient had constructed to explain her own experience. (That is, after all, why people continue to seek the help of the physician.) Sometimes the patient's narrative will point out radical misunderstandings or omissions in the medical narrative. Sometimes the narrative of a third party will reveal problems with both the medical and the patient's narrative. In any event, students of narrative in medicine have begun to show us how we can judge such narratives and make comparative choices among them when they conflict, and bioethics needs both to incorporate and to expand that field of study.

Modernist medicine cannot, and should not, disappear just because of postmodernism; and neither should bioethical principles disappear just because of narrative. Rita Charon[10] and others have reminded us that a narrative approach to bioethics need not exclude any other major approach. Paul Lauritzen,[11] looking at the role of appeals to experience in ethics, suggests that a compelling narration of personal experience can form a sort of reality check on ethical reasoning based on principles—most commonly by showing that the ethical analysis was wrongly framed, or that it does not fully plumb the depths of the case at hand. Lauritzen goes on to suggest an application here of John Rawls's notion of reflective equilibrium.[12] Ultimately, for our ethical reasoning to be sound, we must check the coherence or the "fit" of carefully and truthfully narrated personal experiences against our ethical theories and their applications, and vice versa.

To push this extension of Rawls a bit further, we might recall that Rawls's theory of justice was seen as justified by an appeal to *wide reflective equilibrium,* defined as a state of overall coherence among three general elements of the theory—basic, abstract principles of justice; considered judgments about particular cases or issues; and basic theories of human nature.[13] One of Rawls's special insights was the notion that general principles had to cohere with at least some particular judgments in order for the theory as a whole to be justified; and his account of a "considered judgment" reflects the qualities he thought a particular judgment ought to have in order to serve this function as a potential corrective to abstract theory. If we follow Lauritzen's suggestion, we might discuss an extension of reflective equilibrium that we might christen *deep reflective equilibrium*—made up of the three elements of wide reflective equilibrium, plus selected appeals to narratives of personal experience. Just as with considered judgments, we would be challenged to specify what characteristics an experiential narrative ought to have before we might consider ourselves justified in modifying an otherwise satisfactory abstract principle, because the principle (or more likely, some of its applications) fails to cohere well with that narrative. It might also prove, on further inquiry, that deep reflective equilibrium is not really a revision of Rawls's theory after all; as it might turn out to be the case that what Rawls has called considered judgments are in reality tightly compressed narratives.

Another important lesson Frank's postmodern vision has revealed to us is the emptiness of one of the sanctuaries offered by modernity. The myth of privileged access to the true narrative via scientific objectivity held out the hope, fondly grasped by generations of physicians, of effectively treating the patient while remaining invulnerable and emotionally untouched by the patient's suffering. Frank's analysis of suffering, of testimony, of empathy and the communicative body suffices to undermine this concept. If the professional who seeks to cure the patient is confident that she will remain untouched by the patient's suffering, then *no one is listening to the patient's story, the suffering remains without meaning, and healing has been rendered impossible.* The physician who would seek the state of *"aequanimitas"* in the face of the patient's illness is worse than a mere technician who may be able to cure the body without comforting the person; he is instead a positive hindrance to healing, and a threat to the community of storytellers that is trying to do something seriously about the healing of suffering.

This claim amounts to a massive charge of incompetence against the medical profession and its educators. If invulnerability is bad, and thinking that one can remain invulnerable while still doing the work of medicine effectively is a vain hope, then we have for many years been attracting precisely the wrong sorts of people into medical practice and training them in precisely the wrong way. What little we many have done lately in trying to teach empathy and humanism hardly scratches the surface.

If physicians are as incompetent at this critical aspect of healing as appears to be true, then the work of bioethics is rendered much more difficult. Bioethics is really geared toward instructing the well-motivated and competent physician on resolving difficult dilemmas; it is not well set up to instruct medicine how to clean out its own Augean stables, or to help with the task if medicine were to ask. Moreover, it seems likely that some (perhaps many) were attracted into bioethics for the same reasons that our colleagues were attracted into medicine—we can observe human suffering at close range, allow ourselves to feel good about our desires to help, but remain invulnerable behind the armor of our professional expertise, claiming all along that we cannot allow emotional engagement to interfere with the detachment and objectivity demanded by our craft. To that extent, it is especially hard for bioethics to tell medicine how to begin to clean up its act.

At a minimum, bioethics must be working with whoever within medicine is listening to start to think about what will be needed when the supposed sanctuary of invulnerability and "detached concern" ceases to exist. We have, for instance, usually thought of institutional ethics committees as multidisciplinary panels of inquiry or tools for crafting consensus about moral issues. We may have to begin thinking about them much more as potential sources for emotional and social support for caregivers who are truly willing to confront and to be altered by the story of the patient's suffering.

Of course, just because we have taught ourselves that we remain invulnerable in the face of suffering does not mean that we are. Perhaps a critical task of bioethics is to join forces with those best able to show today's physician or nurse (or ethics consultant) exactly how she has been changed thus far in her career, exactly how she has managed so far not to admit this, and exactly what stresses in her life are attributable to this denial. That we can be changed and yet not be destroyed—that in fact we can grow in unanticipated ways—seems to be both true and largely unappreciated. Talking about this more widely within the system as it exists may be a necessary first step. The moral development of the health professional throughout a career remains a question very little explored within our field.

Conclusion

Up to now, bioethics has tended to address the question of how physicians, nurses, and other expert professionals might best cure diseases and treat patients. Frank forces us to ask why the question has not rather been, all along, how all of us, as a community of humans and hence of fellow sufferers, can live with each other in our suffering and participate fully and responsibly in reciprocal systems of healing. Professional expertise has an important role to play within that community network of healing; but it is only one role, and that role does not necessarily privilege the professional community with the sort of power that it has traditionally claimed and exercised. If patients need to reclaim their voices and their stories from inappropriate professional dominance, then bioethics must first ask whose side it's on, and if it's on the side of the patient, then what it can do to help.

Notes

1. Arthur Frank, *The Wounded Storyteller: Body, Illness, and Ethics* (Chicago: University of Chicago Press, 1995).

2. I am grateful to John Arras and Daniel Goldstein for explaining to me how Frank's "postmodernism" is actually a much less radical criticism of modernity than that of other postmodern thinkers.

3. Giles Scofield, "Ethics Consultation: The Least Dangerous Profession?" *Cambridge Quarterly of Healthcare Ethics* 2 (1993):417–448.

4. Robert M. Veatch, "Abandoning Informed Consent," *Hastings Center Report* 25, no. 2 (1995):5–12; Robert M. Veatch, "The Concept of "Medical Indications,"" in *The Patient-Physician Relation: The Patient as Partner* (Bloomington: Indiana University Press, 1991).

5. Tod Chambers, "From the Ethicist's Point of View: The Literary Nature of Ethical Inquiry," *Hastings Center Report* 26, no. 1 (1996):25–32.

6. RC Smith and RB Hoppe, "The Patient's Story: Integrating the Patient- and Physician-Centered Approaches to Interviewing," *Annals of Internal Medicine* 115 (1991):470–447.

7. GL Engel, "The Need for a New Medical Model: A Challenge for Biomedicine." *Science* 196 (1977):129–136; JH Levenstein, EC McCracken, IR McWhinney, et al., "The Patient-Centered Clinical Method, 1. A Model for the Doctor-Patient Interaction in Family Medicine." *Family Practice* 3 (1986):24–30; KL White, ed., *The Task of Medicine: Dialogue at Wickenburg* (Menlo Park, CA: Henry J. Kaiser Family Foundation, 1988); KL White, "The General Physician: Past and Future," *Journal of General Internal Medicine* 5 (1990):516–521.

8. KL White and JE Connelly, eds., *The Medical School's Mission and the Population's Health* (New York: Springer-Verlag, 1992).

9. Wayne C. Booth, *The Company We Keep: An Ethics of Fiction* (Berkeley: University of California Press, 1988).

10. Rita Charon, "Narrative Contributions to Medical Ethics: Recognition, Formulation, Interpretation, and Validation in the Practice of the Ethicist," in ER DuBose, RP Hamel, and LJ O'Connell, eds., *A Matter of Principles?: Ferment in U.S. Bioethics* (Valley Forge, PA.: Trinity Press International, 1994).

11. Paul Lauritzen, "Ethics and Experience: The Case of the Curious Response," *Hastings Center Report* 26, no. 1 (1996):6–15.

12. John Rawls, *A Theory of Justice* (Cambridge: Harvard University Press, 1971).

13. Norman Daniels, "Wide Reflective Equilibrium and Theory Acceptance in Ethics," *Journal of Philosophy* 76 (1979):256–82.

3

Enacting Illness Stories
When, What, and Why

Arthur W. Frank

"How can it be," asks the surgeon Richard Selzer when he himself is critically ill, "that a lifetime of treating the sick has not prepared him for the role of the patient?" (1994, p. 84). The particular cultural moment when this not only can be but *must* be, given the ideology and organization of modern biomedicine, is the *when* of ill people's stories. Selzer realizes that he cannot speak his personal experience in his professional voice; the voice that has been his is no longer his *own*. Many ill people find they cannot live the story, or just the story, that biomedicine tells of their illnesses; the need for a voice of one's own is a particularity of our times.

People have probably always told each other stories about their pains and discomforts, but our present stories are told when that particular contemporary phrase—"in your own voice"—makes sense to people and can back up claims to a story's interest and importance. But "voice" is not necessarily or exclusively a spoken or written voice. I choose the stories that are retold in this paper as a way of making amends for how my own work (Frank 1995) may have contributed to reducing the notion of story to verbal and written forms. In this paper I want to consider stories that are told by being enacted.

My belief that ill people must tell their own stories and leave medical stories to medical professions is grounded in my own experience as an ill person (Frank 1991). As my treatment for cancer progressed, I realized I was waiting for my doctors or nurses to give my suffering some expression that would turn what was happening to me into . . . what? I didn't know what; filling in what was *what* I expected them to do for me.

Then I began to realize that, despite my cancer center's claims to treat the "whole person,"[1] any sense that was to be made of my experience was going to have to come from me. They were telling a story of my illness, but this story was not my experience, and if I was not to lose the experience that was mine, and lose part of myself with it, I needed to tell my own story. This need to tell was not so much my problem as it was my potential. Storytelling was not another task I had to perform at a time when I was already overburdened; it was the possibility of turning that burden into creativity. Perhaps in learning to tell my story I began to learn, better than I ever had, what my own voice sounded like.

This paper is about not only why I claim a unique contemporary possibility for ill people to tell stories, but why I make a stronger claim for the individual and communal responsibility for storytelling. I begin with the present moment *when* stories are being told, go on to *what* stories are being told, and conclude with *why* it seems valuable to tell stories and attend to others' stories.

When: The Present Context of Stories

Illness stories work differently in the lives of hearers and tellers because "now" is different. If the present "now" of being ill is different from previous present moments, then stories play a different role in our lives. My point, which carries into the section below, is that the distinctive quality of *what* is told may not be in the text of the story. Rather this distinctive quality depends on the social context in which the story is used. And central to the present context of illness stories is, unavoidably, the practice of medicine.

The physician and sociologist Howard Waitzkin has provided an insightful and innovative application of Louis Althusser's concept of ideology to medical practice. Althusser was a French Marxist theoretician who wrote (1984 [1970]) that ideology works by "hailing" people: literally calling "Hey, you!" at someone. If I see a friend and yell "Hey, George!" I call on that person to be George, and to be George in his capacity as my friend; the hail imposes an identity and a relationship. Any "Hey, you!" is addressed to specific individuals, hailing them as specific sorts of people; they are called not only to fill certain functional roles, but to *be* a type of person.

Althusser's story of ideological hailing, told in a medical version, goes like this. One day a person is walking down the street, living a life. Then that person seeks medical advice, either reactively in response to a pain or dysfunction, or proactively in response to a sense of obligation to "look after one's health." Perhaps the advice is to come back next year, which is a minimal hail. In other cases the person can end up being strongly hailed: the person is given the new identity of patient-with-a-diagnosis. The person now has a new way to think about him or herself; the more extreme the diagnosis in its implications, the more imposing this new identity is.[2]

Waitzkin describes a medical interview with a patient who both smokes and drinks:

> medical ideology here hails the patient as a subject, who assumes concrete responsibilities in defined social roles. His self-destructive behaviors become important not just as they injure his body. Rather, these vices also threaten a web of relationships that depend on his performing reliably. The doctor's language hails the patient not only as a wheezing man with a liver swollen by alcohol, but also as a worker, a son, a brother, and a future husband. In all these roles, the patient's behaviors, especially those related to drinking, interfere with what he is expected to do. On behalf of medicine as a social institution, the doctor here speaks the language of ideologic reproduction, prevailing on the patient to march down a more straight and narrow path. (1991, p. 189; see also 299–300, n.8)

Waitzkin describes how medicine *creates* a new person, a new "subject," in its work of hailing; how this particular patient is hailed will also be substantively relevant to an argument below. This creation of the patient is based not on a politically and morally neutral science, but on the social need to keep people "performing reliably" in what they are "expected to do." The patient is hailed "to march [not walk] down a more straight and narrow path." Whether this path is what the patient needs is not the present issue; the problem Waitzkin opens up is how we can possibly say what anyone "needs" when ideology—whether medical, legal, educational, or religious—has already defined the terms of what people "need." The work of an ideological apparatus is to make a particular definition of need appear as a self-evident truth.

Althusser's other descriptive term for how ideology works is *interpellation.* To interpellate a term is to fit it into a slot that is already there, waiting to be filled. The term put into this slot then becomes understood as always-having-been the sort of term that fits that slot. Rather than the slot having been waiting for the term to fill it, the term was waiting for the slot to give it its proper place, or definition, or self-understanding. Ideology works by interpellating people into slots and then making them believe that they are the sorts of people—the sorts of *subjects*—these slots require.

Ideology creates the subject by blending self-definition into institutional definition. To be hailed or interpellated is to be encouraged, even coerced, to think of oneself as what the hailing institution, such as medicine, defines one to be.

Two points follow. First, ideology is powerful because when this hailing is successful, the person hailed assumes the identity that the hailing institution requires him or her to be; again, institutional definition blends into self-definition. Second, in our present culture, medicine is a particularly powerful hailing institution because of the unquestioned and preeminent importance people place on "health."[3] The claim of health has the capacity to trump most other claims, thus giving medical interpellations their force.

The medical interview hails a person to be a patient whose diagnosis carries the responsibility to engage in a treatment. Diagnosis does the work of interpellation: the disease becomes not only what one *has*, but more significantly what one *is*, for example, a cancer patient. Medicine hardly creates the cancer, but it does create the career of cancer patient. Being a cancer patient is not only a role; the social expectations go well beyond medical compliance. Being a patient is also a *moral status*, implying what a person is entitled to ask from society, and what society expects from the person.[4]

What is called "medical power" is thus the power of medicine as what Althusser calls an ideological apparatus, a machine for hailing and interpellating. The power of medicine to hail people as medical subjects has expanded greatly during the last fifty years as the nature of the *medical subject*, which we conventionally call the patient, has changed.[5] This change is often described as the triumph of modern medicine.

Since I myself am alive following a disease that would probably have killed me as recently as 25 years ago, I can hardly dispute the reality of medicine's triumph. But as a sociologist I notice the other side of this triumph: more people are interpellated by medicine more of the time. "Early detection" is one rationale for this hailing, and "risk factors" is another complementary form. To have "risk factors" is to be a virtual patient, not yet sick, but hailed as one who is a medical subject with the restrictions and responsibilities that attach to that status. The patient Waitzkin describes above seems to hover between being a person-with-a-disease and being a person-at-risk. For medical interpellation, the difference is increasingly moot.

Telling stories "in your own voice" thus makes sense as an activity and as a personal goal at a time when people become increasingly self-conscious of being hailed. The premium on speaking in your own voice may make sense only when people are conscious that a good deal of speech is not one's own but consists of speaking the lines that the institutional interpellation sets in place. Many people who have never heard of Althusser and who would regard his jargon as academic obfuscation are, nevertheless, self-consciously aware that institutional systems require them to be certain sorts of people. They hear the hail *as* a hail, coming from a system that they seek but also resist.

People's self-consciousness of being hailed means that the medical ideological apparatus is increasingly cracked, as powerful as it remains. I like to define postmodern times as when opposing trends steam along simultaneously. One trend is that people embrace medical interpellations. The medical apparatus becomes more encompassing as medicine has more "to offer" and thus claims more extensive authority in its patients' lives. The countertrend is that people *resist* interpellations. They refuse to be who medicine, or any other ideological apparatus, calls them to be. A breast cancer activist titles her recent book *Patient No More* (Batt 1994). Thus people both complain when medical services are restricted, and many are also becoming "patient no more." Perhaps there is no contradiction here: as the apparatus gets stretched wider, its cracks show. Interpellation no longer puts the subject into a sealed room that effectively shuts out all other identity possibilities. Stories of people's "own" seep in and out.

People resist medical interpellation ambivalently and ambiguously. Most people want what medicine has to offer, but they do not want to assume the subjectivity that medicine requires in order to receive what it offers. The most commonly told stories that ill people tell when they gather outside the medical gaze—in support groups and in larger survivor organizations[6]—are stories of minor resistances: ironic verbal comebacks to tactless remarks made by medical staff, covert acts of noncompliance, engagement in nonmedically authorized or medically incomprehensible acts of self-healing and recovery, or simply dumb-doctor anecdotes that are themselves performative acts of resistance. I emphasize that these storytellers are, to their doctors and nurses, compliant patients. They provisionally accept the medical interpellation, but they resist it as a total identity.[7]

What, then, is one's "own voice" at the present time? To claim a voice of one's "own" is to stake a counterclaim against the ideologies that hail the person to assume the identity that they require. In Althusserian terms, what is one's "own" is not measured in originality but in self-consciousness of being more than what the person is hailed to be. The expert voice is the voice of interpellation; it claims to know what sort of subject the person is and ought to be. The expert voice asserts the moral responsibility that the person act as the subject she or he is interpellated to be: at best being a good patient, and at minimum not being "in denial," where the medical description of "denial" marks the person who refuses to hear the hail and become a proper sort of patient. I emphasize that in most cases interpellation is still accepted, but the person also seeks to remain someone more than what the hail calls them to be. One's "own voice" is the voice of the identity that people seek to retain when they are confronted with the interpellation of an ideological apparatus.

My contention is that, at our present *fin de siècle,* ideological apparatuses are reaching a crisis that is the historical culmination of two opposing tendencies.

One tendency is the dominance of systems of expertise, represented by the history of medicine: the increasing power of the professional voice backed by a more effective and invasive technology and, in an impressive range of cases, actual cure. The other tendency is resistance to domination. This resistance proceeds from the women's suffrage movement, the labor unionization movement, and anticolonial rebellions through the civil rights movement and on to the proliferation of "liberation" and "pride" movements today. In all of these movements a voice can be heard saying: We are not who you have tried to make us be; we are more, and we now claim the right to discover for ourselves what that "more" is. Among these other movements, communities of the ill are forming. The idea of such communities makes sense in the context of these other movements.[8]

The inside of the crack in the ideological apparatus of medicine, along with other expert systems, is that it cannot sustain its own success. As medicine's institutions became unwieldy and as its claims became inflated, people realized that for all that medicine can deliver, it cannot deliver all that its ideal once promised. The ghost of the kindly and efficient Dr. Marcus Welby, the television icon of medical promise in the late 1960s, lends an irony to people's perceptions of the medical system they do encounter: the maze of referrals to subspecialists, the tests and questions that are repeated because no one effectively coordinates a patient's case, the waiting lists and delayed test results, the promise of diagnostic precision and the reality of uncertainty, the mistakes for which no apology is offered, and—the most recent wrinkle—the nagging doubt as to whether one is being given the best medical advice or advice that steers treatment in a direction that a third-party payer is willing to reimburse. These are problems of the insured, knowledgeable, and well connected; the problems of the poor are something else again (see Abraham 1993; Hilfiker 1994). In this milieu of medical implosion, cynicism begets resistance. Resistance finds its own voice by telling stories *about* the hailing process rather than telling its stories *in* the voice that people are hailed to be.

The claim to speak in one's own voice and tell one's own story is *not*, however, a claim that this story is exclusively one's own.[9] On the contrary, what is claimed is membership in a community of those who share one's story. Here my discussion of the present moment *when* a particular type of story is told fades into my later discussion of *why* stories are told. Stories are told as claims to membership in communities, but the community is not already there, waiting for the story. Communities are formed out of stories; the story is the reflexive affirmation that a gathering of people *is* a community, or even that two people can become a community. The communal act of telling, hearing, and recognizing a story is how a group becomes a community. Further claims, both individual and group, can then be advanced based on the reality of that community. Stories tell individual people's experiences, but in storytelling, individuality folds into community.

As a final note on ideology, let me recognize that storytelling is itself a form of interpellation, but interpellation of a different form.[10] The storyteller hails the listener not on behalf of an ideological apparatus, but as one who shares the experience necessary to share the story. The call to share stories is a call to the common work of *finding out what the experience we share might mean as an identity.* An ideological apparatus already knows what sort of subject it requires the hailed person to be. Medicine has in place its diagnostic categories, treatment options, and protocols before the patient enters the office. Storytelling has nothing already in place. The story is about trying to figure out what sort of subjects *we who share this story* might be.

I began by quoting Selzer asking: "How can it be that a lifetime of treating the sick has not prepared him at all for the role of the patient?" Because: when Selzer treated the sick, he hailed them to be what his treatment required them to be, medical subjects. Now, ill himself, he must figure out who he is. As introspective as Selzer's medical voice has been, to tell his own illness he needs a new voice.

What Stories: Enacted Tellings

Most of the attention to the relevance of stories in medical humanities generally, and in "narrative ethics" specifically, has been limited to literary stories. By literary stories I mean both stories that have some status within a canon of literature (see Brody 1987; Charon 1994; Peschel and Peschel 1986) and those that are if not artistic works, narrative texts that exist in some durable form of publication (Hawkins 1993).[11] I have previously suggested, too briefly and without sufficient examples, that illness stories are less often literary than "enacted" (Frank 1995, p. 116).[12] The decentering of the literary form as the paradigm of storytelling takes more work.

Literary stories are convenient to write about, since writing most effectively quotes other writing, but the analytical preference has deeper roots. Literary stories allow honoring a commitment to people's own voices, since these voices can be quoted directly. To retell enacted stories is to increase the risk of imposing a professional interpretation on the action of the storyteller. The enacted story is reshaped as it is retold; it thus becomes the professional's story of the ill person's story. Recognizing this and other honorable reasons for preferring literary stories (see Davis 1991), here I want to emphasize the enacted stories that are marginalized and excluded by this preference.

To decenter the literary story as the paradigm of what "story" means, I will discuss two different enacted stories. These discussions are intended to tell the stories and underscore the work they do, but they also illustrate the interpretive problems of writing about people's nonwritten stories. In both cases I will be telling a story about someone else's story about what they interpret as the story being enacted. I am comforted by the adage that anything worth doing is worth doing badly; certainly these stories are worth retelling, however refracted that retelling is.

In social scientific considerations of illness, the "story" usually denotes a narrative elicited by a third-person interviewer. The story may emerge with very little prompting, or it may be pieced together out of responses to a variety of questions (for example, see Good et al. 1992). In this tradition the British sociologist Gareth Williams (1993) tells the story of Mrs. Fields, a sixty-two-year-old widow with acute rheumatoid arthritis. Mrs. Fields seems verbally taciturn. She enacts her story through the way she organizes her life.

Mrs. Fields splits her life between treatment, which is her physician's concern, and her everyday independence. Williams writes that "a clear line could be drawn between the progression of her disease as being something over which she had little or no direct control, and the severity of the disabling symptoms of the disease, against which she felt compelled to assume a posture of resistance" (1993, pp. 95–96). Her resistance, then, is not as I have characterized resistance above: it is resistance against the disease itself, with medical treatment constructed as a resource. Mrs. Fields accepts being interpellated as a patient, but only so far; her story is about keeping boundaries around the reach of this interpellation in her life.

Mrs. Fields enacts her story through her actions of remaining physically independent, keeping her house clean, and staying out of debt. One symbol of her independence is her adjustable bath-seat: "You see," she tells Williams, "I can just go upstairs and run that bath anytime. I'm not worried about anybody [that is, about getting help from either one of her sons who live nearby or from a health worker], I could be there all afternoon and be quite happy with the fact that I've done it myself" (1993, p. 97). Thus taking a bath becomes an enactment of a larger story about who Mrs. Fields is; telling herself as independent in the bath interpellates her chosen identity.

This identity is enhanced by keeping her house clean. Mrs. Fields takes pride in telling Williams how a public health nurse who was in the neighborhood asked to use her toilet. "You know," she says, "you think you've achieved something. I know it may sound simple to you, but it's not. That was something important. She [the nurse] can't think I'm careless, and she's not frightened of touching anything in the house" (1993, p. 98). Here Mrs. Fields seeks the approval of a medical professional, but not for her compliance with treatments of her illness. Rather she seeks recognition of the virtue of her life beyond illness; for the nurse to offer that recognition, she must be in Mrs. Field's home. The toilet enacts the story.

Mrs. Field's third sphere of enacted story is financial. Williams comments that for Mrs. Fields, "To be in debt is to have one's virtue questioned in a profound way" (1993, p. 101). One anecdote illustrates how Mrs. Fields uses financial independence as part of her work to limit the interpellation of herself as a patient, with the dependence that status implies. Social services would have paid for her bath-seat, but she prefers to buy it herself despite living on a subsistence budget. The issue again is autonomy: "Now it's mine. Nobody's coming knocking at the door saying 'Have you finished with that?' It's mine, I can go up and use it when I want" (1993, p. 101). Because Mrs. Fields has paid for the bath-seat, she cannot be hailed ("Nobody's coming knocking") as in debt to a third party.

Using her bath-seat, keeping her toilet clean, and paying her bills are how Mrs. Fields enacts a story of herself. "It is in terms of such representations," Williams writes, "that we perceive our own activities as appropriate to the kind of people we take ourselves to be" (1993, p. 102). What Mrs. Fields's story is about is the "pursuit of virtue." Her life is "an attempt to enact a story about herself as she wishes to be understood, regardless of whether the enactment is the optimum way for her to proceed in the given circumstances" (1993, p. 103). The "optimum way" would be to get the bath-seat from social services, but this would violate the coherence of Mrs. Fields's story.

Williams argues the importance of understanding Mrs. Fields's life in narrative terms—with her actions interpreted as the enactment of a story—rather than in the psychological terms favored by professionals. Only in narrative terms can we recognize Mrs. Fields as a moral actor. Williams expresses the considerable shift in perspective that a narrative interpretation effects:

> we have to recognize that the expressive terms people use cannot be reduced to instrumental terms of "adjustment" and "adaptation." These concepts, staple components of the rehabilitation literature, tend to be ethically judgemental because they are unrelated to the context of the moral life of the person concerned. In order to avoid the pitfalls of judgement, we need to see coping strategies as moral practices. (1993, p. 103)

Williams then links moral practices to narratives by quoting Michael Oakeshott: "a moral practice is, in part, a language of self-enactment" (1993, p. 103). Our moral practices are our stories; we tell our stories—we make them public and we hold ourselves accountable to them—in our moral practices. Any story is a self-enactment "in which conduct may be recognized in terms of its 'virtue' and an agent may recognize himself in terms of his 'virtuousness'" (Oakeshott, quoted in Williams 1993, p. 103).

Mrs. Fields would have no interest in claiming any originality in how she enacts herself. Her story is very much her own—her sense of independence is palpable—but the meanings of her symbolic actions derive from the conventional virtuousness of her community. Through her enactments, Mrs. Fields sustains her membership in a moral community that knows itself by its independence, cleanliness, and financial responsibility. Her "own" story is valuable as an expression of membership in this community.

A more complexly enacted story is told by medical anthropologist Martha Balshem in her ethnography of a Philadelphia community, "Tannerstown," where she worked for several years as a public health educator. Balshem tells about Jennifer, a young widow whose husband, John, died of pancreatic cancer. John's illness was marked by repeated misdiagnoses, conflicts with physicians, and many moves between hospitals. One day John's chart is left in his room by mistake, and Jennifer reads: "Patient is married, fairly extensive history of alcohol abuse, none in the last several months. Also there is a 22 year history of cigarette smoking (1 & ½ packs)." Jennifer continues the story:

> So I was looking through it and the doctor comes running back, and of course—
> they can't stop you. But already I'd found the page, you know. So the doctor said,
> "Oh, I forgot the book." He went to take it. I said, "Oh, what's this on here?" And
> he, like, looked at me, you know, and he said, "Oh, that's not important." I said,
> "It's important to *me!*" "You're going to take this report," I said, "saying he's an
> alcoholic and he smokes and this is what causes cancer." And I said, "Then you
> wonder why we get upset because the statistics are wrong!" (Balshem 1993,
> 102–103)

Jennifer is self-consciously proud of not being an educated woman, but she makes a sophisticated argument: charts like John's will be used to compile statistics concerning causes of disease, and if the descriptive information is wrong, the eventual epidemiology will be biased.

After John's death, Jennifer enacts her story in her attempts to have the chart changed so that his habits are no longer presented as the cause of cancer. She has only partial success, convincing a physician to add pencil note in the margin of the chart to indicate that John drank less than one case of beer a week. If Mrs. Fields's story is about autonomy, Jennifer's story is about bitterness over issues of voice and authority. Balshem's summary of Jennifer's struggle is that, in the end, John's physician's "voice is real, and hers is not" (1993, p. 117).

Unlike Mrs. Fields, Jennifer does not trust physicians. Her resistance takes the form of refusing to allow John to be remembered as what medicine interpellated him to be: an alcoholic smoker whose habits caused his death. Her problem, even her tragedy, is that she can imagine enacting this story only by rewriting the medical story. Her failure is foretold when she first complains that John's alcohol consumption was far below the level she considers to be abuse. The physician responds that this is not the relevant issue: "And he just kept saying to me, 'You're concerned about the wrong things,'" (1993, p. 103). This medical response to Jennifer interpellates her as a nonperson. This interpellation is not the chance remark of one hurried professional; we will see below that it is a calculated judgment deeply rooted in the medical narrative of what constitutes virtue in response to disease.

Between Jennifer and John's physician, Dr. Hughes, there is not a problem of communication in the sense of simply not knowing the other's narrative, and if they knew, then all would be well. Theirs is a conflict of two narratives that explicitly reject each other. Jennifer and Dr. Hughes each live in what Arthur Kleinman has called different "local moral worlds" (1995, p. 122). Each moral world tells its own story about what causes cancer. The story told by residents of Tannerstown has to do with pollution, particularly from the factory that provides employment for many residents and fills the air with residues that most locals believe are toxic. The medical story has to do with people's high-fat diet, their smoking, and their alcohol consumption. Jennifer's community members acknowledge their high cancer rates, but they interpellate themselves in a narrative of industrial exploitation. The medical community sees the same cancer rates, cannot make a determinative judgment about the effect of pollution, and claims "lifestyle" is the cause.

Balshem convincingly demonstrates what is nonnegotiable between Jennifer and Dr. Hughes. Their conflict differs in one significant respect from the medical interpellation described by Waitzkin in the quotation above. Jennifer wants Dr. Hughes to recognize that his patient's disease extends outward in a web of relationships that includes her. Dr. Hughes wants to delimit his responsibility to his patient alone.

When Balshem interviews Dr. Hughes and asks about the decisions Jennifer made to move John between hospitals, he interrupts her in a tone she hears as "aggressive" and says, "But why—why should she be the one making [the decisions]? . . . Generally speaking, we feel the patient should make the decisions. Now, obviously family members should be present and should *hear* the information" (Balshem 1993, pp. 114–115). Again we hear Jennifer being interpellated in a nonspeaking part, as an onlooker at her dying husband's bedside. This interpellation as silent "family member" is at the core of Dr. Hughes's medical philosophy, and Jennifer must resist it.

Balshem emphasizes that both stories, Jennifer's and Dr. Hughes's, enact deep emotional investments: "The emotions expressed by both Jennifer and Dr. Hughes are the specific costs to them of life in the context of wider forces" (1993, pp. 123–124). For Jennifer, those forces are the imposition of air and water pollution that threaten her health and the health of her children. The imposition of those forces, and her inability to affect them, seem continuous with the imposition of a medical version of her husband's life (and it is the imposition of a medical narrative on his life prior to illness that is the issue for her). Dr. Hughes's story is "rooted in a complex hope for patient compliance" (1993, p. 124). The same chart entry that enacts her sense of injustice enacts his sense of truth about disease and his frustration with his patients' unwillingness to live according to this truth.

What stories do ill people tell? Stories that are *enacted* through symbols that can be as mundane as a clean toilet or as complex as the correctness of a medical chart entry. These enacted stories call our attention to the embeddedness of stories in *communities*: Jennifer's story is tellable only because it draws on and lends further credence to the Tannerstown narrative of cancer causation, just as Mrs. Fields's enacted story depends on established community symbols of virtue.

Third and finally, stories embody deep *emotion*. This emotion is understandable enough as deriving from what the stories tell: suffering and death. But the emotion of the stories also expresses the depth of narrative conflict over which story it is right to tell about the same event. Narrative conflicts are moral conflicts that cannot be articulated as the claims of some unquestioned ideological apparatus: Jennifer's moral stance lacks institutional backing, and Dr. Hughes understands his narrative as being under attack. Both tell stories that are backed by interpretive communities, but each confronts a different community telling a different story. One facet of people's personal emotional investment in their narratives reflects their lack of perceived institutional backing for their moral stances.

In a world of narrative conflicts, is it legitimate to ask if stories can "get it wrong," as physicians accuse Jennifer of doing, or is asking this question only another ideological hailing? Jennifer's story could be called a failed one, especially when juxtaposed to Mrs. Field's story. Balshem concludes by writing of Jennifer's "pain of unresolvable emotions" (1993, p. 124), and many would read that as a failure.[13] But while literary narrative and clinical practice aspire to resolution, is that aspiration appropriate to enacted stories? Perhaps Jennifer must leave her story unresolved to keep open a wound inflicted by a system of power relations that remains in place, untouched by the ways it mishandled John's diagnosis and treatment. To say that Mrs. Fields reaches "acceptance" while Jennifer remains "angry" distorts both narratives. Mrs. Fields sustains her humanity through her practices of moral virtue, but hers is a world turning inward; her responsibility to her adult children centers on not imposing on them. Unlike Mrs. Fields, Jennifer is trying to create a world for her growing children. Jennifer's moral virtue requires resistance, and all Jennifer has to fuel her resistance is her pain of unresolved emotions.

Jennifer and Mrs. Fields are leading more or less happy lives, and their stories both reflect and create their happiness. But as real as any person's happiness is, to judge this happiness, and to claim that another way of living would make them happier, is precarious. To interpellate any story as a success or a failure is a judgment that is meaningful only from within the ideological apparatus that sets in place the terms of hailing. Yet living in a world crosscut with ideologies cannot require abjuring all values lest we perpetuate these ideologies; that would only create a void of relativism. Awareness of ideology calls us to display our values *as ours*, thus interpellating others as subjects who can choose or refuse these values.[14]

Perhaps the most important lesson to be learned both from Mrs. Fields and from Jennifer is that stories are not optional to an existence that could proceed without them. To live is to enact a story. All that is optional is what sort of story we enact and how self-conscious we are about our enactments. Stories are the ongoing work of turning mere existence into a life that is social, and moral, and affirms the existence of the teller as a human being.

Why Stories: Responsibility and Community

A conventional response to the question of why illness stories are important is that they can inform clinical practice; attention to stories makes better doctors.[15] Howard Brody has clearly recognized that my project is not about offering advice to clinicians. He writes that I "consciously ignore" the lessons that my account of ill people's stories might have for medicine because I have other interests:

> [Frank] is much more concerned to establish the responsibility of patients individually, and the community of patients jointly, for telling stories and hence assigning meaning to their suffering. He knows that each diversion into offering advice for professionals is one more distraction that could undermine his message of the responsibility of the sick for their own fate. (Brody, this volume)

Brody goes on to say that it is up to medical professionals to extract and develop what lessons from my work are valuable to them. I enjoy meeting with physician groups whenever I can, but Brody is right: I believe that the *why* of illness stories is not for their value in informing medical practice. Illness stories matter because they enhance the self-consciousness of the ill and aid them in developing their distinctive community.

The double usage of "responsibility" in the Brody quotation and the linkage he suggests between storytelling and ill people's "fate" expresses a tone of my argument that Suzanne Poirier has objected to, saying that this emphasis on responsibility creates "potentially overwhelming demands, I sometimes felt, on those people who are often most disenfranchised" (1996, p. 79). I want to describe the *why* of stories in a way that defends my assertion of responsibility.

Mrs. Fields and Jennifer teach us that what counts in telling a story is not the resources a person brings to the telling but the resources that can be created through that telling. Neither Mrs. Fields nor Jennifer is at the bottom of the social continuum of resources, but neither one would be called privileged. Their stories are the resources—in the sense of being resources that generate other resources—that keep them each from becoming what Poirier calls disenfranchised.

Mrs. Fields's practices of independence, cleanliness, and solvency are what keep her enfranchised as a moral actor, recreating each day the virtue that is the basis of her personhood. Hers is a narrative enfranchisement, depending on the story she enacts in these practices. Jennifer's bitterness reaffirms the purpose and vitality of her voice, a voice that is perpetually at risk of being silenced. As Jennifer retells the story that keeps her emotions unresolved, she enfranchises herself as a person who is able to see through the multiple ideologies of public health, of institutional authority, and of people who tell her that she is "concerned about the wrong things."

To keep their lives their own, Mrs. Fields and Jennifer must tell their enacted stories. What is "potentially overwhelming" to Mrs. Fields and to Jennifer is the threat of being silenced about their suffering: either being forced to become a passive recipient of care—as Mrs. Fields fears—or being spoken for by experts pressing hard to tell her story for her—as Jennifer resists. Their situations illustrate that those with least resources are often the most eloquent storytellers, though not, usually, of literary stories. Even more important, Mrs. Fields and Jennifer both show why the responsibility to tell stories is most acute for people who are most immediately threatened with being silenced.[16]

The primary responsibility to tell stories is a responsibility to one's own voice; it is a responsibility to remaining what Gareth Williams calls "the kind of people we take ourselves to be" (1993, p. 102). Telling stories is never *another* obligation, because to live is to enact a story about the kind of person we take ourselves to be. Telling stories is the obligation every person confronts as she or he enacts a life; illness only gives the stories a different urgency.

Mrs. Fields's rheumatoid arthritis does not change her conception of virtue; it only intensifies her need to avoid distraction in her pursuit of virtue. If there is a hint of compulsiveness in Mrs. Fields's enactments, it is because she knows how easily she could slip into a life she fears. John's death does not change

Jennifer's sense of herself as struggling to sustain a voice in a world that is oppressive; that sense of self comes from living in Tannerstown. John's death gives Jennifer's resistance a specificity of focus: "they" are those who distorted John's hospital chart in order to preserve their ideology about how "lifestyle" causes cancer in Tannerstown. John's illness and death only raises Jennifer's personal stake in the community narrative.

The complementary level of responsibility for telling stories has to do with community. Mrs. Fields and Jennifer must also tell stories to retain their standing in the communities that support them. The individual story depends on the community from which it draws its symbols and its core narrative, and its telling reaffirms this community. The community of the ill is reflexively recreated in each telling of each story, whatever form that telling takes. This community thus provides the basic moral resources for those who would be its members to tell their stories, achieve that membership, and, through their stories, renew the resources that are then available to other members.

To exercise both levels of responsibility to self and to community, the ill person should realize that physicians, whatever their intentions, have a different job description and take their stories from different communities. The medical message to Jennifer that she is concerned about the wrong things is not a throwaway deprecation; it is the considered expression of a clash of relevances (see Toombs 1993). Some physicians and patients certainly enjoy relationships that bridge their personal and community narratives, but many—I think the vast majority—do not, and as the "doctor-patient relationship" becomes "managed care," I think ever fewer will. For most ill people and their families, the danger is waiting for someone else—particularly someone outside their community—to tell them their story (see Frank 1994).

Let me conclude with that most risky of ventures, a prediction. While the fundamental emotions attached to sickness—the fear and anxiety, the pain, the isolation and loss, and also perhaps the occasional moments of wonder and absolute joy—have not changed much in a very long time and are not likely to change, the terms of medical interpellation may be changing significantly and imminently. Increasing numbers of medical subjects are no longer being hailed as sick persons with the diagnosis as the formal device of interpellation. Instead they are being hailed as persons at risk, with "risk factors" as the formal device of interpellation. Medicine now hails an increasing number of people as *potentially* ill.

If students of medicine and culture are correct in identifying a shift to a medicine that is population-based rather than individual, multidisciplinary rather than being a medical hierarchy, epidemiological rather than diagnostic of individuals, concerned with risk more than with identifiable pathology, and preventive rather than curative,[17] then interpellation certainly will change. The medical subject is increasingly the patient described by Waitzkin in the quotation above: a functionally well person who needs to be convinced to change his or her "lifestyle."

Let me stake my own values on the side of believing that the patient Waitzkin describes is sick and needs "to march down a more straight and narrow path" if he is not to become much sicker. I am often ready to enlist in the cause of health promotion. But as a sociologist, my job description is to express reservations about the overall process that is being effected incrementally by innumerable specific interventions, each of which, taken singly, is reasonable and humane.

This "new" medicine will not tell its story of its patients' lives in charts that are kept unavailable to patients except when inadvertently left in their rooms. Instead medicine will set patients a series of tasks to enact a new story of their lives. This enacted story that medicine sets in place is called *prevention,* tailored to and justified by the patient's risk factors. The new medicine will interpellate medical subjects into a story to be enacted throughout their whole lives: in the air they breathe and the light that touches their skin, in their eating and drinking, their sexuality, their leisure and their "stress." I am not sure which is more frightening: the current fragmentation of the patient among subspecializations, or a medicine that really does treat the *whole* person, with no space left to be more than this interpellation.

This future is not, however, dystopian. As the medical interpellation shifts its terms of hailing from disease to health, from the diagnostically fragmented patient to the new, medicalized, "whole" patient, new stories of resistance will certainly be created, enacted, and told. I believe that people will continue to find their own voices in the next century, whatever the terms of its medicine. What their stories will sound, or look, or feel like, I have no idea, and that is what will make these stories *their* own.

Acknowledgments

Most of this paper responds in some way to comments made by Howard Brody and Suzanne Poirier in their writing, in their presentations during a session devoted to my work at the 1996 meeting of the Society for Health and Human Values, and in our conversations. Hilde Nelson's editorial guidance was insightful. My thanks to all for their ideas and their friendship.

Notes

1. This claim remains conveyed by the bas-relief carvings that cover an entire wall that patients and their families still pass while entering the cancer center. The wall is divided into squares; carved into each square is the logo of each specialization that the center claims to make available to patients. The message I heard was *all* that the center could do for me—what else, the wall seemed to ask, could a patient possibly need or want? That was in the mid-1980s, before managed care came to Alberta.

Today that wall is even more of an illusion that can delay people from searching for resources they need.

2. Lest the description of medicine as ideology appear as another instance of social scientific doctor bashing, let me be clear that the person who hails is as caught up in the ideology as the person being hailed; thus the physician is interpellated every bit as much as the patient is. Althusser is not just compounding jargon when he refers to the "ideological *apparatus.*" Ideology is not something one person does to another. It is an apparatus, a big machine that catches up individuals and their purposes within itself. How physicians resist having their own voices caught up in the ideological apparatus of medicine is another story; the work of David Hilfiker (1994) can be read as one example of a physician's resistance to medical interpellation.

3. At least, middle-class people place this importance on health. David Hilfiker (personal communication) reminds me that people living in the lowest socioeconomic strata may give health considerably less priority, to the consternation of clinic providers who label their behavior as noncompliance. In Hilfiker's example, staying home to receive a welfare check that would otherwise be stolen may be more important than keeping a clinic appointment. The person "failing" to keep the appointment thus refuses the primacy of the medical hail. "Noncompliance" may not be self-conscious resistance to the ideological apparatus, but it involves taking a step outside that system.

4. I draw here on Erving Goffman's essays in the collection *Asylums* (1961a).

5. Although Julia Epstein (1995) does not use an Althusserian theoretical language, her work describes how powerful medicine has been during the last several hundred years in interpellating subjects to fill gendered slots that uphold a larger social hierarchy. For further studies that can be read as instances of medical interpellation, see Komesaroff (1995, especially 180–181).

6. I write this paper shortly after attending the 10th Annual Meeting of the National Coalition for Cancer Survivorship, an umbrella group for numerous local organizations. What I heard at this meeting only confirmed what I have been hearing during the last five years of attending such meetings, large and small, both locally and internationally.

7. My thinking here derives from the sociological work of Erving Goffman (1961b) on "role distance": the techniques that individuals employ to demonstrate to others and to themselves that they are, as subjects, more than what their present social role displays them to be. Insofar as any social role is an interpellation, role distance is the endemic resistance to the ideology that prescribes the expectations that attach to roles.

8. The National Coalition for Cancer Survivorship was formed by individuals who applied to their post-illness experiences skills developed in other community action organizations. AIDS activism is the most obvious example of an illness group applying skills learned through other activity, specifically gay rights. The recent political activism of breast cancer groups self-consciously applies lessons learned by watching AIDS activists. These communities are diffuse, changing, and variably effective, but their presence seems to be part of the landscape for the foreseeable future.

9. The issue of what voice can be called one's *own* and in what sense has received sustained attention since the seminal work of Lionel Trilling (1972). More recently, see Charles Taylor (1991) on problems and possibilities of authenticity.

10. Stories are constantly being appropriated to serve ideological apparatuses. Folklorists bemoan the appropriation of traditional folktales to serve as ideological indoctrination for children, interpellating them within gender stereotypes (Tatar 1987) and political subservience (Zipes 1983).

11. My own editing of the "Case Stories" series of first-person stories by ill people (*Second Opinion,* 1994–1995; *Making the Rounds in Health, Faith, and Ethics,* 1996) reinforces the assumption that stories aspire to be written texts.

12. See also Radley (1993) on "enacted metaphors."

13. My undergraduate students who are preparing for careers in clinical work usually regard

emotional displays as suspect and emotional conflicts—or any lack of "resolution"—as a clear indi-cation that someone has failed. These students' accounts frame failure as personal, not institutional. The complementary issue is how much medical staff desire expressions of gratitude from patients and their family. These expressions not only recognize efforts expended, they also allow the staff to believe that emotions expressed during treatment—often in response to treatment—have been resolved. The "thanks" provides a closure that the events in themselves did not.

14. Contemporary dis-ease over the terms in which one person can assert his or her values, and how far—in practical terms of action—anyone can object when others base their actions on different values, is given its fullest discussion in the work of Robert Bellah and his colleagues, *Habits of the Heart* (1996).

15. Thus Anne Hunsaker Hawkins introduces her study of published illness narratives, which she calls "pathographies," by asking: "What impact, if any, can such a study have on the rapidly changing patterns of medical practice today and—even more important—tomorrow?" (1993, p. x). For Hawkins, the "study of pathography" has its goal "in restoring the patient's voice to the medical enterprise" (1993, p. xii). This is an excellent goal, but my goal is restoring the patient's voice to the patients themselves, or enhancing a developing self-consciousness among ill people that they are more than medical patients.

16. For those at the very bottom of resourcelessness, for example the homeless patients served and described by David Hilfiker (1994), the issues change somewhat, but not entirely. These people do seem unable to tell their own stories, and asserting their responsibility to do so is a cruel misrecog-nition of their lives. But I am convinced by Hilfiker's book that any hope people have of escaping the cycle of homelessness depends on their developing a self-story. Hilfiker's practice of "poverty medi-cine" seems less about offering treatment and cure and more about helping people to create a story of themselves as responsible agents, capable of the kind of acts that Mrs. Fields and Jennifer use to keep themselves out of homelessness.

17. This list draws on, but modifies, Bunton and Burrows (1995), p. 207.

References

Abraham, Laurie Kaye. (1993) *Mama Might Be Better Off Dead*. Chicago: University of Chicago Press.

Althusser, Louis. (1984) [1970]. "Ideology and Ideological State Apparatuses," in *Essays in Ideology*. London: Verso, pp. 1–60.

Balshem, Martha. (1993) *Cancer in the Community: Class and Medical Authority*. Washington, DC: Smithsonian Institution Press.

Batt, Sharon. (1994) *Patient No More: The Politics of Breast Cancer*. Charlottetown, Prince Edward Island: Gynergy Books.

Bellah, Robert N., Richard Madsen, William M. Sullivan, Ann Swidler, and Steven M. Tipton. (1996) *Habits of the Heart: Individualism and Commitment in American Life*. Updated edition. Berkeley: University of California Press.

Brody, Howard. (1987) *Stories of Sickness*. New Haven: Yale University Press.

Bunton, Robin, Sarah Nettleton, and Roger Burrows, eds. (1995) *The Sociology of Health Promotion: Critical Analyses of Consumption, Lifestyle, and Risk*. London and New York: Routledge.

Charon, Rita. (1994) "Narrative Contributions to Medical Ethics: Recognition, Formulation, Inter-pretation, and Validation in the Practice of the Ethicist," in Edwin R. DuBose, Ron Hamel, and Lawrence J. O'Connell, eds., *A Matter of Principles? Ferment in U.S. Bioethics*. Valley Forge, PA: Trinity Press International, pp. 260–283.

Davis, Dena S. (1991) "Rich Cases: The Ethics of Thick Description." *Hastings Center Report* 21 (July-August):12–17.

Epstein, Julia. (1995) *Altered Conditions: Disease, Medicine, and Storytelling*. London and New York: Routledge.

Frank, Arthur W. (1991) *At the Will of the Body: Reflections on Illness*. Boston: Houghton Mifflin.

———— (1994) "Interrupted Stories, Interrupted Lives." *Second Opinion* 20, no. 1 (July):11–18.

———— (1995) *The Wounded Storyteller: Body, Illness, and Ethics*. Chicago: University of Chicago Press.

Goffman, Erving. (1961a) *Asylums*. Garden City, NY: Doubleday Anchor.

———— (1961b) *Encounters: Two Studies in the Sociology of Interaction*. Indianapolis: Bobbs Merrill.

Good, Mary-Jo Delvecchio, Paul E. Brodwin, Byron J. Good, and Arthur Kleinman, eds. (1992) *Pain as Human Experience: An Anthropological Perspective*. Berkeley: University of California Press.

Hawkins, Anne Hunsaker. (1993) *Reconstructing Illness: Studies in Pathography*. West Lafayette, IN: Purdue University Press.

Hilfiker, David. (1994) *Not All of Us Are Saints: A Doctor's Journey with the Poor*. New York: Hill and Wang.

Kleinman, Arthur. (1995) *Writing at the Margin: Discourse Between Anthropology and Medicine*. Berkeley: University of California Press.

Komesaroff, Paul A., ed. (1995) *Troubled Bodies: Critical Perspectives on Postmodernism, Medical Ethics, and the Body*. Durham and London: Duke University Press.

Peschel, Richard E., and Enid Rhodes Peschel. (1986) *When a Doctor Hates a Patient: And Other Chapters in a Young Physician's Life*. Berkeley: University of California Press.

Poirier, Suzanne. (1996) "Expressing Illness: Review Essay of Arthur W. Frank, The Wounded Storyteller." *Medical Humanities Review* 10, no. 1 (Spring):74–79.

Radley, Alan. (1993) "The Role of Metaphor in Adjustment to Chronic Illness," in Alan Radley, ed., *Worlds of Illness: Biographical and Cultural Perspectives on Health and Disease*. London and New York: Routledge, pp. 109–123.

Selzer, Richard. (1994) *Raising the Dead: A Doctor's Encounter with His Own Mortality*. New York: Viking.

Tatar, Maria. (1987) *The Hard Facts of the Grimms' Fairy Tales*. Princeton: Princeton University Press.

Taylor, Charles. (1991) *The Malaise of Modernity*. Concord, Ontario: Anansi.

Toombs, S. Kay. (1993) *The Meaning of Illness: A Phenomenological Account of the Different Perspectives of Physician and Patient*. Dordrecht: Kluwer Academic Publishers.

Trilling, Lionel. (1972) *Sincerity and Authenticity*. Cambridge: Harvard University Press.

Waitzkin, Howard. (1991) *The Politics of Medical Encounters: How Patients and Doctors Deal with Social Problems*. New Haven: Yale University Press.

Williams, Gareth. (1993) "Chronic Illness and the Pursuit of Virtue in Everyday Life," in Alan Radley, ed., *Worlds of Illness: Biographical and Cultural Perspectives on Health and Disease*. London and New York: Routledge, pp. 92–108.

Zipes, Jack. (1983) *Fairy Tales and the Art of Subversion: The Classical Genre for Children and the Process of Civilization*. New York: Wildman Press.

4

Autobiography, Biography, and Narrative Ethics

John Hardwig

There is, it seems to me, a preoccupation with autobiography in narrative bioethics. We need to overcome this preoccupation; autobiographies are both epistemically and morally suspect. Autobiographies remain important, of course, but biographies are also of critical importance, both for the theory of bioethics and for clinical practice. I take my concerns about autobiographies and an ethics based on them to be a concern *within* narrative ethics, not either an attack on it or a defense of it.

Before I begin, a word about how I will be using "narrative ethics." I do not include casuistry (*à la* Jonsen) within my purview.[1] Nor am I considering a view like Nussbaum's that reading literature is good for your character.[2] As will be clear from the examples I use, I am thinking primarily of the use of patients' stories of their lives and their illnesses. However, most of my reflections are general enough to apply to virtually any autobiographical account, and thus to narrative ethics beyond the field of bioethics.

The epistemic and moral weaknesses of autobiography are obvious and commonly recognized. I can claim no special insight here. In fact, once they stop to think about it, I expect most readers will have the sense that they were already aware of these problems.

One interesting question, then, is why narrative bioethics has not already recognized them. I cannot explore this issue in any depth. But I suggest that the causes may lie in our heritage of Cartesianism, together with a patient-centered bioethics. Failure to recognize the *epistemic* difficulties with autobiography seems to me to stem primarily from the ghosts of Cartesianism that continue to haunt us despite all our denials and attempts at exorcism. Blindness to the *moral* weaknesses of autobiography is, I believe, rooted in the much too simple patient-centered ethics that was traditional in medicine and has been taken over uncritically by contemporary bioethics. In its contemporary guise, a patient-centered ethics takes the form of an ethics centered in patient autonomy. Although Cartesianism and patient autonomy are largely separate traditions, they support each other in creating a focus on autobiography in bioethics.

The Epistemology of Autobiography

We are, often without even noticing it, still under the spell of two related Cartesian legacies: (1) Motives, interests, beliefs, desires, and attitudes are primarily mental states; action or behavior is, at most, an effect of these mental states. (2) Mental states exist in a consciousness, and since each of us is aware of our own consciousness, each of us knows her own beliefs, values, feelings, and so on. For convenience, I will call these twin Cartesian legacies the view that we are transparent to ourselves.

This Cartesian notion of self-transparency may seem doubly irrelevant to bioethics. In the first place, we deny that we accept any such pre-Freudian, pre-Hegelian (pre-Socratic?) notions. And, on some level, we do reject them. But they are deeply embedded in our common sense and our culture. Consequently, unless we are constantly vigilant, we find ourselves falling victim to this heritage despite ourselves. Secondly, Cartesian self-transparency may also seem remote from narrative bioethics because we deal in ethics, not epistemology. But ethics is not independent of epistemology. As I shall try to indicate, this tradition is neither remote nor irrelevant.

Within these Cartesian premises, the problem of knowledge is the problem of knowing whether there is a correspondence between our own consciousness and something outside it. Thus each of us knows her own mind, but there is a major problem of knowing other minds. We have direct access to our own consciousness but none to someone else's, and inferences from behavior—including verbal behavior—to mental states are always precarious. Each of us is thus in a position of unique epistemic authority with respect to our own minds—your knowledge of my beliefs, desires, motives, intentions can never be better than mine. Indeed, your knowledge (if any) is derivative from mine, depending as it does on my reports about my mental states.

Within narrative bioethics, this Cartesian legacy yields a nearly exclusive fascination with autobiography. Autobiographies are authoritative. The stories we are concerned with, the stories that are to figure in narrative ethics are *the patient's* stories—as told by the patient, of course. If there is no problem with knowing our own minds, but major obstacles to knowing the minds of others, then autobiographies are the stories we need, the stories to rely on in narrative ethics.

Were we not under the Cartesian spell, we would immediately recognize this as palpably naïve. The authoritative account of someone's life is her own—her autobiography? Of course not! In our everyday lives and dealings with each other, nobody would take a first-person account as the definitive or even the most reliable word on the subject. "I am the only one at work who understands the business." Hmm. "I was just trying to help her get control of her life." I wonder. "My ex-wife. . . ."—*whatever* follows that expression is deeply suspect. Would anyone be fool enough to take a former President's autobiography as the definitive account of what he was doing while he was President?

We may think that President Nixon's account of his White House years is riddled with lies. But lies are only one problem and they arise only at the final stage, the stage at which I tell my story for others. But autobiography plays an earlier and more basic role, too—I tell the story of my life *for myself.* The narrative we tell about ourselves is part of living a life that is *a life,* with unity and coherence, rather than just a bunch of experiences that happened to the same person.

The fact that we tell—and perhaps must tell—ourselves stories about our lives introduces an important ambiguity into what we mean by autobiography. The story I tell myself about my life is not an autobiography to which you can ever have access—probably not even if we are intimate, certainly not if we are strangers. We all have secrets. So you must be content with the story I tell for public consumption. That will not normally be exactly the way I see my life. The autobiographies we can consider in bioethics are thus all "secondhand" autobiographies, stories retold for an external audience. They may contain lies and distortions; they will normally be crafted for their intended audience. We shall return to this point.

First, however, if we escape the spell of Cartesianism, we quickly see that even the stories we tell ourselves contain lies and distortions. Self-deception is an important feature of our lives and an important phenomenon for an evaluation of autobiographies. In fact, there are at least four different sets of epistemic problems with autobiographies: (1) ignorance; (2) innocent mistakes; (3) self-deception; and finally (4) lies. Let us briefly consider each of these.

Ignorance and innocent mistakes are the simplest of these problems, so let's start here. There are many things that we do not know about events in our lives. What I do not know cannot figure in my autobiography, however important it may be to my life. I do not know why my former wife finally decided to move to California with me, or why the philosophy department at Humboldt State voted not to renew my contract. Both are important turning points in any story of my life. Which story I choose to tell may well turn on my beliefs about why these pivotal decisions were made as they were.

Notice, too, that some of the things I do not know about my life I could not even find out . . . without relying on someone else (a biographer, perhaps). Someone else might be able to elicit a much more straightforward and truthful account of important events in my life. My former wife may, for example, tell others things about our relationship that she would never tell me. My autobiography is, then, epistemically limited, not only by my ignorance, but by information unavailable to me, though perhaps available to others.

These are failures to know *others* completely enough. But even more important is the fact that there is also much about ourselves that we do not know. We are not close to being transparent to ourselves. There is much about even our present state of mind that we do not know. This is true even on a very basic level. Many discussions of informed consent seem to be plagued by the assumption that the patient will know what treatment she wants if she is just informed about the pros and cons of the various options. But even outside of a medical context, it is often hard for me to know what I want. The problem here is not only one of envisioning what life would be like under various conditions. Nor am I playing on some fancy notion of what I *really* want. It's simply that I often have trouble knowing what I want right now.

Of course, telling the story of my life requires knowing much more about me than just my present state of consciousness. And as we move into less basic though equally critical elements of my account of myself, the likelihood of errors multiplies rapidly. I am quite capable of major mistakes about my beliefs and values. My own account of my intentions, my motives, my character, my personality are all extremely unreliable. The rage I feel is unnoticed, my desire for revenge unexperienced, and consequently my account of what I was up to is . . . not only fallible, not only faulty or flawed, but fundamentally wrong and wrongheaded. I used to divide the world into "settlers" and "explorers" and thought of myself as an explorer. My partner just hooted at that idea. And she was right.

Thus either desires, motives, beliefs, values, and attitudes are not mental states at all, or I can be mistaken about my own mental states. In addition, we have an "outside," as it were, not just an inside. We are normally known at least as much by what we do as by what we say about ourselves. And what I do is a public phenomenon, not uniquely or immediately accessible to me. I have direct access *at most* to what I intended to do, and if my desire for revenge can be unexperienced by me, I may not know even that. Indeed, on some epistemologies—

notably Mead's—it is only through the responses of others that I come to have knowledge even of what I am saying (as opposed to merely thinking), and thinking is itself derivative from saying.[3]

So much for innocent mistakes. They are innocent and thus not very interesting, though they do raise interesting problems for a narrative ethics based on autobiography. Yet perhaps the most interesting thing to be said about innocent mistakes is that it is hard to find a really convincing example of one. *Why* did you not notice your rage? Everyone else did! And how *could* you have overlooked your desire for revenge? It colored virtually everything you did! You, an *explorer? You?*

The important mistakes in my autobiography may not be innocent. I have an important stake in which story I tell about my life. As a result, autobiographies are often—even standardly—riddled with self-deception. Self-deception is motivated, not innocent. If I am telling the story and the story is about me, I will normally want to leave the audience with a favorable impression about the central character. The first audience of my story is myself, and I desperately want to feel good about myself. The stories I tell myself are imbued with that mission.

Most of us do in fact manage to cast ourselves in a favorable light, at least to ourselves. (Even those who are habitually "down on themselves" usually feel that they are more honest with themselves or have higher moral standards than those who feel good about themselves.) Self-assessment and self-judgment are always epistemically suspect; consequently, autobiography is, in important respects, seldom the most trustworthy story of a life. In fact, one of the reasons I often do not even know what I want is because I have many wants that I don't want to admit to myself.

Let's move on now to stories told for others. I am also very much interested in what the broader, outside audience thinks of me. I would like to leave a good impression. I want almost everyone to be impressed with me and what I have done, everyone to think well of me, everyone to like me. The first thing this causes me to do is to tell my story in light of the ideas I have about the beliefs and values of the audience. I tell different stories for different audiences, and they may all be inaccurate, if only by reason of one-sidedness.

Joanne Lynn argues that most seriously ill and dying patients are desperately trying to be "a good patient."[4] They very much want to do a good job of dying in the eyes of doctors, family, and friends—the audiences. After all, this is their last chance to do well, their last chance to leave a good impression, their only chance to die well. If Lynn is correct, the autobiographies of terminally ill people—including their statements about what kind of treatment they want—will usually be decisively shaped by this desire to meet the norms and expectations of different audiences. Viewed in this light, it may not be surprising that many patients tell one story to one doctor, another to another, yet a third to a nurse, and still other stories to various members of their families. If I detect different expectations, I will tell different stories.

Of course, a variety of stories *may* all be true. All stories of a life are incomplete (or they would take about as long to tell as to live). And it may be that different stories—different emphases perhaps—are appropriate for different audiences and different purposes. I know, for example, that you are a clinician and you are interested in a story focused on health and illness. So I may leave things completely out of my story that are much more important to me than my health. But my motivation in shaping my story to its audience is also normally not purely altruistic. I edit, shade, stretch, distort, and often even lie in an attempt to secure a more favorable response from my various audiences.

Now, lies and self-deception are intimately related. There are at least three important feedback loops between the stories I tell for various audiences and my self-knowledge. First, it is much easier for me to tell you a story that you will find convincing if I believe it myself. Consequently, I can easily fall victim to my attempts to impress or deceive you and end up believing the stories I have told for public consumption. Lying often ends in self-deception.

Second, my desire to leave a favorable impression on you is deeply confusing to me—it makes it harder for me to distinguish my own wants from your expectations or hopes of me. When a patient opts for more treatment for her cancer, how, then, can we assume that she knows what *she* wants, as opposed to wanting what she thinks we expect of her? Lynn thinks she may well not know what she wants. Of course, she may want most *whatever* will leave a favorable impression on the audience. But presumably our ethics of informed consent is not to reduce to an elaborate game in which patients are forced to try to guess what medical treatment we want them to choose.

Third, partly as a result of these first two feedback loops, there may well be limits to how long and how thoroughly I can tell a story for public consumption without becoming what I pretend to be. A very dramatic example is provided by police who work with undercover agents. The very lives of undercover narcotics agents, for example, depend on their ability to tell their cover stories convincingly. Police officers relate that an agent—any agent, anyone—can go underground for only about six months before she literally loses track of who she is.[5] She will, for example, no longer remember that she is a police officer or who her father is. And if we believe that the story we tell about ourselves is the basis of identity, we will be forced to conclude that an agent can only go underground for about six months before she *becomes* a different person.

So much for a brief overview of ignorance, mistakes, self-deception, and lies in autobiographies. There is one more reason for concern about the epistemic trustworthiness of autobiographical accounts: I am normally the central character in my autobiography. But if I see myself as the central character, won't my account tend to overplay the importance of my own role and contribution, and correspondingly to underrate the place and contribution of others? Thus, when I tell the story of the philosophy department at East Tennessee State University during my years as chair, it tends to place too much emphasis on what I did.

Multiple Autobiographies

Autobiographies contain many epistemic weaknesses; they are all epistemically suspect. But even if they are often mistaken, isn't there something privileged about autobiographies? Right or wrong, honest or distorted, an autobiography is, after all, the way *I* see my life; it expresses the meaning my life has for me. And that is what is important for stories of illness and for medical treatment decisions.

But we have already seen that the autobiography I tell myself is not available to you. Should we even say that the story I tell *myself* is the way *I* see my life? "How could it fail to be the way I see my life? My conscious experiences are my conscious experiences, after all! The way I see myself and my life may be mistaken, but it *is* the way I see it!" But that is the voice of the Cartesian legacy again. If we recognize self-deception, doesn't "the story I tell myself" become systematically ambiguous? If my desire for revenge colors virtually everything I do but I deny this to myself, or if I see myself as an explorer but unfailingly choose the familiar and the secure . . . what are we to say?

I think we must say that I am telling myself at least *two* stories simultaneously, one in which the desire for revenge does not figure at all, but also another in which it looms large and is justified. But I am unaware of this second story, unaware of it despite the fact that I am telling it! Strange as this may seem, I think we *must* say that I am telling myself multiple stories, for my *action* (as opposed to my deceptive conscious awareness) is also story-driven. It, too, has narrative unity.

Now, if you take my conscious story that I do not seek revenge as the whole of my story or even the center of it, you will treat me inappropriately, and I will be disappointed, frustrated, or enraged by what you do. For the stories I *consciously* tell myself will be only one part of my own sense of my life. I can articulate for myself only some of the meaning my life has for me; some of that meaning I may be quite unaware of. Thus, dealing most sensitively and effectively with a self-deceived, inarticulate, or unreflective person—any of us to some extent—will involve attempting to ferret out *all* the stories she tells herself, including those she is not aware of.

The meaning my own life has for me is thus never completely captured in the stories I am aware of. Self-knowledge, on the account I am suggesting, would involve coming to acknowledge this multiplicity of autobiographies, learning to ferret out and articulate all of them, dealing with the discrepancies among them, and then ceasing to tell oneself the self-deceptive stories. Only with perfect self-knowledge would my autobiography be single, and only then would it accurately convey the complete sense or meaning my life has for me.

Autobiography and the Clinical Encounter

Exclusive reliance upon patient autobiographies would do more than place narrative ethics on a perilous epistemic foundation. It would weaken the practice of medicine, as well. Wherever accuracy is important, there are serious questions about whether we ought to attend exclusively—or even primarily—to autobiography. Consider, first, small things. Medical students are taught to double the amount of alcohol I say I consume and perhaps also the number of cigarettes I say I smoke. The veracity of the sexual history I give is suspect, as is the story I tell about what I eat or why I am seeking pain medication. Users of illegal substances often deny use. Child abuse, spouse abuse, and elder abuse invite cover stories.

Consider next the following examples: "He says that he hates his job and being on disability would be wonderful. But I know how depressed he is whenever he can't work and how horrible he feels about himself when he doesn't have a job." "He'll tell you that impotence is no big deal at his age, but it bothers him tremendously." "She says she's doing OK, but she stays drunk or high most of the time since her accident." "He says his memory is pretty good, but I'm afraid to leave him alone for even a few hours." "She says she still gets around pretty well, but there are many days when she can barely make it to the bathroom and back. She wants you to think she can take care of herself because she's terrified of going into a nursing home."

Moreover, because health, sickness, and medicine often touch on very intimate features of our lives, they evoke all kinds of very basic attitudes about what is appropriate to tell to whom and how the audience will evaluate me if I reveal this fact about myself. I have seen patients who are unable or unwilling to admit the amount of pain they are suffering for fear of being thought weak or unmanly. Bulimia is something many young women cannot talk about. The spectacle of my death may be too terrifying to mention. Or I may be too ashamed of my terror to mention that.

We have seen that the story a clinician or bioethicist receives is seldom the story the patient tells herself. It may well not be the story the patient would tell another audience. But even if a clinician could elicit the story I consciously tell myself, that would normally not fully capture the meaning my life and action have for me. For all these reasons, sensitive and appropriate treatment of me in the clinic or hospital depends—just as it does in other contexts—on a careful attempt to weave a coherent picture of me and my illness out of the various stories I tell, together with the stories others tell about me.

The import of these points runs deep. In light of the multiple stories I will usually be telling myself and others, how do you respect or honor my autonomy? How do you design a plan of medical treatment for me that will embody or promote the meaning my life has for me? Do you attend only to the story I tell you? If so, why am I so upset when you treat me like the explorer I take myself to be? Or must you also consider the stories I tell others and even try to gain access to the stories that inform my action but not my awareness of myself? If the latter, you must talk with my partner, not just me—she will readily tell you that I am certainly no explorer, however much I may see myself that way. Thus, even promoting patient autonomy must not rest solely on autobiography. If you would respect or promote my autonomy, you must attend to various *biographies* of me, not just to the story I consciously tell myself . . . or you.

Good clinicians must, then, be skilled biographers, not just faithful receptors of patient autobiographies.[6] Part of the training of medical, nursing, and social work students must be—and already is—developing their skills as biographers. In this respect, the practice of medicine and nursing may well be far more sophisticated than our theories of narrative bioethics that are rooted in patient autobiographies.

The Moral Evaluation of Autobiographies

We have so far considered mainly the implications for me of treating me on the basis of my autobiography. Let us now turn to the implications *for others* of my autobiography. With this we move to a more straightforwardly *moral* evaluation of autobiography. We can begin by reflecting on the central role I assign myself in the story I tell about my life: *Shouldn't* I be the central character in the story of *my* life? Especially if it's the story of my life *as told by me!* Isn't there something pathetic or deeply unfortunate about those who do not play the central role even in their own autobiographies? Moreover, don't I have some fundamental right to tell the story of my life? Whose life is it, anyway?

But I am not the only character in my story. The story of my life cannot be simply the story of me, for there is no way to separate my life from the lives of those around me and especially those intimately connected with me. Any story of my life will have to include many other characters. Let's focus our reflections on the role of family and loved ones in my autobiography, since their lives are most closely intertwined with mine, and they are the ones most likely to be deeply affected by the role I assign them in the story I tell.

In contrast with autobiography, there is in many joint endeavors or communities no central character. Often, there is no central character in a neighborhood, an academic department, a business, a government agency, or a team.

That's usually an important part of what makes them healthy. Certainly there is no central character in a healthy family.

Another part of what makes families healthy is that there is, in important respects, not one story for each family member, but only one story among them. The claim that there should be (in many significant respects) only one story in a family is not the claim that families should be monolithic entities, committed to one set of beliefs and values, with no tolerance for deviance. There can be difference, conflict, even basically different perspectives within one story. Rather, the point is that families (couples, friendships) in which too many different stories are told are typically characterized by lack of communication and understanding, and also by an absence of intimacy and sharing.

Who tells the story when lives are intertwined? It is a privilege and a power to have the right to tell the story. In other contexts, it is normally the privilege of the powerful—the dominant man—to tell the official story of "his" family and "his" family life. But in bioethics, we listen to the patient's story.

Reliance upon patients' autobiographies both reflects and reinforces a patient-centered bioethics. The patient-centered feature of bioethics seems entirely justified and even noble—it's just advocacy for the vulnerable. But in bioethics, as elsewhere, when we attend exclusively to one family member's story, we tend to ignore or discount the ramifications on the lives of the rest of the family.[7] They are only bit players of marginal importance in the story we are concerned with. Exclusive reliance upon autobiography thus systematically undervalues others and overlooks or discounts the importance of their interests.

There are at least two forms of oppression involved in reliance upon any one family member's story.

First, it silences the others. A focus on *the patient's* autobiography silences all other members of her family. *Their* interests and *their* autobiographies do not count. And the family *is* in fact all too effectively silenced by our bioethics and in our health care system. Decisions are made every day that promote the patient's interests at truly staggering costs to the lives of other members of the patient's family. These decisions are routinely made as if families were no more than patient support systems or as if the interests of other members of the family were somehow morally irrelevant. We do not even ask whether it is morally legitimate to impose these burdens on the patient's family—in fact, a patient-centered ethics implicitly *requires* that we not consider the interests of the family. Because our ethics has so thoroughly silenced families, we can congratulate ourselves on an ethics that places the patient's interests over all others and on having faithfully served the patient's interests.

But it is wrong to consider only the well-being of one member of a family when the lives of the others will also be dramatically affected. To do so is tacitly to reduce all other family members to means to the well-being of the one family member who is ill. Because this is wrong, it is also wrong to listen exclusively to the patient's story. Doing so always runs the risk of inappropriately discounting the interests of the rest of the family.

All this is true of the autobiographies we tell when we are at our best. Even at our best, most of us assign ourselves the central role in our stories. Most of us are inclined to weigh benefits and burdens to ourselves more heavily than those to others. We all tend to be self-centered. But if illness makes most people more self-absorbed, self-centered, or inconsiderate, more regressed into a primitive or immature self, then the autobiographies of the seriously or chronically ill will be especially likely to shortchange the interests of others. And all of this is further reinforced by an audience of health care professionals and bioethicists who are most interested in the health-related aspects and outcomes of the story and who are all professionally committed to weighing in on the side of the sick. For these reasons, we should be especially wary of relying on a sick person's story.

But even when the interests of others are not inappropriately discounted in the story, it is still a form of oppression for any one person to tell the official story of a group—family, clan, business, team, government, or ethics consult. It is not, for example, morally sufficient if I paternalistically take the interests of the rest of my family into consideration, not even if I am scrupulously fair in doing so. *They* must be allowed to speak for themselves—to define their own interests, to say how they see our present situation. Allowing others also to tell their version of the story is part of what is involved in respecting them as persons. Thus there is a basic moral criticism of exclusive attention to anyone's autobiography . . . with the possible exception of those who are all alone, with no family, friends, or loved ones.

The second way in which people can be oppressed by an autobiography is that they can be forced to live in someone else's story. This form of oppression grows out of the fact that we are not only passive tellers of our stories, but also active agents who are living our lives. We all attempt to live out a script. In order to continue to live our present script, we must often try to fit recalcitrant reality into our stories. One option for fitting reality into a story is, as we have seen, deception and self-deception. But as actors, we have a second option for fitting reality into our scripts. We can actively shape reality to fit the story we are telling. This is not in itself remarkable, uncommon, or morally troublesome; it is an essential feature of action, an inescapable part of forging a life.

But it can easily slide into a form of oppression: we attempt to force others to live as characters in our stories. Take the example—perhaps the caricature—of the traditional husband who "takes care of the little woman." If I am living out that style of masculinity, then I *must* see my wife as "the little woman"—as needing help, perhaps even as fundamentally incapable of taking care of herself.

Otherwise the story I am attempting to live out will lapse into incoherence, and a large part of my life becomes meaningless. I may, as a result, take steps to make reality conform to this perception. I take steps—normally without full awareness of what I am doing—that tend to incapacitate my wife in order that I may be the man who takes care of her. This sometimes takes truly horrific forms. Equally horrific, to mention just one more example, are attempts to create my sons in my own image, to make them "chips off the old block."

(Distance normally insulates outsiders to some extent; they are somewhat more immune than family members to this sort of oppression. But outsiders, too, can be forced to live in the stories of others. In fact, the frustration physicians and nurses feel over providing futile treatment can be a result of the professional debasement that can result when health care professionals are forced to play an assigned role in the patient's or family's preferred story.)

To the extent that I am successful in forcing, manipulating, pressuring, or badgering others to live as characters in my story, I deprive them of the opportunity to author their own stories. There is a fundamental loss of freedom and autonomy in this. It is, at bottom, to deprive the other of the opportunity to live her own life. Although illness can help to free other members of my family from this form of tyranny, it can also serve to strengthen my hand in making them serve my story. Ideally, of course, we should be creating a story *together*.

To summarize, the moral challenge to a narrative ethics based on patient autobiography is that it harbors two forms of oppression. First, others are silenced and often slighted if only my story about our life together is attended to. It is wrong to slight the interests of others; it is wrong to silence others even if they are not slighted as a result. Secondly, I easily wrong others by attempting to mold them to fit into my story. Others aid and abet both forms of oppression if they attend exclusively or even primarily to the story I tell about my life and the place others have in it. For these two reasons, a narrative bioethics based primarily on patient autobiography is morally as well as epistemologically flawed.

The Alternative

What is the alternative to a preoccupation with autobiographies in narrative ethics? I have already hinted at it. The alternative is to acknowledge that an autobiography is only *one* account of a life, a deeply fallible and often unreliable account at that. Moreover, all of us live in and tell many autobiographies. Consequently, insofar as narrative bioethics requires an accurate account of a life or an illness, we need to piece together the narrative by attending to many stories told by many tellers. Acknowledging this would involve coming to see that the patient's *husband* has a perfectly valid "take" on her wishes and values, on what her life has been all about, on "what she is up to" (including what she is up to in telling her story the way she does).

Of course, the point here is not that we are transparent to *others* but not to ourselves. There are limits to others' knowledge of me, too. Other narrators also have agendas; their stories about me also contain mistakes. Their stories are also motivated, shaped for an intended audience, designed to impress us with the narrator, and so on.

This is true even for those of us famous or distinguished enough to have professional—"detached," "objective"—biographers. It is even more true of biographers with whom we have had extended interaction. My physician, in telling the story of my case, is also inevitably telling a story about how she practices medicine and even about who she is. And the biographers who have most at stake in telling our stories one way rather than another are our more common "intimate biographers"—lovers, close friends, and family members. Their self-images and even their lives may turn dramatically on the way they tell the story about us.

There is, then, no detached observer—value-free, motiveless, with no intentions, no plans, no agenda—to tell the authoritative story.[8] There is no authoritative story. Because there is no "view from nowhere," the alternative to autobiography in narrative ethics cannot be simply a return to the physician's privilege to tell the story of the case. Rather, we must recognize that the physician—or bioethicist—tells the story of patients in the way she does because of the limits of her own self-knowledge and the agendas she brings to bear. The person cannot be left out of the story she tells; the person cannot really even be left out of the factual or scientific observations she makes about the case.

This more complex view of narrative and narrative ethics requires a new discipline of us. There may well still be a point to the traditional discipline of trying to achieve and speak from a detached, value-free standpoint. Often we should try to put our selves out of play in telling stories about others, or even about ourselves. But recognizing that we all inevitably fail to achieve an objective, detached, unmotivated account either of ourselves or of others, we need also to learn another, rather different discipline—that of coming to recognize our own motivations, biases, agendas, and then of stating them quite explicitly. This kind of self-knowledge is required of a narrator—and thus of a health care professional—if her account is to be maximally reliable and morally trustworthy.

If someone has the requisites that enable her to offer an epistemically reliable and morally trustworthy autobiography, it will be because she has long participated in a complex, multiperson process, listening to many different accounts of her dreams, fears, plans, actions, activities, and past. She knows herself because she continually tries out various versions of her story—biographies as well as autobiographies—on many audiences to check the reliability of her own view against their responses to what she is saying about her life.[9]

Autobiographies that are both epistemically and morally reliable are thus derivative from biographies: it is only through having attended to many stories about me—including the stories others tell in response to my earlier autobiographies—that I can finally give a trustworthy account of my own life. Still, self-knowledge is never complete. No one's autobiography should ever be taken as the definitive account of her life. And none of us can completely avoid deeply troubling and pervasive forms of oppression that often pass unnoticed in the stories we tell.

In light of all this, we might venture a fundamental reinterpretation of autonomy, including patient autonomy. The autonomous person is not an island or some transparent self who has immediate knowledge of what goes on inside herself and who clings to that in the face of everything anyone else may say. No, an autonomous person develops an autobiography in community—in this complex, multiperson encounter seeking the truth about her and her life with others. On this alternative view, only those who have participated in such a process can become autonomous. For it is only through hearing many stories about ourselves that we can know ourselves, what our life has been . . . or even what it means to us.

The art of weighing these many different and often conflicting stories, and of weaving them together into a reasonably coherent though multivocal account, is the art of the biographer. As bioethicists and clinicians we must, then, become biographers, not simply faithful recorders of autobiographies. Listening to multiple sources is epistemically more reliable than exclusive reliance upon any one source. Attending to many voices is almost always morally preferable to listening to only one. Dialogue is better than monologue.

Acknowledgments

I wish to thank Hugh LaFollette, Stuart Finder, and Hilde Nelson for helpful comments on earlier versions of this paper.

Notes

1. Albert Jonsen and Stephen Toulmin, *The Abuse of Casuistry: A History of Moral Reasoning* (Berkeley: University of California Press, 1988).

2. Martha Nussbaum, *Poetic Justice: The Literary Imagination and Public Life* (Boston: Beacon Press, 1995).

3. George Herbert Mead, *Mind, Self, and Society* (Chicago: University of Chicago Press, 1962).

4. Joanne Lynn, "End of Life Decision Making in Seriously Ill Patients," presented at "Deciding How We Die: The Use and Limits of Advance Directives," Roanoke, VA., 15 September 1995, conference sponsored by Carilion Health Systems.

5. I owe this point to Edwin J. Delattre, in conversation.

6. I owe this point to William Donnally, in conversation.

7. For an argument that a patient-centered ethic should be replaced by a family-centered ethic see John Hardwig, "What About the Family?" *Hastings Center Report* 20, no. 2 (1990):5–10; Hilde L. Nelson and James L. Nelson, *The Patient in the Family* (New York: Routledge, 1995).

8. It should be obvious by now—if not long before—that this paper is deeply indebted to feminist epistemology. See, for example, Sandra Harding, *Whose Science? Whose Knowledge? Thinking From Women's Lives* (Ithaca, NY: Cornell University Press, 1991).

9. I have argued that dialogue is necessary for self-knowledge and thus for moral rationality in a very early article: John Hardwig, "The Achievement of Moral Rationality," *Philosophy & Rhetoric* 6 (1973):171–85.

5

Nice Story, But So What?
Narrative and Justification in Ethics

John D. Arras

Everywhere one looks in the academy these days, theory is out and stories are in. On any number of different fronts—including anthropology, history, literary criticism, and even philosophy—we are currently witnessing a headlong retreat from theory and so-called "master narratives" such as Enlightenment rationalism, Freudian psychoanalysis, and Marxism. Many scholars in the social sciences and humanities seem particularly eager to jettison the last vestiges of the Enlightenment ideals of objectivity, rationality, truth, and universality as these pertain both to matters epistemological and axiological. The consensus seems to be that, just as our ability to know is profoundly circumscribed by the contingencies of time, place, and our own psychological makeup (all knowledge is thus "local"), so our values are said to reach no farther than the bounds of our community or nation. Furthermore, it is maintained that any attempt to extend the boundaries of either our knowledge or our values is not just wrong and ill-fated (because, given our finitude, it cannot be accomplished), but also dangerous because it will inevitably amount to an imposition of our ways of knowing and valuing upon others. Thus, the belief in objectivity and universality that once drove the so-called "Enlightenment project"—a belief that such great but diverse thinkers as Voltaire, Rousseau, Kant, Locke, and Marx once viewed as profoundly liberatory—is now the object of a profound suspicion. Behind the search for universality must lie the will to dominate, to bend others to our ways of thinking and valuing. Objectivity and universality, once thought to be the key to our common deliverance from the narrowness and stupidity of local custom, have come to be seen as the seeds of tyranny.

In the place of the Western mind's traditional quest for the objective and universal laws undergirding nature, history, and morals, we now find the flourishing of narrative, storytelling, anecdote, and autobiography. Here too the argument is both epistemological and moral. All knowing is necessarily bound up with a narrative tradition of one kind or other; and all valuing grows out of and expresses the stories that constitute us as members of a particular family, community, or nation. Rather than lusting after the immutable laws of nature and "Man," historians, social scientists, philosophers, and legal scholars have begun to celebrate the particularity and localism inherent in the medium of the little story, the *"petit récit."* In a litany that has by now become quite familiar, we see anthropologists like Clifford Geertz making the case for "local knowledge,"[1] literary critics like Jane Tompkins lauding the critic's own autobiography,[2] legal scholars like Paul Gewirtz probing the role of narrative and rhetoric in law,[3] and philosophers like Richard Rorty siding with the poets and novelists against the theoreticians.[4]

This flourishing of narrative has brought about what literary critic David Simpson has conceived as a major shift in the "balance of trade" among academic departments of universities.[5] Literature has emerged as the major exporter of methods and themes to other departments once dominated by more objectivist and scientific tendencies. Indeed, the traditionally sharp boundaries between such academic subjects as history, anthropology, literature, and philosophy have recently yielded to make way for the triumph of a "literary culture" that now appears to dominate the academy. Simpson calls this refiguring or abolishing of boundaries between traditional disciplines "the academic postmodern." At my university, this development is strikingly illustrated by the spectacle of the famous philosopher Richard Rorty using the philosophy department essentially as a mail drop while doing most of his teaching in the department of English literature; at the same time, our English professors write books on why literary criticism has to be more philosophical.

The field of bioethics is beginning to take its own narrative turn. Long dominated by the aspirations to objectivity and universality as embodied in its dominant "principlist" paradigm, bioethics is now witnessing an explosion of interest in narrative and storytelling as alternative ways of structuring and evaluating the experiences of patients, physicians, and other health care professionals. To be sure, the universalist mantra of autonomy, beneficence, and justice still holds sway in many quarters, and its principal defenders have proved to be quite adept at ingesting or co-opting much recent criticism without giving up on their central claims regarding the pivotal role of principles in the moral life.[6] Still, one wonders whether the current plethora of conferences, journal issues, and articles devoted to narrative bioethics presages not merely an important shift away from "principle-driven" ethics, a movement that has been proceeding apace for some time now under the auspices of casuistry and feminism, but also the imminent triumph of the literary sensibility in a field that has traditionally wished to appear as a source of "hard knowledge" to its beneficiaries and funders in the medical and research establishments.

In spite of the current enthusiasm for narrative and the plague of stories[7] it has engendered, we have not gained much clarity about the precise meaning of narrative ethics and how it relates, or should relate, to ethics in general. After dutifully plowing through much of the extant literature on this emerging trend, I must confess to being at a loss as to what it all means. In particular, the connection between narrative and moral justification remains maddeningly obscure. What, one wants to ask, is the relationship between narrative and the achievement of moral justification, between the telling of a story and the establishment of a warrant for believing in the moral adequacy or excellence of a particular action, policy, or character? In order partially to dispel some of this unclarity, I shall attempt in the present essay a modest typology of narrative ethics. There are several different conceptions of "narrative ethics," and each carries significantly different implications for the question of moral justification. As we shall see, some conceptions are relatively modest and unthreatening to the claims of principles and theory, while the more robust versions of narrative ethics threaten to replace the regnant paradigm.

Moral Justification in the *Ancien* (Modern) *Régime*

At the risk of gross oversimplification, one might say that the model of moral justification at work in most "theory-driven" accounts of ethics,[8] including the first three editions of the principlism of Beauchamp and Childress, involved an effort to connect with a normative essence, idea, or norm beyond the vagaries of actual human behavior. Whether one purported to find this normative ideal in the principle of utility, the categorical imperative, or Rawls's two principles of justice, one sought to ground one's ethical judgments of right action and sound policy in a source beyond the contingencies of historical accident, beyond the narrow confines of one's community and tradition. Whether one owed ultimate theoretical allegiance to Mill, Kant, or Rawls, ethical rationality was conceived along the lines of a scientific (or at least quasi-scientific) model. From Plato's cave to Rawls's original position, the motivation behind the method remained unchanged: in order to attain truth and justify one's ethical judgments, it is first necessary to purify these judgments of any and all subjective elements involving the agent's "story," that is, his or her inclinations stemming from a particular upbringing, social class, or networks of relationships. This model finds its most thoroughgoing adherent in Kant, whose preoccupation with human nature was limited to our "rational nature as such" rather than to the particularities of human anthropology. This position finds an unintentionally comic contemporary echo in Engelhardt's claim to have established a "transgalactic" foundation for morality.[9]

It was quite natural, then, that the more theory-driven approaches to ethics would have little, if any, use for narrative or storytelling in their quest for ethical justification. Kantians have been more concerned with our ability to universalize the maxims animating our behavior, while utilitarians, in their familiar role as cost-benefit analysts, have sought to achieve a kind of science of desire. In each case, stories play a decidedly limited role in the formulation of moral problems and no discernible role in the justification of their resolutions. This denigration of narrative is not accidental; it is, or so I would argue, a constituent part of the rationalistic, Enlightenment tradition. The spirit of this tradition is nicely illustrated in the figure of Auguste Comte, the nineteenth-century French social theorist who regarded religion as merely a collection of stories, a form of consciousness that had to be surpassed first by philosophy (metaphysics) and eventually by modern science, which occupied the highest rung in the hierarchy of rationality.[10] As Jean-François Lyotard aptly puts the matter, according to the "man of science," narratives are mere "fables, myths, legends, fit only for women and children."[11]

The remainder of this essay will be devoted to an exposition and preliminary assessment of three distinct formulations of "narrative ethics" that each in its own way attempts to redress the balance in favor of narrative. We will first consider narrative as a supplement to (or ingredient of) principle-driven approaches to ethics. From this angle, narrative is seen as an indispensable and ubiquitous feature of the moral landscape. Here narrative not only allows us to delineate moral problems in a concrete fashion, but also plays an important role in the formulation of moral principles and the depiction of character. Then we will briefly inspect the view, powerfully articulated by Alasdair MacIntyre and Stanley Hauerwas, that narrative functions principally as the very ground of all moral justification. Narrative functions here not merely as a supplement or handmaiden to principles and theory, but also as the exclusive basis of ethical rationality itself. Finally, we shall canvass the place of narrative within a distinctly "postmodern" ethical stance, where narrative and the authenticity of the narrator appear to play the role of substitutes for ethical justification. As we shall see, each formulation of narrative ethics poses a progressively greater challenge to currently dominant ways of thinking about the role of stories in moral justification.

Narrative as Supplement to an Ethic of Principles

The most benign and least controversial version of "narrative ethics" asserts that an ethic of principles and theory cannot stand alone, that it must be supplemented by an understanding of the narrative structure of human action in order to achieve a more fully rounded and complete ethic. This assertion itself rests upon three distinct observations about the relationship between narrative and ethics: (1) that narrative elements are deeply embedded in all forms of moral reasoning; (2) that our responses to stories are the ground out of which principles and theories grow; and (3) that narrative is the only medium in which a concern for character and virtue can be intelligibly discussed.

A. The Pervasiveness of Narrative in Ethical Reasoning

Contrary to the vision of the "man of science" quoted above, according to which there exists a sharp division between forms of reasoning driven by stories and those driven by principles and theories, some advocates of narrative ethics insist that stories and moral theorizing are mutually interpenetrating and interdependent. They point out that moral narratives often embody a kind of argument (a "moral"), while much ethical argument is pervaded by narrative elements; and they claim that a keener awareness of these narrative elements embedded in all moral reasoning will permit a more reflective and penetrating mode of moral analysis.

Rita Charon, a physician and literary scholar, highlights a number of ways in which a heightened literary consciousness can augment our reasoning skills in a field like clinical bioethics.[12] For the practicing physician, Charon notes, closer attention to the narrative elements in the situation—and in particular to the patient's own story—would permit the recognition of ethical issues that often go unnoticed. What's really troubling a particular patient—for example, the likely impact of scheduled surgery on her ability to maintain her roles as worker, wife, and mother—will often not find its way into the dominant form of medical narrative, the medical chart. Although the chart and other forms of medical discourse, such as the truncated language of clinical rounds, pretend to have achieved a high level of universality and scientific objectivity, they often screen out the very meanings that the disease or illness has for the patient.[13] In the absence of an understanding of the existential implications of the patient's condition and the meanings of various treatment alternatives, the physician is likely not even to recognize moral tensions or problems latent in the medical encounter.

Charon also usefully points out that the various skills and sensitivities of the literary critic are indispensable in coming to terms adequately with the whole gamut of medical narratives, including not only the chart but also all the stories that caregivers, patients, family members, and authors tell about their experiences surrounding a particular "case." In particular, she notes, closer attention to the way in which medical narratives are presented—including, for example, the way in which the various elements are framed, the content is selected, and the author's point of view is established—can help us read more deeply and critically. Quoting with approval the German literary theorist Walter Benjamin ("The traces of the storyteller cling to the story the way the handprints of the potter cling to the clay vessel"), Charon argues that sensitivity to such questions as authorship and point of view constitute, along with several other important skills, a kind of "narrative competence" that is a prerequisite to doing good ethics.

For Rita Charon, then, "narrative ethics" essentially means a mode of moral analysis that is attentive to and critically reflective about the narrative elements of our experience. It is important to note, however, that Charon's plea for a narrative ethics is not meant as a fundamental challenge to an ethic driven by principles and theories. On the contrary, she explicitly wishes to leave intact the basic structure of principle-driven ethics.[14] On this view, narrative competence is recommended as a supplement, as a way to improve our use of the existing methods of moral analysis by gearing their deployment to the rich particularity of patients' lives. Principles retain their normative force; narrative sensitivity just makes them work better. "Narrative ethics" on this gloss is thus not a newer, better kind of ethics; it simply allows us to apply principles with greater sensitivity and precision.

B. Narrative as Ground and Object of Ethical Principles

A different conception of the relationship between narrative and moral justification, but a conception still faithful to the depiction of narrative ethics as a supplement to principles, might be sought in the notion of reflective equilibrium. This approach to moral methodology was first articulated in the early work of John Rawls,[15] and has since been the subject of much amplification and commentary at the hands of other ethical theorists.[16] I and many others have written elsewhere about this conception of moral justification within the context of bioethics,[17] so I will content myself here with a very brief sketch merely sufficient to make my point about the connection between narrative ethics and reflective equilibrium.

As Rawls and his followers depict it, reflective equilibrium offers an alternative picture of moral justification to the sort of "top-down" account favored by moral "deductivists." Deductivists view the process of moral justification as involving a unidirectional movement from preexisting theories and principles to their "application" at the level of the case. To justify an action or policy on this account is simply to bring it under the relevant theory, principle, or moral rule. According to the partisans of reflective equilibrium, this unidirectional picture distorts or totally ignores the pivotal role of intuitive, case-based judgments of right and wrong. To be sure, the sort of judgments they have in mind are not to be confused with just any responses to cases, no matter how prejudiced, ill-considered, or subject to coercion they might be. Rather, they are referring to those intuitive responses in which we have the most confidence, like those embedded in the conclusions that slavery or the killing of innocent children are wrong. Rawls referred to this class of intuitive responses as our "considered judgments." It is precisely these judgments, it is claimed, that give concrete meaning, definition, and scope to moral principles and that provide critical leverage in refining their articulations.

The partisans of reflective equilibrium claim, in effect, that principles and cases have a dialectical or reciprocal relationship. The principles provide normative guidance, while the cases provide considered judgments. The considered judgments, in turn, help shape the principles that then provide more precise guidance for more complex or difficult cases. Principles and cases thus coexist in creative tension or "reflective equilibrium." Ethical justification is then sought not in any kind of correspondence between our ethical judgments and some sort of transcendent realm of ethical norms or kingdom of ends, but rather in the overall meshing or coherence achieved among our intuitions about cases, our rules, principles, moral theories, and nonmoral theories about society, personhood, and so on.

Now the reason for bringing up this business of reflective equilibrium in the context of the present essay is that the cases about which we have these considered judgments are themselves narratives. They tell stories about what's happening in and around people's bodies and about their social relationships, stories that prominently feature some sort of moral dilemma or conflict. So, rather than viewing stories as being essentially remote from the realms of principle and theory—or, in the "man of science's" words, as "savage, primitive, underdeveloped, backward"[18] and so on—the advocates of this coherentist approach to moral justification would have us view narrative and stories as intimately bound up with the most sophisticated renderings of principle- and theory-driven moral reasoning. For no matter how far we progress toward the ethereal realms of principle and theory, we ought never to lose sight of the fact that all of our abstract norms are in fact distillations (and, yes, refinements) of our most fundamental intuitive responses to stories about human behavior. Our moral vocabulary and the very contours of our moral universe are shaped by the stories that we hear at our parents' knees. Principles and theories do not emerge full-blown from some empyrean realm of moral truth; rather, they always bear the marks of their history, of their coming-to-be through the crucible of stories and cases.

Thus, the defenders of a coherentist theory of moral justification, a theory aptly captured in the metaphor of reflective equilibrium, would claim, like Rita Charon, that narrative and moral theory are not alternatives, but are rather inseparable elements in a perpetual to-and-fro movement from stories to principles and back again. According to both Charon and these moral coherentists, "narrative ethics" is not a new way of doing ethics, but is rather a recognition and full appreciation of the debt that principle- and theory-driven modes of discourse owe to stories. Here too, then, narrative ethics works to supplement, rather than supplant, a principled approach to ethics.

C. Narrative and the Depiction of Character[19]

While some partisans of narrative ethics advance very strong and controversial claims, [20] I think that all would agree that an appropriately complete story or history is a prerequisite to any responsible moral analysis. Before we attempt to judge, we must understand, and the best way to achieve the requisite understanding is to tell a nuanced story.

Thus, when we debate the issue of assisted suicide, for example, we should do so not as some sort of abstract, asocial, and timeless proposition, but rather in the context of a full-bodied case. Dr. Timothy Quill's well-known case study of Diane, a patient requesting assisted suicide, provides an excellent illustration of this narrative approach.[21] Instead of focusing on the derivation and specification of principles, Dr. Quill gives us a rich picture of the "players" and their characters. There was first and foremost his patient, Diane, a courageous but fearful cancer patient seeking control of her dying process, a woman who had already overcome a previous cancer threat and her own debilitating alcoholism; and there was Dr. Quill himself, who emerges as a competent and clearly compassionate physician torn between loyalties to his patient and the ethics of his profession, a man courageous enough to "take small risks for people he cares about." He explores the roles that the players occupy: a doctor trained to preserve life rather than end it, a patient who is also a wife, mother, and respected friend. He tells us about their prior and ongoing relationship, how he had witnessed and rejoiced over Diane's past triumphs over adversity and anguished with her over the current threat. He describes his own doubts and hopes for Diane's future and the future of their ongoing relationship. He wonders whether prescribing a lethal dose might restore her spirits and give her more emotional comfort in her final struggle. And he alludes to the institutional and social context, albeit in my opinion not sufficiently,[22] with references to the current state of the law.

Although a reconstructed principlist might object at this point that all the above matters can and should be folded into a principlistic analysis as components of "the case," it remains true, I think, that the partisans of moral theory and principlism have not given many of these issues their due. This is especially true of Quill's concern to sketch the moral character of his players, the nature of their past and future relationships, and the fine details of their institutional and social context. As Bernard Williams has argued, most of the received moral theories operate with impoverished or empty conceptions of the individual.[23] In order to bring the moral individual into clearer focus, he claims, we must attend to his or her differential particularity, to the desires, needs, and "ground projects" that coalesce into the character of the person. But if we are concerned with the depiction, understanding, and assessment of character, we can do so only by telling and retelling stories.[24]

It is important to note, however, that a salutary concern for the role of character in ethics need not precipitate a wholesale rejection of principles and theory. Although some commentators have contended that an appropriate concern for character and its narrative environment should lead us to reject principle-based ethics,[25] one could just as well view reflection on character as a necessary supplement or extension of an ethic of principles. So understood, narrative ethics emerges once again as an adjunct to standard, principle-based ways of doing ethics.

Historical Narrative and Ethical Justification

The second major conception of narrative ethics I want to consider is a good deal less accommodating to principle-based ethics and poses a greater challenge to principlism's conceptions of moral justification.[26] This view, perhaps best represented by Alasdair MacIntyre and Stanley Hauerwas, constitutes a frontal assault on the so-called Enlightenment project of establishing a rational basis for ethics beyond the constraints of traditions and culture. According to such critics, reason unmoored to a historical community with its own specific canons of rationality is incapable of providing an adequate basis for morality. Reason and rationality, they claim, are always characteristic of a certain historical tradition, whether it be that of Ancient Greece, medieval Paris, or eighteenth-century Edinburgh. Our capacity to view things as reasonable, valuable, noble, appropriate, interesting, and so on is developed within the context of a certain narrative tradition that subtly shapes all of our knowing and valuing. Thus reason and rationality will take on as many forms as there are basic historical traditions; there is no one model of rationality that might be used as a critical vantage point from which to pass judgment on the vast panoply of what Wittgenstein called "forms of life." The Enlightenment project of making ethics "scientific," objective, and rational by stripping it of all subjective elements borne by narrative is, they conclude, a philosophical dead end.

In place of the Enlightenment's deracinated conception of reason, the champions of historical narrative would found ethics on stories and tradition. To be sure, they acknowledge that not just any story will qualify as a ground for our ethical life. Rather, they have in mind what one might call "foundational stories" such as the tradition of Greek or Norse epic poetry, the Bible and traditions of biblical commentary (such as the Talmud and Mishnah), or Confucianism. No matter how much one may strive for a universal and objective picture of things, they claim, at some point one simply has to have faith in a story.[27] The reasoning has to end somewhere, and it ends where it began, with a narrative account of who we are as a people and how we got to be this way. Importantly, even the Enlightenment-inspired projects that attempt to rise above the particularities and vagaries of tradition and culture often betray a nascent awareness of the importance of narrative by portraying themselves as the inheritors of a distinct philosophic tradition, for example, of liberalism, utilitarianism, or social contractarianism.[28]

On this rival view, ethical justification is a matter of squaring one's actions with a social role (or roles) that is, in turn, justified by a fundamental narrative. Far from being justified before some court of abstract reason, our actions are ultimately sanctioned by appeal to the norms, traditions, and social roles of a particular social group. Obversely, according to MacIntyre and Hauerwas, to lack such a distinctive story is to lack a rationale for one's actions, character, and life.[29] For example, a doctor contemplating Timothy Quill's narrative might well object to the latter's embrace of physician-assisted suicide on the ground that throughout history, beginning with the Hippocratic Oath, physicians have defined themselves exclusively as healers, rather than as healers who might on occasion also kill their patients. When confronted with the proposition that our laws against physician-assisted suicide ought to be changed, such a doctor might well respond, not by invoking this or that principle or philosophical theory, but rather by recalling the physician's role in our society, which is, in turn, explicated and justified by an account of the Hippocratic historical tradition.[30]

This aspect of narrative ethics, understood in this stronger sense, generates an ethic that is highly concrete and effectively action-guiding in a manner unavailable to such standard Enlightenment theories as utilitarianism and Kantianism. Because the latter develop their criteria of right and wrong in a realm beyond the particularities of any particular time and place, they provide significant critical leverage; but they do so at the price of an abstractness and remoteness that often render them incapable of definitively guiding action in specific circumstances. The winds of utilitarianism notoriously blow in all sorts of different directions,[31] often simultaneously justifying contradictory positions on important matters of individual morality and public policy, as does Kant's categorical imperative, which seems to function better (at best) as a necessary condition of morality, telling us what we cannot do, rather than as a sufficient condition, telling us what we must do in specific circumstances. For the partisans of this more robust version of narrative ethics, one's story effectively provides the rationale for one's action. ("We are doctors. We don't kill!" "We help the needy, just as Christ bade us to do in the story of the Good Samaritan.")

The difficulties inherent in this particular narrativist project are predictable and serious. While the concreteness of the fundamental narrative indisputably paves the way for a truly practical ethic, it also sets the limits for any given story and thereby serves, in spite of itself, as a vehicle of transcendence beyond the merely local to other stories telling of other times, places, and ways of knowing and valuing. In the first place, foundational stories not only tell us who we are; they also tell us who we are not. In telling us the story of "our people" with our own particular exemplars of good and evil, for example, such stories also tell us about other peoples against whom we define ourselves. We usually do not define ourselves *tout court;* rather, we define ourselves against neighboring families, tribes, cities, states, and nations. Thus, the Israelites defined themselves against the gentiles, Protestants defined themselves against Catholics, Southern whites against African-Americans, and, in the neighborhood where I grew up, the Irish defined themselves against everyone else. At the heart of our own self-conception, then, lies a conception of the Other.[32]

Now, ordinarily this Other figures in our own self-conception not as a subject with his or her own story to tell, but rather as an objectified element in our own story. Thus, for contemporary Palestinians, the only relevant story is the history of their oppression at the hands of the Jewish state; conversely, for contemporary Israelis the relevant foundational story is the history of Palestinian aggression and terrorism. The subjects of these historical narratives are thus locked in a perpetual struggle, not only over land, but also over the meaning of their common history. This kind of struggle for narrative supremacy can obviously go on for a long time; sometimes (as in the Balkans) it can last for centuries. Once the realization sinks in, however, that the Other is not about to simply go away, the road to moral and political progress will usually involve an attempt on the part of warring traditions to hear and attempt to understand the story of the other party. But once one actually sits down to listen to the other's story, one opens oneself not simply to the possibilities for acquiring sympathy and tolerance, but also to the possibility for radical self-transformation. It could well turn out, once I have heard your story, that I judge it to be a better story than the one I was taught as a child.

In this way, an awareness of other stories leads to an awareness of the limits of our own. Obviously, we must begin with our own story, which we learn at our parents' knees and which conditions our entire outlook, but contact with the wider world of other stories usually leads us to question our own story and the various social roles to which it gives rise. Thus, a physician trained in the Hippocratic tradition might be exposed to her patients' stories of suffering, which themselves point to a wider political story of individual freedom struggling to free itself from traditional constraints imposed by the heavy hands of religion, custom, and professional codes of ethics. Such a physician might then experience a genuine moral conflict. In addition to her initial repugnance for physician-assisted suicide ("We're doctors. We don't kill.")—a repugnance founded upon her social role dictated by the story of Western medicine—she may now be attracted by other social roles (for example, that of patient advocate) generated by other stories (for example, that of the tradition of political liberalism). This physician then must confront the difficult business of choosing between social roles with their corresponding foundational stories. Whatever she decides, once the complexity of modern societies is acknowledged, a narrative ethic in this stronger sense no longer seems to offer a ready-made action-guiding solution. Just as the moral theorist must attempt to sort out, say, the respective attractions of various competing *prima facie* obligations in a complex situation of moral choice, so the proponent of narrative ethics not only must ask which story should control her actions in a given situation but eventually must confront the ultimate question of what makes any story morally compelling and worthy of our allegiance. How, in other words, are we to know that the story with which we begin is a "good story" or a better story than the available alternatives?

One way to solve this deep and vexing problem is to set out criteria for the evaluation of stories. Burrell and Hauerwas, for example, contend that "[t]he test of each story is the sort of person it shapes."[33] They elaborate on this answer by positing four additional desiderata that any good story, they assert, will have to display:

1. power to release us from destructive alternatives;
2. ways of seeing through current distortions;
3. room to keep us from having to resort to violence;
4. a sense for the tragic: how meaning transcends power.[34]

While one could quibble with this list of criteria by questioning either the appropriateness of each item or the comprehensiveness of the entire set, the more basic problem for narrative ethics involves the very idea of resorting to a set of abstract criteria for resolving conflicts among plausible stories. For if we are truly able to pick and choose among competing stories by deploying a set of criteria, then it would appear that the criteria themselves, and not the narratives, are fundamental to the critical function of ethics. Although the above list does appear to be rather idiosyncratic, we could easily translate some of its criteria into the traditional language of principles and theory. Thus, criteria one and three above could be recast into the language of "nonmalificence" (that is, do no harm). The second criterion (bearing on release from distortions) could quite plausibly be read as a restatement of Marx's strictures against "false consciousness," a critical position owing more to a theory of social reality and its ideological distortions than to any narrative.[35] By supplementing Burrell and Hauerwas's list with, say, a principle of "beneficence," with respect for individuality or autonomy, or perhaps with an ideal of "human flourishing," we could compile a set of criteria that might look something like W. D. Ross's list of *prima facie* duties,[36] which could then be applied to the various fundamental stories competing for our allegiance. Narrative ethics must on this account have recourse to an independent set of abstract criteria bearing either on the rightness of actions or on the kinds of characters that our stories ought to foster. But the problem with this approach is obviously that it forfeits the supremacy of narrative over abstract principle, thereby returning us to the more benign conception of narrative ethics as a supplement to (or dialectically incorporated ingredient of) principles and theory.

Another way of sorting out the rival claims of competing stories, one more consonant with the whole idea of a robust narrative ethics, is to claim that some narratives do a better job of solving the problems that have claimed the attention of other narratives. As developed by Alasdair MacIntyre, this claim boils down to the notion that the only corrective for a bad, inadequate, or incoherent narrative is a better narrative, not some set of abstract principles. MacIntyre develops this suggestion through his conception of "epistemological crises"[37] in which the members of a narrative tradition come to see that tradition as ultimately unable to resolve its problems or inner tensions. MacIntyre views the fundamental narratives as engaged in a quest to discern "the good life for man." At a certain stage in its development, a narrative tradition may experience an epistemological crisis or breakdown in which its resources no longer prove adequate to the task at hand. At this point, the members of such a tradition might look to other narratives as resources for solving the very problems that had proved so intractable within their inherited story. Adherents of the original narrative may find that the new tradition shows them not only a new story with new social roles to supplant the old ones, but also a way out of their former epistemological impasse.

Importantly, MacIntyre contends that when an outside narrative assumes this role, epistemological and moral progress has taken place. We have not merely witnessed the abandonment of one story and accompanying social roles for another story and other roles. If that were all that has happened, then we could speak only of the temporal succession of one story by another and narrative ethics would have to remain silent on the fundamental question of which story might be better than another, thereby settling for a disquieting relativism. Rather, MacIntyre wants to claim that we have moved from a relatively narrow and (by now) dysfunctional narrative to a more encompassing and more adequate story that effectively solves the problems of the first tradition. When this happens, we have, in effect, moved from the particular to the (more) universal without abandoning our commitment to narrative as the driving force behind ethics. In other words, narrative ethics can remain critical without ultimately abandoning narrative in the fashion of Burrell and Hauerwas.

In order to maintain this position, MacIntyre must insist that the adherents of the faltering story must be able to see the succeeding story as holding the key to the resolution of their former problems. They must, moreover, be able to see the new story as constituting an advance over the old story in terms that would be comprehensible to the adherents of the old story.[38] Without this sort of linkage, we would be back to a mere succession of stories instead of the hoped-for moral progress from the particular to the more encompassing view. While this is not the place for a full-blown critique of MacIntyre's position, it should be noted that his view on narrative and justification is controversial and problematic. In particular, if foundational stories of the meaning of human life are to have the sort of globally pervasive influence that MacIntyre ascribes to them, if they condition our modes of thought, language, sensibility, and frames of reference, then it is hard to understand how the substitution of a new foundational narrative for a faltering story could leave intact all those old modes of thought and evaluation that are supposed to evaluate the new story in terms of the old.[39]

Narrative and Postmodern Ethics

So far we have canvassed two distinct approaches to the question of narrative ethics and its relation to ethical justification. The first, articulated by Rita Charon, conceived of narrative ethics as an enriching supplement to the more standard forms of principle-based ethics. On this view, ethical justification resides either in the conformity of our actions to various ethical rules and principles that are themselves justified by some deeper philosophical theory, or in the process of reflective equilibrium. According to the second approach, represented by Hauerwas and MacIntyre, ethical justification must be sought in social roles, which are themselves grounded in foundational historical narratives. I now want to take up a third approach to narrative and ethical justification under the rubric of "postmodern" ethics. As I shall try to show in this final section, the postmodern storyteller has come to see narrative not as a substrate, but rather as a substitute for the entire enterprise of moral justification.

A. What is a Postmodern Ethic?

As I (dimly) understand it, "postmodernism" can be understood from one angle as a wholesale retreat not only from traditional theories—such as Marxism, Freudian psychoanalysis, or utilitarianism—but also from attempts at achieving some sort of grand coherence in our epistemological, ethical, and social views. In the place of theory and overarching coherence, the postmodernist asserts the virtues of the *petit récit* or "little narrative." Instead of probing history, for example, for its "deep structure" or laws of social development, the postmodernist historian dwells on small-scale narratives and anecdote. Thoroughly disabused of grounding or justifying her discourses on such basic and traditional distinctions as between fact and fiction, knowledge and custom, truth and ideology, the postmodernist observer (historian, anthropologist, philosopher, literary scholar, legal theorist, and so on) seeks a kind of legitimation through the telling and retelling of stories.[40]

Richard Rorty's endorsement of an "ironist culture" provides an illuminating example of this eclipse of explanation and justification by narrative.[41] While Rorty concedes that on the most mundane level, within a particular narrative or historical tradition (for example, the common law), we can still make use of the notion of justification, he argues that at the more global level, where rival narratives, vocabularies, and traditions clash, we cannot speak meaningfully of justifying any one of these rival views by anchoring it in the bedrock of a true theory of history, human nature, or the natural world. When confronted with a sustained narrative that now shows signs of budding incoherence or newly perceived insensitivity to the sufferings of others—for example, a society (such as ours) that has traditionally and systematically degraded women—Rorty's "liberal ironist" must resort, not to logical argument, but rather to a kind of poetic redescription that allows us to see the world in new ways. Instead of presenting one's interlocutor with a logical argument that cannot be denied on pain of self-contradiction, the feminist must work with other like-minded people to forge a new vocabulary, a new set of meanings, and encourage others to begin to describe the world in similar ways.[42] For Rorty, then, the poet, not the traditional philosopher, is the vanguard of the human species.[43]

The ultimate goal of Rorty's culture of liberal ironism is not the replacing of falsity and distortion with truth (about "Man," "human nature," "History," "Reality"), but rather the mere continuation of the "conversation." Whereas both explanation and justification seek and require closure at some point—always lusting after that "QED"—Rorty's notion of conversation desires only its own continuation in a limitless quest for novelty. It refuses to seek a final resting place in some moral, social, or scientific bedrock that will put an end to disputation and conversation once and for all. One important ethical maxim that Rorty would have us derive from his notion of conversation—a kind of postmodern categorical imperative, if you will— is thus that we should always strive to keep "moral space" open for more dialogue.[44]

Another way to depict the implications of postmodernism for ethics is to describe it as an "ethics of voice."[45] In contrast to the standard brands of Enlightenment ethics that highlight either the content (for example, utilitarianism) or form (for example, Kantianism) of what is said, postmodernist ethics seems to be primarily concerned with who gets to tell the story. More specifically, the postmodern categorical imperative seems to come down to an insistence that everyone gets to tell his or her own story. Thus, Arthur Frank, a self-described postmodernist, sets out in his remarkable book, *The Wounded Storyteller*,[46] to rescue the first-person illness narratives of his fellow cancer sufferers from the "colonialism" of modernist (that is, scientific) medicine. According to Frank, those who suffer should be allowed and encouraged to speak for themselves, to find their own voice, rather than submit to the reductionistic and objectifying categories of modern medicine. Instead of the professionals' "case studies," narratives that objectify the experience and sufferings of people grappling with illness, Frank advocates the "case story" in which the ill are allowed to discover for themselves what it means to be a good person by telling and then reflecting on their own story.[47]

At this point, one might very well be moved to exclaim, "Nice story, but so what?" What is the connection, in other words, between all this storytelling and what might quaintly be called "the truth"? According to Frank, the stories that convey the subjective quest of the ill person "are their own truth," and he confesses to being unsure "what a 'false' personal account would be."[48] While prepared to grant that some personal narratives might be "evasive," Frank considers this evasiveness to be their truth. The more I reconstruct (distort?) the details of my own story, the more I manifest the truth of my desire to have experienced a different narrative course in my life (p. 22). Against an ethic of principles and rules, Frank claims that narrative ethics offers the ill person the freedom or "permission" to allow his story to lead in a variety of different directions in order to facilitate the process of self-discovery through the trial of illness (p. 160). And lest the reader begin to wonder about the potentially solipsistic consequences of such a view of truth in narrative, Frank concedes in the end that narratives are ultimately based upon an appeal to something more than our desires: "What is testified to remains the really real," he writes, "and in the end what counts are duties towards it" (p. 138). Still, although the act of providing "testimony" forges a connection for Frank to the "really real," this particular kind of postmodern testimony makes no pretense of grasping the whole or presenting a full panorama connecting my testimony to that of others. We are left with the ill person's *petit récit.*

As I mentioned at the beginning of this essay, this postmodernist privileging of the "little story" has both an epistemological and ethical dimension. We ought to favor such narratives, first, because we can't do any better. It is an epistemological error to believe that we can transcend the local, anchoring our science and ethics on the bedrock of the objectively and universally real. But we also have an ethical motivation to prefer the "little story" in the tendency of larger or more "totalizing" narratives, such as Marxism or Frank's portrayal of modern medicine, to silence, coerce, or, at the extreme, physically annihilate those who do not conform to their norms and expectations. As Lyotard mordantly observes, "The nineteenth and twentieth centuries have given us as much terror as we can take. We have paid a high enough price for the nostalgia of the whole and the one."[49]

B. Some Problems and Reservations

While I do not consider myself sufficiently well versed as yet in the literature of postmodernism to hazard a global assessment of this movement and its implications for ethics, the brief sketch I have presented above should provide us with a rich agenda for further elaboration, reflection, and critique. I will therefore limit myself to the expression of some initial doubts and worries regarding the promise of a postmodern ethic founded on *petits récits.*

1. The Threat of Subjectivism. As developed by Arthur Frank, postmodern ethics risks sacrificing ethics at the altar of personal self-development. Not entirely satisfied with Rita Charon's portrayal of narrative ethics as a necessary adjunct to an ethic of principles, Frank argues that beyond the delimited sphere of "patienthood," in which the suffering individual is subjected to the norms and projects of health care providers, narrative ethics achieves autonomy and completeness in its own sphere, which is the sphere of "personal becoming" (p. 158). As noted above, this ethic cannot provide us with guidelines or principles; instead it provides each suffering individual with the moral space and "permission" to develop his or her story in ways that seem appropriate to her or his own life. While Frank says many important and interesting things on this theme, the overall effect of his argument seems to privilege the search for individual coherence over one quite central function of ethics, traditionally conceived, which is the passing of judgment on actions, policies, and character traits.

For example, Frank confesses to being unsure what a "false" personal account might be. I must admit to having a lot less trouble on this score. Although each and every one of us no doubt shades the truth or even intentionally distorts crucial facts in the stories we tell about our own lives, one need think only of the life story or personal testimony of Ronald Reagan to find a staggering example of duplicity and self-deception. As recounted and amply demonstrated in Gary Wills's fine biography,[50] Reagan was chronically and systematically incapable of telling fact from fiction about any of the defining events in his own life. Whether the issue concerned his boyhood days in Illinois, his wartime "service" in Hollywood, his behavior as president of the Screen Actors' Guild during the McCarthy era, or (I might add) during the Iran-Contra affair, Reagan seemed congenitally incapable of telling a story about his own life that was even remotely related to what had actually happened. In each and every case, the story told had more to do with what Reagan wished were true than it did to people and events in what might be referred to as the real world. But this, of course, should come as no great surprise. Although Reagan was perhaps more doggedly systematic in his penchant for self-deception and buffing his personal record than most people, all of us tell stories that deviate in greater or lesser measure from what really happened. Come to think of it, psychiatrists would probably be out of a job if all of us were more truthful, self-aware, and trustworthy in the stories we tell about ourselves.[51] If correspondence to what actually happened—making due allowance, of course, for the necessity and vagaries of interpretation—is an indispensable measure of the verisimilitude of stories, then it would seem that we have no more reason to place unquestioning trust in these "little narratives" than in some of the theorists' metanarratives.[52]

Frank seems willing to concede our penchant for self-deception, but he immediately spots "the truth" involved in distorted narratives: that is, our desire for a reformulated story. While I would agree with Frank that duplicitous or self-deceptive narratives (truly) betray a desire on the storyteller's part to have a different story from the one he or she has lived out and for which she or he is (in part) responsible, this is certainly not the only or the main thing we mean when we say that a story is "truthful." It appears that Frank is so eager to give suffering individuals sufficient "moral space" and "permission" to develop their own personal stories that he risks undercutting our ability to make moral judgments. It sometimes seems as though he is willing to substitute the "authenticity" of the storyteller for the more traditional concern for ethical justification. So long as the narrator has suffered and claims the mantle of authenticity, that in itself justifies the story told.

We encounter here a broader and more fundamental problem with narrative as a vehicle for ethics. We have already seen, through Rita Charon's work, just how important narrative is to ethics as traditionally conceived. Narrative provides us with a rich tapestry of fact, situation, and character on which our moral judgments operate. Without this rich depiction of people, their situations, their motives, and so on the moral critic cannot adequately understand the moral issue she confronts, and any moral judgments she brings to bear on a situation will consequently lack credibility. To paraphrase Kant, ethics without narrative is empty. But if all we do is strive to comprehend, if we are exclusively concerned with discerning coherence within a person's narrative, then we have no moral space left over for moral judgment. And this becomes a problem as soon as we realize that some internally coherent stories may yet be morally repugnant and fit objects for moral disapproval. To round out the allusion to Kant, we might say here that ethics without judgment is not ethics. Pace Frank, stories may well have their own (internal) truth, but that is not the only truth with which we must be concerned if we mean also to do ethics. The partisans of narrative ethics must therefore begin to think harder about the implications of "bad coherence" for their enterprise.[53]

2. Localism and Social Criticism. A related problem for Frank, and more generally for postmodernism, is the temptation to fetishize "little narratives" at the expense of broader social understanding and critique. While there is unquestionably an important place for such narratives, and while Frank's book makes an eloquent and powerful case for them within the context of an often-stifling modernist medical culture, it is also no doubt true that an overemphasis on the little story can render us purblind to larger social patterns and events that must also be grasped and understood if we are to achieve a fully rounded and adequate picture of our social world. It is an enduring temptation for Frank and the postmodernists, in their single-minded embrace of creativity, empathy, and compassion, uncritically to buy into the essentially romantic myth of the isolated individual or group, and thereby to ignore larger patterns and relationships that a more critical and socially attuned approach might recognize. At the very least, someone like Frank should be concerned not just with individual stories, but also with larger sets of relationships or recurring patterns that might cast new light on these stories and suggest common strategies for social improvement.

One might also entertain doubts in this connection about the extent of the postmodern critique of transcending the local. It is certainly true, as Lyotard points out, that a "totalizing" mentality has often led to oppression of dissenting minorities, but it is equally true that the rationalist tendencies of the Enlightenment tradition have also had a profoundly liberatory effect in many instances. Indeed, important movements of liberation from the provinciality of custom and tradition may well find themselves theoretically eviscerated by the postmodernist embrace of the local.

Consider the case of feminism. In contrast to Rorty's assessment,[54] many thoughtful feminists see theirs as an essentially modernist movement opposed to the arbitrary authority of men over women, as an assault on every social norm or institution resting on the ideology of male superiority.[55] Whereas Lyotard views a dogged attachment to the local and the *petit récit* as a liberation from the enslavement of "master narratives," these feminists see the Enlightenment ideals of freedom and equality as liberatory from the enslavement of women manifested in just about every local culture known hitherto. While communitarians like MacIntyre uncritically accept the social roles handed down by tradition and foundational narratives, feminists are bound, in the words of Sabina Lovibond, sooner or later to call the parish boundaries into question.[56] For them, the total reconstruction of society along rational lines—assuming the rationality of gender equality—is not so much a shopworn and discarded Enlightenment ideal as an indispensable blueprint for fundamental and desperately needed social reform. Crucial to this agenda is the critical idea of false consciousness, that is, the ability of dominant social classes to impose their own values and ideals on all other groups so that the latter are often impaired in their ability to discern their own true best interests. For many contemporary feminists, the gradual but systematic transcendence of pervasive local rationales for male domination constitutes the first order of business in social theory. To be sure, these feminists seek out and honor the individual experiences of individual women; that indeed is a large part of what "consciousness-raising" is all about. But it is also about linking the common experiences of individual women into a cohesive and global social critique and accompanying program for large-scale social action. For such activists and theorists, the postmodern attachment to the local represents a fundamental threat to feminism as a critical theory of society. Defenders of the postmodern outlook in ethics thus need to reflect on the implications of their localism for the prospects of effectively criticizing pervasive, ideologically inspired injustices. And we all need to think much harder about how to acknowledge our individuality and situatedness without abandoning the possibility of social criticism. Instead of just noticing (and even celebrating) our differences, we also need to understand better how our differences are intertwined in a larger social tapestry. In spite of the manifest virtues and attractions of the *petit récit,* there is still room, in other words, for considering the bigger picture.

Success?

In this essay I have canvassed three distinct approaches to the relationship of narrative ethics to ethical justification. I have come to the provisional conclusion that the first approach, which conceived of narrative as an essential element in any and all ethical analyses, constitutes a powerful and necessary corrective to the narrowness and abstractness of some widespread versions of principle- and theory-based ethics. The second approach, staked out by Burrell, Hauerwas, and MacIntyre is initially plausible, but risks either falling back into a more principled version of ethics (compare Burrell and Hauerwas's search for abstract criteria) or sinking into a relativistic slough of incommensurable fundamental narratives (MacIntyre). Finally, I have argued that self-consciously postmodern approaches to ethics risk mistaking the authenticity of the narrator for ethical truth, and often ignore the larger social picture. While it should be obvious by now that narrative and narrative methods of inquiry are pervasive and indispensable for ethical analysis, it remains less clear whether any of the more fundamental assaults on principle- or theory-based ethics can be successful. Narrative is thus indisputably a crucial element of all ethical analysis, and we would all do better to be more self-conscious about the literary nature of ethical understanding and assessment. It remains to be seen, however, whether narrative will ever be in a position to supplant an ethic also undergirded by principles and theory.

Notes

1. Clifford Geertz, *Local Knowledge: Further Essays in Interpretive Anthropology* (New York: Basic Books, 1983.)

2. Jane Tompkins, "Me and My Shadow," in Linda Kauffman, ed., *Gender and Theory: Dialogues on Feminist Criticism* (New York and Oxford: Blackwell, 1989), pp. 121–139.

3. Peter Brooks and Paul Gewirtz, *Law's Stories: Narrative and Rhetoric in the Law* (New Haven: Yale University Press, 1996).

4. Richard Rorty, *Philosophy and the Mirror of Nature* (Princeton: Princeton University Press, 1979); *Contingency, Irony, and Solidarity* (Cambridge: Cambridge University Press, 1989).

5. David Simpson, *The Academic Postmodern and the Rule of Literature: A Report on Half Knowledge* (Chicago: University of Chicago Press, 1995).

6. Indeed, Beauchamp and Childress have made so many concessions to casuists, feminists, communitarians, and other critics in the fourth edition of their monumental and justly praised *Principles of Bioethics* (New York: Oxford University Press, 1994) that this observer has been moved to describe them as the "Borg of bioethics." (In the late lamented TV series, "Star Trek: The Next Generation," the Borg was an enormously powerful and unrelenting entity that subsisted by attacking and then assimilating other beings and whole civilizations into its neural network. The Borg's mantra was, "Resistance is futile. You will be assimilated!")

7. Simpson speaks of an "epidemic of storytelling" (see *The Academic Postmodern*, p. 25), and Daniel Callahan has recently objected to the "tyranny of the story" in "Does Clinical Ethics Distort the Discipline?" *Hastings Center Report*, vol. 26, no. 6 (November-December 1996):28.

8. By "theory-driven" I mean here principally utilitarianism and Kantian deontology, including Rawlsian theories of justice. Excluded from this definition are all forms of Aristotelian ethics, virtue ethics, and coherentist models of ethical justification.

9. H. T. Engelhardt, Jr., *The Foundations of Bioethics*, 1st ed. (New York: Oxford University Press, 1986). Interestingly, the moral tone of Engelhardt's transgalactic theory bears a striking resemblance to a kind of flinty Texas individualism.

10. I owe this account of Comte to David Burrell and Stanley Hauerwas, "From System to Story: An Alternative Pattern for Rationality in Ethics," in H. T. Engelhardt, Jr., and Daniel Callahan, eds., *Knowledge, Value and Belief* (Hastings-on-Hudson, NY: The Hastings Center, 1977), p. 125.

11. Jean-François Lyotard, *The Postmodern Condition: A Report on Knowledge* (Minneapolis: University of Minnesota Press, 1984), p. 27: "The scientist questions the validity of narrative statements and concludes that they are never subject to argumentation or proof. He classifies them as belonging to a different mentality: savage, primitive, underdeveloped, backward, alienated, composed of opinions, customs, authority, prejudice, ignorance, ideology."

12. Rita Charon, "Narrative Contributions to Medical Ethics: Recognition, Formulation, Interpretation, and Validation in the Practice of the Ethicist," in E. R. DuBose, R. Hamel, and L. J. O'Connell, eds., *A Matter of Principles? Ferment in U.S. Bioethics* (Valley Forge, PA: Trinity Press International, 1994), pp. 260–283.

13. For a well-developed autobiographical account of how such a truncated medical vision can adversely affect the care (and lives) of patients, see Oliver Sacks, *A Leg to Stand On* (New York: Summit Books, 1984).

14. "The principlist methods of ethical inquiry remain as the structure for clarifying and adjudicating conflicts among patients, health providers, and family members at the juncture of a quandary. The principles upon which bioethics decisions have been based . . . continue to guide ethical action within health care" (p. 277).

15. John Rawls, *A Theory of Justice* (Cambridge, MA: Harvard University Press, 1971), pp. 48–51.

16. Norman Daniels, "Wide Reflective Equilibrium and Theory Acceptance in Ethics," *Journal of Philosophy*, vol. 76 (1979):256; "Wide Reflective Equilibrium in Practice," in L.W. Sumner and J. Boyle, eds., *Philosophical Perspectives on Bioethics* (Toronto: University of Toronto Press, 1996), pp. 96–114. See also Dwight Furrow, *Against Theory* (New York: Routledge, 1995), ch. 1.

17. My account here draws on my previous article, "Principles and Particularity: The Roles of Cases in Bioethics," *Indiana Law Journal*, vol. 69 (1994):992ff.

18. Lyotard, *The Postmodern Condition* at p. 27.

19. This section is drawn from my article, "Principles and Particularity: The Roles of Cases in Bioethics," pp. 983–1014.

20. Nussbaum, for example, argues that narrative is the only proper medium for some philosophical issues. See "Introduction: Form and Content, Philosophy and Literature," in *Love's Knowledge: Essays on Philosophy and Literature* (New York: Cambridge University Press, 1990), pp. 3–53.

21. Timothy Quill, "Death and Dignity: A Case of Individualized Decision Making," *New England Journal of Medicine*, vol. 324 (1991):691ff.

22. Indeed, in my opinion, Quill's major failing is to have inadequately considered the implications of introducing the practice of assisted suicide within the context of a society that fails to provide adequate health care, including pain relief and treatment for depression, to millions of potential candidates.

23. Bernard Williams, "Persons, Character, Morality," in *Moral Luck* (New York: Cambridge University Press, 1981), pp. 1–19.

24. For a more fully developed statement of the fit between narrative and the depiction of character, see Tobin Siebers, *Morals and Stories* (New York: Columbia University Press, 1992), p. 15.

25. Burrell and Hauerwas, "From System to Story."

26. I say "conceptions" here to underscore the fact that principlism embraces both correspondance and coherentist approaches to moral justification.

27. Samuel Fleischacker, *The Ethics of Culture* (Ithaca: Cornell University Press, 1994).

28. See John Rawls, *Political Liberalism* (New York: Columbia University Press, 1993), pp. xxi–xxix.

29. MacIntyre, *After Virtue* (Notre Dame: Notre Dame University Press, 1981), p. 201: "[M]an is in his actions and practice, as well as in his fictions, essentially a story-telling animal. . . . I can only answer the question 'What am I to do?' if I can answer the prior question 'Of what story or stories do I find myself a part?' "

30. Willard Gaylin et al., "Why Doctors Must Not Kill," *Journal of the American Medical Association*, vol. 259 (1988):2139–2140.

31. Geroge Sher, "Justifying Reverse Discrimination in Employment," *Philosophy & Public Affairs*, vol. 4, no. 2 (1975):159.

32. This dialectical aspect of self-definition has received its most memorable expression in Nietzsche's *On the Genealogy of Morals*, trans. W. Kaufmann (New York: Vintage, 1969). See especially the "First Essay: Good and Evil, Good and Bad," pp. 24–56. See also Hegel's *Phenomenology of Mind*, trans. William Wallace and A. V. Miller (Oxford: Clarendon Press, 1971).

33. "From System to Story," p. 136.

34. *Ibid.*, at p. 137.

35. Karl Marx, "Preface to a Critique of Political Economy," in D. McLellan, ed., *Karl Marx: Selected Writings* (Oxford: Oxford University Press, 1977), pp. 388–391.

36. W. D. Ross, *The Right and the Good* (Oxford: Clarendon Press, 1930).

37. Alasdair MacIntyre, *Whose Justice? Which Rationality?* (Notre Dame: University of Notre Dame Press, 1988), p. 362. MacIntyre also addresses this theme in "The Relationship of Philosophy to Its Past," in Richard Rorty, Jerome B. Schneewind, and Quentin Skinner, eds., *Philosophy in History* (New York: Cambridge University Press, 1984), p. 44.

38. MacIntyre plays out this theme in the context of the philosophy of science in the following way: "[T]his solution can now be formulated as a criterion by means of which the rational superiority of one large-scale body of theory to another can be judged. One large scale of theory—say, Newtonian mechanics—may be judged decisively superior to another—say, the mechanics of medieval impetus theory, if and only if the former body of theory enables us to give an adequate and by the best standards we have true explanation of why the latter body of theory both enjoyed the successes and victories that it did and suffered the defeats and frustrations that it did, where success and failure, victory and defeat are defined in terms of the standards for success and failure, victory and defeat provided by what I earlier called the internal problematic of the latter body of theory. . . . It is success and failure, progress and sterility in terms both of the problems and the goals that were or could have been identified by the adherents of the rationally inferior theory." See "The Relationship of Philosophy to Its Past," p. 43.

39. For a fuller development of this criticism, see Furrow, *Against Theory*, pp. 49–59.

40. Simpson, *The Academic Postmodern*, p. 62. In this connection Lyotard remarks, "narrative knowledge does not give priority to the question of its own legitimation and . . . certifies itself in the pragmatics of its own transmission without having recourse to argumentation and proof" (p. 27).

41. Rorty, *Contingency, Irony, and Solidarity*; see also Rorty, *The Consequences of Pragmatism* (Minneapolis: University of Minnesota Press, 1982).

42. Richard Rorty, "Feminism and Pragmatism," in Grethe B. Peterson, ed., *The Tanner Lectures on Human Values*, vol. 13 (Salt Lake City: University of Utah Press, 1992), pp. 3–22.

43. Rorty, *The Consequences of Pragmatism*, p. 150; *Contingency, Irony, and Solidarity*, p. 20.

44. Margaret Urban Walker, "Keeping Moral Spaces Open," *Hastings Center Report* (March/April, 1993).

45. Arthur Frank, *The Wounded Storyteller* (Chicago: University of Chicago Press, 1995), p. xiii. Later on, Frank writes, "The idea of telling one's own story as a responsibility to the commonsense world reflects what I understand as the core morality of the postmodern" (p. 17).

46. *Ibid.*

47. Postmodernism is characterized by Simpson as exhibiting a nostalgia for the preprofessional. See Simpson, *The Academic Postmodern*, p. 47.

48. Frank, *The Wounded Storyteller*, p. 22.

49. Lyotard, *The Postmodern Condition*, p. 81. In this connection Simpson notes that even Hegel,

the great Satan of postmodernism, saw a need to allocate some role in his totalizing system to the individual, to "the little guy." According to Simpson, the distinctive claim of postmodernism is that "[i]n these times we are all little guys" (*The Academic Postmodern*, p. 60).

50. Gary Wills, *Reagan's America: Innocents at Home* (Garden City, NY: Doubleday, 1987).

51. For an amusing novelistic portrayal of this fallible human tendency, see Irvin D. Yalom, *Lying on the Couch* (New York: Basic Books, 1996).

52. Simpson is particularly discerning on this point: "There is nothing whatever in our participation in little narratives, our own or those of a few natural hearts or professional colleagues or fellow sufferers, that guarantees an avoidance of the blind spots or even of critical errors. Telling one's own story, or the story of one's imagined group or subculture, with an implicit or explicit reliance on the dubious category of 'experience,' has in itself no more or less authority than the grandest of grand narratives" (*The Academic Postmodern*, p. 30).

53. In Frank's defense, one might recall his apparent acknowledgement of a referent for narrative ethics beyond the subjectivity of the individual storyteller: "What is testified to remains the really real, and in the end what counts are duties towards it" (p. 138). The problem with this, however, is that "what is testified to" remains precisely the pain and suffering of the individual storyteller, presumably as interpreted by that storyteller. So what began as a possible link to some tangible external check on the truth of stories ends up being one more manifestation of the subjectivistic nature of Frank's approach.

54. Rorty, "Feminism and Pragmatism."

55. Sabina Lovibond, "Feminism and Postmodernism," *New Left Review*, no. 178 (November/December 1989):5–28; Seyla Benhabib, "Feminism and the Question of Postmodernism," in *Situating the Self: Gender, Community and Postmodernism in Contemporary Ethics* (New York: Routledge, 1992), pp. 203–241.

56. Lovibond, "Feminism and Postmodernism," p. 22.

TWO

Reading Narratives of Illness

6

The Ethical Dimensions of Literature
Henry James's The Wings of the Dove

Rita Charon

Prologue

Bioethics has entered a time of intensive and productive renewal. Aware that doctors and patients need more than abstract rules, overarching principles, and legal precedents as they try to find fitting and authentic solutions to ethical dilemmas, medical ethicists have turned to literary studies for help in addressing the particulars of human life. Aware, too, that ethical issues arise not only in quandary cases and highly publicized conflicts but also in the ordinary, everyday experiences that patients have with illness or doctors with doctoring, ethicists have intuited that textual methods might help in examining the fabric of lives, the moral texture of lived experience, and that which takes place between one landmark case and the next or before and after a final choice is made. Their intuitions—in retrospect accurate and productive—led them to literary texts that illuminate the lives of patients and the work of medicine, theories that sort out the roles of the tellers and listeners of complex clinical stories, and practices that guide readers toward reliable interpretations that a community of readers can share.

In their haste to appreciate and use what literature has to offer to bioethics, ethicists may have missed some of the richer and more generative aspects of literary studies that can help them in their work. In a parallel lapse, literary critics may not be aware of the enormous debt they owe to moral philosophers in rehabilitating the field of literary ethical criticism. With mutual gratitude, the moral philosopher and the literary scholar can review the background of their current collaboration so that they can make all the more salient that which they have to say to one another.

Literary scholars cannot talk about abstract principles or theories without glossing a particular text. Henry James's *The Wings of the Dove* provides a majestic field for examining the ethical dimensions of literature that pertain to the work of bioethics. Not only is this magnificent novel built around the grave illness and death of its protagonist; the methods James uses to tell his story instruct his readers in the fundamental and profound skills of apprehending, amid great conflict and human pain, the good and the right—whether in a fictional world or in the ordinary world of one person with another. Reading this novel, that is to say, provides the reader with practice in the very skills basic to clinical bioethics. At the same time, literary elements that contribute to the ethical dimensions of literature—the narrator's stance, point of view, and the reader's response, among others—sit at the heart of this caring and generous novel. In the name, then, of care and of generosity, let us—with attention to *The Wings of the Dove*—examine the bases of ethics in literature, the better to serve doctors, patients, and their families as they struggle toward human goodness in their lives and their deaths.

Ethical Criticism

The branch of literary studies that equips readers to grapple with questions of the moral imagination and to unearth knowledge of human goodness, as embodied in works of literature, is called ethical criticism. Ethical critical methods recognize and describe the moral climate in which literary works are produced and received and the moral consequences of their having been written and read, tracing the efferent forces that lead from culture, through author, narrator, and characters, to reader, and ultimately—with the reader as the transforming agent—to the world of human actions. Ethical criticism voices the fundamental concerns of any writer or reader: Why do we read and write? What is the relation of our creations to our lives? What are our responsibilities to the books we read? How do books change lives? Such concerns cannot help but form the prologue to any serious attempt to engage a literary text. Ethical criticism provides methods to examine the relations between literary acts and human acts in the ordinary world, between the life one lives before and after having read a particular book, and between knowledge of art and knowledge of life, all of these culminating in the value and meaning (and evanescence) of a knowledge of the good.

Unfortunately, contemporary literary criticism is inhospitable to questions about the ethical dimensions of literature and to those who raise them. Matthew

Arnold's confidence that literature "serve[s] the paramount desire in men that good should be for ever present to them" and that literature nourishes "our instinct for beauty, our instinct for conduct" has long ago lost its authority in literary studies.¹ Scholars today who examine the moral implications of the actions of characters in literary works risk being labeled "thematic" by a critical culture that demeans an interest in what happens in a plot. To write of the personal meaning of a text marks the writer as a naïf, a prestructuralist, a functionalist, one who has not mastered Nietzsche and Foucault, one who accepts the realism of a text as if it were real. Furthermore, much of what does appear to be critical examination of ethical concerns in contemporary literary studies is, sadly, hostile and regressive. Several critics writing today of ethics in literature recoil against such developments in literary studies as Marxist, feminist, semiotic, and deconstructionist methods of analysis, accompanying their concerns with such hidden agendas as inserting partisan religious interests into the academy, legitimating censorship, or recanonizing the traditional canon.²

However, several literary scholars appear to be facing fundamental questions about the ethical conduct of criticism, the responsibilities of authors, the responsibilities of readers, and the moral climate of literature. Inspired, genealogically, by Aristotle and Horace, and more recently by Matthew Arnold and Lionel Trilling, such scholars as Wayne Booth, J. Hillis Miller, Barbara Herrnstein Smith, and James Phelan have articulated questions and elicited dialogue about the moral implications of the acts of reading and writing.³ Rather than withdrawing from the contemporary critical conversation, as do other so-called ethical critics, these writers take up the challenge of integrating the vast knowledge of how texts work with universal questions about the right ways to live, using methods from schools of reader-response, Marxist, feminist, and psychoanalytic criticism to raise questions about the responsibilities and consequences of the text. Once freed to recognize and discuss the responsibilities that author, narrator, character, and reader hold toward one another, the attentive critic finds that all (or most) of literary studies occurs within an enveloping ethical climate. Paul de Man situates the moral at the heart of the reading act, no matter how destined to failure he concedes the act to be. "Behind the assurance that valid interpretation is possible, behind the recent interest in writing and reading as potentially effective public acts, stands a highly respectable moral imperative that strives to reconcile the internal, formal, private structures of literary language with their external, referential, and public effects."⁴ If de Man calls something respectable, no doubt he is calling into question its respectability. Nonetheless, to name the necessity to reconcile the private with the public functions of literature a "moral" act expands literary study from the examination of cultural artifacts to the comprehension of the consequences of literary acts on individual lives, consequences for which writers and readers bear responsibility.

In trying to explain why ethical criticism "fell on hard times," Wayne Booth suggests that ethical criticism differs from other schools of criticism—and is therefore particularly vulnerable to such local conditions as fears of censorship and privileging of the sardonic—in its universality, reflexivity, and reciprocity. Naming the distinctions not only between ethical criticism and other literary schools but also between the ethics of narrative and other forms of ethics (medical ethics, ethics of the marketplace, and ethics of nuclear warfare, for example), Booth describes a high and encompassing plane upon which his enterprise sits. No humans are untouched by stories; a reader judges a story using the same mind that has been itself influenced by other stories; and both teller and listener must be engaged in examining the ethics of a story. Harking back to Arnold, Booth admits that he is concerning himself with an ethics of life, an ethics of being that strikes to the heart of human experience, as stories exist close to whatever it is that tells human beings who they are, where they are from, and where they are going.[5]

If literary critics feel queasy talking about goodness, moral philosophers consider such talk their responsibility. A surprising cross-disciplinary movement has occurred in the past few years. Moral philosophers—including Charles Taylor, Bernard Williams, Martha Nussbaum, and Iris Murdoch (herself a novelist as well as a philosopher)—have turned to literature to examine the nature and sources of goodness. Claiming that the language of literature alone is complex and nuanced enough to express moral ambiguities and to address human relations to goodness, these philosophers have, with touching humility, approached great works of fiction to continue their search for terms and evidence of goodness. Although they do not, on the whole, read literary texts with the theoretical complexities available to the literary scholar, they are able—perhaps because of their professional commitment to such embarrassing entities as virtue and morality and their distance from cynical or even nihilistic currents of contemporary literary studies—to see in novels and poems that which literary critics cannot.[6]

Free from worries about the literary canon or the academic pitfalls of thematic criticism, Martha Nussbaum, for example, can examine Henry James's *The Golden Bowl* for evidence of the workings of moral responsibility in the novel and to support, conceptually, her project of defining methods that human beings use to discover the right ways to live. In her remarkable study, *Love's Knowledge*, informed by Aristotelian moral considerations and Jamesian literary theory, Nussbaum asserts that "only the style of a certain sort of narrative artist . . . can adequately state certain important truths about the world, embodying them in [the narrative form's] shape and setting up in the reader the activities that are appropriate for grasping them."[7] Fresh in its direct wrestling with the human consequences of the actions of Maggie, her father, Charlotte, and the Prince, Nussbaum's reading of *The Golden Bowl* relies on Williams and Murdoch, among others, for theoretical foundations. Murdoch emphasizes the perceptual consequences of close readings of literary texts: "[T]he most essential and fundamental aspect of culture is the study of literature, since this is an education in how to picture and understand human situations,"[8] and suggests the moral consequences of attentiveness, literary or otherwise: "Where virtue is concerned we often apprehend more than we clearly understand and *grow by looking*."[9] To literature, then, these philosophers move to discover how they can "picture and understand human situations," the better perhaps to apprehend them, perhaps growing *in virtue* in the process.

The work of moral philosophers in the fields of literature provides the literary critic with conceptual and linguistic support for talking about and thinking about goodness. Simultaneously, the work of literary critics enables moral philosophers to approach literary texts with the theoretical discrimination and canonical knowledge required of robust and generative study. Once the confluence of interest between the moral philosopher and the literary critic is observed, one can see the reason and the rightness of such a confluence: these concerns belong neither to the student of fiction nor to the student of moral codes. Instead, these concerns tend to be transhistorical and transdisciplinary—as wide and as deep as are traditional humanistic concerns for the future of the species.

The Moral Novel

Although the study of ethical dimensions of literature could proceed by studying any work of fiction, Henry James's novels are particularly generative subjects for such scrutiny. James is often described as a moral novelist or as a philosophical novelist. Some critics mean, by such designations, that James's novels usually pivot on characters' moral dilemmas and the means by which they think or act themselves out of their conflicts, or that he was concerned, predominantly, with the restrictions on human freedom imposed by social structures or psychological forces.[10] Others develop theories about James's affinity with one or another formal school of philosophy or theology.[11] Literary critics writing during James's lifetime recognized the power of the ethical moment in his fictions, placing him alongside George Eliot and Joseph Conrad, not only for the primacy of moral considerations in his fiction but also for the neutrality of his authorial judgment.[12] When, in the 1940s, F. R. Leavis included James in the "great tradition" of English novelists, he recognized in James "a vital capacity for experience, a kind of reverent openness before life, and a marked moral intensity."[13] In 1944, Lionel Trilling wrote of James's moral courage: "He could bear what most of us shrink from—the knowledge of how dangerous, subtle and complex the social world and the moral life are."[14] And, finally, James himself was not shy about including moral considerations in his own conceptions of literature: "[T]o count out the moral element in one's appreciation of an artistic total is exactly as sane as it would be (if the total were a poem) to eliminate all the words in three syllables, or to consider only such portions of it as had been written by candle-light."[15]

Several features of fiction develop and convey ethical meaning: the plots themselves, the narrative forms that contain them, and the personal consequences, for the individual reader, of having read the fiction. Slim though many charge them to be, the plots James imagines are shot through with moral conflict and ambiguity, revolving around the choices humans make regarding the right way to live. Throughout his fictional oeuvre, but most fully in the novels of his late (so-called major) phase, James creates characters only to free them, within the text, to brood and to deliberate, to envision and then to weigh alternatives, to choose and then to act.[16] Through his control of point of view, James provides as his fictional material the human actions of thinking, seeing, imagining, and deciding. The novels are big because these human movements take time and space in which to occur convincingly, or, as Joseph Warren Beach writes of *The Wings of the Dove*, "The amplitude of the record gives room for the carrying out of those large operations, or manoeuvers, which amount to nothing less than a revolution in someone's life."[17]

James's good friend Edith Wharton said of him: "For him every great novel must first of all be based on a profound sense of moral values and then constructed with a classical unity and economy of means."[18] Not only, that is, do the predicaments of the characters in his novels raise moral questions; the aesthetic forms he perfected through his life themselves force considerations of freedom and goodness. In noting that "[t]he moral implications of James's fiction are to be found not only and not principally in the judgments he passes on his characters but in the fully creative function of James's form," Laurence Holland emphasizes that this second source of ethical meaning, the form, *does* something in the fiction, that the generative form itself invents, imagines, and acts not only toward progression of plot but also toward the creation of moral distinctions regarding modes of perception, elasticity of judgment, imaginative agency, and impossibility of closure.[19] The use James puts language to differs from conventional uses, including other literary uses. Through his commitment to fine perception and through his bravery in facing both the abyss of meaning inherent in story and the abyss of reference in words themselves, James lays bare both language's indeterminacy and the human triumph in choosing to act, despite confusion, in a reality that exists, like its counterpart fiction, only by virtue of having been told. It is as if, a century before the deconstructive movement, James already knew that experience, coming as it does through the agency of a language without closure, itself is refused any but the most tentative and temporary closure, and that even that temporary grasp of meaning arrives only through words.[20]

The individual reader of a novel by James undergoes, or may undergo, profound moral experiences in the acts of reading; this moral effect that the fiction itself exercises on the reader constitutes the third source of ethical meaning. In the Preface to *The Wings of the Dove,* James addresses the reader in a parenthetical exhortation:

> Attention of perusal, I thus confess by the way, is what I at every point, as well as here, absolutely invoke and take for granted. . . . The enjoyment of a work of art, the acceptance of an irresistible illusion, constituting, to my sense, our highest experience of "luxury," the luxury is not greatest, by my consequent measure, when the work asks for as little attention as possible. It is greatest, it is delightfully, divinely great, when we feel the surface, like the thick ice of the skater's pond, bear without cracking the strongest pressure we throw on it.

The act of reading takes on corporeal and bracing vigor, as the reader reads with all the concentrated gravity of his or her body against the result of the author's work, figured as an elemental force of nature. Reader and writer are engaged simultaneously in both a test of strength—will the skater crack the ice?—and a shared attainment of luxurious levitation, the skater floating above the dark cold depths on a solid lighter than its corresponding liquid.

James consistently brings his reader through the coils of human experience that are ordinarily hidden from view, whether in the fictional or real world. Uncoiled to their dramatic length, the characters' inner experiences and deliberations are made visible to the reader, who is then able, by virtue of having read James, to imagine or to discern hidden inner experiences of other characters or even of other human beings.[21] As John Carlos Rowe notes in situating James's formalism *vis-à-vis* his phenomenology, "More than any other modern author, James helps shape an esthetic of experience, which by means of its characterization as the 'reader's experience' helps in the recuperation of the vanishing subject as well as the battered claims of literature for some truth and reality."[22] Although assertions that reading fiction changes lives are on their face suspect, James's fictions lend themselves to such analysis because of the cumulative effects of a consistent (and chronologically graded) challenge offered to his reader: James requires that his reader lend the full force of his or her imagination and consideration to characters whose actions become transparent and revelatory only in the light of unselfish attentiveness. That is to say, the process of reading James's fictions exercises and rewards human qualities of goodness that, in the willing reader, may persist into ordinary life. Laurence Holland emphasizes the part the reader plays in creating moral issues in James's fiction: "[James] neither ignored the reader out of concern for the objective integrity of his novel nor was content simply to tell and show the reader things. . . . [H]e wanted not only to *show* things to the reader but to *act upon* him. . . . The result in James's fiction is an intimacy of address to the reader which has all the contingencies and moral resonance of intimacy."[23] Not only, that is, does the implied reader develop a relation with the implied author; in reading James, the reader himself or herself enters a living relation with the author. Over a long career reading James, one can achieve the levitation of skating on the ice of the works and can, at the same time, dive, with the author himself, into that "dim underworld of fiction, the great glazed tank of art" to find—at least provisionally—the sources of meaning, not only for the fictions, but for life itself.[24]

The Wings of the Dove as Ethical Fiction
The Plot

The plot, as James himself admitted, is simple. Orphaned and unwell, American millionairess Milly Theale falls in love with Merton Densher, a penniless London journalist on assignment in New York. When Milly comes to London, accompanied by her loyal friend Susan Stringham Shepherd, she falls in with the impoverished Kate Croy and her rich aunt Maud Lowder, each member of their set more brutal and manipulative than the next. Although Kate and Milly never speak of Densher, Milly learns that Kate and Densher are secretly engaged but cannot marry because of Densher's want of means. Upon Densher's return to London, Milly forgoes any sign of her love for him out of loyalty to her friend Kate. Milly consults with Sir Luke Strett, a great London physician, and learns that she has not long to live. When Kate discovers that Milly is gravely ill, she sets Densher up to marry Milly for her money, which upon Milly's death will allow Kate and Densher to marry. Passive, Densher goes along with Kate's plan and allows Milly to think that he loves her. Milly "turns her face to the wall" when she learns of Densher's and Kate's engagement from Lord Mark, a rejected suitor, and she dies a prolonged and horrible death after having forgiven Densher for his deceit. Only upon Milly's death does Densher realize the evil he has colluded in, and only upon her death does Densher realize he loves Milly. He declines to accept Milly's stunning bequest, thereby surrendering a future with Kate, who refuses to marry him without Milly's money.

Milly and Densher dominate the novel, both because of the actual events of the plot and because of distinguishing mental and moral powers conferred on them by James. The novel's two interlaced plot movements are Milly's slow realization of her impending death and Densher's slow realization of his guilt. Parallel in language and structure, these two portentous events—Milly waiting to die and Densher recognizing the immorality of his acts—require one another as they mirror one another, for Densher's deceit hastens (or even causes) Milly's death, while Milly is, after all, the occasion of Densher's sin. Structurally, the two movements beget one another, for Milly's experience of illness follows her growing consciousness of the unspoken love relation between Densher and Kate.[25]

As interior states of developing consciousness rather than discernible events, these plot elements cannot be registered dramatically; instead, they leave evidence through the language of retrospective knowledge. Beginning in Book V, Milly and Densher are repeatedly shown to recognize, retrospectively, the meaning of events and of language. Such scenes occur 28 times in the novel—usually at critical points in the plot—ten times for Milly (for example, "She recalled, with all the rest of it, the next day piecing things together in the dawn, that she had felt herself alone with a creature who paced like a panther") and 18 times for Densher (for example, "She was never, never—did he understand?—to be one of the afflicted for him; and the manner in which he understood it . . . constituted, he was very soon after to acknowledge, something like the start for intimacy") (I, p. 282; II, pp. 73–74).

In the course of learning of her dying, Milly consults Sir Luke, the "greatest of medical lights" (I, p. 226). Of all the novel's characters, that is to say, Sir Luke is described as having the power to illuminate. Milly detects pity in Sir Luke's attitude toward her, and decides that "when pity held up its telltale face like a head on a pike, in a French revolution, bobbing before a window, what was the inference but that the patient was bad?" (I, p. 240). Given the intersubjective signs that Sir Luke offers, Milly herself realizes the gravity of her illness. Walking through the Regent's Park after her second visit with the doctor, she recognizes "that her only company must be the human race at large, present all round her, but inspiringly impersonal, and that her only field must be, then and there, the grey immensity of London" (I, p. 247). Finding communion with strangers, Milly finds herself "just in the same box. Their box, their common anxiety, what was it, in this grim breathing-space, but the practical question of life?" (I, p. 250). Universal and universalizing, Milly's illness confers a realization of human commonality and shared fate to a woman otherwise decorously withdrawn, by virtue of her fortune, from the chaos of human action, raising not the "practical question of life" but the universal question of death.

If Milly's ruminations in the Regent's Park bring her into universal communion with the human race, Densher's brooding—also begun in the Regent's Park—leads to his isolation and, ultimately, his metaphoric death (II, p. 12). Densher's reluctant though persistent moral self-examination is delayed by rationalizations, refusals to accept blame for his actions, and misrepresentations of his deceit of Milly as the exercise of gentlemanly tact. First, he tries to convince himself of the triviality of moral action: "In default of being right with himself he had . . . the interest of seeing . . . whether . . . that might be quite so necessary to happiness as was commonly assumed" (II, p. 183). He then attempts to absolve himself of guilt because his acts have been but omissions: "[H]e hadn't really 'begun' anything, had only submitted, consented, but too generously indulged and condoned the beginnings of others" (II, p. 183). Even after Lord Mark has descended on Milly and has revealed Densher's and Kate's deception, Densher persists in self-absolution. Lord Mark becomes, in Densher's imagination, the villain, whereas Densher himself, through circuitous reasoning, becomes: "blameless. . . . [T]he only delicate and honourable way of treating a person in such a state was to treat her as *he*, Merton Densher, did" (II, p. 265). Taking comfort from Sir Luke's implication that Densher "had meant awfully well," Densher clings to his innocence until Milly dies, bolstered even by Milly's final interview with him in which he feels "forgiven, dedicated, blessed" (II, p. 332; II, p. 343).

Only in the last three (of 36) chapters does Densher acknowledge his moral failure. Only after Milly dies does Densher abandon his rationalizations and look full in the face at what he has done. Haunted by the knowledge of what he and Kate have done and unable to undo it, Densher commits his final moral choice. He gives to Kate Milly's unopened posthumously sent letter; he sends, still sealed, the official report of Milly's bequest to Kate. Affixing blame to Kate even at the end, noting to her "how you 'have' me," Densher nonetheless accepts his own role in Milly's death and, by her death, achieves a final stillness—his own metaphorical death that had started in Venice is here in London completed—in will, in engagement, and in life (II, p. 401). An inverted redemption—Kate suggests to Densher that Milly "died for you then that you might understand her"—Milly's death grants not life but knowledge, which for Densher results in renunciation (II, p. 403). Having surrendered both Milly's fortune and Kate, Densher is left living the consequences of his moral conversion: he has died to life, he has escaped into Milly's memory;[2] he has, to commemorate Milly, turned his face to the wall. Despite the losses thereby incurred, Densher seems to accept willingly and gratefully this belated recognition of the moral dimensions of his actions.

Both Milly and Densher are instructed, ironically, to act with freedom. Sir Luke tells Milly that: "You say you can do exactly as you like, Oblige me therefore by being so good as to do it," while Kate instructs Densher, in delivering her plan of deceit, that his role is: "Not worrying. Doing as you like" (I, p. 245; II, p. 64). They both figure themselves as Sir Luke's patients, even though Densher is never under the doctor's medical care (II, p. 305). Although the narrator reveals the points of view of Kate Croy and Susan Stringham in early books, by Book VII the narrative focus has narrowed to Milly and Densher. After the move to Venice, Kate's and Susan's interior voices are silenced, leaving the reader in the presence—heightened through concentration—of Milly and Densher alone. These multiple parallels between Milly and Densher underscore the reader's realization that they are "doing" the same thing in the novel. If the journey toward death is equated with the journey toward guilt and eventual moral straightness, then the means by which such journeys proceed may too be equated. Both journeys are personal conflicts that engender moral growth. By having been gifted with a language that can contain and express their continual thoughts and that can apprehend perceptions and then move those perceptions around within the self, Milly and Densher become fully moral agents. They attend to their moral predicament, as Murdoch describes: "The task of attention goes on all the time and at apparently empty and everyday moments we are 'looking,' making those little peering efforts of imagination which have such important cumulative results."[26] Characterized throughout the novel by stillness rather than action (Milly motionless in her palace, Densher achieving a stillness in Venice that approaches death), they hardly act except to use language, and yet James convinces his reader that such use of language constitutes moral action of the highest kind. By allowing thoughts to achieve the status of language, Milly and Densher—and they alone in the novel—finally read their predicaments and finally choose moral action in the world as a result of their actions in language.

Ethical in nature, the actions of the novel directly address the right way to live, heightened by the dramatic tension of death's nearness (and unfairness). The plot, that is, centers on the development and consequences of the moral imagination. To use Charles Taylor's formulation, the two central protagonists, in their doubled and intertwined struggle toward the right way to live, search "to be rightly placed in relation to the good."[27] What is goodness in this novel, and how do characters try to attain it? Although the directions of the individual searches differ—Milly's story, essentially told in reverse, is that of a young woman who will have died an early death (for James knew before writing the novel that Milly would die, and other characters too know that she will die),[28] and Densher's story is prophetic, filled with omens whose significance is revealed only in the light of the story's end[29]—both characters search for a moral compass that can direct their choices.

The measure of a theoretical approach to a novel is the extent to which the approach illuminates otherwise hidden aspects of the work. Examining the sources of goodness and moral failure within the plot of *The Wings* reveals the balance in which Kate and Milly are poised, the oppositional forces of ethical gravity to which Densher is exposed (that he remains still through most of the novel attests to the gravitational forces' near-equivalence), and the ultimate triumph of Milly's dove over Kate's panther. The dove triumphs, not because the panther does not have compelling interests to champion and to protect, but because the dove is able to be faithful to her vision of goodness, unified, as it is, by economic power and the knowledge of the future. That Kate herself is divided—by the pull of family loyalty, the lure of that which life with Aunt Maud offers, the revulsion toward her sister's state of poverty and helplessness, and her honest and passionate love for Densher—repeats the major plot of moral gravity in a minor key. Attention to the ethical dimensions of the plot, that is to say, allows the reader to behold and to decode the story as one governed by the opposing fields of contradicting beliefs about right ways to live, and then to judge—within the economy of the story—the ultimate balance struck between them.

The Form

Plot elements, then, contribute to the ethical climate of *The Wings* because the story itself turns on moral choices made by, witnessed by, or attended by the novel's characters. At the same time, the novel's formal characteristics midwife these moral events by revealing to the reader—very subtly, specifically, and powerfully—the ground upon which to stand to behold and enter these ethical moments. James tailors the novel's structure, points of view, and narrative persona to grant the reader intimacy with the characters and personal stake in the outcome of their choices. Reading *The Wings* approaches living—living with doubt, living with irreversible conflict, living in the face of mortality. By the end of the long novel, not only has the reader dwelt in the presence of the fictional characters—such is the case in any decent novel. More compellingly, *The Wings* relentlessly presents its characters' ethical decisions as seen from the inside, choices that develop not only in the lived time of real life but also in the recesses of a brooding and generative self-examination that rewrites actual events, denying to biography any element of truth and giving it, instead, to consciousness.

"Style is character, it is the quality of a man's emotion made apparent; then, by an inevitable extension, style is ethics, style is government."[30] At once personal disclosure and public force, Trilling suggests, style, or form, becomes the site for reconciliation between individual passion and societal action. To find the center of ethical action, then, the reader attends not only to the "matter" or plot of the novel but to the style of composition, that which can reveal the "character" of the writer and the ethics of the work. James chose a structure of ten books, five in Volume I and five in Volume II, the break between volumes occurring immediately after Merton Densher returns to London from New York. Each book has between two and seven chapters. The center of consciousness, that is, the character from whose point of view the narrator appears to see, shifts from book to book, sometimes from paragraph to paragraph, giving multiple dimensions to the novel and perspectival choices to the reader. Kate Croy, Merton Densher, Susan Stringham, and Milly Theale alternate as the centers of consciousness. Any reader ethically fit for reading this novel must have the intellectual capacity and the empathy required to adopt consecutive and contradictory points of view. The experience of weighing, of balancing, of trying first one and then the next perspective, as demanded by the alternation of the books' center of consciousness, mimics the real-life experience of reaching ethical decisions or of helping others to reach them.

Although critics sometimes label narrators of James's late novels impersonal, meaning that the speaker who tells the story is not personified in the fiction, the teller of *The Wings*—however disembodied—exerts great influence on the plot itself and on the experience of the novel's reader. Neither named nor assigned a gender, *The Wings*'s narrator seems to have intimate knowledge of all the characters. He or she is able to step into dialogues and inner monologues to elaborate the meanings of characters' spoken words or unspoken thoughts. For the first chapter of the novel, the narrator is fully absorbed into the consciousness of Kate Croy, the center of consciousness of Book I, Chapter 1. That is to say, the narrator's voice is offered as if in ventriloquism for Kate herself and is not textually individuated from Kate's thoughts. However, on the twenty–sixth page, the narrator emerges in the first person to explain Kate's feelings toward her Aunt Maud: "[O]ur young woman's feeling was founded on the impression, quite cherished for years, that the signs made across the interval just mentioned had never been really in the note of the situation" (I, p. 26).

From then on, James uses the first-person-plural pronoun as the stamp of the narrator, who seems able to adopt, sequentially, the perspective and worldview of one of the several centers of consciousness.[31] "There were moments again— we know that from the first they had been numerous—when he felt with a strange mixed passion the mastery of her mere way of putting things," the narrator intersperses into a conversation between Kate and Densher at a critical point in the romantic and economic deceit of the plot (II, p. 371). Or, later, in describing Densher's state of mind *vis-à-vis* the dying Milly: "Never was a consciousness more rounded and fastened down over what filled it; which is precisely what we have spoken of as, in its degree, the oppression of success, the somewhat chilled state—tending to the solitary—of supreme recognition" (II, p. 400). These examples serve to show that the narrator's intrusions are by no means trivial. They move the plot forward. They offer information that is otherwise unavailable. Technically, the first-person utterances signal which character ought to be considered as the source of illumination of each particular stretch of narrative. The reader follows the movement of narratorial ventriloquism from one character to another, and at times it changes more than once every page.

Who is included in the "we" and the "our"? Are there perhaps several narrators telling this story? Do they take turns? Leo Bersani suggests that "the psychological center of the drama in James's late novels is in the narrator's mind," the novel, ultimately, revealing James's own attempt to resolve moral issues.[32] Other readers disagree with Bersani, suggesting that James's use of the first-person-plural narrator signals a desire, on James's part, to involve the reader in complicity in assigning fates to the characters.[33] No one seems present at these musings except for the narrator and the reader, as they consult on the state of affairs of "their" characters. The use of the "we" confers a solidarity and a unity of purpose on the person narrating the story and the person reading it, while it opens an intimacy with the characters about whom they brood. Through the technical device of adopting the first-person-plural narrator, James appears to merge his narrator with his reader, and then to merge both narrator and reader with the characters, one at a time, through the intimacy attained by knowledge of their inner states and the unison, signalled by the "our" and "we," of their field of vision or point of thought.

There are 52 uses of the adjective "our" in relation to a character or a pair of characters, as in "our young woman" or "our slightly gasping American pair": 18 for Milly, 13 for Densher, seven for Susan Stringham, six for Kate, six for Milly and Susan, and two for Kate and Densher. There are 49 uses of the pronoun "we" by the narrator. All sentences with first-person-plural subjects use verbs of narration or perception: "we shall sufficiently take the measure, we have presented, at which we have already glanced, we give it in her words, we shall come close, we hasten to add, we already know, we have gathered, as we thus note, a process we have described, we get a far impression," for example. This pronominal being identifies itself three times. The first personification, occurring as Susan Stringham looks at Milly, applies a general description to the narrating presence, "Her friend looked at her . . . a little harder than the surface of the occasion seemed to require; and another person present at such times might have wondered to what inner thought of her own the good lady was trying to fit the speech" (I, p. 186). A more specific, albeit oblique, personal reference occurs in the next chapter: "It had sprung up, we have gathered, as soon as Milly had seen [Kate] after hearing from Mrs. Stringham of her knowledge of Merton Densher; she had *looked* then other and, as Milly knew the real critical mind would call it, more objective; and our young woman had foreseen it of her, on the spot, that she would often look so again" (I, p. 212). "Another person," then, has become "the real critical mind," at least in the inner thoughts of Milly.

Finally, the critical mind distinguishes itself from the characters' inner thoughts while narrating Milly's response to Kate's late evening "panther" monologue: "[The American mind] had to be led up and introduced to each aspect of the monster, enabled to walk all round it, whether for the consequent exaggerated ecstasy or for the still more (as appeared to this critic) disproportionate shock" (I, p. 277). That the teller is a critic—James's term for the committed reader—confers all the more the weight of judgment onto not only the telling but the listening (or reading), too.

What are the ethical implications of this narrative method? James inserts the reader into the process of telling this story. At every moment of narratorial action, the "we" that includes the reader makes of the reader a cocreator of the tale. What "our" characters choose to do or happen to think becomes at least as much the reader's responsibility as the implied author's or narrator's. Cumulatively, such insertions of the reader into the sphere of power of the narrator exert considerable moral pressure on the reader. By virtue of the narrative method, the reader must align his or her loyalty with each of several characters in sequence, often having to accept the point of view of one character immediately after another character has been deeply wounded at the first character's hands. Deconstructive criticism has advanced the concept that the reader holds responsibility for "how the story turns out." In this novel the reader's contributions are immense: first, keeping straight the abstract or personal referents and ambiguous pronouns;[34] second, making sense of the thoughts of all characters even when the narrative focus excludes them; and third, imaginatively presenting oneself with the world as experienced by contradicting points of view, that is, accepting, without flinching, the vertigo required to attentively read *The Wings*.

The Reader's Experience

Considerations of method, then, merge into considerations of the experience of the reader in living through this book. From the opening sentence of *The Wings of the Dove*, the reader feels himself or herself placed in an intimate relation with the narrator: "She waited, Kate Croy, for her father to come in, but he kept her unconscionably, and there were moments at which she showed herself, in the glass over the mantel, a face positively pale with the irritation that had brought her to the point of going away without sight of him" (I, p. 3). Not only is the reader suspended in *waiting* with Kate Croy, but the person telling the story is placed immediately over Kate's shoulder, so that the teller can see the reflection when Kate looks into the mirror. A dual intimacy begins: the teller placed quietly over the shoulder of Kate and willing to be her instrument, and the reader, attentive, waiting—like Kate—to hear.

At the same time, the attentive reader laughs at James's joke—a protagonist is waiting, with irritation, *in the first sentence of a long novel,* for someone to come in. Who is it who enters a novel on its first sentence if not the reader? Oddly, then, James jokingly equates the reader, who has just managed to open the covers of the book, with Kate's father, the base liar and cheat Lionel Croy. By this opening gambit, James places before anything else the reader's responsibility to assume a fully realized role in the fiction that follows. Although James taunts the reader with the notion that Kate, and by extension all the characters in the novel, exists quite apart from the fact of being read, the characters need the reader to animate their action in order for the novel to unfold.

This opening sentence gives the reader a sense of the enormity of his or her role; it also presents Lionel Croy as the first of a series of surrogate readers offered to the real reader. Most fictions include a character who is, explicitly or implicitly, the figure of the reader—that character who fictionally lives out the activities that the real reader, by agreeing to read the book, has assumed. Not restricted to James, surrogate readers are commonly encountered in fiction— Dilsey in *The Sound and the Fury,* Captain Vere in *Billy Budd,* Knightley in *Emma,* Lily Briscoe in *To the Lighthouse.* Sometimes—as is true of Dr. Hugh in James's "The Middle Years"—the surrogate reader indeed acts, in the narrative, as a literal reader or critic. In other fictions, the surrogate reader, in whose persona the real reader travels through the book, is not an actual reader but instead an interpreter of signs, a weigher of evidence, a decoder of signals. Often in novels, and often indeed in James's, to identify the surrogate reader gives the real reader a deep clue about what will be needed to read this book.

Why, though, should James offer Lionel Croy as one's surrogate reader? Croy has, through an unnamed crime, debased himself. Upon Kate's mother's death, Kate was taken up by her rich Aunt Maud, on the condition that Kate sever all relations with her father and sister. Nonetheless, Kate appeals to her father to take her in, to allow her to make her home with him. Described as "the first and last unequivocally moral gesture Kate makes in the course of the novel," her offer to remain with her father, thereby renouncing the worldly benefits of a life with Aunt Maud, presages not only other renunciations to come in the novel but other surrogate readers as well.[35] Kate says to her father: "It's simply a question of your not turning me away—taking yourself out of my life. It's simply a question of your saying: 'Yes, then, since you will, we'll stand together.'" (I, p. 16). The only parent in a novel of orphans, Croy turns Kate down, renouncing his parental responsibilities. In symmetry, Lionel Croy returns at the end of the novel, begging for protection and care from Kate's sister: "He looked as wonderful as ever. But he was—well, in terror. . . . He wants, he says, to be quiet. But his quiet-ness is awful. . . . He cries" (II, p. 383). Parodying, then, the actions of the major characters—Densher's attempted stillness, Kate's extreme want, and Milly's death—Croy forms the background for the reader's exit from the novel, just as he assisted at the entrance.

There are two other characters who effectively live out such an accompanying role within the novel, thereby modeling the reader's role: Susan Stringham Shepherd and Sir Luke Strett both "stand together" with Milly through her ordeal, offering the value of their accompaniment as their highest contribution. After Sir Luke has confirmed to Susan the seriousness of Milly's illness, Milly says to Susan: "You must simply see me through. Any way you choose. Make it out together" (II, p. 101). Susan's accompaniment, however genuine, falls short of selflessness: "She had wanted, very consciously, from the first, to give something up for her new acquaintance, but she had now no doubt that she was practically giving up all. . . . She had now no life to lead; and she honestly believed that she was thus supremely equipped for leading Milly's own" (I, pp. 84, 86). Susan's personal renunciation, then, is not only an act of generosity toward Milly but simultaneously an act of personal salvation. Appearing in Book V, the physician Sir Luke Strett models accurate attentiveness and selfless presence as his only therapeutic intervention: "[S]o crystal-clean the great empty cup of attention he set between them on the table" (I, p. 230). Asked what he will do for Milly's condition, Sir Luke answers: " 'You can depend on me,' the great man said, 'for unlimited interest' " (I, p. 242). Psychoanalytically inflected (the therapeutic relation is his medical intervention, and the doctor enables Milly to learn of her own unconscious thoughts), Sir Luke's treatment of Milly provides a climate of truth within which Milly herself discovers how badly she is ill, and shows the deeply humanistic absence of self-interest required to make of Sir Luke a complete healer and, simultaneously, a fully realized model for the reader. When Milly's condition worsens in Venice, Sir Luke is called for immediately: "[W]here was the voice of Sir Luke Strett[?] If they talked of not giving her up shouldn't *he* be the one least of all to do it? 'Aren't we, at the worst, in the dark without him?' " (II, pp. 278, 279).

James, then, offers three potential models of the attentive accompanying presence—Lionel Croy fails, Susan Stringham is compromised by her own personal weakness, and Sir Luke Strett is the ideal attentive presence. On rereading the novel, the reader accepts the odd realization that James at the start equates him or her with Lionel Croy because Croy burlesques a relation that occupies the center of this novel and also, perhaps, the center of the experience of reading it. The task of reading the novel becomes the genuine attempt— perhaps through the surrogacy of Sir Luke—to see Milly through her ordeal, ultimately her death, not only with attention but with truth.

In view, however, of the narrative contract implied by the first-person-plural narrator, it may be more accurate to consider the narrator as the surrogate reader of this fiction. In addition, that is, to offering a character as the figure upon whom to model oneself as reader, James makes the unusual gesture of offering himself as the reader's model. For example, as Densher vacillates in his moral paralysis, the narrator dutifully records each instance of the character's moral failure, although only from within Densher's own consciousness. The absence, of course, of perspectives critical to Densher conceal whatever judgments other characters may harbor toward Densher. The reader faithful to the book has no choice but to imagine the interpretations of Kate, Susan, and Sir Luke, interpretations that perhaps judge Densher harshly. The reader also has to provide, provisionally at least, the inner lives of those characters who have moved out of textual reach. What might Kate herself feel after her visit to Densher's rooms? What must she go through in the final "success" of her plan? In these and countless other instances in the novel, then, "the reader does quite half the labour" of creation side by side with James, determining plot and meaning of the novel in part through his or her own creative powers.[36]

By consistently making room, as it were, beside himself in the telling of the story, James grants the reader a share in the imaginative power of creating the story, challenging the reader to invest in the outcome of these characters with the force of so-called real life and granting, in addition to intimacy with fictional characters, a powerful intimacy with James himself. If earlier works, for example the short story "The Middle Years," seem to implicate a parental relation for James toward his reader, then *The Wings of the Dove* offers to the reader a metaphorical role of parent, alongside James himself, to the novel's characters, who are begotten, if you will, in creative acts between the author and the reader. The moral effect on the reader, then, implicates not only the reader's literary skills but also the deep personal sources of his or her notions of goodness and moral failure. Not discriminating between autobiography and fiction but eliciting a seamless evaluation of the particularities of these characters' actions and choices, the novel—or rather the process of reading it—makes explicit a reader's perceptions and beliefs about how individual persons can search out and grasp the right ways to live. Rather than a morality play, the novel acts on the reader as would genuine human experience in the ambiguity of real ethical choice. The reader who gives himself or herself over to James's desires, who skates on that levitating ice, will have experienced and taken part in the inner lives of these humans deeply afflicted with their ultimately incurable ailments.

Epilogue

The ethical dimensions of literature include elements of plot, form, and the moral influence on the reader. Such dimensions of literature clarify, for the ethicist, the professional and personal experiences of grappling with the chaotic and ultimately narratively grasped experiences of patients and doctors who seek ethical guidance. Once bioethicists have developed our analytic skills, we must begin to develop our skills of deep involvement—with selfless disinterest—in the lives of others. Our engagement with our patients and their families must be deep enough to grasp the texture, the conflicts, the regrets, and the hopes of these lives, and it must be disciplined enough—by virtue of attention to the conflicting predicaments of other human actors within the drama—to achieve balance and fairness. The legacy of Henry James grants to the selfless and skilled reader experience in such healing discernment. The plot, form, and process of reading James's late novel together provide conceptual models and affective experience in recognizing and articulating sources of goodness and evidence of moral failure. It is the hope of this work that literary texts, theories, and practices can contribute to that motion within bioethics that strives toward singular clarity, personal engagement, and deep recognition of "the practical question of life."

Notes

1. Matthew Arnold, "Literature and Science," in *Discourses in America* (London: MacMillan and Co., 1889), p. 117.

2. David Parker's *Ethics, Theory and the Novel* (Cambridge: Cambridge University Press, 1994) stands as an example of a study of evaluative criticism which dead-ends into defensive posturing against contemporary critical studies to protect the traditional canon. For a balder and less nuanced visit of the same territory, see Charles Altieri, *Canons and Consequences: Reflections on the Ethical Force of Imaginative Ideals* (Evanston, IL: Northwestern University Press, 1990). For a more thoughtful study of moral concerns, see Christopher Clausen, *The Moral Imagination: Essays on Literature and Ethics* (Iowa City: University of Iowa Press, 1986).

3. Wayne Booth, *The Company We Keep: An Ethics of Fiction* (Berkeley: University of California Press, 1988); J. Hillis Miller, *The Ethics of Reading: Kant, de Man, Eliot, Trollope, James, and Benjamin* (New York: Columbia University Press, 1987). See a number of recent anthologies and proceedings of conferences devoted to questions of ethics and ideology in literary studies: *Reading Narrative: Form, Ethics, Ideology*, ed. James Phelan (Columbus, OH: Ohio State University Press, 1989); *Understanding Narrative*, ed. James Phelan and Peter J. Rabinowitz (Columbus, OH: Ohio State University Press, 1994); and David H. Richter, *Falling into Theory: Conflicting Views on Reading Literature* (Boston: Bedford Books of St. Martin's Press, 1994). Barbara Herrnstein Smith addresses fundamental questions of evaluation of texts in her *Contingencies of Value: Alternative Perspectives for Critical Theory* (Cambridge, MA: Harvard University Press, 1988), questions that indeed precede those of the ethical dimensions of literature to probe the contingencies of all textual judgments.

4. Paul de Man, *Allegories of Reading: Figural Language in Rousseau, Nietzsche, Rilke, and Proust* (New Haven: Yale University Press, 1979).

5. Booth, *The Company We Keep*.

6. Not all moral philosophers agree that the literary or narrativist turn is appropriate. Nonetheless, a vigorous and disciplined debate has opened, both among philosophers and between philosophers and literary scholars. See the 1983 issue of *New Literature History* devoted to the ethics of narrative. If some moral philosophers and literary scholars—Martha Nussbaum, Cora Diamond, D. D. Raphael—defend philosophy's right and obligation to examine the philosophical and moral

content of literary texts, some of their colleagues—including Murray Krieger and Angel Medina—query their motives and their methods.

7. Martha Nussbaum, *Love's Knowledge: Essays on Philosophy and Literature* (New York: Oxford University Press, 1990), p. 6.

8. Iris Murdoch, *The Sovereignty of Good* (New York: Schocken Books, 1971), p. 34.

9. Ibid. p. 31.

10. See, for example, Charles Samuels, *Ambiguity and Henry James* (Urbana, IL: University of Illinois Press, 1971) and R. P. Blackmur, *Studies in Henry James,* ed. Veronica Makowsky (New York: New Directions Publishing, 1983). Yvor Winters asserts that "[James] was so obsessed with the problem of moral judgment in its relation to character, that he not only constructed his plots so that they turned almost wholly on problems of ethical choice, but he sought to isolate the ethical problem as far as possible from all determining or qualifying elements" in *Maule's Curse: Seven Studies in the History of American Obscurantism* (Norfolk, CT: New Directions, 1938), p. 215.

11. Merle Williams, *Henry James and the Philosophical Novel: Being and Seeing* (Cambridge: Cambridge University Press, 1993); Quentin Anderson, *The American Henry James* (New Brunswick, NJ: Rutgers University Press, 1957); Paul Armstrong, *The Phenomenology of Henry James* (Chapel Hill, NC: The University of North Carolina Press, 1983).

12. Joseph Warren Beach, *The Method of Henry James* (New Haven: Yale University Press, 1918).

13. F. R. Leavis, *The Great Tradition; George Eliot, Henry James, Joseph Conrad* (New York: New York University Press, 1969), p. 7.

14. Lionel Trilling, "The Head and Heart of Henry James," in *Speaking of Literature and Society,* ed. Diana Trilling (New York: Harcourt Brace Jovanovich, 1980), pp. 202–206, p. 203.

15. Henry James, "Charles Baudelaire," in *Selected Literary Criticism,* ed. Morris Shapira (Cambridge: Cambridge University Press, 1981), pp. 26–31, p. 30.

16. In *The Later Style of Henry James* (Oxford: Basil Blackwell, 1972), Seymour Chatman counts "verbs of mental action" in samples of James's late novels and compares his findings with counts of such verbs in samples of contemporary fiction of similar length. He finds 250 verbs of mental action in a 200-sentence segment of *The Wings,* three times as many as in the sample of Samuel Butler's *The Way of All Flesh* and five times as many as occur in Joseph Conrad's *Typhoon.*

17. Beach, *The Method of Henry James,* p. 256.

18. F. O. Matthiessen, *The Major Phase* (London: Oxford University Press, 1944), p. xi.

19. Laurence Holland, *The Expense of Vision: Essays on the Craft of Henry James* (Princeton: Princeton University Press, 1964), p. x. Of the vast number of critical works addressing the relation of James's aesthetic form to his ethical or moral considerations, see also Sallie Sears, *The Negative Imagination: Form and Perspective in the Novels of Henry James* (Ithaca: Cornell University Press, 1968); Naomi Lebowitz, *The Imagination of Loving: Henry James's Legacy to the Novel* (Detroit: Wayne State University Press, 1965); Daniel Mark Fogel, *Henry James and the Structure of the Romantic Imagination* (Baton Rouge: Louisiana State University Press, 1981). Millicent Bell addresses the pluripotent narrative meanings of James's never-closed endings, as if the reader is asked to entertain multiple alternatives to the stated plot. See *Meaning in Henry James* (Cambridge, MA: Harvard University Press, 1991), pp. 1–44.

20. See Myler Wilkinson, "Henry James and the Ethical Moment," *The Henry James Review,* 1990; 11:153–175 for a discussion of James's conceptual foreshadowing of de Man, as discussed by J. Hillis Miller.

21. How often in *The Wings of the Dove* does the narrator comment, quietly, that a passage describing an action or event takes longer to read than the event took to occur?

22. John Carlos Rowe, *The Theoretical Dimensions of Henry James* (Madison: University of Wisconsin Press, 1984), pp. 228–229.

23. Holland, *The Expense of Visions*, p. x.

24. Henry James, "The Middle Years," in *The Novels and Tales of Henry James*, The New York Edition, vol. XVI (New York: Charles Scribner's Sons, 1909), p. 81.

25. Henry James, *The Novels and Tales of Henry James*, vols. XIX (vol. I of *The Wings of the Dove*) and XX (vol. II of *The Wings of the Dove*) of The New York Edition (New York: Charles Scribner's Sons, 1909). Page numbers appearing in parentheses in the text refer to this edition. Milly swoons after seeing the Bronzino portrait at Matcham, for example, to defend against her vision of Kate as she imagines Densher sees her. As Kate hovers over her, "saying to her that she hoped she wasn't ill" and the other guests have been led away, Milly ruminates that "she had in a manner plunged into [the illness] to escape from something else . . . something that was perversely *there*. . . . 'Is it the way she looks to *him*?'" (I, p. 225). The same simultaneity of plot elements occurs when Milly, wandering in the National Gallery in order to avoid hearing Sir Luke's news about her illness, meets Densher and Kate. Her reunion with Densher, although characterized by her realization that "she should still like him" (for James, an expression of the deepest love), is overshadowed by her anxious awaiting of Sir Luke's prognosis (I, p. 300).

26. Murdoch, *The Sovereignty of Good*, p. 43.

27. Charles Taylor, *Sources of the Self: The Making of the Modern Identity* (Cambridge, MA: Harvard University Press, 1989), p. 44.

28. James wrote unequivocally about the germ of the novel within the idea of a young woman condemned to an early death, a germ created in the short life of his beloved cousin Minny Temple who died of tuberculosis in her twenties. James's Preface and notebooks follow the development of "a very old—if I shouldn't perhaps rather say a very young—motive; I can scarce remember the time when the situation on which this long-drawn fiction mainly rests was not vividly present to me. The idea, reduced to its essence, is that of a young person conscious of a great capacity for life, but early stricken and doomed, condemned to die under short respite, while also enamoured of the world" (I, p. v). Susan Stringham realizes in the Alps that physical illness is the "light in which Milly was to be read" and that "talk of early dying was in order" (I, p. 116; I, p. 134). Kate guesses early on the severity of Milly's illness, telling Densher that Milly will "really live or she'll really not. She'll have it all or she'll miss it all. Now I don't think she'll have it all" (II, p. 54).

29. "Having so often concluded on the fact of his weakness, as he called it, for life—his strength merely for thought—life, he logically opined, was what he must somehow arrange to annex and possess" (I, p. 51). Although these thoughts relate to Densher's love and desire for Kate, the words take on ominous meaning in view of his hastening of Milly's death. Densher's "private inability to believe he should ever be rich," which he regards as "in truth quite positive and a thing by itself" remains true to the end, foretelling his renunciation of Milly's fortune and his subsequent loss of Kate's hand (I, p. 62). And Densher's casual comment to Kate after his conversation with Aunt Maud, "I may be safely left to kill my own cause," rings with horror with the climax of the novel in sight (I, p. 89).

30. Lionel Trilling, *Matthew Arnold* (New York: Harcourt Brace Jovanovich, 1977), p. 30.

31. Very rarely, the narrator speaks in the singular. "They sat together, I say, but Kate moved as much as she talked; she figured there, restless and charming, just perhaps a shade perfunctory, repeatedly quitting her place, taking slowly, to and fro, in the trailing folds of her light dress, the length of the room, and almost avowedly performing for the pleasure of her hostess" (I, p. 275). There seems to be little difference between the moment of the phrases in which the narrator appears as an "I" and as a "we," but this observation requires further testing.

32. Leo Bersani, "The Narrator as Center in *The Wings of the Dove*," *Modern Fiction Studies*, Summer 1960; VI:131–144, p. 131.

33. Douglas Paschall, "Complicit Manoeuvres: The Form of *The Wings of the Dove*," in *Modern*

American Fiction: Form and Function, ed. Thomas Daniel Young (Baton Rouge: Louisiana State University Press, 1981), pp. 13–27.

34. See Seymour Chatman, *The Later Style of Henry James* and Shlomith Rimmon, *The Concept of Ambiguity—The Example of James* (Chicago: The University of Chicago Press, 1977) for extended discussions of the consequences of the ambiguity of pronouns' referentiality in James's late novels.

35. Sallie Sears, *The Negative Imagination: Form and Perspective in the Novels of Henry James,* (Ithaca: Cornell University Press, 1968), p. 69.

36. In an essay on the novels of George Eliot, James elaborates his theory of the reader's collaboration. "In every novel, the work is divided between the writer and the reader; but the writer makes the reader very much as he makes his characters. When he makes him ill, that is, makes him different, he does no work; the writer does all. When he makes him well, that is, makes him interested, then the reader does quite half the labour." "The Novels of George Eliot," in *Discussions of George Eliot,* ed. Richard Stang (Boston: D.C. Heath and Company, 1960), pp. 3–7, 4–5. First printed in the *Atlantic Monthly* in 1866.

7

Film and Narrative in Bioethics

Akira Kurosawa's Ikiru

Charles Weijer

The projected film was born just over a century ago. The subject of early cinema was the real world: images of people, trains, cities, and foreign places filled early movies. In many ways, the remarkable innovation of film was that "[t]he screen image provided the closest copy of the real world that had yet been achieved by technology."[1] In 1896, *Strand Magazine* said of one film of the seaside that "the spray is thrown up in so realistic a fashion as to make the people in the stalls actually start involuntarily, lest they should be drenched"![2] Cinema did not become a mass medium, however, until directors (and audiences) tired of travelogues and began to explore fictional narratives involving actors. In short, film captured the world's imagination only when it began to tell stories.

Given the growing interest of bioethics in narrative, it is surprising that film as a storytelling medium has been largely ignored. For example, Howard Brody, in his well-known book, *Stories of Sickness,* refers to "novelists, poets, and playwrights" as storytellers from whom we can learn, but doesn't mention filmmakers.[3] Indeed, a search of the Bioethicsline database (1973 to February 1996) revealed that none of the 33 articles on "narrative" dealt with film. (Three articles in the Bioethicsline database discuss using film to teach bioethics;[4] one analyzes the portrayal of bioethical issues in several recent films.)[5]

Cinema represents a rich source for bioethicists interested in stories and how they are told. In this paper I want to do two things. First, I want to discuss one remarkable film, Akira Kurosawa's 1952 classic *Ikiru,* and some of the storytelling devices used in it. Second, I want to examine how the underlying view of life-narrative—that is, the real or ultimate nature of a person's "lifestory"—presented in *Ikiru* challenges current conceptions of the life-narrative in bioethics.

Ikiru, translated literally as "to live," tells the story of the last five months of life of a bureaucrat, Kanji Watanabe, from his diagnosis with stomach cancer until his death. The central irony of the film is that Watanabe has been more or less dead for the last twenty-five years. Only when he comes to terms with his cancer diagnosis does he begin to live truly, if only for a brief period.

The opening image of the film is an X ray of Watanabe's stomach. The narrator tells us that "[t]his is the stomach of the hero of our story. There is a stomach cancer in the pyloric region, but the man himself doesn't know this yet."[6] We are then shown an image of Watanabe working at his desk: he stamps papers, checks his watch, stamps some more papers, winces, and takes some stomach medicine. The narrator continues:

> This is the hero of our story. But to tell anything about this man right now would be extremely boring. Why? Because all he is doing is killing time. . . . There is no time during which he actually lives. In other words, one cannot really say that this man is alive at all. . . . It's no good! This won't make a story at all. Why he's just like a corpse.[7]

Shortly thereafter, Watanabe learns of his cancer diagnosis and the fact he has only a short time to live. Alienated from his family and coworkers, Watanabe sets out on a quest for meaning that occupies the first two-thirds of the film.

Watanabe's first impulse is to engage in a reckless pursuit of pleasure, but nightclubs, dancing, and alcohol only bring on a violent hemorrhage. The answer for him does not lie in the epicurean. He then attaches himself (platonically) to a beautiful young girl from the office, who herself seems so full of life. But here too Kurosawa will not allow him an answer. When Watanabe implores her to tell him how, if only for a day, he can live just like her, she replies, "But, all I do is just move around and eat. . . . That's all" (Kurosawa 1970, p. 151).[8] Only when freed from desire and immature attachments to others can Watanabe achieve enlightenment. As another group in the restaurant begin to sing "Happy Birthday," the answer comes to Watanabe: he will help a group of impoverished citizens cut through red tape and have a filthy drainage pond cleared to build a park for children.

After Watanabe announces his resolve to see the park constructed, the narrator tells us that five months has elapsed and Watanabe is dead.

The last third of the film is devoted to Watanabe's funeral. His family and co-workers have gathered in his home to pay their last respects. The park has been built, but many questions remain: Was Watanabe responsible for the park being built? Why did his behavior change so suddenly five months prior? Did he really know that he had cancer? (He had told no one who was present at the funeral of his diagnosis). As the evening builds to a drunken climax, all present finally realize Watanabe's modest but heroic act. Intoxicated, they swear to cast off their bureaucratic torpidity and emulate Watanabe's example of action. "I'll work as if I've been reborn!" one shouts; "We all will," the group replies.[9] In the next and last scene of the film, Watanabe's coworkers are back in the office, and it is painfully clear that nothing whatsoever has changed.

Stephen Prince, in *The Warrior's Camera*, rightly observes that the intense cinematic formalism of *Ikiru* is a conscious emulation by Kurosawa of techniques developed by Bertold Brecht.[10] Brecht's notion of "complex seeing"—conveying the meaning of a play through the full range of theatrical devices, not just dialogue—is translated into the film's intensive use of sound track, frame composition, camera, lens, and editing in relaying the film's message.

Also, Brecht's (connected) notion of distancing the spectator from the play's characters is a central influence on the film. "Above all," notes Prince, "Brecht emphasized the position of the spectator as observer, rather than as one implicated in the stage action through processes of identification, and the play as non-linear structure as jumps, curves, and montage that would emphasize human life as a process of change."[11] By distancing the spectator from the characters on stage, Brecht is consciously attempting to reduce the spectator's *empathy* with stage characters so that *understanding* has room to develop. Brecht himself explains that:

> Before a correct attitude can be imitated it must first have been understood that the principle is applicable to situations that are not exactly like those portrayed. It is the theatre's job to present the hero in such a way that he stimulates *conscious rather than blind imitation* [emphasis added].[12]

Kurosawa consciously employs these Brechtian techniques in order to maximize the impact of the film's moral lesson. Without some distance between the spectator and Watanabe, the film would lapse into sentimentality and become more like a television movie of the week rather than an exploration into human nature. In order to distance us from Watanabe, Kurosawa structures the film around a series of disappearances. Watanabe disappears from the narrative rather conspicuously several times during the first two-thirds of the film (and then all together for the remainder of the film). This leaves us, the spectators, wondering where he has gone; even characters on screen ask each other this question and offer theories to account for Watanabe's disappearance.

Techniques related to "complex seeing" are often employed in the film in order to achieve this effect. Camera, lens, and editing are used at several points during the film to build up an expectation of seeing Watanabe, only to have us suddenly discover that he is gone. For example, after Watanabe learns of his cancer diagnosis, the camera follows him leaving the hospital. Mirroring his shock and isolation, the sound track is completely silent as he walks down a busy street. Only when he is almost run over by a truck do the sounds of the street return. Suddenly, as Watanabe stands on the sidewalk, the camera tracks across the street, threatening to leave our main character behind. The next shot has the camera tracking toward a house we have not seen before. Someone is singing. (Is it a character in the film or the sound track?) When the camera reaches the door of the house, using a reverse-field shot (a 180-degree rotation in the camera's axis), Kurosawa shows us that we have been following not Watanabe, but his son and the son's wife. Where is Watanabe? What has happened to him? These are questions we will ask over and over while watching this film.

Watanabe is the central narrative enigma in *Ikiru*. Prince describes his character as "a textual gap that the narrative tries to fill in and reclaim by inventing hypotheses for his behaviour."[13] Watanabe's story thus proceeds in a halting and fragmented fashion. Hypotheses are put forward; sometimes they are confirmed, sometimes they are denied. At the funeral, when Watanabe has disappeared for the last time, the search for Watanabe's story is at its most intense. Some present think he has killed himself as a political act, others suggest that he had a mistress, others believe that he knew he had cancer, and still others are sure he did not know his diagnosis. As the characters become progressively more drunk, they recollect stories about Watanabe and argue. Gradually, a more or less coherent picture of the last months of Watanabe's life emerges.

As I have indicated above, Kurosawa employs Brecht's technique for an important reason: to prevent our empathy for the main character from lapsing into lachrymose sentimentality. This task is, in itself, a recognition of the fact that film is a medium capable of imparting a powerful emotional impact. Consider the the scene in which Watanabe learns he has terminal cancer. The scene opens with Watanabe in a hospital waiting room: he has been suffering from stomach pains and is waiting for X ray results. A strange man confronts him in the waiting room and tells him all the signs of stomach cancer. The escalating discomfort in the scene is palpable as we slowly realize that he is describing Watanabe's symptoms: trouble eating, heaviness in the stomach, blood in the stool. Without uttering a word, Watanabe's anxiety is obvious: he shifts uncomfortably in his seat, moves to another seat, looks away from the strange man (and toward us, the spectators). But the strange man is relentless: Watanabe learns that if the physician tells him it is a mild case of ulcer and nothing is to be done, he is done for. Silently, Watanabe walks into the physician's office. The doctor tells him in a reassuring tone, "You have a light case of ulcer." Watanabe's coat drops to the ground and he stares into the camera, wide-eyed with terror.

Films draw us in emotionally in a way that perhaps no other medium can. Consider the following account of a movie theater (written in 1914):

> I happened to take my eyes from the screen and look at the man sitting beside me, when lo! His face was moving in response to every contortion upon the face of the actor. Again, I have noticed some much-affected young women swaying to and fro, obeying every moment [*sic*] of the sorrowing heroine. One thing can surely be said of the pictures, they absorb the attention of the people who see them even more completely than the speaking dramas of the ordinary theatre.[14]

In the scene from *Ikiru,* we not only witness Watanabe's anxiety and pain, we feel it. Considering the scene's obvious emotional impact, the most remarkable thing about it is that Watanabe does not utter a single word.

In the last section of this paper I want to talk about how *Ikiru's* narrative challenges conventional understandings of life-narrative. Underlying this discussion will be the following premise: what we take to be the essence of life-narrative influences how we collect information for a story about a life and how we tell that story.

Consider one conventional view of the life-narrative, what I will call the *self-authored life-narrative.* This view holds that the individual herself is the sole author of her life-narrative. The parallels with contemporary individualism are obvious: if a person's life is a text, she is the sole author and interpreter of that text. If this is the view that we hold of a person's life-narrative, the implications for the bioethicist trying to put together a story about a life are clear. When the person is competent, she is the *only person we need speak to* about the events in her life and what they mean.

If the person in question is incompetent, our task becomes very difficult. We must attempt, by whatever means, to capture her subjective experience in order to reconstruct her life-narrative. Rebecca Dresser, for example, argues that an approach to decision-making for incompetent adults must consider their subjective experience, and at times experiential interests (the pleasure or pain individuals derive from merely experiencing life) must outweigh prior expressed wishes (critical interests).[15] Just how we access the privileged subjective world of the cognitively impaired patient is, of course, a problem. Dresser suggests that family members can be used to help reconstruct the person's life-narrative. But since family members provide us with indirect evidence, at best, as to the state of the patient's mind, we must regard them as unreliable witnesses:

> Many [patients] fail to exhibit signs of distress, and caregivers frequently note that patients' families seem to suffer much more than the patients themselves. In balancing the burdens and benefits treatment could confer on this group, observers must be especially careful to identify and keep separate their personal discomfort about aging and mental decline from the patient's own subjective reality. As others have warned, such feelings can too easily shape the perceptions of those observing the cognitively impaired patient, yielding a flawed judgement that treatment should be forgone for the patient's "own good."[16]

This view of a life-narrative seems problematic. For one thing, my life-narrative is intimately connected with the life-narratives of others. For another, my own life-narrative (and ultimately my own identity) is constructed in relation to those around me. (Ask me who I am, and I'll begin by telling you the ways in which I am different from my parents.) Charles Taylor, arguing that we understand ourselves in narrative terms, makes the point simply: "A self can never be described without reference to those who surround it."[17] Taylor's point is not merely that a complete account of a life must include a description of intimate relationships. Rather, he asserts that *my identity itself is formed in conversation with others*:

> This is the sense in which one cannot be a self on one's own. I am a self only in relation to certain interlocutors: in one way in relation to those conversation partners who were essential to my achieving self-definition; in another in relation to those who are now crucial to my continuing grasp of languages of self-understanding—and, of course, these classes may overlap. A self exists only within what I call "webs of interlocution."[18]

MacIntyre argues for another commonly held view of the life-narrative, one we might call the *jointly authored life-narrative*.[19] A life, MacIntyre tells us, is held together by a narrative unity. A single comprehensive story of my life answers the question: Who am I? I am accountable for past actions because of this narrative unity; and the purpose of life involves finding a satisfactory completion to the narrative. But, MacIntyre continues, my own narrative is inextricably linked with those of people close to me:

> I am part of their story, as they are part of mine. The narrative of any one life is a part of an interlocking set of narratives. Moreover this asking for and giving of

accounts itself plays an important part in constituting narratives. Asking you what you did and why, saying what I did and why, pondering the differences between your account of what I did, and *vice versa*, these are essential constituents of all but the very simplest and barest of narratives.[20]

What follows from this view? In contrast with the *self-authored life-narrative*, when collecting data for a story about someone's life, it will not be sufficient to speak to that person alone. It is important to see how others view that life and how they participated in its formation. (I am not always the best judge of my own character or actions.) Ultimately, though, MacIntyre believes that only one true account of a life exists. As he puts it, "stories are lived before they are told."[21] Presented with differing accounts of one life, according to MacIntyre, "it clearly makes sense to ask who is right, if anyone."[22] Thus, when contradictory views of a life exist, at least one of those views is false. So, then, one of the tasks of the bioethicist when collecting information for a story of a patient's life will be to decide which of the views of persons close to the patient is to be discarded and which is to be retained. In short, contradiction among accounts of a single life must be resolved.

The narrative approach in *Ikiru* argues against both the *self-authored* and the *jointly authored life-narrative*. In short, Kurosawa does not believe that a wholly true story of a person's life-narrative can ever be told. In his well-known film *Rashomon* (1950), Kurosawa relates five mutually contradictory versions of a rape and murder relayed by eyewitnesses to the crime. Although each of the stories agrees on some basic facts, there is no objective way to resolve the differing accounts. Commenting on the film's message, Kurosawa says that:

> [h]uman beings are unable to be honest with themselves about themselves. They cannot talk about themselves without embellishing. This script portrays such human beings—the kind who cannot survive without lies to make them feel they are better people than they really are.[23]

This is a deep problem for those who would attempt to construct a true version of a patient's life-narrative. If even the patient herself will embellish the past, how can we ever generate a true version of her life-narrative? The answer is, of course, we can't. Having arrived at the same conclusion, Long points out that life-narratives are invariably the result of "authorial aspect."[24]

> [J]ust as the novelist is selective with respect to character development, plot, etc., so the person "who seeks the connective threads in the history of his life . . . has singled out and accentuated the moments which he experiences as significant; others he has allowed to sink into forgetfulness." The result of this process is

narrative unity as something akin to *fictionalized history*. . . . [T]he narrative unity which results from this process is not *discovered*; it is the result of selective attention, emphasis, dim remembrance, and possibly even forgetting. The person makes choices about the importance of persons and events, decides on their meanings, though there may only be a minimal awareness of the resulting order as a partially created one. These choices and decisions—like those of a novelist— are not arbitrary; they are guided by the desire for the "good story." The finished product is the "fictionalized" history of a life, neither a lie nor "the truth," but instead a work of imagination, evaluation and memory.[25]

We are left then with what one might call a *postmodern life-narrative*: an objective telling cannot be achieved, and contradiction among differing accounts may not be resolvable. The funeral scene in *Ikiru* is a prime example of this sort of narrative. It is, in many ways (excluding the drunkenness, of course), reminiscent of the sorts of meetings that bioethicists have with health care workers and families every day. When a patient is cognitively impaired, in a persistent vegetative state, or otherwise unable to decide for herself, she has become, like Watanabe, a "textual gap." We attempt to fill this narrative space by asking family members and others close to the patient to tell us about the patient's wishes, values, and life experiences. In short, we ask them to tell us stories about the patient. What emerges is a multivoiced picture of the patient relayed in the stories told about her. Told in this way, the picture of the patient is a complex one: fragmented, relative, and filled with contradiction.

What does this imply for the bioethicist? First, even if the patient in question is competent, a full version of that person's life-story cannot be constructed without reference to the perspectives of intimate others on her life. While no "true" version of the life-narrative can be constructed, the multivoiced story of a single life will provide a fuller, richer picture of that life. Second, if no canonical version of the patient's life can be appealed to, contradiction among stories about a person's life will often be irresolvable. While we may speak of one story being better than another, it is problematic to speak of it as "truer." Each of the voices describing a life will—like a fugue—converge at times and diverge at others.

An interesting question remains as to how the written bioethics case should be presented if we accept the *postmodern life-narrative*. One approach might be to present the case as a transcript of the encounter involving the bioethicist, the patient (if possible), and those intimate with the patient. Following the format of *Ikiru*'s funeral scene, each of the views of the patient's life-narrative—those of persons close to the patient, that of the patient, possibly those of health care workers, and even the emerging view of the bioethicist—could be put into dialogue with one another. Ultimately agreement may be reached on many points, but substantial disagreements may remain among the various accounts. The task, then, of the bioethicist is to catalog these varying perspectives and to highlight points of agreement and disagreement.

Tod Chambers[26] presents a written bioethics case that is quite similar to the format described above. In it he retells the story of a physically and cognitively impaired man derived from interviews with various health care workers involved with the case (the man had died by the time the interviews were done and Chambers chose not to interview family members). Although the interviews were done on a one-to-one basis, each of the individual testimonials is edited together into an overall account of the man's story. Importantly, each of the speakers is identified, and contradictions among the accounts is left intact. Unlike the approach outlined above, though, the bioethicist has no voice in the story. Clearly, further work is needed to elucidate an approach (or approaches) that is both true to the concept of the *postmodern life-narrative* and practical in a clinical setting.

The cinema represents yet another resource available to bioethicists studying stories and how they are told. *Ikiru* has also allowed us to examine the adequacy of conventional views of the life-narrative—the *self-authored* and the *jointly authored life-narratives*. The ensuing critique has, if convincing, left us with a *postmodern* understanding of life-narrative: in short, an objective telling of a life-narrative cannot be achieved, and contradiction among different stories about the same life is often not resolvable.

If we imagine a life as a single musical "voice," it is a voice in which the theme is reexamined and often reworked. As a result, the musical theme grows and changes; elements are discarded in one incarnation, only to be changed and included in a later one. If we wish to understand a life fully, this single voice is in itself insufficient; other voices must be added. As these multiple voices relate the story of one life, they will converge at points and diverge at others. And so, by this complex telling, a life in its richness is revealed.

Acknowledgments

The author is grateful to the following individuals for their helpful comments on earlier drafts of this paper: Carl Elliott; Tod Chamber; Hilde Nelson; Bette-Jane Crigger; Benjamin Freedman; Karen Lebacqz; and Anthony Belardo. An abbreviated version of this paper was presented at the Spring meeting of the Society of Health and Human Values in Knoxville, Tennessee, April 11–13, 1996. The author's research is funded by a fellowship from the Medical Research Council of Canada.

Notes

1. S. Bottomore, "The Coming of the Cinema," *History Today* 46, no. 3 (1996):14–20, at 15.

2. *Ibid.*

3. Howard Brody, *Stories of Sickness* (New Haven: Yale University Press, 1987), p. xi.

4. D. J. Self, D. C. Baldwin, and M. Olivarez, "Teaching Medical Ethics to First-Year Students by Using Film Discussion to Develop Their Moral Reasoning," *Academic Medicine* 68 (1993):383–385; D. J. Self and C. Baldwin, "Teaching Medical Humanities Through Film Discussions," *Journal of Medical Humanities* 11 (1990):23–29; and A. Smith, "The Teaching of Medical Ethics," *Journal of Medical Ethics* 11 (1985):35–36.

5. E. L. Erde, "Bad-Guys, Buccaneers, and Bureaucrats: Images of Bioethics in Film," in D. H. Brock and R. M. Ratzan, eds., *Literature and Bioethics: Literature and Medicine* (Baltimore, MD, 1988), pp. 148–169.

6. A. Kurosawa, "Ikiru," in *Complete Works of Akira Kurosawa*, vol. 6 (Tokyo: Kinema Jumpo Sha, 1970), pp. 105–176, at 107.

7. *Ibid.* at 108.

8. *Ibid.* at 151.

9. *Ibid.* at 174.

10. Steven Prince, *The Warrior's Camera* (Princeton, NJ: Princeton University Press, 1991).

11. *Ibid.* at 100–101.

12. *Ibid.* at 101.

13. *Ibid.* at 103.

14. Bottomore, *supra* note 1, at 18.

15. Rebecca Dresser, "Dworkin on Dementia: Elegant Theory, Questionable Policy," *Hastings Center Report* 25, no. 6 (1995):32–38.

16. Rebecca Dresser and Peter J. Whitehouse, "The Incompetent Patient on the Slippery Slope," *Hastings Center Report* 24, no. 4 (1994):6–12, at 11.

17. Charles Taylor, *Sources of the Self: The Making of the Modern Identity* (Cambridge, MA: Harvard University Press, 1989), p. 35.

18. *Ibid.* at 36.

19. Alasdair MacIntyre, *After Virtue* (South Bend, IN: Notre Dame University Press, 1981), pp. 204–225.

20. *Ibid.* at 218.

21. *Ibid.* at 212.

22. *Ibid.* at 213.

23. Akira Kurosawa, *Something Like an Autobiography*, trans. Audie E. Bok (New York: Vintage Books, 1983), p. 183.

24. T. A. Long, "Narrative Unity and Clinical Judgement," *Theoretical Medicine* 7 (1986):75–92.

25. *Ibid.* at 87.

26. Tod Chambers, "Voices," *Second Opinion* 19 (1993):81–91.

8

Perplexed about Narrative Ethics

Tom Tomlinson

Stories are everywhere in the practice of health care. There are a million stories in the Naked City (an archaic reference young readers might not get). There are 400 or so in a good-sized hospital, counting just the patients. They are often compelling stories, too, whether they are tragic or triumphant. We make hit TV shows out of them, from *Marcus Welby, M.D.* to *ER.*

What might stories provide for us besides the pleasure of reading and telling them? Could they deepen our understanding of ethical problems and choices? This is a live question in large part because the dominant mode of ethical reflection practiced within health care ethics has come under increasingly skeptical scrutiny. We postmodernists are suspicious of methods of ethical reasoning that apply foundational principles from the top down (there's a mixed metaphor for you). There are a number of complaints lodged against this "principlism," and I won't survey them all here. The one of most immediate relevance is that in their abstractness, high- or even medium-level ethical principles are too removed from and insensitive to the specifics of the very particular living cases to which they are "applied." By contrast, stories are all about particular people, places, and events. If abstractness is the problem, stories (or "narratives") would seem to be part of the solution. And so "narrative ethics" is born.

Sounds pretty reasonable . . . in the abstract. When we get down to specific claims and arguments concerning just how narrative might contribute to reasoned ethical reflection, however, the water becomes a good deal murkier.

Before descending for a closer look, it will be helpful to distinguish between two different sorts of roles commonly envisioned for narratives in health care ethics. The first sees stories playing a part in moral or professional development. The reading and study of stories, it is said, has salutary effects on moral development through the enhancement of perceptiveness, sensitivity, sympathy, or other virtues. This claim will not be the focus of my attention on this occasion. Before setting it aside, I'll just note that my more literary acquaintances are nice to sit down with for a chaw and a chat, but I can't say that I've noticed any generally higher level of ethical acumen among them than is found among the rest of us in the herd.

It is the second role for narrative that interests me more. This sees narrative serving a central epistemic function in the discovery, justification, or application of ethical knowledge—a role that fills the gaps inherent in any analytical, rule-based method. What is that epistemic role? How does it work? Why should we have confidence in it? There are a variety of answers to these questions.

Enriching Moral Knowledge

One of the most common claims is that stories can enlarge our base of morally relevant knowledge. This idea is expressed in a variety of ways.

"It is the precise role of narrative to offer us ways of experiencing [the] effects [of destructive alternatives] without experimenting with our own lives as well" (Burrell and Hauerwas 1977, p. 138).

A novel like *David Copperfield* can "enlarge the moral imagination" in a way that "makes plain [the moral] cost" of a set of beliefs, attitudes, or policy. Dickens does this not so much by presenting facts hitherto unknown, but by doing so in a way that "engages" us so that we are brought to care about them (Diamond 1982, p. 33).

The reading of literature provides:

> vicarious experience [that serves] as a means of sympathetically participating in the lives of others. . . . By cultivating experience through imagination, through metaphor, through creative reading, a bridge can be established between the world of the patient (the other) and the world of the nurse or the physician or ethicist (the self). (Radey 1992, p. 40)

So long as we don't press any questions about how this role is to be played in the context of medical ethics, all of this seems innocuously and vaguely true. For the Victorian distant in space and class from the people of Dickens's world, a novel like *David Copperfield* may perhaps have been the best and certainly the most agreeable way to gain some sympathetic understanding of people who were otherwise alien.

But reading novels is not the only way to enlarge my understanding of people I don't know. Couldn't I do so by working with them, sharing experiences with them (real, not vicarious), talking with them? Isn't this in fact the way that we most commonly improve upon our understanding of others?

To put this question into the context of medical practice, isn't it by talking to the actual patient, seeing his real suffering, feeling sympathy for her genuine plight, that we cross the bridge between the patient on the one side and the doctor, nurse, or ethicist on the other? A vicarious literary experience or second-hand story would be a poor substitute.

Of course I recognize that no one would advocate wholesale substitution of literary experiences for real ones: rather, we should think of stories as useful *supplements* to our understandings of patients. Even this more modest sugges-tion raises an important difficulty. As all advocates of narrative ethics observe, a good story is about a very particular set of circumstances inhabited by charac-ters with specific and unique histories, identities, and trajectories. But then how will even a very good story, even a very good story about a person in circum-stances just like my patient's, provide me with useful and accurate insights about that real person's feelings, motives, or outlook? Well, perhaps the story will suggest to me some of the ways that a person in such circumstances may respond, and then I can explore those possibilities with my patient.

So the story can illustrate some general truths about human nature, which I may then tentatively apply? This is no doubt true of many good stories, but this feature would not distinguish narrative ethics from other modes of moral knowledge. Remember that the special virtue of narrative, the mark that distin-guishes it from the arid abstractions of ethics engineering, is that it remains in the world of the particular. Which kind of knowledge about patients *is* provided in stories—knowledge of the particular or knowledge of the general?

Neither choice is a comforting one for the claim that narrative provides a special source of morally relevant knowledge, useful for deliberating about real people's lives. For if the truth of the story is truth only for the characters portrayed in it, then it tells me nothing directly about those who don't live in that particular story. And if the truth of the story is alleged to be truth for all simi-larly situated, then the deliberately constructed particulars of the story provide scant evidence by themselves that the character is Everyman. Novels and stories become at best vivid illustrations of knowledge verified through other means.

None of this is to say that stories are not a valuable source of moral senti-ments. Diamond comes closest to the humble truth when she points out that what is notable about Dickens's art is not the presentation of facts, like a tract from some nineteenth-century Childrens' Defense Fund, but the creation of fellow feeling in the reader. That feeling is morally animating, and the having of it may be indispensable to moral judgment. Reading, seeing, or hearing a story is one way to get that feeling. But the feeling can't be morally warranted merely by the fact that a story creates it; and stories are only one source of moral sentiments, and one of the weaker ones at that.

Bridging the Gap

Another kind of epistemic claim made on behalf of narrative is that it bridges the gap between abstract ethical principles and the concrete circumstances of real cases. As Hunter puts it, "Narrative negotiates the application of general truths about human experience to the individual case" (Hunter 1995, p. 1791). Leder contends that narrative understanding is essential because a "'top down' methodology, wherein one commences with high-level theory, can obscure the rich complexity of cases." Rather than whether to tell the patient the truth about his cancer, we need to know how much truth to tell, what counts as the "truth," what the patient will hear when we tell the truth, and so on. "A hermeneutic approach, oriented toward the close reading of narratives, may better note the significance of such elements imperceptible from the heights of ethical theory" (Leder 1994, p. 251).

How? What is the medium through which narrative makes this connection? The one most frequently invoked is "interpretation." So far, however, it's been impossible for me to find a clear-eyed account of what "interpretation" refers to, how it is distinct from appeals to principled moral commitment, or how it ties principles to particulars. A few examples will illustrate my perplexity.

Drew Leder describes a case of a mother deciding whether to authorize surgery for a severely deformed newborn, and asserts that the case "provokes broad *interpretive* conflicts. . . . Is this newborn a full-fledged person in danger of being subjected to the cruelest form of discrimination . . . a dying child whose suffering may be needlessly prolonged . . . not a 'person' at all?" (1984, pp. 243–244; my emphasis).

How is it useful or illuminating that these disagreements are about matters of "interpretation," rather than about the substance and relevance of ethical principles? How will we decide among these alternatives if not by critically examining our principled commitments regarding respecting persons, having a right to life, avoiding discrimination, and so on? And if interpretation is a form of reflection to be employed in addition to, rather than instead of, principled reasoning, what is it that distinguishes "interpretive" from "principled" modes of critical ethical judgment?

As if to clarify this distinguishing feature, Leder remarks that hermeneutics (understood here as the discipline of interpretation) is a "communal dialogue which progresses through revelatory give and take" (1984, p. 254). In a similar direction, Rita Charon asserts than one "locates the authority for judging a conclusion's rightness of fit [with the narrative] on its acceptability to others doing similar work" (Charon 1994, p. 273).

Not very helpful. *Any* social system of reasoned reflection involves a "communal dialogue" of "give and take," including those deliberately rooted in principle. (I'm ignoring Leder's "revelatory" because I don't know what it means.) Charon's Kuhnian account gets us no further: it doesn't distinguish ethics from science, from anthropology, from literary criticism, because it glides over the question of what features govern "acceptability."

The failure to provide any more precise account of the nature and role of "interpretation" is a symptom of the tendency to wave it and "narrative" as banners that fly over everything bright and beautiful being ignored by those crude and insensitive principles. In standard bioethics discussions of surrogate motherhood, for example, Leder claims that:

> so much remains unconsidered . . . market pressures and alienating labor-options that may lead women to become surrogate mothers; the fetishism of commodities described by Marx, and how this infiltrates our treatment of human beings; the way gender roles as conceived of within our society shape our notions of "motherhood." (1984, p. 253)

(Notice, incidentally, that these are all concerns motivated by worry over the genuineness of the surrogate mother's "autonomy," and hence they all arise out of allegiance to a moral principle.) Now, if all these different inquiries involve the use of "interpretation," then the term has come to apply to virtually any account whatsoever, framed within any set of methods. Conceived so globally, "interpretation" can't be a construct useful for demarcating any distinctive way of understanding and resolving ethical problems.

Can we get a better fix on the relevant features of "interpretation"? Advocates of narrative ethics need to, because some of the characteristics that one would naïvely attribute to "interpretation" belie the claim that a narrative ("interpretive") ethics avoids the reliance upon abstractions that is the chief sin of "principlism." In one sense of the word, to "interpret" a set of events is to assign it a meaning, not readily apparent in the bare facts, which places those events within some larger framework. That framework will of necessity be composed of more general and abstract commitments and beliefs. An example comes from Charles Radey's discussion of a man facing death in an ICU:

> One way of considering our ICU case is to see this man in terms of myth. Surely he is coming to grips with death, its meaning in his life, and the possibilities of

rebirth. . . . The mythical realm opens, requiring courage and inviting discovery. Familiarity with the grand stories and myths of the ages prepares the practitioner as well as the patient for terminal-care decisions. (1992, p. 42)

Unfortunately, Radey never gets any more specific than this, but we know the sort of "myths" and metaphors that he's probably referring to. Our culture offers us images of Death as the Grim Reaper, or as the merciful angel delivering us from the mortal coil, or the endless sleep, or the door to eternity, and so on. Any of these metaphors might shape in some way the patient's or practitioner's response to impending death. But their connection to specific choices and responses is, if anything, even more amorphous and abstract that the most general ethical principle. How could "interpretation" provide the missing link between abstract ethical principle and concrete specifics if interpretation itself is inherently an act of abstraction?

Another difficulty with employing "interpretation" as a tool for concretizing ethical principles gets uncovered when we ask when it is that we most feel the need to supply interpretations. One answer is that we are driven to interpretation when situations present us with recalcitrant ambiguities and apparent contradictions. Interpretations are attempts to resolve or account for these in some coherent way; the more complex the circumstances and the better our imaginations and other interpretive resources, the greater the variety of alternative interpretations. If the situation is one that presents us with an ethical problem, a central ethical question will then become, "Which interpretation *should* we act on?" It remains a mystery how this question is to be answered through the medium of interpretation. Interpretation has supplied the alternatives; it has not provided any resolution. If interpretations are to help resolve choices, it will be because they supply reasons for preferring one alternative over another. And supplying reasons is to appeal to abstractions and generalizations of some magnitude. Before you know it, you're up to your neck in that damn principle of universalizability (which, by the way, tells us to treat like cases alike; not to treat all cases alike!).

Indeed, the richer the story, the less the resolution offered for the ethical questions raised. It's instructive here to compare Richard Selzer's "Mercy" with Timothy Quill's "Death and Dignity" (the story of "Diane"). "Mercy" invites competing interpretations of facts and motives at every turn. This is what makes it a pleasing work of art; but it is also what leaves the reader at sea with respect to any final judgment of whether the physician acted rightly in the story by not giving the final, fatal dose, let alone with respect to any more general judgment about the ethics of assisted suicide and euthanasia. By contrast, Quill's story of Diane is a set piece constructed deliberately at every turn to persuade the reader that Quill acted ethically, and to make the case for assisted suicide as an option for patients. But in order to accomplish this, Quill has to submerge any opportunities for the reader to supply alternative interpretations of events. So, for example, he tells us that it was "clear that preoccupation with her fear of a lingering death would interfere with Diane's getting the most out of the time she had left" (Quill 1991, p. 693). We don't get to hear the conversations that led Quill to that conclusion, and so we're presented with no opportunity to provide our own, perhaps very different, interpretation of their meaning.

The point is not to attribute any subterranean dishonesty to Quill, but to emphasize a common feature of interpretation: it might just as often complicate choice as clarify or resolve it. Not that complicating choice is a bad thing, or useless as an element in ethical deliberation. We should fully appreciate the genuine complexity that faces us, and if alternative interpretations can expose that complexity, then that is an honorable role for interpretive skill. Interpretation simply can't play the mediator between principles and particulars, where the gap looms just as large as before narrative stepped up to the plate.

This point has implications for the plausibility of the idea that casuistry provides the normative method of choice for narrative (a notion advanced by Carson Strong, among others). It's always been striking to me that what are usually offered as paradigm cases (in both classical and contemporary casuistry) are incredibly thin "narratives." And how could it be otherwise? Thicken them up and you get ethics gumbo. Their status as paradigm cases (which must by definition evoke an unambiguous moral response) evaporates, and their comparison with problematic cases becomes hopelessly complicated. In order to function as moral paradigms, they must be archetypes immune to interpretation, not narratives.

Narrative Rationality

Finally, I want to examine the idea that any ongoing narrative, and especially the "narrative" of an individual life, carries with it an internal rationality that elevates one choice over another as the right or best one. Alasdair MacIntyre points out that we cannot understand any individual human action without placing it within a history of some sort: "in successfully identifying and understanding what someone else is doing we always move towards placing a particular episode in the context of a set of narrative histories . . . action itself has a basically historical character" (MacIntyre 1984, pp. 211–212).

It is not just other people's lives that we understand properly as stories, but our own. "Man is in his actions and practice, as well as in his fictions, essentially a story-telling animal. . . . I can only answer the question 'What am I to do' if I can answer the prior question 'Of what story or stories do I find myself a part?' (MacIntyre 1984, p. 216). He means to refer here to more than the fact that, in order to comprehend the consequences of my choices, I must understand how others are likely to respond to them, where their responses will be shaped by historically conditioned expectations and conventions. Rather, the story of my life demands a narrative coherence that makes one choice more intelligible than another: "In what does the unity of an individual life consist? The answer is that its unity is the unity of a narrative embodied in a single life. . . . To ask 'What is the good for me?' is to ask how best I might live out that unity and bring it to completion" (MacIntyre 1984, p. 218).

This view is carried over into medical ethics by proponents of narrative who assert that we can best gauge the ethics of choices made by or for patients by attending to how those choices fit into the fabric of the patient's story. Writing about the ethics of decisions for incompetent elderly persons, Howard Brody argues: "that among those things to be considered are the elements of the life narrative that is drawing to a close, and which sorts of endings *make the most sense* within the context of that narrative" (Brody 1987, p. 164: my emphasis).

The fundamental fallacy in these views is the inference from the claim that my life is best *described* by a narrative to the normative claim that my life choices are best judged by their coherence within my life-narrative. My history (my story so far) will shape what I do no matter what I do. And no matter what I do, it will be intelligible within the narrative of my life. MacIntyre and others reify "my narrative" as if it were a kind of script being followed. Hence the phrase "the narratives we live out." Unless we assume that our stories are being written by someone else (God or the Fates), we don't live out a narrative, we create one by living a life. Of course, the narrative we create is a unity, as MacIntyre says. It is the story of our life. But the narrative of the individual life (of the single choosing agent) is necessarily a unity. It may end up a tragic narrative, or a fool's narrative, or a noble narrative. They will all equally be unities.

So the question of how best to live out "that" unity is not answered by the notion of narrative unity. It's answered by appeal to extranarrative ideals that elevate some kinds of narratives over others. Howard Brody incorporates ideals of moral integrity and human relationship into his conception of narrative ethics: "When we have a momentous decision to make, we often ask ourselves how that decision would fit within our our unfolding life story. Would it cohere in a meaningful and authentic way as the sort of action that the principal character of this narrative would be likely to perform?" (Brody 1992, p. 249). Elsewhere, he suggests that a coherent life story is one in which my actions "appear reasonable and responsible" rather than "whimsical and aberrant," and is "a story of a person who cares what his close associates think of him" (Brody 1994, p. 210). Well, that's one kind of story, and a pretty dull one from the sound of it. The lives of an expedient scoundrel or a moral chameleon or a flinty loner would equally well be narratives, and *as narratives* they could be equally coherent (and maybe more interesting). They may not be equally worthy *as lives*, but if so it is because we are judging them against conceptions of the best way to live, not conceptions of the best way to write a story.

I might concede that my life's narrative unity demands some coherence with my history of values, relationships, and choices. But since that coherence can be achieved through indefinitely many routes, the "demand" of narrative coherence becomes so easily met as to lose virtually all of its prescriptive force. Margaret Urban Walker agrees that in deciding what to do, an individual will feel the need to take account of his or her individual, historically shaped hierarchies of ideals and values. But in so taking account, the person is engaged in what she calls "moral self-definition"—not merely living out an identity, but creating one. One's particular judgments are "undertakings." They are not contracts binding on some future self, because my future self retains the capacity for moral self-definition and redefinition. "Particulars presumed to apply on the basis of past concerns and commitments may be revoked or revised, as well as renewed. . . . To affirm a moral position on the basis of weighting certain particulars is either . . . to sustain an extant moral course or to chart . . . a new one" (Walker 1987, p. 179). The need for moral self-definition, like the need for narrative coherence, leaves open the questions of which past concerns and commitments will be revoked, how they may be revised, and how past choices will be interpreted. My choices must be made only *within* a historical, narrative context; they are not made by it.

Take as an example the sort of situation that Howard Brody suggests would be best understood by attending to narrative coherence. An elderly man has completed a durable power of attorney appointing his son as decision-maker and specifying that he does not want heroic treatments employed if he has a terminal illness. One week after a stroke, he remains in the intensive care unit, unconscious, with severe, unstable hypotension managed only with maximum doses of medication. The chances for the return of blood pressure control and for substantial neurological recovery are low, but not impossible. His son wants to consider withdrawal of the medication, even given its probably lethal consequences. How would an inquiry into narrative coherence help us evaluate this request? Is there a course of action that would "make the most sense" as the last chapter in this man's story?

I don't think there is, just because there are an indefinitely large number of next chapters that could make sense. We can start first with the obvious fact that what he meant to commit himself to when he wrote his advance directive is open to multiple interpretations. What did he mean by "heroic" treatment or "terminal" illness? Why did he give his son durable power of attorney—to administer his wishes, or to interpret them? What was most important to him: adherence to his expressed preferences, or fatherly trust in his son's love and judgment? Of course, further details of his story might help rule out some answers as improbable and lend support to others. But further questions of interpretation will invariably arise at this next level as well. Even if we could settle on a single, unambiguous interpretation of his intentions when he signed the advance directive, we would still have the further question of what he would make of those intentions now. Would he reaffirm them; reinterpret them (in what directions?); repudiate them? Finally, to what extent is "his" story a product of his own devising? The last chapter the father would write might well be different from the last chapter his son would write. Each would present a coherent narrative of a life, albeit from a different point of view.

Because there are so many coherent narrative possibilities, the standard of narrative coherence can do little to warrant one line of narrative over another. We will instead turn to other considerations, derived from principle and policy. A principle of respect for autonomy will privilege the father's narrative over the son's equally coherent one. The desirability of preserving the integrity of family decision-making may justify our giving the son the authority to select among competing but equally coherent interpretations of his father's wishes, and so on. As I suggested earlier, the pursuit of narrative and interpretive possibilities may appropriately complicate our moral choices, but by itself offers little help in making them.

A Narrative Link

So how can narrative thinking aid us in warranting our moral judgments? I've identified a few modest ways. Stories can expand our understanding of other people and perhaps of ourselves, so that our ethical judgments become better informed. They may awaken moral sensibilities, so that we more keenly feel the wrongfulness of circumstances we had become hardened or blind to. The imperative to "get the whole story," and the interpretive skills that help to do so, can help uncover ethically relevant complexities.

What is untenable is the idea that narrative provides a mode of ethical justification that is independent from or superior to appeals to moral principles. Neither interpretation nor narrative coherence offers the tools needed for choosing from among all the interpretive and narrative possibilities.

What remains tantalizing but so far poorly explored is the idea that narrative understanding can provide a link between principles and particulars. The failures and inadequacies of the accounts of this link that I've examined have their source in an ironic cause—discussing and defending narrative ethics in the abstract, rather than by example. The unique virtue of narrative is its capacity for organizing particulars. Its contributions to principled ethical argument, then, will be clarified and documented only through detailed and careful analysis of a genuine narrative (not the pale and superficial cases found in the current narrative ethics literature) that pays sustained attention to the interplay between narrative and principled methods. Only an argument by illustration can show how ethical principle is mediated in its application to complex circumstances by special narrative competencies.

References

Brody, Howard. (1987) *Stories of Sickness*. New Haven: Yale University Press.

Brody, Howard. (1992) *The Healer's Power*. New Haven: Yale University Press.

Brody, Howard. (1994) "The Four Principles and Narrative Ethics," in R. Gillon, ed., *Principles of Health Care Ethics*. London: John Wiley and Sons, pp. 207–215.

Burrell, David, and Hauerwas, Stanley. (1977) "From System to Story: An Alternative Pattern for Rationality in Ethics," in H. Tristram Engelhardt, Jr., and Daniel Callahan, eds., *Knowledge, Value, and Belief*. Hastings-on-Hudson, NY: Hastings Center, pp. 111–152.

Charon, Rita. (1994) "Narrative Contributions to Medical Ethics: Recognition, Formulation, Interpretation, and Validation in the Practice of the Ethicist," in Edwin R. Dubose, Ronald P. Hamel, and Laurence J. O'Connell, eds., *A Matter of Principles? Ferment in U. S. Bioethics*. Valley Forge, PA: Trinity Press International, pp. 260–283.

Diamond, Cora. (1982) "Anything But Argument?" *Philosophical Investigations* 5:23–41.

Hunter, Kathryn Montgomery. (1995) "Narrative," *Encyclopedia of Bioethics*, ed. Warren Thomas Reich, vol. 4. New York: Simon & Schuster and Prentice Hall International, pp. 1789–1794.

Leder, Drew. (1984) "Toward a Hermeneutical Bioethics," in Edwin Dubose, Ronald Hamel, and Laurence O'Connell, eds., *A Matter of Principles? Ferment in U.S. Bioethics*. Valley Forge, PA: Trinity Press International, pp. 240–259.

MacIntyre, Alasdair. (1984) *After Virtue*. 2nd ed. Notre Dame, IN: Notre Dame University Press.

Quill, Timothy A. (1991) "Death and Dignity: A Case of Individualized Decision Making." *New England Journal of Medicine* 324:691–694.

Radey, Charles. (1992) "Imagining Ethics: Literature and the Practice of Ethics." *Journal of Clinical Ethics* 3:38–45.

Selzer, Richard. (1982) "Mercy." *Letters to a Young Doctor*. New York: Simon and Schuster.

Walker, Margaret Urban. (1987) "Moral Particularity." *Metaphilosophy* 18:171–185.

9

Bioethics' Consensus on Method
Who Could Ask for Anything More?

Mark Kuczewski

At first glance, a consensus on methodological issues in bioethics seems an unlikely accomplishment, because people treat method in several ways. Lay people tend to turn directly to the hot issues of the day, such as assisted suicide, and overlook questions of method. Conversely, some professional philosophers exaggerate the problematic nature of method. They believe that there is no distinctive method to medical ethics. There are only the various ethical theories, for example, deontological systems of principles, types of utilitarian calculus, and the like, which can be applied to the moral problems of medicine. Because theories diverge at their foundations, these philosophers assume that answers to moral problems will also take different directions. Furthermore, some argue that if medical ethicists deliberate without committing to a particular ethical theory or tradition of inquiry, one or more bad consequences will follow: (a) they will lack a decision procedure for tough questions;[1] (b) a forced, sociologically based consensus will predominate;[2] or (c) the history of ethical disagreements in society at large will merely repeat itself within the field of medical ethics.[3] Of course, the problem with the arguments of these professional philosophers is that nothing like the consequences they predict has actually come to pass. Instead, the commonsense approach of the layman has shown itself to be fruitful.

The history of method in biomedical ethics is a fascinating one and is a story showing that practice can guide theory in ethical deliberations. In this way, medical ethics is not singular but harkens back to the more moderate premodern approaches to ethics, most notably to Aristotle. Medical ethics has been successful in hammering out consensus on issues such as the need for informed consent to treatment or research and the right of patients to refuse life-sustaining treatment.[4] Proceeding by the examination of cases, both in the courts and the clinic, a set of legal and ethical concepts were articulated to guide decision-making. Reflection on this process of working back and forth between cases and concepts is producing a methodological consensus. That is, a consensus is also emerging on the best approach to bioethical problems.

Consensus is not unanimity. It does not mean that every person in the field agrees on every point. But it does mean that, as one reviews the major writings in the field, certain themes emerge and consistently recur. Those who dissent from these are noteworthy because they dissent on "settled" points. I will outline the recurring themes that form the core of bioethics' consensus on method. We will see that the consensus is built around a conception of narrative ethics and a corresponding person of a certain character, judgment, or virtue who is the *sine qua non* of narrative. When put forward in their most basic form, these two centerpieces of the consensus on method are difficult to reject completely. Nevertheless there are detractors. I will explore their criticisms and argue that there are more fundamental motivations behind these critiques. These criticisms reduce to concerns about our ability to know what is right and, of even more importance, to convince others of what is right. The former is easily answered. However, I shall argue that the latter problem persists for all forms of ethics, not only that which has come to dominate medical ethics.

The Consensus on Method

Undergraduate lectures on method in medical ethics don't usually begin with the claim that there is a consensus on method in bioethics. Instead, a capsule synopsis of the good old "high theories" of ethics, such as deontology and utilitarianism, is put forth. Then highly contrived cases are trotted out, and students try to apply these theories. The results are usually less than satisfying. As a consequence, higher-level courses take a more sophisticated approach.

In a graduate-level or continuing-medical-education lecture on method, the capsule summary of the high theories is followed by a well-accepted conclusion that the undergraduates discover at first hand. Namely, deontological and utilitarian theories are often too general to resolve difficult cases. For that reason, approaches are proposed that rely not on the singular foundational principles of high theory but on the more maximlike, midlevel principles of autonomy, beneficence, nonmaleficence, and justice.

Balancing and interpreting these or similar commonsense concepts is the key to the major approaches in bioethics. Principlism ("the four-principles approach") claims that we can balance these principles through the use of certain prudential maxims.[5] Casuistry (case-based reasoning) claims that by comparing cases to a paradigmatic case in which the principle or common ethical maxim that should predominate is clear, we can arrive at a sound moral judgment.[6] Communitarian ethics, an import from political philosophy, argues that moral concepts must be given meaning and weight through the deliberations of the citizenry or the participants in the scheme of health care delivery.[7] Communitarian ethics is sometimes distinguished from, sometimes considered the same as, virtue ethics. Virtue ethics emphasizes the development of certain states of character that make possible knowing and doing good.[8] The goals and the process of character development are usually considered communal in nature. For this reason, communitarian and virtue ethics may be coextensive. So there are three, possibly four, candidates for *the* method of medical ethics, but we must not be distracted by their seeming differences.[9]

Notice that all are in agreement on several points. First, starting with high theory and attempting to apply it to particular problems is ruled out. We might say that the first point of the consensus is that (1) there is no such thing as "applied ethics." Applied ethics has traditionally been conceived as a two-step process in which you first work out an ethical theory in the abstract and then plug in the content from the particular field.[10] This is a deductive model of moral reasoning, and the solution is supposed to follow of its own accord. This is clearly not how medical ethics operates, and virtually no major thinker in medical ethics holds this position.[11] However, that does not mean we should merely dismiss the notion of method.

The second point of the consensus is that (2) methods are useful. This point has a tradition beginning with the *Belmont Report* of the National Commission for the Protection of Subjects of Biomedical and Behavioral Research. In that report, the commissioners self-consciously married common concepts borrowed from the liberal democratic and civil rights traditions—namely, respect for persons (autonomy) and justice—to the concept of beneficence from the medical tradition. The four-principles approach divides the three principles of the *Belmont Report* into four *prima facie* duties (respect for autonomy, beneficence, nonmaleficence, and justice) and gives us several useful "prudential maxims" to assure that the ethicist does not neglect alternative strategies in balancing the mid-level concepts.[12] The casuist calls for examination and reexamination of cases, resulting in their arrangement in a taxonomy under the appropriate common moral concept or maxim based upon the salient circumstances.[13] The communitarian seeks to ensure the participation of the relevant members of the community and to create a process of examining cases and balancing moral maxims and concepts such that genuine deliberation results.[14] In other words, all agree on the need for certain mid-level concepts in which to discuss moral experience. Much of the give and take among the methods is about the best way to interpret, articulate, and refine the content of these concepts. Despite the fact that each method initially takes a different approach to dealing with this articulation, there is also widespread agreement that rote method alone will not solve ethical problems.

The third and perhaps most central tenet of the consensus is that (3) all methods in medical ethics presuppose a kind of narrative construction.[15] Whether one is balancing principles in the particular case,[16] allowing the circumstances to determine the proper solution,[17] or arriving at a solution that preserves the goods of particular relationships or the community at large,[18] one presupposes that there is a skillful way to construct the case such that its salient features will become thematic, and acceptable resolutions will surface. Whether in a case consultation, the deliberations of an institutional ethics committee, or the workings of a governmental commission, the person of sound moral judgment wades into murky waters. He or she is usually asked first to clarify the issue. Often a variety of hypotheses are put forward by different parties regarding the constitution of the problem. The ethicist(s) investigate the problem and construct the story so that both the problem and the possible resolutions become clearer.[19] Much of the ethicist's skill consists of an ability to transcend the limits of the readily available perspectives from which to construct the narrative.

The perspective of the health care providers and the perspective that can be gleaned from a chart review often characterize the patient in terms of the limited setting, time frame, and orientation of the hospital. These perspectives conceal much that is of great importance in understanding the moral issues at hand. The knack is to reconstruct the case such that the problems and conflicts have discernible origins and form a coherent story. This is usually a process of weaving together a number of different narratives: the patient's, the family's, the various health care providers'; the institution's.[20] It may be seen as a process of making these different narratives "transparent" to each of the parties, who see the conflict only through their own perspectives.[21] This constructive process is similar for the principlist, the casuist, and the communitarian.

The narrative(s) of medical ethics receive structure from, and are punctuated by, a wide variety of substances. This is the fourth point of the consensus. (4) Ethically relevant material comes from many sources, especially legal precedent, standards of care, and the general cultural milieu, including its multifarious traditions.[22] When we ask "where does ethics come from?" medical ethicists might provide answers that trace to a philosophical thought experiment such as the "original position,"[23] but they are just as likely to cite the history of medical practice and show how a resolution is in accord with what is best in it. This ability to reach for any of a variety of sources in constructing a narrative leads us to the fifth point of the consensus.

It is widely agreed that in medical ethics there is no Archimedean point that can serve as the foundation of ethical inquiry or as the ultimate teleological aim by which all solutions are judged. When dealing with an ethical issue, one is usually starting *in medias res*. We do not start with the same principle each time but find that cases often lead us to the relevant concepts. One might begin with respect for the patient's autonomy, but soon find oneself discussing the physician's duty to protect the patient from harm because the patient's decision-making capacity is in question. And vice versa. Similarly, cases suggest various maxims to the experienced casuist, but a casuist of good judgment will consider a wide variety of similar cases that exhaust the potentially relevant factors, no matter how he began the inquiry. The communitarian, likewise, cannot always start and end with some reified conception of the good of the community or institution, but must explore a variety of scenarios concerning what the good of the community means and how the good of this particular patient is tied in with such related goods. Although we are in the middle of things, we can always work back and forth between these cases, maxims, concepts, duties, and revise each in the light of new understandings and interpretations of the others. In other words, the fifth tenet of the consensus is that (5) medical ethicists seek a "reflective equilibrium" in which perceptions of particular cases and the more general levels of reflection are brought into balance.[24] Medical ethics is, therefore, coherentist in that there is no absolute starting point, but the overall "fit" of the cases, principles, and solutions produced is the measure.[25]

The first five points presuppose the sixth tenet of the consensus. (6) The usefulness of method is largely character-dependent. Each method provides useful tools to those who wish to deal with bioethical issues. Using the tools of method in a maximally beneficial way requires a person of requisite experience. When trying to resolve an ethical issue in a particular case, some people are better than others at facilitating the expression of perspectives and processing of concerns. Similarly, some persons have an ability to hit the mark in piecing together all the circumstances and factors in a particular case and determining which solution fits best in this instance. We can say that method presupposes a person of judgment, of sound practical reasoning or, to use the Aristotelian formulation, a person of practical wisdom.[26] To understand this point properly, it must be clear that medical ethics is not usually about a person of practical wisdom who sits alone and arrives at answers. This is clarified by the seventh tenet.

The seventh point of consensus is that (7) medical ethics is as much about process as events, outcomes, or solutions. In medical ethics, "process" is a thick ethical concept with meanings and implications that function on many levels. On the simplest level, a notion of process has elucidated the doctrine of informed consent, the cornerstone of medical ethics. Process models of informed consent have taken medical ethics beyond the static notions of rights and have described the relationships essential to quality medical decision-making.[27] Once again, it is not that informed consent and rights are useless concepts, but it is only within the context of physician-patient-family relation-ships and the process of shared decision-making that the scope and meaning of rights and patient autonomy are fully intelligible.[28] These same deliberative processes that characterize case resolution also make conflict manageable on the level of ethics committees and government commissions.[29]

Medical ethics has formed a consensus on consensus: the process of coming to consensus, the process of deliberation, is as much a part of the fabric of morality as the particular "solution." So, although I have at times spoken of prac-tical reasoning or judgment as if it applied to a lone ethicist analyzing a case, this language is misleading. The narrative construction of the ethical decision-making is an interpersonal process in which an ethicist is just one character.

Critiques of the Consensus

The consensus on method is a moderate and balanced approach distilled from several decades of the "doing" of medical ethics. As with any moderate consensus, critiques from each extreme are possible. Some criticize the consensus as too "inflexible" or too "rigid." Simply stated:

> (1) The consensus on method reflects a western philosophical view that is highly individualistic in nature. In many other cultures, the rights of the individual are not as important as the values of the group.[30] Therefore, the consensus fails to take other cultures seriously. Even in many white Anglo-Saxon Protestant fami-lies, the values of the family are more important than the primacy of the patient's autonomy. This phenomenon is not captured by our patient-centered ethic.[31]

This criticism is easily dismissed. From what I have already said, we can see that this complaint is lodged against the rhetoric of medical ethics rather than its substance. At times, with the constant talk of informed consent, patient self-determination, respect for patient autonomy, and so on, it can sound as if medical ethics is hopelessly libertarian. However, the points of consensus, espe-cially the seventh tenet, show that this is not so.

More challenging to the consensus on method are those criticisms that suggest it is too "soft," indeterminate, or intuitive in nature. This complaint takes several forms but generally it reduces to certain claims:

> (2) The consensus on method is intuitionist in nature and intuitionism is discredited. Proceeding on intuitions, different persons will come to different

conclusions, and there will be no decision-making procedure to help in hard cases. Thus we need to move away from these interdisciplinary dialogues and return to the rigor of theoretical philosophical ethics.[32]

Similarly, some who are sympathetic to the consensus on method and have been responsible for developing certain of its tenets fear that it lacks sufficient resources to deliver us from the moral prejudices of our age:

> (3) Without some way to anchor the consensus, we are in danger of rolling down slippery slope after slippery slope. As we focus on each case and construct each narrative, we are in danger of succumbing piecemeal to a particular bias. For instance, autonomy, as the natural bias of a liberal democratic society, might come to dominate every major question in medical ethics.[33] This point has been made by communitarian authors who suggest either the conscious embrace of a tradition of inquiry to provide an ordering hierarchy of values[34] or the development of explicit community mechanisms to deliberate upon and select the fundamental values that guide decision-making.[35]

The attacks against the "soft" nature of the consensus on method mix together metaphysical, epistemological, and pedagogical concerns. This is in itself not a problem, since the consensus also mixes these elements liberally. However, when we separate these elements, we find that the metaphysical and epistemic concerns can be answered satisfactorily. Criticisms that suggest that the consensus cannot convince those outside the mainstream in bioethics are more difficult. Nevertheless, all the objections are answered in the same way— by highlighting the characterological assumptions of the consensus (Tenet 6), including the requisite character of those who wish to dialogue with bioethicists. Let us examine in greater detail how the consensus can respond to each criticism.

"Rigid" Bioethics? The Cultural Bias Criticism

A very interesting but easily dismissed criticism asserts that bioethics is dominated by the rights claims of individuals as expressed in the concept of autonomy and operationalized in the doctrine of informed consent. This criticism concludes that, since bioethics reflects this bias of the Western liberal democratic tradition, it is culturally nearsighted and must be transformed in order to become more than just our own codified cultural biases. This criticism gains support from such highly esteemed authors as Hilde and James Lindemann Nelson, who claim that medical ethics has been so individualistic in its formulations that it fails to create a satisfactory framework even for cognizing the role of the family in medical decision-making.[36]

This criticism of the consensus has force only if we do one of two things: (1) assume that when the term "autonomy" is used, we should think in terms of an extreme individualism; or (2) assume that those theorists in bioethics who strongly emphasize rights are the mainstream thinkers rather than those who advocate the consensus.[37] Respect for patient autonomy or patient self-determination is certainly the fundamental concept in medical ethics. Its triumph, at least in theory, over physician paternalism marks the modern era in medical ethics. However, we must be quick to point out that patient autonomy does not vanquish the physician's duty to guard the well-being of her patient (beneficence); rather, these duties must be balanced appropriately. Another way of saying this is that the consensus sees a certain richness to the physician-patient relationship that transcends the mechanical application of rights claims. The patient is not simply a consumer who calls all the shots while the physician brings mere mechanical skills to the encounter.[38]

As I noted in the exposition of the seventh point of the consensus, advances in the theory of informed consent have shown how consent is a process in which there are roles for physician-patient-family relationships in medical decision-making. In effect, the critics of extreme individualism in medical ethics have been so well received and have become so established that they are now the mainstream. The language of medical ethics continues to be that of patient autonomy, self-determination, and informed consent, but medical ethicists operating within the consensus have built a place for beneficence and for close others into this terminology.[39] Of course, bioethicists are still sometimes misled by their own terminology, but this is a rectifiable error and must be addressed on an issue-by-issue basis.[40]

The charge of cultural bias is exaggerated. When autonomy is considered in balance with beneficence, when informed consent is conceived as a process that includes many parties rather than as an individualistic event, subcultures have a place within the clinic. The problem of multiculturalism is often conceived as pitting cultures that place a premium on the cohesion of the group against the culture of medicine, which values the individual. However, this is a caricature of modern medical ethics. Instead, medical ethics has a framework that can accommodate both the patient who values his privacy rights and the patient who is equipped with an entourage that has its own dynamic. As Dena Davis has hinted, the real problems of multiculturalism are empirical. The health care team must become familiar with the beliefs of the subculture and also the relationship this patient has to those beliefs and to the group.[41] Yes, medical ethics never ceases to speak a patient-centered language. But this language contains thick ethical concepts that can capture the realities of a contextualized patient.

Too Soft? Archimedes, Where Are You Now?

The second set of criticisms of the consensus is more challenging. Is medical ethics in trouble without a decision procedure to help it in difficult cases? Can a method that contains few, if any, timeless and absolute principles rise above cultural prejudices, or is it doomed continually to reify the dominant culture's values in a conventionalist bioethics?

Certainly, it would be simpler to have clear, indubitable, first principles from which to construct a complete ethical system. However, anything that approaches such a status is unable to fulfill our practical needs. And those concepts that we call principles in medical ethics (autonomy, beneficence, and the like) are not bright shining stars, but need a good deal of interpretation and elaboration. Thus, if the consensus on method is to prove relatively stable, it must claim that its interpretive method and critical approach are sufficient without an additional anchor. Several considerations can be cited in support of this claim.

First, we must wonder why intuition seems to be so discredited that these critics favor a more theoretically based, mechanistic decision procedure. It is easy to see that intuition must generally guide theory *at least as much as* the reverse. Why would anyone respect a theoretically based decision procedure? Precisely because it yields results that square with our firmest intuitions and most deeply held considered opinions. When it doesn't, the philosopher must revise the theory or the mechanism. (Any graduate student in philosophy can recite certain stock cases that make rigid deontological or utilitarian action guides untenable and that have caused deontologists and utilitarians to make innumerable additions to their theories.)

Of course, a formal mechanism can help in cases where intuitions are lacking. But such a consideration only pulls the formal decision procedure into a tie with the consensus. The methods of the consensus are about finding help for difficult cases through analogy to our best and clearest intuitions. It seems that introducing a contrived mechanism is simply redundant. Given these considerations, perhaps the search for an "objective" mechanism should arouse suspicion. Maybe those who oppose the consensus are not really concerned with the results yielded by its methods but have other motives—for example, they are interested in convincing those who do not share the firmest intuitions and most deeply held considered opinions of mainstream bioethicists. I shall return to this concern.

What of the slippery slope of autonomy? Elsewhere I have constructed a casuist response to the slippery-slope argument.[42] I suggested that the casuist can use the appreciation of multiple principles and goods to offset the momentum of the single value of the slippery-slope argument. That is, the slippery slope assumes that the more often you decide in favor of one value, such as autonomy, the more likely you are to settle future cases in the same way. Each time you do so, your appreciation of that value grows while you appreciate the competing good, say, beneficence, less and less. The casuist prides herself on being familiar with a wide array of cases whose solutions appropriately honor a variety of values. Thus the experienced casuist has the tools to maintain a self-critical approach. This same answer is available to all methods that are within bioethics' methodological consensus. For instance, the four-principles approach explicitly staves off the unbridled march of a single value by considering each of the four principles to be equally weighty *prima facie* duties that must be appropriately balanced in accordance with specific features of the situation. The four-principles approach married two values that were dominant throughout the history of medicine, namely, beneficence and nonmaleficence, with two drawn from our political heritage, namely, autonomy and justice. Modern medical ethics has been successful not by bringing the theoretical systems of philosophers to bear on medical ethical questions but, as the *Belmont Report* demonstrates, by bringing two areas of moral experience into dialogue with each other. To avoid the slippery slope, medical ethics must continue to give each of these kind of voices—those of the medical traditions and those that reflect our liberal demo-cratic heritage—their due. Whether one believes one is practicing casuistry, principlism, or communitarian ethics, this goal is the same.

As I noted in the exposition of the tenets of the consensus, there is a charac-terological element to medical ethics. The consensus squarely embraces virtue theory in claiming that character and the needs of interpersonal relationships anchor medical ethics. We are now in a better position to see why this is so. Because bioethics lacks foundational principles, a critical approach that tries to balance a variety of considerations provides the vehicle for self-criticism. In other words, ethicists construct a narrative that makes the salient features of the case thematic. Through a process of continuing narrative construction, a reso-lution or an outcome comes to pass that is as ethically sound as possible. The values, goods, principles, prudential requirements, maxims, and so on provide a checklist of considerations that can be used as self-critical tools by the ethicist. In the tenets of the consensus, I alluded to one way in which the character of the ethicist was important. Namely, the narrative construction is a skill that has been developed by experience and may vary with the ethicist's experience. The answer to the criticism of the slippery slope points out that bioethics is dependent on the character of the ethicist in an additional way: the narrative construction and the self-criticism from which the ethicist may learn are functions of the humility of the ethicist.

Although we can provide checklists of considerations that should not be overlooked when an ethicist "works up" a case, there is no formula for constructing the story of the case and no algorithm for arriving at an appropriate resolution. The ethicist must be continually vigilant to allow the elements of the narrative to surface and to avoid reading her own biases in its construction and resolution. This demands a willingness to be open to criticism continually and to be willing to learn from each case.

An openness to the ethos of medicine and that of the larger society, an acquaintance with many values and cases, and a certain kind of ethicist may be sufficient for the methodological consensus to avoid a slide down the slippery slope. However, this does not mean that the consensus will be able to achieve unanimity among all parties in society. The consensus is likely to gain greater acceptance in the near future than it currently enjoys, since achieving consensus is a semiperformative activity.[43] The consensus on method has emerged as a product of years of multidisciplinary scholarly activity, the deliberations of professional societies, the work of governmental commissions, the grassroots activities of institutional ethics committees, and legal precedents. Nevertheless, when one says, "we have reached a consensus on method," this reinforces the consensus. However, such a statement cannot convince everyone.

As I noted earlier, it is this desire to be convincing to everyone that lies hidden behind the major criticisms of the consensus on method. Criticizing the consensus for being too rooted in liberal individualistic ideology can be a philosophical way of saying that the conclusions of bioethics are not persuasive to certain subcultures: ardent religious supporters of a vitalist theology, for example. Certainly, the radical communitarian criticisms of bioethics are based in the fact that some debates, such as abortion, seem to go on aimlessly forever.[44] Staring at such a problem for too long can blind one to those large areas of consensus that have emerged, such as that on forgoing life-sustaining treatment.[45] Bioethicists must not be blinded in this way.

Failure to be persuasive to everyone is not only a criticism of the methodological consensus in bioethics, but a criticism of all thought throughout time. No ethical framework or first principle can persuade everyone. Someone can deny it. Of course, the proponents of "high theory" or first principles will say: "But, then those dissenters are being *irrational* or *unreasonable*." Of course, if we define rationality or reasonableness as a willingness to take part in consensus-building processes, then this same answer is open to bioethicists who champion the consensus on method.

Through the miracle of public opinion polls, we know that there is nothing unique about ethics' inability to persuade everyone of its conclusions. Physics, mainstream medicine, and the *New York Times* also have detractors who don't believe many of the most supported claims each makes. It will be a mark of the wisdom of the bioethics community if it accepts the limits of persuasiveness rather than becomes distorted in a process of overreaching itself. This is not yet a point on which there is consensus.

Some, such as Ezekiel Emanuel, have suggested organizing health care into small, community-based programs (CHPs) in which the members set the agenda and citizens may choose a program that shares their fundamental value assumptions. In this way, each program can exclude "fundamental dissent" and achieve consensus within the program on all major issues, including abortion.[46] However, it is easy to see why such a strategy is doomed to failure. Once all those who are pro-life have joined pro-life CHPs, the radical element among them will not desist from their pro-life activities. These people do not want only their CHP to be free of abortions; they will want all CHPs to be abortion-free. The same problem arises if the question of fundamental assumptions is raised to the macrolevel.

Alasdair MacIntyre favors society's coming to embrace a tradition of philosophical inquiry *in toto.* By settling the fundamental philosophical assumptions for an entire society, the problems the CHP encountered in resolving the abortion question should not resurface. However, that society could ever settle the fundamental value questions for everyone does not seem plausible even if a sincere effort to do so were made. Dogmatists who insist on a certain principle will not be hoodwinked by showing them that they have previously agreed to more fundamental values that contradict their principle. They will simply insist on the principle, revise their value commitments, or create some other narrative that does not demand reconciling their thesis with the societal hierarchy of values. When one is willing to adhere to a thesis at all costs, philosophical inquiry can make no headway. It would be strange to judge any philosophy or methodological consensus by how well it does in this regard, since they all do equally poorly.

In order to be persuaded by the better case, one must manifest a certain degree of humility. One must accept that it is at least possible that one is wrong and wish to know and to do what is right. No principle, theory, or tradition can persuade the person who lacks all humility. Bioethics' consensus on method can fare no better. The consensus demands humility on the part of those who claim to be bioethicists. Humility is the condition of ethical truth within bioethics. It is also the condition of truth beyond the bioethics community. Those who wish to engage bioethics in a genuine dialogue must have this attribute.

Ramifications

I have outlined the central tenets of the consensus on method in bioethics and have considered the major objections. This consensus is always open to revision.

Nevertheless, it has and should continue to prove a relatively stable structure and be useful for guiding moral inquiry in the near future.

There are ramifications of articulating this framework, both for those within bioethics' mainstream and for those who would seek to undermine the consensus. First, attempts to argue that one method in bioethics is definitively superior to the others seem unimportant and a waste of energy when the amount of common ground is mapped out. Instead, fruitful dialogue among those within the mainstream will probably take the form of efforts to contribute additional points of consensus. A particular methodological approach may demonstrate that it has a useful feature of which all bioethicists should be aware and should seek to incorporate into their analyses. This is how the consensus has developed, and there is no reason it cannot continue to do so. For example, each method endorses giving attention to particular circumstances, but casuistry made this point thematic; all methods are enhanced by attention to communal deliberative processes, but many neglected this factor until the communitarians made the point obvious; other methods have made other contributions. Proponents of the methods I have surveyed may demonstrate that I have overlooked additional important points on which all can agree. However, it is likely that the most important additions may be made by methods that I have not directly considered. For instance, feminist ethicists and phenomenologists each have their own starting points that make them sensitive to particular matters of method. As a result, they may make additional relevant factors thematic.

The consensus also sets the limits. It shows the general points with which other methods need concur to be within bioethics' mainstream. Of course, a radical method might argue against the mainstream. In such an effort, the tenets of the consensus are also useful. These tenets expose the assumptions that must be undermined by any method that wishes to be a serious competitor. The major objections to the consensus that we have already surveyed should also help objectors to focus their criticisms and to avoid repeating facile complaints.

The remarks I made to defend the consensus against the major objections point to the need for a person of experience and judgment to navigate through difficult ethical issues or to facilitate a process that allows an appropriate resolution to emerge. Similarly, I highlighted the fact that the success of method also depends on the humility of the ethicist. Furthermore, humility is demanded by any who would engage the consensus. I do not think bioethicists ask too much in requiring this of all objectors before taking them seriously. In fact, it may be that bioethics has lacked a "prophetic" voice by asking too little of those who disagree, and thereby has reinforced vicious tendencies under the justification of pluralism.

In sum, we have found that method demands virtue. I began by asking, "who could ask for anything more" than the methodological consensus? I have suggested that the person of humility does not do so, but asks only to be a part of these consensus-building processes. Bioethics now has the opportunity to invite others beyond its own community into these deliberations and to call them to rise to the standards of virtue that these processes demand.

Acknowledgments

I'd like to thank John Arras, Francoise Baylis, and Carson Strong for their helpful comments on an earlier draft of this essay.

Notes

1. K. Danner Clouser and Bernard Gert, "A Critique of Principlism," *Journal of Medicine and Philosophy* 15(1990):219–236.

2. Alasdair MacIntyre, "Does Applied Ethics Rest on a Mistake?" *Monist* 67(1984):498–513, at p. 513.

3. *Ibid.*, p. 500

4. Alan Meisel, "The Legal Consensus about Forgoing Life-Sustaining Treatment: Its Status and Prospects," *Kennedy Institute of Ethics Journal* 2(1992):309–345.

5. Tom L. Beauchamp and James F. Childress, *Principles of Biomedical Ethics* (New York: Oxford University Press, 1989, 3rd ed.), pp. 44–55; (1994, 4th ed.), pp. 34–38.

6. Albert A. Jonsen, "Casuistry as Methodology in Clinical Ethics," *Theoretical Medicine* 12(1991):295–307.

7. Ezekiel J. Emanuel, *The Ends of Human Life: Medical Ethics In a Liberal Polity* (Cambridge, MA: Harvard University Press, 1991).

8. Edmund D. Pellegrino and David C. Thomasma, *The Virtues in Medical Practice* (New York: Oxford University Press, 1993).

9. Beauchamp and Childress, *Principles of Biomedical Ethics* (1994, 4th ed.), p. 19.

10. Loretta A. Kopelman, "What Is Applied About 'Applied' Philosophy?" *Journal of Medicine and Philosophy* 15(1990):199–218.

11. Baruch A. Brody, "Intuitions and Objective Moral Knowledge," *Monist* 62(1977):446–456; Tom L. Beauchamp, "On Eliminating the Distinction Between Applied Ethics and Ethical Theory," *Monist* 67(1984):514–532; Ronald A. Carson, "Interpretive Bioethics: The Way of Discernment," *Theoretical Medicine* 11(1990):51–59; Albert A. Jonsen, "Of Ballons and Bicycles or The Relationship between Ethical Theory and Practical Judgement," *Hastings Center Report* 21(1991):14–16.

12. Beauchamp and Childress, *Principles of Biomedical Ethics* (1994, 4th ed.), p. 34.

13. Jonsen, "Casuistry as Methodology in Clinical Ethics," pp. 301–303.

14. Emanuel, *The Ends of Human Life*, pp. 162–167.

15. Rita Charon, "Narrative Contributions To Medical Ethics: Recognition, Formulation, Interpretation, and Validation in the Practice of the Ethicist," in Edwin R. Dubose, Ronald P. Hamel, and Laurence J. O'Connell, eds., *A Matter of Principles? Ferment in U.S. Bioethics* (Valley Forge, PA: Trinity Press International, 1994), pp. 260–283.

16. Edmund D. Pellegrino, "The Metamorphosis of Medical Ethics: A 30-Year Retrospective," *Journal of the American Medical Association* 269(1993):1158–1162, at p. 1161.

17. Jonsen, "Casuistry as Methodology in Clinical Ethics," p. 298.

18. Ezekiel J. Emanuel and Linda L. Emanuel, "Four Models of the Physician-Patient Relationship," *Journal of the American Medical Association* 267(1992):2221–2226; Alasdair MacIntyre, *After Virtue: A*

Study in Moral Theory (Notre Dame: University of Notre Dame Press, 1984, 2nd. ed.), pp. 205–225.

19. Tod Chambers, "From the Ethicist's Point of View: The Literary Nature of Ethical Inquiry," *Hastings Center Report* 26(1996):25–32.

20. Mark G. Kuczewski, Mark R. Wicclair, et al., "Make My Case: Ethics Teaching and Case Presentations," *Journal of Clinical Ethics* 5(1994):310–315, at pp. 313–314.

21. Howard Brody, "Transparency: Informed Consent in Primary Care," *Hastings Center Report* 19(1989):5–9.

22. Meisel, "The Legal Consensus about Foregoing Life-Sustaining Treatment," pp.311–314; Jonathan D. Moreno, *Deciding Together: Bioethics and Moral Consensus* (New York: Oxford University Press, 1995), p. 25; Carl Elliot, "Where Ethics Comes From and What to Do about It," *Hastings Center Report* 22(1992):28–35.

23. John Rawls, *A Theory of Justice* (Cambridge, MA: Harvard University Press, 1971); Norman Daniels, *Just Health Care* (Cambridge, MA: Cambridge University Press, 1985).

24. Baruch A. Brody, "Quality of Scholarship in Bioethics," *Journal of Medicine and Philosophy* 15(1990):161–178; John D. Arras, "Getting Down to Cases: The Revival of Casuistry in Bioethics," *Journal of Medicine and Philosophy* 16(1991): 29–51, at pp. 48–49; Ezekiel J. Emanuel, *The Ends of Human Life: Medical Ethics In a Liberal Polity,* pp. 155–156.

25. Baruch A. Brody, *Life and Death Decision-Making* (New York: Oxford University Press, 1988), p. 13; Ezekiel J. Emanuel, *The Ends of Human Life: Medical Ethics In a Liberal Polity,* pp. 34–35; Tom L. Beauchamp and James F. Childress, *Principles of Biomedical Ethics* (1994, 4th ed.), pp. 20–37.

26. Albert R. Jonsen and Stephen E. Toulmin, *The Abuse of Casuistry: A History of Moral Reasoning* (Berkeley, CA: University of California Press, 1988), pp. 257, 263, 314; Albert A. Jonsen, "Casuistry as Methodology in Clinical Ethics," pp. 303–304; Tom L. Beauchamp and James F. Childress, *Principles of Biomedical Ethics* (1994, 4th ed.), p. 107; Edmund D. Pellegrino and David C. Thomasma, *The Virtues in Medical Practice,* pp. 84–91; Mark G. Kuczewski, "Casuistry and Its Communitarian Critics," *Kennedy Institute of Ethics Journal* 4 (1994):99–116 pp. 109–111; Kathryn Montgomery Hunter, "Narrative, Literature, and the Clinical Exercise of Practical Reason," *Journal of Medicine and Philosophy* 1996, 21(3):303–320.

27. Charles W. Lidz, Paul S. Appelbaum, and Alan Meisel, "Two Models of Implementing Informed Consent," *Archives of Internal Medicine* 148(1988):1385–1389; Howard Brody, "Transparency: Informed Consent in Primary Care."

28. Mark G. Kuczewski, "Reconceiving the Family: The Process of Consent in Medical Decision-making," *Hastings Center Report* 26(1996):30–37.

29. Jonathan D. Moreno, *Deciding Together: Bioethics and Moral Consensus,* (New York: Oxford University Press, 1995), p. 115.

30. Lawrence O. Gostin, "Informed Consent, Cultural Sensitivity, and Respect for Persons," *Journal of the American Medical Association* 274(1995):844–845.

31. Hilde Lindemann Nelson and James Lindemann Nelson, *The Patient In the Family: An Ethics of Medicine and Families* (New York: Routledge, 1995).

32. Ronald M. Green, "Method in Bioethics: A Troubled Assessment," *Journal of Medicine and Philosophy* 15(1990):179–197; K. Danner Clouser and Bernard Gert, "A Critique of Principlism," p. 233.

33. John D. Arras, "Getting Down to Cases: The Revival of Casuistry in Bioethics," *Journal of Medicine and Philosophy* 16(1991): 29–51 at pp. 45–47.

34. Alasdair MacIntyre, *Three Rival Versions of Moral Inquiry: Encyclopedia, Genealogy, and Tradition* (Notre Dame, IN: University of Notre Dame Press, 1990), pp. 226–227.

35. Emanuel, *The Ends of Human Life.*

36. Hilde Lindemann Nelson and James Lindemann Nelson, *The Patient in the Family.*

37. Examples of such theorists might be H. Tristam Engelhardt, Jr., *The Foundations of Bioethics*

(New York: Oxford University Press, 1st edition, 1986); and Robert Veatch, *A Theory of Medical Ethics* (New York: Basic Books, 1981).

38. Emanuel and Emanuel, "Four Models of the Physician-Patient Relationship."

39. Mark G. Kuczewski, "Whose Will Is It, Anyway? A Discussion of Advance Directives, Personal Identity, and Consensus in Medical Ethics," *Bioethics* 8(1994):27–48.

40. Kuczewski, "Reconceiving the Family," p. 31.

41. Dena Davis, "It Ain't Necessarily So: Clinicians, Bioethics, and Religious Studies," *Journal of Clinical Ethics* 5(1994):315–319.

42. Mark G. Kuczewski, "Casuistry and Its Communitarian Critics," *Kennedy Institute of Ethics Journal* 4 (1994) 99–116, at pp. 107–112.

43. Moreno, *Deciding Together*, p. 52.

44. Alasdair MacIntyre, *After Virtue: A Study In Moral Theory* 2nd edition, (1984), p. 6.

45. Emanuel, *The Ends of Human Life* (Notre Dame: University of Notre Dame Press), pp. 42–96.

46. *Ibid.* p.182.

THREE

Literary Criticism in the Clinic

10

Medical Ethics and the
Epiphanic Dimension of Narrative

Anne Hunsaker Hawkins

I will argue in this essay that epiphany is a recurrent feature of the genre of literary narrative, and that any approach to ethics that calls itself "narrative" needs to take account of this fact.[1] I will also argue that what I am calling "epiphanic knowing" is an integral part of ethical decision-making; that it is an aspect of the way in which physicians make decisions about their patients (and learn from those decisions) in the course of practicing ethical medicine, and that it is therefore deserving of careful study.

In recent years bioethical discourse has come under criticism for focusing on what *should* go on in ethical decision-making rather than what actually happens. For many ethicists, the overriding assumption seems to be that decision-making should involve only the rational or logical faculties of mind. Leon Kass observes that this emphasis results in a lack of attention to "what genuinely moves people to act—their motives and passions . . . [their] loves and hates, hopes and fears, pride and prejudice, matters that are sometimes dismissed as nonethical or an irrational because they are not simply reducible to *logos*" (Kass 1990, p. 7). Physicians are clearly aware of this breach between ethical discourse and ethical practice. In reality, decisions are usually not made exclusively through a process of skilled deductive reasoning. Many other factors are also involved whenever we make important decisions about our own lives or the lives of others—and in this medical decisions are no different from any others.

Furthermore, it would seem that this is the way we *should* make decisions. Moral choice is an act of the whole person: it should involve all our mental faculties—reason, intuition, emotion, imagination—working in concert. Epiphanic knowledge does, and should, coexist with the kind of knowledge that is arrived at through deductive reasoning.

Narrative ethics—along with feminist ethics, hermeneutical bioethics, casuistry, and other new or revived approaches—is today enjoying popularity as a counterpart, or correction, to what has come to be called "principlist" ethics. A narrative approach is useful in countering the tendency in philosophy-based ethics to overemphasize moral principles and rules in considering a particular ethical situation. It is of interest that the call for a narrative approach to ethics originally came from scholars outside literature—from theologians and psychiatrists. In an essay published in 1977, David Burrell and Stanley Hauerwas use the term "narrative" with a sense of its context in the traditional stories of Judaism and Christianity. They introduce the term as a corrective to the hyperrationalism of contemporary ethical theory, arguing that practical reason cannot be separated from narrative contexts—particularly the contexts of religious narrative—and that the attempt to do so results in "a distorted account of moral experience." Burrell and Hauerwas do use literary terms such as "plot" and "character" in discussing narrative, but they do so as nonliterary scholars. Narrative is "the connected description of action and of suffering which moves to a point"—this being "the connected unfolding that we call plot" (Burrell and Hauerwas 1977, p. 128). And character they treat as something that unfolds or develops during the story in such a way as to "offer insight into the human condition" (p. 130).

Similarly, the psychiatrist Robert Coles, writing at about the same time as Burrell and Hauerwas, uses the term "narrative" more as a metaphor than as a specifically literary term. The novels he uses in his teaching make possible "a kind of medial ethics that has to do with the quality of a lived life" (Coles 1979, p. 445). Coles goes on to observe that the kind of moral inquiry he wants to teach is much like what one finds in great novels: "intense scrutiny of one's assumptions, one's expectations, one's values, one's life as it is being lived or as one hopes to live it" (p. 446).

A subsequent study by a nonliterary scholar who calls for a narrative approach to ethics is Howard Brody's *Stories of Sickness*. Brody argues for a medical ethics that can take into account the narrative dimensions of an individual's life—the recognition "that certain sorts of events can be fully understood only as portions of an ongoing narrative" (Brody 1987, p. xiii). Though Brody's discussion of particular texts is as insightful as any literary critic's, he does not intend his book as literary criticism and does not approach narrative in a technical way. For Brody, "each of us *is* a biography, a story. Each of us *is* a singular narrative" (p. xi).

Only recently have scholars in literature and medicine taken up the call for a narrative approach to ethics, with Anne Hudson Jones's "Literary Value: The Lesson of Medical Ethics" in 1987 and Stephen Miles's and Kathryn Montgomery Hunter's "Case Stories" series in the journal *Second Opinion* in 1990. Literature and medicine scholars are in a unique position to contribute insight about a narrative approach to ethics because they can take advantage of narrative theory. Suzanne Poirier has effectively used the literary theories of Bakhtin and Derrida in analyzing medical records and medical case reports. Rita Charon brings to a discussion of medical ethics such literary elements as point of view, narrative frame, simultaneous multiple meanings, temporality, and plot, and perhaps most important, the implications of the act of reading itself, with the complicated relationship between author, text, and reader, that are so much a part of contemporary narrative theory (1993, 1994). Tod Chambers analyzes discussions of medical ethics in terms of point of view—the position or vantage point from which events are observed and presented. He demonstrates convincingly that the way in which ethicists construct cases—even when these are based on a real case—inevitably reflects the particular point of view of the author.

The various elements of literary narrative have their correlatives in the ways in which we experience our lives or understand the lives of others. Indeed, sometimes the devices of narrative literature reflect an important way of apprehending experiential truths. The idea of stream of consciousness was "in the air" at the turn of the century, but it was literature—specifically, James Joyce's *Portrait of the Artist* and *Ulysses*—that helped us crystallize our understanding of this aspect of our mental functioning. Henry James, in his "Prefaces," insists that every story is told from a specific point of view, most commonly that of an omniscient narrator, a first-person narrator, or a third-person narrator, and that a given narrator may even be unreliable. This principle, which he manipulates so skillfully throughout his fiction, has contributed to our awareness today that any particular account of things must be seen as only a partial understanding of a situation, one that reflects the assumptions, character, and life experiences of the teller. All literary scholars today are aware of the fact that our subjective perceptions condition—and sometimes distort—our understanding of a particular situation, both in literature and in life.

In this essay I hope to contribute to the tendency toward more specificity in the narrative approach to medical ethics by examining the concept of epiphany, a device that is widespread in narratives of all kinds. An epiphany is a moment of recognition or revelation, a sudden insight or understanding that gives a deep sense of meaning and value. Though it may be prepared for over long periods of time, the experience is not gradual but immediate. Epiphanic knowledge is experienced as abrupt and total and "all of a piece"—it is not a knowledge arrived at through discursive reasoning. Usually we conceive of narrative temporally: experience is configured as linear, progressive, and chronological. In these terms our concern is with the unfolding of a life through time as this is manifested in narrative frame, temporality, and plot. The epiphany, though, concerns those dimensions of narrative that one might think of as "vertical," not horizontal or linear; total, rather than sequential. Narrative, then, whether in literature or in life, could be said to move through nodes of the epiphanic; it moves toward and then away from moments of recognition, insight, and the sudden apprehension of meaning.

There is often an epiphanic element in the way physicians perceive and resolve ethical issues, even though they may not recognize or acknowledge this element in their decisions and even though they are not likely to give it such a literary name. The epiphanic dimension may range from a specific intuition to deeper and more general insight; from the instinctive hunch to the sudden and total apprehension of meaning. As physicians sometimes say, "The penny drops." There seems to be no one word for this way of knowing: "intuition" serves for some; but for others, intuition suggests something irrational, even mystical. And this kind of knowledge is not irrational *per se;* rather, it is simply not arrived at through a sequential process of deductive thinking.

Many physicians would acknowledge the role that this "epiphanic" way of knowing plays in the art of diagnosis and in relating to and communicating with patients. The skilled physician is attentive not just to what a patient says, but also to tone of voice, body language, facial expression, and so forth. Such physicians know that the offhand phrase or the elliptical comment can yield knowledge as significant as the formal story, the explicit narrative account, that the patient constructs for the clinical interview. What is thus revealed is often more than just a medical condition: suffering patients grant physicians access not only to their bodies but to their minds and souls. The physician Michael Radetsky describes these "sudden intimacies with total strangers—those moments when the human barrier cracks open to reveal what is most secret and inarticulate" (Radetsky 1988, p. 29). Rita Charon observes that "even when the problem at hand is trivial . . . the hesitant glance, the inarticulate sigh, or, as William Carlos Williams says, 'the hunted news I get from some obscure patient's eyes' carry with them profound challenge about the meaning of lives and the meaning of deaths" (Charon 1986, p.12). Such epiphanic recognition of meaning in the commonplace and the ordinary—even if that meaning cannot be articulated—is an important dimension of the physician's narrative competence. Again, there is no single word or phrase for this kind of knowledge about patients. It is similar to what physicians call "pattern recognition" in diagnosis. It also reflects what Michael and Enid Balint, in their seminars with general practitioners years ago at the University College Hospital in London, called "the flash" or "the flash technique"—"an intensity of observation, of identification, and of communication" between patient and physician. The epiphanic realization does not necessarily occur *between* doctor and patient; it can also occur in the flash of understanding that will come to the physician about a given patient.

The intuitive skills that are so obvious in diagnosis and in patient interaction also play a part in ethics and in ethical decision-making. Bioethics is sometimes criticized for too narrow a focus on certain kinds of ethical problems—namely, problems that are able to yield to a solution of some kind and problems that occur in tertiary care hospitals. There is general consensus among physicians (if not among bioethicists) that ethical issues are much more comprehensive than this. Indeed, physicians often do not draw the fine distinctions favored by philosophers between what should and should not be called "ethics." As both Rita Charon and Leon Kass declare, there are ethical issues involved in every encounter between a doctor and a patient (Charon 1994, p. 264; Kass 1990, p. 7). Recognition of such ethical problems is itself an important step in the process of ethical consideration. Physicians who are aware of the epiphanic dimension of their work—the profound but often latent meanings in ordinary interactions with patients—will be better able to recognize ethical issues embedded in a patient's narrative.

Epiphanies in Literature

Though the term "epiphany" (as applied to a literary technique in fiction) has now passed into common usage, it was James Joyce who first articulated the concept. For Joyce, the epiphany is not the manifestation of the divine, as in the biblical epiphany where the Christ child is revealed to the Magi; rather, it is an apprehension of the ordinary, the prosaic, or even the vulgar as deeply meaningful. Such things have a "radiance," Joyce would say. A part of the artist's mission (which for Joyce was akin to the priesthood) was to bring forth epiphanies, looking for them not in lofty themes and subjects but in casual, commonplace, even trivial events. In 1900, quite early in his career as a writer, Joyce began to write a series of prose poems that he called "epiphanies." These were brief sketches of ordinary life, often of conversations overheard. An epiphany would capture the single word that tells a whole story or the simple gesture that reveals a complex set of relationships. For a time Joyce thought of compiling his epiphanies into a book (in *Ulysses* he mentions his youthful resolve to leave copies of his epiphanies to all the libraries in the world). Later they became a part of *Stephen Hero*—the autobiographical narrative that subsequently became *A*

Portrait of the Artist as a Young Man. The best statement of what is meant by epiphany comes from this early book, *Stephen Hero.* While walking down a Dublin street, Stephen Daedalus remarks of what he sees: ". . . we recognize that it is that thing which it is. Its soul, its whatness, leaps to us from the vestment of its appearance. The soul of the commonest object, the structure of which is so adjusted, seems to us radiant. The object achieves its epiphany" (Joyce 1963, p. 213). Epiphanic knowledge for Joyce is rooted in the particular, in the givenness of the real. An epiphany is not a symbol of something else, it is an apprehension of the "whatness" of the thing—its unique character.

Though Joyce is responsible for calling attention to this dimension of narrative and for the use of "epiphany" as a literary term, the phenomenon he describes seems almost universal in Western literature. Epiphanies are widespread in narratives of very different kinds from widely separated cultures and periods; they can be found in ancient Greek epic and tragedy as well as in much modern fiction both before and after Joyce.[2] Moreover, there are many types of epiphany in narrative—indeed, it seems most accurate and most useful to conceive of literary epiphany not as any single model or prototype but as a spectrum of possible forms. This spectrum ranges from recognition to revelation, from realizations that are human discoveries of self or other to those occasions when life seems to reveal itself in some numinous moment.

In ancient literature of the West, the epiphanic dimension of narrative manifests itself primarily through the divinities of the Greek or Roman pantheon. Throughout Homer's *Iliad,* for example, gods appear to mortals as an epiphanic representation of the meaning and consequences of their action. In the very first book, when Achilles is angered enough by Agamemnon to draw his sword and run him through, Athena suddenly intervenes to stop him, pulling his hair so that he turns around "and straightway / knew Pallas Athene and the terrible eyes shining" (Homer, I. 199*ff*). Athena's appearance marks the hero's sudden awareness of the nature and consequences of his intended action, and with this insight he changes his mind, thrusting his sword back in its scabbard. Most often epiphanies in the *Iliad* occur on the battlefield, as particular gods appear in person during a hero's *aristeia* to help him accomplish feats that seem impossible, to save him from injury or death, or even to destroy him. Human action is thus represented as open to influence from another level of being: as inspired and impelled or checked and defeated by agencies that transcend the human.

In Virgil's *Aeneid,* likewise, the gods intrude on human action as epiphanic realizations of meaning and purpose. When Troy is burning and Aeneas is still fighting furiously, Venus appears to him and announces: "Look now—for I / shall tear away each cloud that cloaks your eyes / and clogs your human seeing" (Virgil, II. 817–819). Aeneas now sees Neptune, huge, towering over the city and tearing apart its walls; he sees fierce Juno at the gates of Troy; and he sees Tritonian Pallas with her storm cloud standing tall on the loftiest tower. It is a powerful and overwhelming epiphanic realization that the city is doomed to fall. And with this realization, Aeneas stops fighting and flees.

In these examples from Greek and Roman epic two themes are represented simultaneously: divine revelation—the appearance of a god or goddess—and the human discovery of self or other. In the case of Achilles, the epiphany of Athena is a divine mandate that he realizes he must obey, but also a recognition of the imprudence in allowing anger to dictate his action. In the case of Aeneas, Aphrodite appears in an epiphany to prevent him from murdering Helen in his rage and to show him that it is the gods who are destroying the city. It is also a recognition that, instead of giving vent to his rage, his "fanatic anger," he should realize that the city is fated and that he should now save himself and his family.

With Greek tragedy, the two dimensions of epiphany, revelation and recognition, appear separately in the moments of *anagnorisis,* the recognition or understanding that a character achieves, and the formal epiphany of the god that sometimes occurs at the end of the play. In *Philoctetes*, for example, the two protagonists Philoctetes and Neoptolemus proceed through a series of human recognitions to the divine revelation of Herakles (a god in this play) that is needed to complete and correct them. In *The Bacchae*, likewise, there are epiphanies of human recognition throughout that are consummated in the divine epiphany of Dionysus at the very end of the play. Queen Agave's epiphany is perhaps one of the finest (and the cruelest) in all Greek tragedy. It occurs near the end of the play, as the mad Agave realizes that the bloody head impaled on the thyrsus she carries is not that of a lion but that of her son, Pentheus, whom she has dismembered in dionysian frenzy. Cadmus first tells her to raise her eyes to the heavens, whereupon she finds that things look different—clearer—than before. He asks her about her husband, then about her son, and with this, she suddenly becomes aware of "the greatest grief there is" (Euripides, I. 1282). But Agave's terrible discovery, as well as her madness, are elements in Dionysus' plot of revenge, and the god himself appears in the final epiphany to drive this lesson home.

Of course, not all Greek tragedies are characterized by the formal epiphany of a god at the end of the play. But even in these other plays, the divine dimension to human motive and human action is in some way represented. The plot of *Oedipus Tyrannus*, for example, turns on a powerful moment of self-recognition when Oedipus realizes that he is himself the slayer of his father, Laius, the murderer he has been seeking so that he can punish him and purify the city. But Oedipus' life-story throughout is shaped by oracular utterances: he fled Corinth and came to Thebes in order to avoid fulfilling the oracle that he would kill his father, and he is driven to avenge Laius' murder first by a divinely inflicted plague and then by another oracle mandating that the killer of Laius be detected and punished. And the same terrible conclusion that the riddle-solving Oedipus reaches by human means has already been voiced by the prophet, Tiresias.

The literary history of the epiphany from ancient literature to modern fiction is a movement from the sacred to the secular. It is true that Tolstoy and Dostoyevsky, in their consciously realist fiction, include epiphanies that are religious and visionary: "The Death of Ivan Ilyich" ends with a deeply religious epiphany of light and transcendent joy through which Ivan's fear of death is overcome; in *The Brothers Karamazov*, Alyosha has an epiphany of the marriage at Cana that overflows into an affirmation of life itself. But increasingly, moments of insight in the modern novel and short story are entirely secular or wholly separated from any credal system. Symbolically and historically, Joyce is the turning point: it is fitting that he should use the religious term, "epiphany," to describe moments of insight that have little or nothing to do with religion.

Examples of epiphanies in the modern novel include works as varied as Proust's *A la Recherche du temps perdu*, which is studded with epiphanic realizations that the past is embodied in the present, Conrad's *Heart of Darkness*, with Kurtz's terrible epiphany of horror, the novels and stories of Henry James, and the works of Chekhov or Kafka (one thinks of "In The Penal Colony," with its instrument that tortures and teaches at the same time). Morris Beja, in his book on epiphany in the modern novel, would add to these authors Flaubert, Virginia Woolf, Thomas Wolfe, Faulkner, Durrell, Barth, Hemingway, Katherine Mansfield, and Sherwood Anderson. And today, most readers of contemporary fiction or of current book reviews are aware that "epiphany" has become part of the accepted critical parlance of authors and reviewers.

It may be helpful at this point to examine in some detail several examples of epiphany in modern fiction. It seems fitting to begin with Joyce, whose stories in *Dubliners* are organized around epiphanies and who ends *Ulysses* with an overtly sexual epiphany that is Molly Bloom's (and Joyce's) great affirmation of life. Joyce's epiphanies are invariably sudden moments of profound understanding of a situation, another person, or one's self. In "The Dead," the culminating story of *Dubliners* (and, some would argue, his finest short story), there are three very different epiphanies. The first—let us call this a positive epiphany—occurs when Gabriel gazes up at his wife, who is standing in the shadows near the stairtop and listening to a plaintive Irish song. "There was grace and mystery in her attitude," remarks Gabriel, "as if she were a symbol of something" (Joyce 1969, p. 210). The second epiphany in the story—it is a negative epiphany—occurs when Gabriel, after the party is over and he has retired to a hotel room with his wife, looks at himself in a full-length mirror and sees a

"pitiable fatuous fellow . . . a ludicrous figure . . . a nervous well-meaning senti-
mentalist, orating to vulgarians and idealising his own clownish lusts"(p. 220).
It is a moment of bitter self-recognition. But there is a final epiphany in "The
Dead" that concludes not only this story but also the whole book. Let us call this
the transcendent epiphany. Gabriel is at first hurt and irritated to find that his
wife, Gretta, who he thinks shares his own amorous feelings, is actually
absorbed in the romantic memory of a youthful sweetheart. But these feelings
become submerged in an epiphanic experience of profound and generous
empathy for his wife as, nearly asleep himself, he watches the snow falling
outside and imagines it covering all Ireland, even the grave where his wife's
young suitor lies buried. As befits Joyce's conscious appropriation of a term
from religion as a literary device, this last epiphany is a fully secular one, but it
is permeated with latent religious overtones. Michael Furey is a Christ-like
figure who "braved death" and "died for her sake" (p. 222). And the story ends
with a frankly apocalyptic image of the snow falling on the living and the dead
alike "like the descent of their last end" (pp. 223–224). There is nothing quite like
this final epiphany in all of *Dubliners*. It combines aspects of the earlier positive
and negative epiphanies—the radiant vision of Gabriel's wife on the steps and
the savage self-judgment of the "pitiable fatuous fellow" glimpsed in the
mirror—but it also transcends them in an epiphanic realization that is as
profound as it is inarticulable.

Henry James in his fiction subtilizes the epiphany and seems to remove it
even further from a religious context. "The Beast in the Jungle" is structured
around an epiphanic moment of terrible self-recognition when John Marcher,
standing beside the grave of the woman who had loved him, realizes "the beast"
that threatened him in his own failure to have really lived. "Everything fell
together, confessed, explained, overwhelmed" (James 1982, p. 218). The escape
from the beast, he now realizes, "would have been to love her; then, *then* he
would have lived" (p. 219). But more often, epiphanic elements in James's stories
and novels are present as a dimension of experience rather than as a discrete
event. James is superb at allusive language that always points beyond itself
toward some inexpressible, inarticulable otherness. Readers of the novels sometimes misperceive James, with his careful description of the upper-middle-class
manners and conventions of late-nineteenth-century America (and England), as
concerned with the superficialities of a society now defunct. But experienced
readers almost always realize at some point (if they did not know from the
beginning) that, far from being concerned only with manners and conventions,
James uses these superficial things to point toward the deep, inarticulable, often
dark realities that are at the heart of human motivation and action. In *The Wings
of the Dove*, the social niceties that make up a dinner party mask the predatory

needs and destructive urges of host and guests alike. Goodness is likewise mysterious and inscrutable: Milly is a sacrificial victim: she is a "dove." We never learn
the extent to which she realizes that she is being used by others, and what she
makes of this. Milly's interview with the famous physician Sir Luke, when she
learns that she is going to die, illustrates James's particular way of representing
the epiphanic dimensions of experience. The episode is radiant with meaning,
but the reader doesn't even know what Milly's illness is. Nor, at the end of the
book, are we allowed to witness her death. James's art here is to deny us the
factual presentation and, instead, point toward deeper things: we apprehend the
meaning of an event or an interchange through its radiant allusiveness rather
than through any factual description.

In *The Golden Bowl* James gives the reader an image for this in referring to
Poe's story of the shipwrecked Gordon Pym, who, drifting in a small boat,
suddenly comes up against "a thickness of white air that was like a dazzling
curtain of light, concealing as darkness conceals" (James 1985, p. 56). James uses
this image to point to the state of mind of the characters in his story, which
"had resemblances to a great white curtain" (p. 56). Images of veils, curtains,
white mists permeate the novel: they point toward those mysterious elements
in the psyche of the individual that are always concealed and yet always dimly
intuited. The veil or curtain seems an apt metaphor for what best characterizes
James's sometimes maddeningly oblique prose style, which points toward the
inexpressible mystery that is the heart of his narrative and the center of its
meaning.

A final example, one much closer to the world of medicine, is Chekhov's
"Ward Number Six." Andrey Yetimovich Ragin is a physician in a small provincial Russian village. He is responsible for the care of patients with mental problems who are confined to a psychiatric ward that is backward, corrupt, and even
brutal. Midway through the story, Andrey Yetimovich indulges in the unheard-
of practice of visiting with a patient on the ward, talking with him because he
finds him "intelligent and interesting," even sitting side by side with him on the
bed. He feels that he understands Ivan Dmitrich Gromov's experience—that it is
the human condition to feel imprisoned; that solace can be found only within
the self, through "free and profound thought"; and that no one, not even the
denizens of Ward Number Six, are worse off than anyone else. Eventually Andrey
Yetimovich's colleagues conclude that his actions are a sign that he is deranged,
and he becomes incarcerated in the same mental ward that he used to visit as a
doctor. He has to exchange his clothing for regulation hospital garb. He is
assigned a bed. He tries to leave, but his way is barred by the guard, Nikita. When
he protests, he is badly beaten. Lying on his bed in pain, he has a sudden
epiphanic understanding of what it is *really* like to be a patient on Ward Number

Six: ". . . all of a sudden out of the chaos there clearly flashed through his mind the dreadful, unbearable thought that these people, who now looked like black shadows in the moonlight, must have experienced this same pain day in and day out for years. How could it have happened that in the course of more than twenty years he had not known, had refused to know this?" (Chekhov 1965, p. 58). Chekhov's doctor is able to understand his patients' experience only when he himself is incarcerated in Ward Six.

The Epiphanic Dimension of "Ethical Medicine"

It seems certain that there are dimensions of medical practice and medical ethics that might also be called "epiphanic." Of course in the twentieth century, no god will emerge *ex machina* to reveal ultimate meaning and resolve a dilemma; rather, we are left to our fallibly human resources to make the best decisions we can and then live with them. There are today, as there have always been, doctors whose insights and values are shaped by their religious faith; and there are also doctors who would distrust and dismiss any claims of the mystical or the transcendent. Yet both groups, I would argue, can and do have the kind of experiences that I call epiphanic, and such experiences can have a powerful impact on the way they practice medicine.

One kind of experience that seems often to be epiphanic for physicians is a serious illness of one's own. The terrible epiphany of Chekhov's doctor, who finally understands his patients' experience when he is himself incarcerated on Ward Number Six, has a counterpart (usually with a happier dénouement) in the experiences of physicians who themselves become ill. Physicians who write pathographies often experience their own illness as a dramatic and transforming event—an epiphany of sorts. They maintain that they never before really understood what it is like to be sick and they often claim that the personal experience will make a profound difference to the way they practice medicine in the future. Oliver Sacks observes about his own illness experience: "Being a patient taught me, changed me, as nothing else could. Now I *knew*, for I had experienced [this] myself. And now I could truly begin to understand my patients. . . . I came to realize, as did my patients, that there is an absolute and categorical difference between a doctor who *knows* and one who does not" (Sacks 1984, pp. 202–203). For Sacks, the whole experience of illness is like an epiphany.

Epiphanic knowing in medicine may be most recognizable in the act (or process) of diagnosis. Most physicians will recognize the similarity between the epiphanic dimensions of ethical decision-making in medicine and what is called "pattern recognition" in the art of diagnosis. As one neonatologist observed about this in conversation, "patterns come into focus and then you just know what's going on. And you base your decision on that knowledge." It is worth observing here that physicians often do not make the same distinctions that ethicists maintain between "ethics" and a variety of aspects of medical practice, from diagnosing a condition to exercising clinical judgment. When physicians are asked about ethical issues or ethical decisions they confront in practicing medicine, they will frequently respond in such a way that medical issues, clinical judgment, and ethical considerations are inextricably combined (Charon et al., 1996).

In an attempt to better understand the nature and role of epiphanic thinking in medical ethical judgment, I have begun interviewing senior medical students and physicians. In talking with medical students, epiphanic experiences readily emerge: their first dying patient, the event that determined their choice of specialty, some observed procedure or patient interaction that they are determined either to emulate or to avoid. Senior physicians may find such experiences harder to isolate, for particular events such as these have been absorbed into the shape and texture of their whole way of being, both professional and personal. But these experiences and the insights they evoke help shape the moral sensibility that a physician brings to ethical decisions.

The following examples were provided by a fourth-year medical student and a third-year resident. Each was asked to think of a case that would illustrate the role that "epiphanic knowledge" might play in medical ethical decisions about a particular patient. Epiphanic knowledge was described as a sudden apprehension of meaning or of "what to do"; as a kind of knowledge not arrived at through discursive reasoning; as the kind of experience referred to by the phrase "the penny dropped." I took extensive notes on the cases as they were described by each interlocutor. I have decided to present the resultant narratives in the third person in acknowledgment of my role in eliciting the cases in the first place, in writing down what I heard (necessarily an interpretive role), and in editing my notes for the purposes of this essay. I returned the edited cases to the original authors, asking for verification not only of facts but also of overall meaning and interpretation. The versions presented here have been checked and approved by both authors. All information that might identify patients has been changed for purposes of confidentiality.

My first example is a case reported to me by Larry Beecher, a fourth-year medical student on his Medicine clerkship. Beecher was responsible for several weeks for the care of Mrs. A., a 56-year-old woman who had been admitted to the Intermediate Care Unit with severe hypoxia. Before coming to Memorial Hospital, Mrs. A. had spent a month at a local hospital where she was treated, wrongly, as it turned out, first for pneumonia and then for bronchitis and chronic obstructive pulmonary disease. When a mediastinal mass the size of a grapefruit was discovered to be constricting her airway, she was referred to Memorial. Beecher reports that when he first saw her she looked haggard and worn, much older than her 56 years; she was dressed oddly and she carried a teddy bear. "It was hard to take a history," he remarked, and the reasons for this became clear when Mrs. A.'s chart (which arrived several hours later) verified mild retardation. Beecher continued: "There are few things as terrifying and painful as severe hypoxia." "From the very beginning," he observed, Mrs. A. was hypoxic from acute respiratory distress, and her condition seemed to worsen each day.

Radiation treatment seemed the best course of action for Mrs. A., since it could shrink her tumor in a relatively short time and thus ease her difficulty breathing. But proper irradiation required knowledge of the specific kind of tumor, and this knowledge could be obtained only by means of a surgical or transbronchial biopsy. Given her present difficulty breathing, both were high-risk procedures. The pulmonologist decided to forego the biopsy, reasoning that the risk factor was too high, and thus referred her to the radiation oncologist to treat the undiagnosed cancer as best he could. Though the radiation oncologist was understandably uncomfortable with this, he agreed to give it a try. But another problem emerged: Mrs. A. was unable to lie still enough for the procedure. And again, sedation was not possible because it would interfere too much with her breathing.

Mrs. A.'s difficulty breathing kept getting worse. She was unable to sleep at night and would lie awake moaning, "Help me, help me." This situation continued for some ten days. The nurses could do nothing to alleviate her pain, and the medical staff were unwilling to undertake responsibility for causing her death if their attempts at intervention went awry. Mrs. A. was not able to demonstrate any capacity for making a competent decision, and her already borderline mental functioning was being further hampered by chronic hypoxia. Attempts had been made to contact her family. A brother living in Tucson vaguely advised "trying something," but admitted that he really didn't know what she might be feeling; on the other hand the brother's wife, who had recently spent time in an ICU caring for her father-in-law, felt that the best course of action was "to just make her comfortable." Decisions about how to treat Mrs. A. were left to the staff.

Beecher was on his way home one Sunday night after being on call for 24 hours. Mrs. A., he reported, seemed to be suffering a good deal. His epiphany occurred as he heard the engines of the hospital's helicopter: he turned to watch it lift off and veer away into the clouds. He reports thinking, "Wouldn't it be great to be the EMT guy or the helicopter pilot where you know what you can do and you have a protocol that you follow. They're dealing with life-and-death situations; there's no time to think and think day after day about what to do, you just have to do something." And then he realized, "How different, really is Mrs. A.'s situation? It's also about life and death. She's clearly going to die if we don't do something. So the question is, why are we making her suffer? Why don't we do something? She's just lying here getting worse and there seems to be nothing we can do." He reported that with this epiphany came the unwelcome recognition that he and the staff had permitted Mrs. A. to suffer because no one was willing to be responsible for the chance that the diagnostic interventions necessary for treatment might cause her death. He remarks about this:

> I realize that patient autonomy is important, but when a patient can't make decisions about treatment and when there is no family member to do this in their stead, then it's in your hands, and you need to go ahead and make a decision. You've got to take on this responsibility. Risk the sedation for the radiation; just do the trach or the bronchoscopy despite the risk. Or else face the fact that this woman cannot be helped and just make her comfortable. This is especially important when there's a great deal of suffering involved.

He concludes, "I think this came to me suddenly, in this way, because it was something that I really didn't want to know. This would mean that we had done the wrong thing, that we had allowed her to suffer for nothing."

My second example was given me by a third-year resident, Carla Weinberg. Carla described a patient whom she cared for last year. Mr. V., a 65-year-old man with end-stage liver disease, had been hospitalized on her unit in a small community hospital for some three weeks. She reports that two weeks ago he was put on a feeding tube and that one week ago he began receiving a morphine drip to control possible pain. Mr. V.'s status was "no-code," but the staff continued to check his electrolytes, adjust his IV, and so forth. His family, who lived nearby, had been very attentive, especially an older brother, who seemed to have taken on the role of spokesperson for the family (it was he who held power of attorney).

One particular night, Weinberg reports, something seemed to be different, even though there was no change of any kind in Mr. V.'s health status. Mr. V.'s brother was visiting him (as he did regularly) and at one point, as the nurses adjusted his IV, the brother said to Weinberg, "Is it going to make a difference?" She responded to his question, though she was not certain as to what he meant. He repeated his question, "But is it going to make a difference?" Weinberg reports: "He said that one phrase, and the light came on. I realized all at once that the family, who at first had been so sure that Mr. V. would come out of this, had over the past weeks finally come to terms with the fact that he wasn't going to get better, that he was going to die. It was really like a light had come on. I went out and called my Attending and explained the situation and he said to me, 'Carla, do what seems best; do the right thing.'"

Weinberg reports that she returned to where Mr. V.'s brother was waiting for her and told him that the tubes could be removed and that Mr. V. would probably die within 24 hours, adding that he would not feel any pain. But Mr. V's brother shook his head and said, "I don't like being responsible for this; I don't want him to starve to death or die of thirst." Weinberg describes her response to this: "Somehow, I knew just what to do." She told the brother that it wasn't necessary to deprive Mr. V. of food and water, but that the staff could "do less," that they could "make some adjustments and keep him comfortable." Fluids were continued, but at a lower level. Predictably, Mr. V.'s blood pressure dropped not long afterwards, and within two hours he started Cheyne-Stokes breathing. Weinberg had anticipated this, and was there ready to tell Mr. V.'s brother that the end seemed near and that he might want to call other family members. Many of them did come to the hospital, where they "said their goodbyes" to Mr. V. He died an hour or so later.

Weinberg reports, "I feel right about what I did. The family even seemed grateful when they said goodbye to me. I believe that when you are in a situation where you need to act in the patient's best interest, you have to ask, 'what would be right for him?' Or in terms of the family, 'where are they coming from?' And when you can answer these questions, then you can really serve your patient, whether he's going to get better or not."

These two examples exhibit certain parallels: for example, both concern the issue of ending life. In one instance, the narrator reaches what seems a right decision, while in the other the narrator recognizes a mistake. Neither moment of insight involves some profound new ethic or controversial medical procedure: both are close to the ethics of "ordinary practice" in a hospital setting. They relate to choices or decisions that the hospital-based physician must repeatedly confront, though this certainly does not mean that such decisions are easy, simple, or insignificant. In both examples, realization comes to the narrator suddenly, not as the result of a logical or analytic process. Both involve images. While Beecher's conscious focus is on the helicopter pilot, the image of the aircraft taking flight surely resonates, if only unconsciously, with the need to release Mrs. A. from her pain. Weinberg's illumination is less direct: her comment that "it was like a light had come on" reflects the sudden understanding of another individual's state of mind. The brother's reluctance to take responsibility suggests that he has himself not reached any conscious decision, but Weinberg intuits a change in feeling and attitude that enables her to help Mr. V.'s brother do so. Both his decision and her gentle intervention are the "right thing." Much is unspoken here: the Attending does not tell Weinberg what is best; the brother does not tell her of his change in attitude. But intuition comes to her like a light turning on. The image is surely retrospective, but it captures the sense of abrupt clarification and enlightenment, resonating with the meaning of epiphany (in one root etymological sense) as a "shining forth."

Let me emphasize again that I am not in any way advocating a process of decision-making that ignores the need for careful, deductive reasoning. My concern here is to suggest that epiphanic thinking is an important and heretofore largely neglected dimension of the way we make decisions—in medical ethics as in everything else—and to urge that advocates of "narrative ethics," given the widespread presence of epiphanies in narrative of all kinds, include recognition of the epiphanic in describing and analyzing ethical decision-making in medicine. I have added cases, or examples, to my discussion in order to broaden the reader's understanding of these things. I would invite others to gather and analyze formal cases in which epiphanies seem to play a role in medical decision-making.

Imaginative Insight, Intuitive Understanding

Narrative ethics often emphasizes the importance of attending to the patient's "life-story." But we should remember that every ethical decision marks the intersection of two stories, the patient's and the physician's, and epiphanic moments of imaginative insight or intuitive understanding occur in both. These are the lyric moments in the prose of our ordinary everyday experience. Their occurrence in stories and novels is often marked by a heightening of style; in real life there is a similar heightening of awareness and intensity of feeling. Of course, the insights that come to us in this way need to be checked against other ways of thinking and knowing. It is possible to be misled by a mood, an instinctive bias, or an ideological conviction—even by stress and fatigue. No one would argue that important decisions in medicine should be made simply by relying on hunches and intuitions. Epiphanic knowledge must be integrated with other modes of ethical consideration. But the way in which this kind of awareness plays a role in ethical decisions has not received the attention it deserves. Whether the epiphany is a moment of inspiration, or a sudden new perspective on a person or a situation, or a new sense of direction and purpose, or the terrible admission of error, failure, and guilt, these are experiences that influence our decisions, shape our lives, and deepen our interactions with others. They are crucial elements in the narrative of our life experience. The ethic that ignores them is not only impoverished, but also unreal.

Notes

1. This essay extends and develops an earlier article published in *The Journal of Clinical Ethics* in which I focused on lyric poetry, instancing the poetic epiphany as relevant to medical ethics and its epistemology.

2. I have deliberately restricted my discussion to texts that are—at least for the modern reader—

secular (even though they may include religious themes). Of course epiphanies recur throughout both the Old and New Testaments: the divine manifestations to Moses and Job, or the transfiguration of Christ and the conversion of Paul are examples that spring at once to mind. But the narrative in which these epiphanies occur is a religious text that is sacred to many readers, whereas the approach of this essay is strictly literary. A full consideration of epiphany would necessarily include religious as well as literary perspectives (to say nothing of psychological, sociocultural, and historical approaches), and would extend to other religions besides Judaism and Christianity.

References

Balint, Enid, and Norell, J. S., eds. (1973) *Six Minutes for the Patient: Interactions in General Practice Consultation*. London: Tavistock Publications.

Beja, Morris. (1971) *Epiphany in the Modern Novel*. Seattle: Univ. of Washington Press.

Brody, Howard. (1987) *Stories of Sickness*. New Haven: Yale University Press.

Burrell, David, and Stanley Hauerwas. (1977) "From System to Story: An Alternative Pattern for Rationality in Ethics," in *The Foundations of Ethics and Its Relationship to Science: Knowledge, Value, and Belief*, vol. 2, ed. H. T. Engelhardt, Jr., and D. Callahan. Hastings-on-Hudson, NY: Hastings Center, 111–152.

Chambers, Tod S. (1994) "The Bioethicist as Author: The Medical Ethics Case as Rhetorical Device." *Literature and Medicine* 13, no. 1: 60–78.

Chambers, Tod S. (1996) "From the Ethicists' Point of View: The Literary Nature of Ethical Inquiry." *Hastings Center Report* 21, no. 1:25–32.

Chambers, Tod S. (1996) "Dax Redacted: The Economies of Truth in Bioethics." *Journal of Medicine and Philosophy* 21, no. 3:287–302.

Charon, Rita. (1986) "To Listen, To Recognize." *The Pharos* 49, no. 4:10–13.

Charon, Rita. (1993) "Medical Interpretation: Implications of Literary Theory of Narrative for Clinical Work." *Journal of Narrative and Life History* 3, no. 1:79–97

Charon, Rita. (1994) "Narrative Contributions to Medical Ethics: Recognition, Formulation, Interpretation, and Validation in the Practice of the Ethicist," in *A Matter of Principles? Ferment in U. S. Bioethics*, ed. Edwin R. Dubose, Ron P. Hamel, and Laurence J. O'Connell. Valley Forge, PA: Trinity Press, 260–283.

Charon, Rita, et al. (1996) "Literature and Ethical Medicine: Five Cases from Common Practice." *Journal of Medicine and Philosophy* 21, no. 3:243–265.

Chekhov, Anton. (1965) "Ward Number Six," in *Ward Number Six and Other Stories*, trans. Ann Dunnigan. New York: New American Library.

Coles, Robert. (1979) "Medical Ethics and Living a Life." *New England Journal of Medicine* 301 (23 August:444–446.

Euripides. (1960) "The Bacchae," trans. William Arrowsmith, in *Greek Tragedies*, vol. 3. Chicago: Univ. of Chicago Press.

Hawkins, Anne Hunsaker. (1994) "Literature, Medical Ethics, and 'Epiphanic Knowledge'." *The Journal of Clinical Ethics* 5, no. 4:283–290.

Homer. (1951) *Iliad*, trans. Richmond Lattimore. Chicago: Univ. of Chicago Press.

James, Henry, (1982) "The Beast in the Jungle," in *Henry James: Selected Tales*, eds. Tom Paulin and Peter Messent. London: J. M.Dent; Everyman's Library, pp. 177–219.

James, Henry. (1985) *The Golden Bowl*. New York: Penguin.

Jones, Anne Hudson. (1987) "Literary Value: The Lesson of Medical Ethics." *Neohelicon* 14, no. 2:383–392.

Jones, Anne Hudson. (1988) "Literature and Medicine: Illness from the Patient's Point of View," *Personal Choices and Public Commitments: Perspectives on the Medical Humanities*, ed. W. J. Winslade. Galveston: Institute for the Medical Humanities, pp. 1–15.

Joyce, James. (1963) *Stephen Hero*, ed. J. J. Slocum and H. Cahoon. New York: New Directions.

Joyce, James. (1969) "The Dead," in *Dubliners*, ed. Robert Scholes and A. Walton Litz. New York: Viking Penguin, pp. 175–224.

Kass, Leon R. (1990) "Practicing Ethics: Where's the Action?" *Hastings Center Report* 20, no. 1:5–12.

Miles, Stephen H., and Kathryn Montgomery Hunter. (1990) "Commentary." *Second Opinion* 15 (November):60–63.

Poirier, Suzanne, and Daniel J. Brauner. (1988) "Ethics and the Daily Language of Medical Discourse: Lessons from a Conference in Geriatrics." *Hastings Center Report* 18 (Aug/Sept):5–9.

Poirier, Suzanne, and Daniel J. Brauner. (1990) "The Voices of the Medical Record." *Theoretical Medicine* 11:29–39.

Radetsky, Michael. (1988) "Sudden Intimacies," in *A Piece of My Mind: A Collection of Essays from JAMA*, ed. Bruce B. Dan and Roxanne K. Young. Los Angeles: Feeling Fine.

Sacks, Oliver. (1984) *A Leg to Stand On*. New York: Simon & Schuster, pp. 202–203.

Virgil. (1971) *The Aeneid*, trans. Allen Mandelbaum. Toronto: Bantam.

11

What to Expect from an Ethics Case (and What It Expects from You)

Tod Chambers

In the appendix to the first edition of *Principles of Biomedical Ethics*, Tom Beauchamp and James Childress included not only various oaths and codes of medical ethics but also detailed accounts of the cases they referred to in their analyses. By the third edition of this work, the authors had greatly expanded the number of cases in the appendix yet altogether eliminated the section on oaths and codes. And in the fourth edition, though Beauchamp and Childress provided only ten cases in the appendix, they state in the preface that "more complete versions" of the cases have been incorporated into the text itself and that "although the appendix of cases is now smaller, more discussion of cases is provided throughout the text" (Beauchamp and Childress 1994, p. vii). The modifications in this classic bioethics textbook suggest a general decrease in concern with oaths and codes in medical ethics and a rise of interest in case stories. The ethics case story had become, even before the revival of casuistry and the appearance of narrative ethics, bioethics' key genre. In some ways this focal interest in cases marks the transition from what Edmund Pellegrino (1993) has recently termed "the Quiescent Period" of Hippocratic ethics to the "Period of Principlism" that Beauchamp and Childress's text exemplifies.

Prior to moral philosophy's invitation into hospitals and medical schools, biomedical ethics was predominantly the domain of the insiders (that is, physicians), and the genres of discourse during the Quiescent Period were largely the oaths and codes passed from one generation of health care professionals to the next. These were genres bound to rites of communal solidarity, that is, pledging an alliance to the medical profession, explicitly for oaths and implicitly for codes. Moral philosophers, though, who came into hospitals during the sixties and seventies to help clarify ethical issues took no oaths to perform this task.[1] With biomedical ethics' entrance into the Period of Principlism came the extinction of those oaths and codes as sources for moral guidance and the ascendancy of thinking about ethical dilemmas primarily through story.

In the present state of the art, bioethics, like medical discourse itself (see Hunter 1991), is entrenched in stories. Ethical case narratives with commentaries are regularly published in national journals, like the *Hastings Center Report*, *Making the Rounds*, and the *Journal of Clinical Ethics*, as well as many small biomedical ethics newsletters. And, as in many communities, medical ethicists speak to each other through shorthand references to a shared folklore; ethicists do not have to retell an entire story but can simply say "Dax," "Helga Wanglie," or "Debbie" (Brody 1988: 144), and one cannot sit through an extended discussion with medical ethicists without hearing cases "presented" to test some abstract argument.

Although ethics cases have been compared to medical cases (Hunter 1988), I contend that they represent a genre with distinct and distinctive narratological features. Much recent literary scholarship has demonstrated that literary texts are understandable to us because they refer to other texts. This intertextuality is not simply the various influences and allusions within a particular text but the condition of communication itself. Readers must understand one text to understand another text, just as you must understand each of the words in this sentence prior to reading them. Because readers have built up expectations about the text, genres are the essence of intertextuality. For readers to be told that a text is a "bioethics case" creates expectations about the narrative because readers have read other texts referred to as "bioethics cases." Each case thus exists within a web of other texts which place expectations in the reader. In this paper, I explore some of the expectations that readers bring to the bioethics case through four narratological features: reportability, action, tempo, and closure. I contend that these features are part of the defining characteristics of the bioethics case as a distinct genre and these characteristics bring with them expectations of what is relevant in moral discussions.

Reportability

One of the principal features that distinguishes a narrative from a nonnarrative is temporal disruption; in a narrative something "happens." Juri Lotman in *The Structure of the Artistic Text* argues that we can divide texts into "those with plot and those without plot" (Lotman 1977, pp. 236–239). For Lotman, texts that lack a plot bear a "classificatory character." One of such a text's properties is that it consists of a particular way of ordering the world, and "it does not permit its elements to move in such a way as to violate the established order" (p. 237). Paul Ricoeur remarks, concerning Lotman's text without plot, that it is "a purely classificatory system, a simple inventory—for example, a list of places, as on a map" (Ricoeur 1984, p. 167). A text *with* plot entails a disruption in a classificatory system: "The movement of the plot, the *event*, is the crossing of that forbidden border which the plotless structure establishes" (Lotman 1977, p. 238). In other words, an event occurs and thus becomes what narratologists refer to as "reportable" (see Prince 1987) when some form of transgression takes place.

Readers have different expectations of reportability with a particular genre, for each genre represents a crossing of different classificatory fields, and a reader, when given a particular genre, anticipates a distinct type of transgression. For instance, suppose you go to a bookstore and in the section marked "murder mysteries" find an interesting book that you buy and over the next week read. This novel entails family conflicts, some turning quite violent, but no one is killed. Although you found the story interesting, you are disappointed, but what is the reason for your disappointment? Because the story does not have the reportability of the murder mystery genre, it has not fulfilled your expectations. Suppose that in this novel the violence does result in the murder of the father by his brother, and this is witnessed by the entire family. In such an instance, you are still disappointed, because you read about a murder but there was no mystery. Reportability is therefore not self-evident, but must be placed within the context of the genre, that is, the reader's expectations of a particular form of transgression (*cf.* Lotman, 1977, p. 234).

Ethics cases and medical cases differ in terms of their reportability. An interesting example of the differences in reportability can be found in a case presented in a *New England Journal of Medicine* piece explaining the "Basic Curricular Goals in Medical Ethics." Culver and colleagues argue that "medical students should be able to identify the salient moral components of" the following "case":

> a competent patient with an obvious malady consults a physician who suggests a treatment that will almost certainly be effective. The physician informs the patient that the treatment has one minor risk; the patient asks a pertinent question about that risk and then decides to proceed. The treatment is carried out, and the patient recovers from the malady. (Culver et al. 1985, p. 34)

The case has reportability (and "salient moral components") but it is not the reportability of an ethics case. Instead it is the reportability of a medical case but, I imagine, for most clinicians a very dull one. This raises the question of what clinicians mean when they refer to a case as an "interesting" one. Similarly, ethicists have their own criteria of an "interesting" case, which is qualitatively different from the clinician's. A single case may be interesting for both clinician and ethicist, but this would be for different reasons. The problem with the Culver case is that it lacks a moral violation and thus—in the same manner as the murder mystery without a murder or a mystery—does not fulfill the reader's expectations of the genre. Essentially these authors wish students to see all medical practice as a moral enterprise, but one would suspect that they would have a hard time teaching an entire ethics course based simply on this kind of case. Or if such a course were taught, it would in turn be redefining the genre of the ethics case. The reportability of the medical case is the result of a transgression in a person's "previous state of health"; the reportability of the ethics case arises from a transgression in morality. Reader have these differing expectations of reportability when they come upon cases defined either as "medicine" or "ethics." The bioethics discipline has been called into the medical setting to respond to a particular form of transgression and has as its central goal responding to reportability.

Look at a case that fulfills the expectations of the genre of a "medical ethics case."

> A 35-year-old Puerto Rican male was found on the street unconscious and was brought to the emergency room at a large hospital. He was believed to be an alcoholic suffering from withdrawal symptoms. Tests revealed he had a severe case of pneumonia. He was febrile, and the pneumonia was becoming more severe.
>
> When he was approached for consent to treat the pneumonia, he had made it clear he wanted no treatment whatsoever. His only family was a sister who could not be reached. The house staff questioned his competency and called in a psychiatrist. The psychiatric interview found him competent and aware of the severity of his illness.
>
> No treatment was administered, and the patient experienced a rapid deterioration. When he became comatose, the house staff decided to treat him, but their efforts proved fruitless. The patient died within 30 hours after his admission to the hospital. (Abrams and Buckner 1983, p. 622)

The first paragraph of this narration by itself could be considered a medical case, but in order for this story to become reportable as an ethics case it requires the second paragraph. When the patient refuses to consent to the treatment the case shifts to an ethics case. If this case entailed a patient accepting the treatment or the house staff being certain that he was competent then this would not be a moral dilemma; nonetheless, there would still be moral features. The reader comes to an ethics case, however, with expectations not of the first paragraph, but of the second paragraph. The genre of the medical ethics case is, thus, a deviation from the medical case presentation. The first case of Culver and colleagues may possess salient moral features, but it is in this second case, which deviates from the genre of the first case, that the reader's expectations for an ethics case are fulfilled.

Action

Bioethics cases tend to be plot-driven narratives that focus on action rather than setting and character development.

Action within bioethics cases generally occurs in a neutral setting. Rarely is there a break in the narrative discourse to describe the environment in which a person's actions take place, and one can often imagine these cases occurring anywhere in which allopathic medicine is practiced. This is similar to what Mikhail Bakhtin has noted concerning classical romances, which can take place in almost any place of that period (1981, p. 100). Contrast this with how many contemporary novels such as *The Moviegoer* and *Midaq Alley* depend on a sense of place (Percy's New Orleans and Mahfouz's Cairo) for their narratives to cohere. Bioethics cases, in contrast, rarely give a sense of place. Occasionally a hospital setting is defined as rural or urban, but there is no sense in which the city of Chicago would differ from San Diego or east Texas from upstate New York. A description of place is not a part of the reader's expectations of a bioethics case. If there are passages of description in the bioethics case, they usually relate to the body, but once again these descriptions are tied to action in that they are most often a part of a clinical examination. Description in this genre is subordinated to the action.

Action also triumphs over characterization in the bioethics case. Tzvetan Todorov divides narratives into those that focus on character and those that focus on plot. Todorov described these as psychological versus apsychological narratives. Apsychological narratives are those in which "the actions are not there to 'illustrate' character but in which, on the contrary, the characters are subservient to the action; where, moreover, the word 'character' signifies something altogether different from psychological coherence or the description of idiosyncrasy" (Todorov 1977, p. 66). Like other apsychological genres, the bioethics case presents character traits only when they directly relate to the cause of actions. For instance, in a case included in Beauchamp and Childress's *Principles of Biomedical Ethics*, a man who has cancer is not told his full diagnosis.

After describing his treatment, the case states: "The patient, a hard-driving entrepreneur who dominated both his family and his business, was first told that there was a probability of 'malignant cell transformation' in his thyroid" (1989, p. 405). In the narrative, this characterization then results in the man going back to work "against medical advice—until he exhausted himself." Like many examples in this genre, this description becomes predictive of later action, and no characterizations are provided that do not immediately relate to the character's action.

Structuralists in literary criticism have generally been more interested in apsychological narratives and have regarded the concept of character purely in terms of action (see Rimmon-Kenan 1983; Martin 1986; Culler 1988). The forms of analysis structuralists have developed often have been tested upon folktales and adventure novels, which, like the bioethics case, are plot-driven and apsychological; consequently the insights of structuralists are particularly relevant to understanding the genre of the bioethics case. For many structuralists, narratives can be broken into a pattern of binary splits, and bioethics cases are particularly agreeable to such a form of structuralist analysis, for most ethicists incorporate into their plots a binary split between two confliciting principles. The structuralist A. J. Greimas (1983), for instance, proposed that the deep structure of all narratives consists of a series of "actants": sender, receiver, subject, object, helper, opponent. In a story a sender sends a subject to get an object for a receiver and the subject's efforts are either helped or opposed. A single agent can take the role of several actants, and actants need not be persons but can be inanimate objects as well. Greimas perceived these actants in terms of binary pairs: sender-receiver, subject-object, helper-opponent. Each of these pairings results in different forms of narrative; for example, an emphasis on subject-object is the focus of quest narratives. Bioethics cases emphasize the pairing helper-opponent.

Consider for example another case used in Beauchamp and Childress's *Principles of Biomedical Ethics*:

> After experiencing dry, persistent coughing for several weeks and night sweats for ten days, a bisexual male visits his family physician. When the patient describes his symptoms and admits that he is bisexual, the physician orders a test to determine if the patient has antibodies to the human immunodeficiency virus (HIV), the virus that causes AIDS. The test results are positive and indicate that the patient has been infected with the virus, will probably develop full-blown AIDS over time, will probably die from the disease, and is probably capable of infecting others through sexual contact. In a long counseling session, the physician explains all this to the patient and discusses the risk of unprotected sexual intercourse to his wife, as well as the possibility that their children, now one and three

years old, would be left without parents if his wife contracts the disease too. The patient refuses to allow the physician to disclose his condition to his wife. The physician finally and reluctantly accedes to this demand for absolute confidentiality. After surviving two episodes of opportunistic infection, the patient dies eighteen months later. Only during the last few weeks of his life does he allow his wife to be informed that he has AIDS. She is then tested and is found to be antibody positive, but she does not yet have any symptoms. However, a year later she goes to the doctor with dry cough, fever, and loss of appetite. She angrily accuses the physician of violating his moral responsibility to her and her children; she insists that she might have been able to take steps to reduce the risk to herself if she had only known the truth. (1989, pp. 403–404)

One can with little effort break this narrative into a series of actanial relationships:

sender-disease
subject-patient
object-keeping confidentiality
receiver-patient
helper-physician

One should take note that I have left out the position of the opponent, which some may wish to see as the wife. Yet the issue of the opponent is a key one in the bioethics case genre. When we used this case in an introductory ethics course for first-year medical students, we did not give them the complete narrative; instead we stopped at the point where they had to make a decision concerning the case. In such a situation, the reader's main decision is whether the physician should be a helper or an opponent. At this point of the narrative the bioethics case departs from the medical case, for once the body has been described and the subject and object defined, the question becomes how the physician will respond. The narrative as told with the wife as the subject would perceive the physician as an opponent to her object. Greimas has been known to continually "refine" his original set of actantial relationships. In some of his later models he added the anti-subject, which is after a different object. In this case, one could analyze the wife as an anti-subject (Greimas and Courtés 1982). Of course, the definition of an agent as a subject or an anti-subject relates in some manner to the point of view within the narrative (Scholes 1974: 105). One could propose that if the case were told from the wife's point of view she would be the subject and her husband would be the anti-subject. Still, the physician must decide whether to be helper or opponent for each of the subjects in these narratives.

This binary split of helper-opponent is central to most bioethics cases, and it reflects what H. Tristram Engelhardt refers to as the "conflict at the roots of bioethics" (1986, p. 66), the split between beneficence and respect for autonomy.

Tempo

Literary genres have been traditionally distinguished not only by their reportability and action but also by the way time is used. For example, a novel is distinguished from a short story not in terms of how language is used but in terms of reading time. One of the expectations of a bioethics case is that it will take a "short" period of time to read or hear, far shorter than a short story, perhaps the length of a parable. With attention to this feature of a narrative, one can, however, compare the relationship of the time narrated to the time of narration. As narratologists have pointed out, the concept of duration in reading narrative discourse is an inherently imprecise one, for how does one classify different rates of reading a text (cf. Genette 1980; Rimmon-Kenan 1983)? One can compare, however, the relation "between duration in the story (measured in minutes, hours, days, months, years) and the length of text devoted to it (in lines and pages), that is, a temporal/spatial relationship" (Rimmon-Kenan, p. 52). In the case presentation of the man found on the street unconscious, two days pass in the story but the entire narrative is told in 13 lines.[2] Case presentations can be longer, although when they are they break from the genre's conventions (e.g., Miles and Hunter 1990). But I wish to argue that the genre of the bioethics case can be defined not only in terms of the overall period of reading but in terms of a particular textual tempo. Through a study of the bioethics case's tempo, one reveals how the narratives focus primarily on events within the space of the clinical setting.

The tempo of a narrative is one of either acceleration or deceleration (Rimmon-Kenan 1983, pp. 52–53). This can be accomplished through ellipsis (where events are omitted), summary (where events are shortened through summarization), scene (where events are recorded in a manner that is close to the time of the story), stretch (where the description takes longer than the events of the story themselves), and pause (where no time has passed in the story) (cf. Genette 1980; Rimmon-Kenan 1983). I am not aware of an ethics case that employs stretch in its discourse, but the other four forms can be found throughout bioethics cases. The tempo of bioethics cases tends, however, to move between summary and ellipsis. Like the medical case history, there can be space devoted to descriptive pauses, primarily because it is the body that is being described. Some case presentations try through dialogue to create a sense of scene. John Lantos in "Leah's Case," a case concerning the medical treatment of a Jewish Orthodox 18-year-old, writes the case primarily in the form of dialogue that draws most heavily on scene. The ethics committee discusses whether the woman should be told of the need to remove a tumor, news which may result in her refusal to have it done.

> "Her life might not be worth living if she is sterile. That should be her decision to make. If she chooses to die rather than be infertile and live, her choice should be respected. But she can't make that choice unless she knows what we all now know. She must be told and must be allowed to decide."
>
> "How can an 18-year-old make a decision like that?"
>
> "According to the law, she can make it."
>
> "According to your law. Not according to her law."
>
> "She would not have to consent to treatment. Parental consent would be sufficient."
>
> "What if she was 17 instead of 18, and was here?"
>
> "Legally, her parents could decide." (1983, p. 83)

Although Lantos's case presentation consists predominant of scene it also has periods of ellipse and summary. And the points in the story at which the tempo enters into ellipse rather than summary and scene are a telling feature of bioethics case presentations. Look for example at the tempo of the confidentiality case presented above. The first 13 lines of the narrative discourse is a form of summary in which the physician discusses the issues of his diagnosis and informing his wife. Following this, there is an ellipsis of 18 months, then a summary of three lines: "Only during the last few weeks of his life does he allow his wife to be informed that he has AIDS. She is then tested and is found to be antibody positive, but she does not yet have any symptoms." An ellipse of a year follows. Finally, in three lines, there is a summary of her angry accusation of the physician. The narrative discourse lengthens with the patient's interaction with the physician. Like many narratives in this genre, there are often descriptive pauses and an increase of space devoted to the narration of medical events (although rarely equal to a medical case history).

Ellipses usually occur, as they do in this confidentiality case, between periods of entrance into the medical setting. This raises an important point about tempo in medical narratives, and that is how it is tied to story-space. As Bakhtin (1981) has pointed out, genres can be distinguished by their differing use of what he called "chronotopes," or the interrelationship of time and space in narrative discourse. In the genre of the bioethics case, the tempo of the discourse is often directly related to the patient's entrance into the space of the medical world. The farther the character goes from the medical world, the greater the chance for ellipses. Of course, the tempo of the discourse is always related to the reportability of events, for there can be extensive medical care condensed into a single sentence, but the tempo rarely includes periods when the characters outside the space of the medical world discuss problems and thus provide a greater degree of space in the discourse. In other words, in an almost Einsteinian manner, the tempo of the narrative expands as the patient enters into the sphere of the health care professional. The physical space of the text increases as the characters enter the space of the hospital or medical office and decreases when the events of the story take place outside this setting.

Closure

In the introduction to a collection of essays on ethics consultation, John C. Fletcher, Norman Quist, and Albert R. Jonsen give a group of case examples to "illustrate the nature and range of ethical problems which arise in the clinical setting." Here is the fourth case, entitled "Should Her Husband Know the Truth?":

> The child was born with cystic fibrosis, a hereditary disease which causes cysts and too much fibrous tissue in glandular organs like the pancreas and lungs. Excess mucous secretions cause a blocking of the lungs and pancreatic ducts. The disease is caused by one gene inherited from each parent, which means that both parents of a child with the disease are carriers of the cystic fibrosis gene. The mother confides in the genetic counselor who comes to see her that the biological father of the child is a man other than her husband. Yet her husband now falsely believes that he has a gene for cystic fibrosis. The counselor returns to her office and asks the physicians in the genetics program, "Should her husband know the truth?" (1989, p. 4)

Like the other narrative features presented already, this case possesses the reportability, characterization, and tempo of many bioethics cases. Like all the case examples used in Fletcher's, Quist's, and Jonsen's introduction, this case ends with a question. This ending is a feature of many bioethics case narrations, and it signifies the unique closure that bioethics narratives impose on their readers; a bioethics case is a genre that requires that the reader bring closure to the plot.

All literature requires closure in some form; I am employing the concept of closure in the way Barbara Herrnstein Smith defines it: "Whether spatially or temporally perceived, a structure appears 'closed' when it is experienced as integral: coherent, complete, and stable" (1968, p. 2). Bioethics cases ask *the reader* to bring closure to the narrative. The Culver et al. case presented at the beginning of this paper seems odd because it neither possess the reportability of bioethics cases nor the closure. Closure in the bioethics case occurs either through the lack of an ending (as in the genetics case above) or through requiring that the reader rewrite the narrative.

Gustav Freytag's diagram of tragedy has been often extended to indicate the essential structure of all narratives (Prince 1987, p. 36): stories begin with an exposition (A) followed by complication (B) and then a reversal (C), which ends with a resolution to the conflict (D).

The cases presented in the Fletcher, Quist, and Jonsen work can be diagrammed in the following manner:

The narrative ends essentially with the climax and asks the reader in some manner to write the ending, that is, to finish the narrative. The second type of bioethics case gives the narrative with an ending, but an ending is not necessarily closure. A narrative with an ending may still require the reader to bring closure to the narrative; in the bioethics case this may be done by requiring the reader to write it with a different ending. When the *Journal of the American Medical Association* published the case, "It's Over, Debbie," there was an extreme response by individuals who were outraged by the actions portrayed. The case told of a resident who "killed" a terminally ill woman (1988). Many of those who have responded to this case have described how the resident *should* have acted. Ethics is frequently defined as the relationship between what "is" and what "ought" to be. This is essentially a question of narrative ending; a desire to take an account of things and rewrite it. In Freytag's diagram, the bioethics case that provides closure in terms of rewriting can be represented in the following manner:

Here D represents the first ending, and closure is brought about by the reader offering D2. This depends upon one's acceptance that the actions of D were wrong and there should be an alternative ending. But I argue that if one agrees with D and sees no reason for D2, then one would *not* classify this case as an ethics case, for it already possesses closure. The genre of the bioethics case has a unique relationship to closure in that it requires a high degree of participation by the reader. Bioethics cases that have closure within them—as the Culver case does—are not ethics cases, for there is no separation of ought and is. This narratological feature of the bioethics case in turn reflects an essential drive within bioethics to give moral guidance to life's plots.

Conclusion: The Tyranny of the Genre

I do not wish to imply that it is solely by reportability, action, tempo, and closure that the bioethics case as a genre can be defined. These narratological features must, however, be taken into account when defining the bioethics case as a distinctive genre. Just as the reader brings expectations for this genre, the genre in turn determines what kind of information is relevant to discussion of ethics in health care. This raises important issues of how the cases are the data for the testing of ethical approaches. In arguing for the importance of ethical issues in medicine for moral philosophers Stephen Toulmin notes that "it required writers on applied ethics to go beyond the discussion of general principles and rule to a more scrupulous analysis of the particular kinds of 'cases' in which they find their application" (1982, p. 737). Yet how one defines a case is of central issue here. For the writer of the case, the expectations of the genre in turn condition the type of information included and excluded.

Virtue ethicists have been highly critical of bioethics for being too focused on quandary solving (Burrell and Hauerwas 1977; May 1983; Pellegrino 1989). Yet one may wonder if it is quandaries per se that are the problem or the style in which the cases are written. Bioethics cases tend to be apsychological narratives and thereby do not provide the kind of information that virtue ethicists deem as essential. Furthermore, because the reportability of cases is based on action rather than inner identity, the virtue ethicist's concern with moral development and motivation does not seem relevant. Care ethicists have strongly advocated that the central issue in ethics is responding to the needs of others, not simply deciding what moral actions should be accomplished. For them the tendency of the bioethics case genre to be apsychological makes care ethics seem superfluous. As Nancy Jecker and Warren Reich point out concerning care ethics, "when bioethicists emphasize impersonal ethical principles, such as autonomy, nonmaleficence, beneficence, and justice, this can have the effect of making the particular persons and relationships involved in ethical dilemmas incidental, rather than essential, to the crafting of moral responses" (1995, p. 338). Some narrative ethicists have advocated the importance of knowing a moral problem within the context of a patient's life story (Miles and Hunter 1990); the concerns of constructing a coherent narrative based on this issue are of primary importance to the narrative ethicist. As seen in its tempo, the bioethics case genre portrays life in detail within the clinical setting, slowing down the narrative discourse when it comes to discussing the problem within the clinical environment. Time passes rather quickly outside of the hospital environment; entire lives can go by in a single sentence. The concerns of narrative ethicists are thereby left out of the case presentations.

The conventions of the bioethics case can exclude from the narrative discourse features of essential value to those advocating approaches to ethics that attempt to broaden the scope of principlism. Yet the particular stylistics of the case genre—as seen in its reportability, action, tempo, and closure—determine what forms of analysis are relevant. The genre, thus, rather than being the data for critique, already includes its own critique of approaches that require a different stylistics to be relevant. By testing the relevance of such moral analysis against this genre, rather than the relevance of the case's presentation to the analysis, it is the genre that in the end triumphs. Understanding the theoretical slant of the narrative in turn permits one to ask what narrative features are excluded from the genre and to be aware of the possible tyranny of this genre.

Acknowledgments

I would like to thank Kathryn Montgomery Hunter and Carl Elliot for reading earlier drafts of this paper and providing insightful criticism.

Notes

1. There have been recent internet conversations in which some ethicists have been advocating for creating an oath to be taken by ethicists.

2. All references to textual space are from the space required in my quotations from these texts and not from the number of lines in the cited version.

References

Abrams, N. and M. D. Buckner, eds. (1983). *Medical Ethics: A Clinical Textbook and Reference for the Health Care Professions.* Cambridge, MA: The MIT Press.

Bakhtin, M. (1981). "Forms of Time and of the Chronotope in the Novel." *The Dialogic Imagination.* M. Holquist. Austin, University of Texas Press: 84–258.

Beauchamp, T. L. and J. F. Childress (1979). *Principles of Biomedical Ethics.* New York: Oxford University Press.

Beauchamp, T. L. and J. Childress (1983). *Principles of Biomedical Ethics.* New York: Oxford University Press.

Beauchamp, T. L. and J. F. Childress (1989). *Principles of Biomedical Ethics.* New York: Oxford University Press.

Beauchamp, T. L. and J. F. Childress (1994). *Principles of Biomedical Ethics.* New York: Oxford University Press.

Brody, H. (1988). *Stories of Sickness.* New Haven: Yale University Press.

Burrell, D. and S. Hauerwas (1977). "From System to Story: An Alternative Pattern for Rationality in Ethics." In *The Foundations of Ethics and Its Relationship to Science: Knowledge, Value and*

Belief. ed. H. Tristram Engelhardt and Daniel Callahan. Hastings-on-Hudson, NY, Hastings Center.

Culler, J. (1988). *Structuralist Poetics: Structuralism, Linguistics, and the Study of Literature.* Ithaca, NY: Cornell University Press.

Culver, C. M., K. D. Clouser, et al. (1985). "Basic Curricular Goals in Medical Ethics." *The New England Journal of Medicine* 312 (Jan. 24): 253–256.

Engelhardt, H. T. (1986). *The Foundations of Bioethics.* New York: Oxford University Press.

Fletcher, J. C., N. Quist, et al., eds. (1989). *Ethics Consultation in Health Care.* Ann Arbor, MI: Health Administration Press.

Genette, G. (1980). *Narrative Discourse.* Ithaca, NY: Cornell University Press.

Greimas, A. J. (1983). *Structural Semantics: An Attempt at a Method.* Lincoln: University of Nebraska Press.

Greimas, A. J. and J. Courtés (1982). *Semiotics and Language: An Analytical Dictionary.* Bloomington: Indiana University Press.

Hunter, Kathryn Montgomery. (1991). *Doctor's Stories: The Narrative Structure of Medical Knowledge.* Princeton, NJ: Princeton University Press.

Hunter, K. M. (1988). "Making a Case." *Literature and Medicine* 7: 66–79.

Jecker, N. S. and W. T. Reich (1995). "Contemporary Ethics of Care." *Encyclopedia of Bioethics.* ed. W. T. Reich. New York: Simon & Schuster Macmillan. 1: 336–344.

Lantos, J. D. (1983). "The Case: What Should Leah Be Told?" *Second Opinion* 18 (April): 81–86.

Lotman, J. (1977). *The Structure of the Artistic Text.* Ann Arbor: University of Michigan Press.

Martin, W. (1986). *Recent Theories of Narrative.* Ithaca: Cornell University Press.

May, W. F. (1983). *The Physician's Covenant: Images of the Healer in Medical Ethics.* Philadelphia: The Westminster Press.

Miles, S. and K. M. Hunter (1990). "Case Stories." *Second Opinion* 15: 60–69.

Pellegrino, E. D. (1989). "Character, Virtue and Self-Interest in the Ethics of the Professions." *The Journal of Contemporary Health Law and Policy* 5: 53–73.

Pellegrino, E. D. (1993). "The Metamorphosis of Medical Ethics: A 30-Year Retrospective," *JAMA* 269(9):1158–1162.

Prince, G. (1987). *Dictionary of Narratology.* Lincoln: University of Nebraska Press.

Ricoeur, P. (1984). *Time and Narrative.* Chicago: University of Chicago Press.

Rimmon-Kenan, S. (1983). *Narrative Fiction: Contemporary Poetics.* London: Routledge.

Scholes, R. (1974). *Structuralism in Literature: An Introduction.* New Haven and London: Yale University Press.

Smith, B. H. (1968). *Poetic Closure: A Study of How Poems End.* Chicago: University of Chicago Press.

Todorov, Tzvetan. (1977). *The Poetics of Prose,* trans. Richard Howard. Ithaca, NY: Cornell University Press.

Toulmin, S. (1982). "How Medicine Saved the Life of Ethics." *Perspectives in Biology and Medicine* 25: 736–750.

12

Narrative Competence

Martha Montello

In more than twenty years of studying literary narratives with medical students and physicians, teachers and scholars of literature and medicine have articulated medicine's conceptual framework and have clarified the variety of ways close reading and interpretation enhance competence in the human aspects of practicing medicine (Charon et al. 1995). Common to their experience has been the discovery of the multiple benefits of introducing literary study into medical education (Charon 1986). Using the methods and texts of their discipline, literary scholars have been teaching medical students and clinicians to comprehend patients' experiences of illness, to form effective therapeutic alliances with patients and their families, to reach accurate diagnoses, and to discern appropriate treatment goals. At an increasing number of medical schools, skilled teachers have been guiding readers in strengthening the focused attentiveness and critical questioning that close textual analysis and interpretation demand.

Perhaps no area of medical education and practice, however, reaps the benefits of narrative knowledge and methods in more fundamental and far-reaching ways than does ethics. Until recently, the practice of medical ethics has relied primarily on the analytic frameworks of philosophic ethics to attempt to discern solutions to bioethical problems. Although physicians need to know the principles and rules of medical ethics, an analytic approach alone to resolving moral issues in medicine reduces ethics to a branch of decision theory, neglecting the meaning of the human experience of the problem at hand (Hauerwas and Burrell 1977). Applying a narrative approach to ethical problems reframes the issues by focusing attention on the context of a patient's and family's life in all its moral complexity. The same literary skills that critical readers use to interpret the meaning of events in a story allow clinicians to see the way ethical issues are embedded in the individual and contingent nature of people's beliefs, culture, and biography.

In combination with a sound understanding of the salient categories of traditional moral theory, *narrative competence* is a necessary element of overall competence in moral reasoning.[1] Increasing interest in narrative approaches to ethics among scholars and practitioners in the medical community acknowledges that while clinical ethics requires good listening skills and accurate, empathic, interpretive abilities, most fundamentally it requires the capacity to make sound moral choices. And as empiric evidence in the classroom and clinic continues to indicate that skill with narratives helps in addressing and handling difficult moral issues in clinical care, literary critics and teachers need to clarify what constitutes narrative competence, how we acquire it, and the ways it enhances physicians' capacities for moral reasoning.

Narrative Frames for Moral Reasoning

Central to any understanding of the relationship between *narrative competence* and moral reasoning is the primary role of narrative in the way we represent the world to ourselves and others. Narrative might be said to comprise, as Arthur Danto suggests, "a metaphysics of everyday life" (Danto 1985, p. xiv). Peter Brooks observes the way "our lives are ceaselessly intertwined with narrative, with the stories that we tell and hear told, those we dream or imagine or would like to tell, all of which are reworked in that story of our own lives that we narrate to ourselves in an episodic, sometimes semi-conscious, but virtually uninterrupted monologue" (Brooks 1992, p. 3). Constantly seeking out linear, time-bound patterns to construct meaning out of our experience and a sense of wholeness in living out our identity, we invoke what James Hillman calls "the insighting power of the mind to create a cosmos and give sense to it" (Hillman 1983, p. 40). Within a framework of beginnings and endings, of turning points and crises, we shape the images that give form to our lives, out of which we make all of our moral decisions (MacIntyre 1981, p. 216).

The intrinsic connection between narrative knowledge and moral reasoning has been described by a growing number of contemporary scholars from disciplines as varied as psychiatry, literary theory, cognitive psychology, history, philosophy, and theology (Spence 1982, Bruner 1990, Sarbin 1986). Common to them all is scholarship that describes how stories portray the way a culture's values and an individual's biography form the foundations for ethical choices within a narrative understanding of the virtuous and worthy life. Philosopher Alasdair MacIntyre insists that we are tellers of stories in large part because, "I can only answer the question, 'What am I to do?' if I can answer the prior question, 'Of what story or stories do I find myself a part?'" (MacIntyre 1981, p. 216). Human actions acquire their moral meaning within narrative constructs, for practical reasoning is inseparable from the particularities of context unfolding over time. Omitting such narrative features as meaning, character, and contingency from ethical thinking distorts any account of a moral experience (Hauerwas and Burrell 1977).

Philosophers and literary critics in the expanding field of ethical criticism concur with theorist J. Hillis Miller's conviction that "narrative, examples, stories . . . are indispensible to thinking about ethics" (Miller 1987, p. 3). Exploring the vital connection between the experience of reading and the process of moral reasoning that readers use in living out their lives, contemporary ethical critics such as Wayne Booth and Martha Nussbaum analyze the way our engagements with literary narratives supplement, interpret, and even restructure our perceptions about our lived lives (Booth 1988, Nussbaum 1990). For these theorists, ethical thinking is at the heart of the experience of reading. From our first engagement with stories as children, we learn to recognize, evaluate, and justify choices and behaviors by vicariously experiencing the way characters think about their lives, make choices, and justify their decisions. Listening to the informal stories of family talk and fairy tales becomes what author Eudora Welty refers to as an early form of participation in the values of the life around us (Welty 1983). And in the pages of children's literature, we are surrounded early in our lives by narratives that emerge as a primary vehicle for moral reasoning. From such classic stories as *Stuart Little* to *Charlotte's Web* and *To Kill a Mockingbird*, children follow the way characters make sense of events and use specific reasons to make moral choices. A mouse decides to run away from home, a spider accepts her death as part of life's ongoing mystery, and a girl begins to comprehend the quality of her father's courage. Even in these early narratives, stories allow us to see how what we value as significant is deeply embedded in its context, and to follow the consequences of specific moral decisions over an extended time, exploring along the way the multiple possibilities for action in any one circumstance. In the unique fleshed-out narratives of literature, we gain unique access to a variety of views of the world, discovering through readerly acts of discernment, perception, and evaluation the moral reality of others. At the same time we become more conscious of our own moral life, understanding with increasing clarity what it means to live by certain values.

Moral knowledge, for philosophers such as Nussbaum and Richard Rorty, is revealed through literary narratives to require more than an intellectual grasp of facts and rules; it engages the emotions and requires what Aristotle calls "perception," the ability to see, as Nussbaum articulates, "a complex, concrete reality in a highly lucid and richly reponsive way" (Nussbaum 1990, p. 152). And certain works of fiction—such as those by James, Woolf, Joyce, and Proust—not only capture the morally salient particularities of our experience but also render the very processes by which we achieve moral understanding and make our choices. Understood this way, fiction is a kind of "moral laboratory," in the words of John Gardner, an exploratory, philosophical method through which a reader discovers the way a singular person with a certain character, situated in specific circumstances, might live a life (Gardner 1978, p. 108).

Entering Narrative Worlds

Literary narratives, then, can be powerful vehicles for moral reasoning. As critic Frank Lentricchia confesses, "All literature is travel literature, all true readers shut-ins" (Lentricchia 1996, p. 63). One of the most common phenomenological aspects of the experience of reading is the feeling of being transported, of losing oneself in the narrative world. Inviting the reader to abandon the here and now and facilitating the journey, the act of reading sets into motion three core processes within the reader—departure, performance, and change—all of which have significant implications for the development of narrative competence.[2]

Reading a story requires that to some extent we depart, leave behind the here and now to enter the world of the narrative. In the same way a moviegoer feels disoriented when the lights come up in the theatre at the end of a film, readers can feel disoriented upon finishing a story and "reentering" the actual world. Akin to the cognitive process of dissociation described by psychology, immersion in the narrative world partially disconnects the reader from the reality of the empirical world. "Once upon a time" transports us and partially isolates us from the lived world, often astonishing us by the depth of the experience (Bruce 1981). The hero of Paul Theroux's novel *My Secret History* describes his experience of being propelled out of his narrow life in his limited world and into the world of the narrative as he reads his travel journal:

> For a moment in my reading I have been transported, and I had forgotten everything—all my worry and depression, the crisis in my marriage, my anger, my jealousy.... It was half a world away, and because it was so separate from me, and yet so complete, I laughed. It was a truthful glimpse of a different scene. It cheered me up. It was like looking at a brilliant picture and losing myself in it. (Theroux 1989, p. 402).

Submitting to the pull of the text, we perform roles required of us by the narrative in order to give substance to the created world and the psychological life of its inhabitants. The various terminologies used within literary criticism to describe the roles of the reader articulate the way performance figures into the process of constructing meaning from narrative texts. From Walker Gibson's "mock reader" to Wolfgang Iser's "implied reader" and Umberto Eco's "model reader," contemporary literary reader-response theorists have focused on reading as an active process (Gibson 1980, Iser 1978, Eco 1993). The text, avers Eco, is "a lazy machine that expects a lot of collaboration from the reader" (Eco 1993, p. 128). Like travelers expected to adapt to local customs in order to participate in the surrounding life, readers must assume the set of attitudes and values that the language of the text requires us to assume in order to become immersed in the narrative world. In *The Company We Keep: An Ethics of Fiction*, Wayne Booth explores the "shaping power" of Jane Austen's novels in the way readers experience patterns of desire and satisfaction:

> In living with Jane Austen's favored characters for many hours and many days, I learn to long for what those characters long for (or in the case of Emma Wood-house, what the character *should* long for, if she knew all along what she learns only toward the end). I learn how to long *in that way* for that special kind of happiness. I am taught both how to desire and what to desire. (Booth 1988, p. 427)

Drawing on readers' own desires, memories, psychological defenses, and imaginations, this quality of performance enables readers to experience and understand things entirely unfamiliar, offering virtually limitless opportunities to engage their faculties in different ways of perceiving the world. As a result, says Booth, readers are able to try on more lives in a month of reading than they ever could in a lifetime of living.

During the act of reading, we are most often unaware of the extent to which we can be changed in the process. Literary critics Richard Eldridge, John Gardner, and J. Hillis Miller remind us that we absorb the values of the worlds we live in when we read. "And even when we do not retain them," insists Wayne Booth, "the fact is that we have lived its values for the duration: we have been *that kind of person* for at least as long as we remained in the presence of the work" (Booth 1988, p. 41). From Aristotle to Norman Holland, philosophers and literary critics have debated the capacity of literature to bring about more than catharsis or repetition of an already-ingrained identity in readers. Recent studies in cognitive psychology and psychoanalytic theory, however, support the contention that our very mental structures are altered during the act of reading (Alcorn and Bracher 1985). Using object-relations theory, some psychoanalytic critics, for instance, explain the way that reading offers readers the opportunity to "reform" the self (Hymer 1983, Roland 1981). Literary narratives can have long-term effects on the structure of the self by extending a reader's psychic map to include unfamiliar territory, taking in new values and knowledge of other ways of seeing the world. Old boundaries can give way to allow the absorption of new understandings. One result is what Rorty refers to as "solidarity" with others, a goal to be achieved not by rational inquiry but by the imaginative ability to see strangers as fellow sufferers. Fiction by Henry James, Gabriel Garcia Marquez, and Nabokov, according to Rorty, also expands our comprehension of ourselves to include the kinds of cruelty of which we are capable and allows us to redescribe ourselves (Rorty 1982, p. xvi). Psycholanalyst Meredith Skura describes this shock of recognition to which readers are often privileged as similar to "moments of integration and insight" that characterize successful analysis (Skura 1981, p. 12). In a complex resonance of reader and text, confrontations between strangers reveal in the reader hidden primary values, repressed or denied, and raise them to the surface to be explored as questions of justice and virtue and moral choice about the lives we choose to lead.

Forms of Narrative Competence

In seeking understanding of complex human problems in order to make effective moral decisions with patients and their families, physicians are often unaware of how much they rely on proficiency that is in the domain of what might be called narrative knowledge. Solving problems of meaning in clinical work and increasing skills in the areas of empathy in ways that enhance the ability to make sound moral choices involves facility with comprehending the motivations and consequences of behaviors and choices. Always context-embedded and particular, narrative knowledge is concerned with examining and understanding singular events within the specific time and place of a unique life-story. In order to find coherence in seqences of events and to form meaningful wholes, physicians need to use not only the logicoscientific knowledge that enables them to gather and evaluate generalizable, replicable, and empirically verifiable data, but also the narrative knowledge that enables them to use the epistemology and interpretive abilities of a good reader. Recognizing multiple contradictory meanings of a story and various possible courses of action calls into play a reader's ability to contextualize a patient's story within multiple dimensions of time, place, and perspective. Recently physicians, ethicists, and literary scholars have been presenting in full contextual detail stories of difficult clinical-ethical cases in which a narrative analytic approach appears critical in reaching a satisfactory outcome for both patient and physician (Charon 1993, Farrow 1995). Rich cases such as these demonstrate the importance and value of aspects of narrative competence that are necessary features of overall competence in moral reasoning in medicine. At the same time, these cases demonstrate the results of what Rita Charon calls "narrative incompetence," where, as she puts it, physicians "get the story wrong," often with highly unfavorable outcomes (Charon 1993, p. 151).

Three specific forms of narrative competence that readers intuitively exercise to discern the meaning of stories enhance the ability of physicians to find meaning in the complex lives of unique individuals. And each of the three forms of competence is strengthened in particular by one of the three core processes that readers undergo in the act of reading—departure, performance, and change.

In the first place, the reader's experience of departure, of being transported from the actual lived world to the world of the narrative, parallels a physician's competence in negotiating a balance between involvement and detachment. Aesthetic distance mirrors clinical distance. Even as medical students, physicians are trained to view their own emotional responses as threatening to the ideal of "detached concern" (Halpern 1983, p. 163). From the first days in gross anatomy labs, students learn to separate from their patients, and throughout their training to fear both a loss of control over their emotions, by becoming too involved in identifying with the patient's predicament, and a loss of humanity, by becoming too detached from the patient's humanity. Overinvolvement with suffering patients is feared to be too great a burden on their limited time and emotional energy. On the other hand, empathic care depends in large part upon developing an emotional resonance with the patient. Readers arbitrate the same sort of conflict, constantly balancing detachment with absorption. Roland Barthes speaks of the pleasure of the text by introducing an erotic metaphor to describe the way a story seduces the reader, leads us on, delays our gratification, and finally leaves us with a sweet, though confused memory of a passionate encounter (Barthes 1975, pp. 9–10). But reading well is also reading with detached control. Bertolt Brecht describes this facet of the reader's stance as that of a cigar-smoking viewer, someone who has a distance from the action on the stage, someone who smokes dispassionately while the play goes on (Brecht 1957, p. 71). Reserved, objective, with arms crossed and gaze askance, the reader/viewer sits judging and weighing the text (Willett 1957). The literary theorist Hans Robert Jauss describes what is at stake as readers negotiate an identification with a protagonist: "Identification in and through the aesthetic attitude is a state of balance where too much or too little distance can turn into uninterested detachment from the portrayed figure, or lead to an emotional fusion with it" (Jauss 1982, p. 11). What the psychoanalyst Donald Spence calls "empathic witnessing" suggests the way reading literature offers a model for listening to patients. Entering the world of the patient, he says, "we listen to the patient and become accustomed to his manner of speaking. [We] learn to hear his store of private meanings reflected in the words he uses. . . . Listening in this manner is similar to making a close reading of a poem; it attempts to get 'behind' the surface structure of the sentence and to identify with the patient as he is expressing the thought" (Spence 1982, p. 8). Skilled readers are like narratively competent physicians who learn to move fluidly between empathic understanding and critical detachment for, as Jauss suggests, "neither mere absorption in an emotion nor the wholly detached reflection about it, but only the to-and-fro movement, ever renewed disengagement of the self from a fictional experience, the testing of oneself against the portrayed fate of another, makes up the distinctive pleasure in the state of suspension of aesthetic identification" (Jauss 1982, p. 12). Narratively competent physicians who listen to patient's stories and concomitantly retain the professional objectivity to gather data and make reliable evaluations perform the kind of cognitive activities that allow readers to be transported to the narrative world and can achieve the kind of resonance a reader finds with a character in a compelling story.

Second, by performing the role required of us by the story, the reader gains access to the lifeworld of the characters, exercising a reader's competence in shifting perspectives. As Janie tells us in the pages of Zora Neale Hurston's *Their Eyes Were Watching God,* "You got tuh go there tuh *know* there" (p. 183). According to critic Walker Gibson, "Every time we open the pages of another piece of writing, we are embarked on a new adventure in which we become a new person. We assume, for the sake of the experience, that set of attitudes and qualities which the language asks us to assume, and if we cannot assume them, we throw the book away" (Gibson 1980, p. 1). Entering another person's world means seeing from the inside out. Adopting the unique frame of reference from which an individual perceives and interprets the world of experience offers readers what F. Scott Fitzerald calls "privileged glimpses of the human heart" (Fitzgerald 1925, p. 6). In the same way, physicians need the narrative competence to change perspectives in listening to patients' narratives. Recognizing moral issues—questions of value and meaning—embedded in the context of individual lives demands the capacity to imagine the richly textured complex lives to which their patients' narratives grant them access. We need to use what Mark Johnson terms "empathetic imaginative understanding," for "we cannot know what it means to treat someone as an end-in-himself, in any concrete way, unless we can imagine his experience, feelings, plans, goals, and hopes. We cannot know what respect for others demands of us, unless we participate imaginatively in their experience of the world" (Johnson 1993, p. 200). The highly individual frame of reference from which each of us perceives and interprets the world of experience can with practice be shifted at will to provide our consciousness with access to unfamiliar reality. In phenomenological terms, we alter our "perceptual stance" every time we read a story (Husserl 1975). With practice, we gain proficiency in using the empathetic imagination. The poet Shelley describes the imagination as "the great instrument of moral good that strengthens . . . the moral nature of man, in the same manner as exercise strengthens a limb" (Shelley 1965). Narrative fiction, especially novels, through detailed description of unfamiliar people, increases our sensitivity to the specific context of the lived lives and moral experience of others, through which we come to see others as one of "us." Through reading we learn compassion in the root sense of the word, "to suffer with," as a profound form of presence with another person.

Another facet of this second form of narrative competence is linked to the reasons novels and short stories are so often principal vehicles of moral vision and change. In altering our perceptual stance with each story we enter, we relinquish our hold on a single vision of experience. An inherent relationship exists between empathizing with others and grasping the complex truth of a situation, the multiple views from which a single event might be seen. In particular, reading narratives such as those by Faulkner, Woolf, and James, in which various points of view form a whole, we come to see that the truth of a moral experience lies in the aggregate of subjective realities, transformed by the reading mind through reflection, that reveals the sum of what matters in a specific human situation.

The literary experience allows us to see beyond ourselves not only in terms of point of view and context but also in terms of temporality, in ways that reveal multiple alternatives and consequences to our ideologies and ethical decisions. Though people generally experience time as having an inescapable directedness from past to future, literary narratives, according to literary theorist Gary Saul Moreson, are able to convey temporal openness through a device he terms "sideshadowing," in which time is portrayed not as a line but as a shifting set of fields of possibility. For example, narratives by Dostoyevsky and Tolstoy suggest that to comprehend an event is to perceive what else might have happened. Multiple possibilities "cast a shadow 'from the side'" so that along with an event, we see two or more alternatives; "the actual and the possible . . . are made simultaneously visible" (Moreson 1994, p. 117). This view of time reveals the ethical pluralism of our experience, encouraging us to forgo the false, shallow certainties of ideology and allowing us to perceive the possibilities for moral choice open to us.

Finally, a third kind of narrative competence that reading yields is a greater facility with pattern recognition and re-formation. By becoming more skilled readers, we increase our ability to recognize patterns and make connections, not only within stories, literary and clinical, but among them. Although reading can never be a substitute for lived life, as literary critic Roger Shattuck reminds us, it "can acquaint us with specific and intensified repertories of emotions, experiences, and possibilites such that later, coming upon an event, we may have a counter-part at hand . . . available. And the movement of our minds is to say, 'This is it.' For we have lived it once already" (Shattuck 1963, p. 134). Students and clinicians often articulate the sense of having "been here before" in an unfamiliar clinical situation after reading a literary narrative that has captured the essence of the event (Montello 1995, p. 121). Forming an empathic connection with a fictive companion, they integrate the values, moral concerns, and responses of the characters with their own experience, allowing them, in Shattuck's words, "to achieve personal experience sooner, more directly, and with less groping" (Shat-tuck 1963, p. 134).

> Literature can foreshorten the complex, two-part process of living, what we participate in through reading becomes the first half of that double process. Our own life, our personal experience, can then move directly into the second beat: recognition. (Shattuck 1963, p. 133)

Entering narrative worlds, students and clinicians can be encouraged to sharpen their ability to find patterns of moral valuing and interpret them in that world's terms. Later, when they come upon a similar event in a patient's story, they can use the same skills, joining one story with another, accurately to observe and make sense out of the chaos of suffering and loss. Reading Tillie Olsen's *Tell Me a Riddle* and Tolstoy's *The Death of Ivan Illych*, for instance, revealed to one physician patterns of moral experience she was discovering in a patient of her own who was dying of cancer, allowing her to interpret and comprehend the specific, unique quality of his suffering at a profound level of understanding and empathy (Connelly 1990).

In the same way that reading changes readers, such depth of understanding leaves the physician open to being changed through experiencing the suffering of another. As the philosopher of science R. Sawyier suggests, "When we fill in the concept of empathy, part of what we imply is that the empathizer has himself had something happen to him right then; it is not just that he has thought hard, or tried to figure something out" (Sawyier 1974, pp. 37–47). In the same way, when we read, we see and hear and feel the same things the characters do and from their same perspective, so that when we close the book to reenter our own lives, that set of emotions and way of knowing is embedded in us, a part of us. And the patterns physicians form in making sense of similar events in the narra-tive world of fiction and lived world of patient care may also have long-term effects on the attunement to questions of value and meaning, with the concomi-tant possibility of change in perspective and behavior (Skura 1981, p. 12). A clin-ician who reads the Book of Job, Chekhov's "Grief," or Styron's "A Tidewater

Morning" with an ear tuned to the moral questions at the center of the characters' agony may never perceive patients' experiences of suffering in the face of
death in quite the same way again. Each specific set of fictive experiences weaves
a thread in the complex texture of the reader's understanding and alters the
picture as a whole.

The Well-Storied Physician

The act of reading itself is not all that matters. How and why one reads is at least
as important. Particularly for medical students, who face a major transition in
their lives, reading for narrative competence offers valuable benefits in the
process of professionalization. At the heart of the transition from student to
doctor is the struggle to reconcile one's values with the demands of patient care
(Branch et al. 1993). Maintaining empathy for patients while becoming accultur-
ated to medicine challenges students to gain a perspective on events, which
allows them to retain their best instincts and values. At the same time, these
primarily young adults are often consciously seeking an ethical being-in-the-
world that seems right and good for both their professional and private lives, one
that achieves the ripeness, coherence, and wholeness that Erik Erikson calls
integrity (Erikson 1978). Recent studies in the cognitive experience of reading
literary narratives suggest that readers pass through predictable Piaget-like
stages as they mature, following a kind of evolution in the way they make sense
of texts and the uses to which they put their reading (Appleyard 1991, Gerrig
1993, Johnson 1993). Young adult and mature adult readers tend to be pragmatic
readers, consciously choosing the uses they make of reading. Victor Nell distinguishes between readers who read to dull consciousness and those who read to
heighten it (Nell 1988). And for those readers who look to literary narratives in
a "purposive" way, as Mark Johnson suggests, as instruments for strengthening
skills in moral reasoning and understanding, what happens during the reading
process can be critical for ethical development. Students and clinicians alike
often discover that stories read us as much as we read them. The ethical truths
that serious readers search for in literature require a personal gaze, a turning
inward to absorb the meaning we formulate in a text into the context of our own
existence. Helping physicians to recognize and respond to moral issues in a way
that integrates their own affective selves with their behaviors with patients can
serve both to heighten consciousness of experiences of human suffering and to
find a balance between detachment and compassion. Using the skills of a reader,
clinicians equip themselves with both a method and a content for discovering
what is "narratively right" for an individual patient in a singular situation. In a
sense, physicians need to be "well-storied," for narrative competence not only
enhances the ability to deal effectively with ethical issues in patient care but also

increases self-knowledge in ways that reorient physicians toward the ideals of service and care with which they entered practice.

Notes

1. The term has been used by Rita Charon, who suggests that without "narrative competence" physicians cannot deliver empathic care (Charon 1993).

2. Cognitive psychologist Richard Gerrig suggests that readers undergo six processes in the act of reading, emphasizing how narrative information influences perceptions and judgments in the actual world.

References

Alcorn, M., and Bracher, M. (1985) "Literature, Psychoanalysis, and the Reformation of the Self: A New Direction for Reader-Response Theory." *Publications of the Modern Language Association*, 100(3):342–354.

Appleyard, J. (1991) *Becoming a Reader: The Experience of Fiction from Childhood to Adulthood.* London: Cambridge University Press.

Barthes, R. (1975) *The Pleasure of the Text.* Richard Miller, trans. New York: Hill &Wang.

Booth, W. (1988) *The Company We Keep: An Ethics of Fiction.* Berkeley: University of California Press.

Branch, W., et al. (1993) "Becoming a Doctor: Critical Incident Reports from Third-Year Medical Students." *New England Journal of Medicine*, 329:1130–1132.

Brecht, B. (1957) *Brecht on Theatre: The Development of an Aesthetic.* John Willet, trans. New York: Hill & Wang.

Brooks, P. (1992) *Reading for the Plot: Design and Intention in Narrative.* Cambridge: Harvard University Press.

Bruce, B. (1981) "A Social Interaction Model of Reading." *Discourse Processes,* 4:273–311.

Bruner, J. (1990) *Acts of Meaning.* Cambridge: Harvard University Press.

Charon, R. (1986) "To Render the Lives of Patients." *Literature and Medicine,* 5:58–74.

Charon, R. (1993) "The Narrative Road to Empathy." *Empathy and the Practice of Medicine,* eds. H. Spiro et al. New Haven: Yale, pp. 147–159.

Charon, R. et al. (1995) "Literature and Medicine: Contributions to Clinical Practice." *Annals of Internal Medicine,* 122:599–606.

Connelly, J. (1990) "The Whole Story." *Literature and Medicine,* 9:150–161.

Connelly, J., and DalleMura, S. (1988). "Ethical Problems in the Medical Office." *Journal of the American Medical Association,* 260(6):812–815.

Danto, A. (1985) *Narrative and Knowledge.* New York: Columbia University Press.

Eco, U. (1993) *Six Walks in the Fictional Woods.* Cambridge: Harvard University Press.

Eldridge, R. (1989) *On Moral Personhood: Philosophy, Literature, Criticism, and Self-Understanding.* Chicago: University of Chicago Press.

Erikson, E. (1978) *Adulthood.* New York: Norton.

Farrow, L. (1995) "Commentary on Narrative Ethics: The Case of the Missing Cases." *Meta-Medical Ethics: The Philosophical Foundations of Bioethics.* M. A. Grodin, ed. Boston: Kluwer Academic Publishers.

Fitzgerald, F. S. (1925) *The Great Gatsby.* New York: Charles Scribner's Sons.

Gardner, J. (1978) *On Moral Fiction.* New York: Basic Books.

Gerrig, R. (1993) *Experiencing Narrative Worlds: On the Psychological Activities of Reading.* New Haven: Yale University Press.

Gibson, W. (1980) "Authors, Speakers, Readers, and Mock-Readers." *Reader-Response Criticism*, ed. J. Tompkins. Baltimore: Johns Hopkins University Press.

Halpern, J. (1983) "Empathy: Using Resonance Emotions in the Service of Curiosity." *Empathy and the Practice of Medicine*, ed. H. Spiro et al. New Haven: Yale University Press.

Hauerwas, S., and Burrell, D., (1997) "From System to Story: An Alternative Pattern for Rationality in Ethics." In *The Foundations of Ethics and Its Relationship to Science*, ed. H.T. Engelhardt, Jr., and D. Callahan. Hastings-on Hudson, NY: The Hastings Center.

Hillman, J. (1983) *Healing Fiction*. Barrytown, NY: Station Hill Press.

Holland, N. (1975) "Unity Identity Text Self." *Publications of the Modern Language Association*, 90:813–822.

Hurston, Z. (1937) *Their Eyes Were Watching God*. New York: Harper & Row.

Husserl, E. (1975) *Ideas*. New York: Collier Books.

Hymer, S. (1983) "The Therapeutic Nature of Art in Self-Reparation." *Psychoanalytic Review*, (70):57–68.

Iser, W. (1978) *The Act of Reading*. Baltimore: Johns Hopkins University Press.

Jauss, H. (1982) *Aesthetic Experience and Literary Hermeneutics*. Minneapolis: University of Minnesota Press.

Johnson, M. (1993) *Moral Imagination: Implications of Cognitive Science for Ethics*. Chicago: University of Chicago Press.

Lentricchia, F. (1996) "Last Will and Testament of an Ex-Literary Critic." *Lingua Franca*, September/October.

MacIntyre, A. (1981) *After Virtue*. Notre Dame, IN: Notre Dame University Press

Miller, J. (1987) *The Ethics of Reading: Kant, de Man, Eliot, Trollope, James, and Benjamin*. New York: Columbia University Press.

Montello, M. (1995). "Medical Stories: Narrative and Phenomenological Approaches." In *Meta-Medical Ethics*, M. A. Grodin, ed. The Netherlands: Kluwer Academic Publishers.

Moreson, G. (1994) *Narrative and Freedom: The Shadows of Time*. New Haven: Yale University Press.

Nell, V. (1988) *Lost in a Book*. New Haven: Yale University Press.

Nussbaum, M. (1990) *Love's Knowledge*. New York: Oxford University Press.

Roland, A. (1981) "Imagery and the Self in Artistic Creativity and Psychoanalytic Literary Criticism." *Psychoanalytic Review*, (68):409–424.

Rorty, R. (1982) *Contingency, Irony, and Solidarity*. New York: Cambridge University Press.

Sarbin, T. (1986) *Narrative Psychology: The Storied Nature of Human Conduct*. New York: Praeger.

Sawyier, R. (1974) "A Conceptual Analysis of Empathy." *Annual of Psychoanalysis*, 3:37–47.

Shattuck, R. (1963) *Proust's Binoculars: A Study of Memory, Time, and Recognition in "A La Recherche du Temps Perdu."* New York: Random House.

Shelley, P. (1965) "A Defense of Poetry." *The Complete Works of Percy Bysshe Shelley*, ed. R. Ingpen and W. Peck. New York: Gordian, 7:109–140.

Skura, M. (1981) *The Literary Use of the Psychoanalytic Process*. New Haven: Yale University Press.

Spence, D. (1982) *Narrative Truth and Historical Truth: Meaning and Interpretation in Psychoanalysis*. New York: W.W. Norton.

Theroux, P. (1989) *My Secret History*. New York: G. P. Putnam's.

Welty, E. (1983) *One Writer's Beginnings*. Cambridge: Harvard University Press.

Willet, J. (1957) *Brecht on Theatre*. New York: Hill and Wang.

13

Toward a Bioethics for the Twenty-First Century
A Ricoeurian Poststructuralist
Narrative Hermeneutic Approach to Informed Consent

Jan Marta

Informed consent is one of the pillars of bioethics, a cornerstone of all ethical medical decision-making, and the enshrinement of the dominance of the principle of autonomy in contemporary North American bioethics to date. Despite or because of this, there is great dissatisfaction with the dominant disclosure model of informed consent, the one reprised in professional codes of ethics,[1] and given the greatest currency in mainstream theoretical and practical (clinical and pedagogical) conceptualizations. The standard elements of this model—disclosure, comprehension, voluntariness, competence, and consent or refusal—are familiar enough, as is the practical definition: an informed consent to an intervention exists only where the patient receives a thorough disclosure regarding the intervention, comprehends the disclosure, acts voluntarily in giving consent, is competent to give consent, and consents to the intervention.[2]

Among the dissatisfactions with this model are the skepticism that genuine informed consent can ever be obtained, given a variety of factors including: patients' lack of medical knowledge; physicians' lack of clinical empathy and communication skills; power, socioeconomic, linguistic, and gender differences; as well as the emotional distress and temporal urgency often clouding the situation. In addition, informed consent is culturally bound to mainstream North American valorization of autonomy, and of a specific version of autonomy, one that construes independence as radical individualism. Anthropologists have demonstrated that this view is a minority one, confined not only to North America but to so-called mainstream North American society, whereas other cultures, including ethnic and racial minorities and North American subcultures, tend to emphasize relationalism, contextuality, and trust. Case reports of immigrants and natives in conflict with the mainstream view and those of Europeans in conflict with bioethics codes derived from imported North American models support the anthropological literature on this account.[3] Indeed, research tends to show that even "mainstream" patients prefer to be informed but not necessarily to share in medical decision-making.[4]

This study will explore how a poststructuralist narrative hermeneutic approach to informed consent, based on the philosophy of Paul Ricoeur,[5] can increase sensitivity to individual, relational, and cultural factors through reformulating informed consent as an experiential, expressive, and interpretive action (process) and act (outcome). For the purposes of this study, informed consent refers to the process and outcome involving the voluntary, competent person in consent to, or refusal of, a medical investigation, procedure, act, or treatment—in other words, to the most common informed consent situation.[6] It encompasses both the oral consent process and the signing of a written consent.[7]

The study begins with a brief introduction to relevant aspects of Ricoeur's theory of narrative.[8] Each of the three key elements—identity, action, and history—and its relation to informed consent, both the current dominant model and a narrative hermeneutic model, is elaborated separately and then integrated into a Ricoeurian poststructuralist narrative hermeneutic approach to informed consent. The study concludes by situating this approach in relation to Hilde Lindemann Nelson's definition and critique, "What's Narrative Ethics?"[9]

The contemporary French philosopher Paul Ricoeur is internationally recognized across disciplines (philosophy, literature, history) as a significant contributor to current theories of narrative. Ricoeur's work on narrative deals with the interrelationships of experience, language, thought, action, and history; his poststructuralist hermeneutic approach integrates semiotics, semantics, phenomenology, hermeneutics, and metaphysics. His work is remarkable in philosophic circles, and particularly relevant to a philosophic approach to informed consent, for its integration of Continental philosophies with the Anglo-American analytic tradition (which underpins the current dominant model of informed consent). Elements of his theory of narrative are present at various stages throughout his long and fecund philosophic inquiry, and predominate in the later works *Temps et récit* (Time and Narrative) in three volumes (1983–1985), and *Soi-même comme un autre* (Oneself as Another) (1990).

For Ricoeur, narrative is a temporally ordered function, genre, and activity of human discourse that structures the subject's experience of the self, others, and the world; the perception and apperception of events; and their expression in time. It is one modality of semantic innovation that creates new meaning through the transformation of semiotic linguistic elements (words) at the discursive level (that of the sentence and larger linguistic units, including eventually the text). While narrative classically describes, imitates, or figures human action (the mimetic function), for Ricoeur narrative also has referential and ontological functions: that is, narratives configure disparate agents, experiences, intentions, affects, and events into meaningful explanations that enable increased comprehension of oneself, others, and the world; and narratives lay claim to and are accorded truth value about oneself, others, and the world.

In Ricoeur's theory the minimal elements of a narrative are a subject, events, and time. Subjects have intentions and identify themselves through their actions in relation to others. Although they are capable of postulating atemporality, subjects experience the world in time. Narratives, through their portrayal of the temporal nature of human experience, imaginatively resolve the aporia of a rationalistic metaphysics, where time is existing yet nonexistent, measured yet nonspatial. For Ricoeur, "time becomes human time to the extent that it is organized after the manner of a narrative; narrative, in turn, is meaningful to the extent that it portrays the features of temporal experience" (*Time and Narrative* 1, p. 3).

The ordering of human experience as a triple present—the past is present as memory, the present is present as attention, the future is present as expectation—subtends the subject's emplotment of actions taken by persons (self or others), and the intentions, affects, and consequences surrounding those actions, into a temporally ordered meaningful narrative. Emplotment, the act of creating narrative plot lines, of putting together characters, events, and time, is always an act of productive imagination, whether the characters and events are held to be "real" or not. The plots created are always to some extent "feigned plots." They also become autonomous from the narrator's intention. The selective process of narration that engages productive imagination has, by its very selectiveness, ethical and moral implications. Because of their constructedness and autonomy, narratives are open to constant refiguration and reinterpretation. These qualities, rather than trapping narrative in a vicious hermeneutic circle, enable narratives to transform currently accepted "truths" about "reality."

Individual and Collective Narrative Identities in Informed Consent[10]

For Ricoeur "identity," whether of an individual or a community, answers a practical question of "who?" posed in four modalities: Who speaks? Who acts? Who recounts oneself? Who is the moral subject? "Who?" asks about authorship and agency: Who is the author or agent of this speech, action, recounting, moral responsibility? The answer to the question "who?" is a narrative. Identity, individual or collective, is narrative identity. Only narrative identity resolves the distinction between sameness and difference over time, escaping the substantialist or formalist *idem* (sameness outside of time) and its counterargument (discrete identities within time) through *ipse* (similarity to oneself over time).

Narrative identity is grounded in language (semantics) and manifested in discourse (pragmatics). "I" is primarily the answer to the question "who?" posed as: Who speaks (in thought or in conversation)? "I" do, and "I" speak about "me" to "you." "I" and all pronouns are deictic linguistic elements, functions that change referent dependent on the context: "I" is the person speaking and "you" the person listening, until we change roles and "I" become "you" and "you" become "I." "I" is the agent of speech no matter which named person is speaking.

When "I" speak about "me" I speak about my "self" as an object of discourse. "-self" is an element that combines with all the personal pronouns; in other words, it is part of a reflexive pronoun structure inclusive of all persons. Ricoeur develops his narrative identity based on the inclusive "oneself" (whether individual or collective) rather than the "I" that defines itself in linguistic opposition to "you."

This grounding of narrative identity in language and discourse interconnects the subject's mind and body through the importance of speech and action—of speech as action. In contrast to the substantialist Cartesian *cogito*, a radically disembodied subject in a state of "hyperbolic" doubt, spatiotemporally disengaged from an already spatiotemporally destroyed metaphysical world (*Soi-même comme un autre*, pp. 15–16), Ricoeur's subject, bodily engaged in a spatiotemporal world, is one who analytically identifies a likeness created through the narrative structure of individual action and praxis (action in relation to others). Through this identification or recognition, a subject is self like another, that is, self similar to an other, and self as other.

The dialectic of sameness and ipseity ultimately engages a dialectic and an ethic of ipseity and alterity. The fundamental relationship of self as being, resembling (like but not the same as), another and an other, that is, the narrative identity of the subject (individual or collective), entrains individual moral and collective ethical dimensions to the subject's actions. These dimensions result from the interconnectedness with others, and from the process of creating one's narrative identity, since telling and privileging a particular story about oneself is a moral and ethical choice—for the individual or collective subject and for others. More specifically, through the narrative identifications of oneself as another, the autonomy of self is intimately connected to solicitude for another, and to justice for all others.

"Oneself as another" also recognizes mutability within the coherence of an individual or collective identity over time. One's identifications are constantly refigured by all the stories one tells about oneself, and which are told about one, whether "one" is an individual, a collective, a community, or a people. These stories are constantly refigured by reflexive (ulterior) configurations. Narrative identity is dynamic, the stories and their retellings constantly changing, their meanings open, their interpretations open works.

Contrary to the current dominant model of informed consent, which relies on a substantialist, rationalistic, disembodied, and disconnected subject that equates (as *idem*, same) an individual's personhood and social role, in a Ricoeurian poststructuralist narrative hermeneutic approach to informed consent, the subjects involved, both physician and patient, would each have a narrative identity as a person and as a role defined by the narrative identity of the collective that currently privileges informed consent as a moral imperative requiring the physician to protect and respect patient autonomy. Physician and patient would engage in the stories of the patient's illness and the physician's medical interventions as interconnected persons, alternately narrator and listener, and interconnected roles, informer and consenter. Each would define the other, both as a person and as a role. Their individual narrative acts would constantly reconfigure their stories, their selves, and each as another. Their narrative acts would mutually reconfigure their narrative identities.

Narrative identity interconnects patient and physician and intertwines their moral and ethical concerns. Where the current model opposes patient and physician, autonomy and beneficence, a narrative hermeneutic model of identity would include the potential for patients and physicians to share common values of autonomy, solicitude, and justice with regard to the self, the other, and all others. To view the persons involved in informed consent, patient and physician, as having narrative identities would transform both the individual experience and the collective paradigm of informed consent, including its ethical justification.

The distinction made through narrative identity between the subject's personhood and his or her assigned role in a collective narrative would allow one to respect the person's unique humanness while recognizing the expectations built into the role, expectations the role has of itself and of the other in the collective narrative identity that figures individual narrative identities. The ipseity of the subject's personhood with role, self as another, would provide for cohesiveness even when these two conflict—as when, using the current dominant model, the person does not wish to adopt the role as assigned by the collective narrative (for example, where an individual patient subject does not wish to exercise the autonomy currently imposed, except, let us say, to autonomously choose to defer to the physician's medical expertise); or where an individual physician subject may personally resent the roles of informer and executor of the patient's consent, yet fulfill them in respect of his or her physician role. In each case the uniqueness of the subject's personhood would be preserved within the collectively assigned role. In moral terms, both individual and collective values would be respected. In the terms of current moral philosophy, narrative virtue theory[11] and principlism could be dialogically wedded (brought together as discourses but not dissolved into each other). The cohesiveness would be part of the collective dominant paradigm and not dependent entirely on the whim of the individuals involved in a given instance of informed consent.

Similarly, the integration of mind and body through narrative identity would facilitate, from within a new collective paradigm, the development[12] of an empathic, narrative, and cultural connectedness that would respect the importance to both patient and physician of the medical explication—the biological, as well as the psychological and social—of the patient's illness as conarrated with the physician. In addition, since identity and alterity are connected through ipseity, narrative identity would assist subjects, patients or physicians, from different cultures to respect their own cultural identities within the collective narrative, including by transforming the collective identification of the roles of informed consent, themselves an open work, open to new interpretations and new configurations.

Informed Consent as Narrative Action[13]

In Ricoeur's theory, action, whether individual or praxis (action in relation to others) is narratively structured. It is implicitly ordered in time, before the act of telling about an action orders it as one of the events of a narrative. The subject perceives and apperceives action in time as it occurs, before it is explicated through narration or understood through narrative comprehension. Action itself is meaningful. It has content that autonomously detaches from the agent and develops social consequences of its own. It persists and flees in time through oral registration (speaking, hearing, retelling) and written recording. Action is open to practical interpretation, that is, it generates new actions; and it is open to constant reinterpretation. Action has a referential function of developing new paradigms and constituting new worlds of interpretation. Action also has an ontologic function. It can be validated against the "logical criteria" of a collective action paradigm and can itself take on the power of a dominant action paradigm.

For Ricoeur, speech acts, which comprise the act of communication, are similarly narratively structured. They create meaning through their "locutionary," "illocutionary," and "perlocutionary" forces—that is, respectively, the act *of* speaking, the actions done *in* speaking (for example, christening or pronouncing dead, where the spoken words perform the action referred to), and the effects generated *by* speaking (on the feelings, thoughts, or actions of the listener). Speech acts can be explicated and understood through speech-act theory and the linguistics of discourse, as Ricoeur does through the original work of J. L. Austin and John Searles. Like other actions, speech acts persist in time through oral and written discourse. They can be interpreted and reinterpreted. Speech acts and communication also have referential and ontological functions, and can take on the power of a dominant collective discourse.

According to Ricoeur, the question of "who?" or "who speaks?" is simultaneously a question of "who acts?" The subject who acts is a person with feelings, thoughts, goals, intentions. The events enacted are related through emplotment to those attributes. Because of this, actions are not simply physical movements but subjectively mediated events in time. The "one who acts" is also the "one who suffers"—joy, pain, sorrow, triumph, defeat. The "one who acts," who suffers, bears the ethical and moral responsibility of his or her actions in relation to another and to others.

On this account a given instance of informed consent is the narratively structured action of patient and physician in relation to each other. Both experience informed consent narratively in time as it occurs, before the speech acts are gathered together into a communication process and narrated as the patient's consent and the physician's understanding of that consent. As a narratively structured action, an informed consent generates new actions, for example those of enacting the agreed-upon medical intervention. The action of informed consent is open to constant reinterpretation. It can be validated, or not, against the "logical criteria" of a dominant model agreed upon by the collective. A dominant model represents informed consent as a collective moral action paradigm to be interpreted and reinterpreted in each instance of informed consent. Each instance has the capacity to develop new paradigms and constitute new worlds of interpretation, even to become a new dominant moral action paradigm. In other words, a given act of informed consent takes on mimetic, referential, and ontological functions beyond the control of the agents, patient and physician, of that particular consent.

Informed consent is an illocutionary speech act. Saying (or writing) "I consent" constitutes the performance of the act of consent itself. In saying "I consent," I exercise a right and give a decision in favor of a certain course of action. My consent is based on another's informing. "I inform" is an expositive illocutionary speech act: that is, in informing one gives an exposition about a topic. However, it is also a perlocutionary speech act in that it produces certain consequential effects on the feelings, thoughts, or actions of the listener. It does this in a nonconventional, nonritualized, personal way, through the personal rhetorical style of the individuals involved, as well as in the collective conventional way, or acknowledged ritual, of an illocutionary act as determined by the collectively agreed-upon "rules" for an informed consent.

Both the dominant collective moral narrative and action paradigms and the individualized narratives, actions, and interpretations of them condition the process of the informing. To understand informed consent as a performative speech act is to focus on the subjects speaking as having personal thoughts, feelings, and intentions, and mutual powers of persuasion that are important to the meaningfulness of informed consent as a particular speech action within a collective paradigm, and to emphasize the interdependence of the particular patient and physician within that paradigm. One's consent constitutes a comment on and communicates an attitude toward the informing and the informant. One's consent commits one *and an other* to a certain course of action— the patient informs the physician of his or her consent and the physician consents to act on this information. In signing a written consent, the patient publicly (medicolegally) names him- or her-self as the agent or author, "I," of the consent and designates the physician as the executor of the agreed-upon intervention. The physician who signs the chart note or procedure report publicly names him- or her-self as the agent or author, "I," of the information of the patient's consent and of the physician's consent to execute its mandate. Physician and patient, informer and consenter, executor and trustee are, like these mirror signatures, twinned authorial and agential deictic functions within individual and collective narratives.

Informed consent as narrative action is thus primarily praxis, action in relation to another. Yet informed consent in the current dominant disclosure model is usually thought of as a series of discrete unidirectional acts *on* or *to* an other, that is, informed consent is comprised of a sequence of acts done *onto* an other: the physician discloses information *to* the patient; the patient consents *to*, or refuses to consent *to*, the physician's execution of the intervention; the physician performs the intervention *on* the consenting patient. Informed consent is also usually thought of as a mental exercise between patient and physician—indeed, often as an unequal and thus unfair duel of wits—one that results in physical movements by the physician on the patient's body. In this way the current dominant model of informed consent reproduces and reinforces the mind-body dualism that continues to dominate medical discourse despite the advent and propagation of the "biopsychosocial" model. Moreover, while the right to informed consent in the current dominant model belongs to the patient, the responsibility for both the procurement of the consent and the results of any intervention is usually thought to fall solely on the physician—or at least is experienced so by physicians. The burden of this responsibility is reflected in the metaphors physicians live by,[14] where, in the medical vernacular, patients "have complications *on*," "go sour *on*," or "die *on*" physicians (as in: "I don't want this guy to die *on me*, not *on my* shift"). The suffering, the emotion, of the physician as "one who acts" is ignored, neglected, or dismissed in a paradigm that privileges the patient as the (etymological) "sufferer" in a restricted negative emotional sense; and splits rights and responsibilities between an (infantilized) patient who must be protected and a (demonized) physician who must be held in check.

While this paradigm may reflect certain "truths," it artificially segregates and categorizes patient and physician, dehumanizing each in the process, reducing each to a formalist substantive sameness of the person with the role narrowly defined (as, for example, *all* patients are *only* submissive, *all* physicians are *only* authoritarian) and of the person over time, each impenetrable to dialogue with the other or with the broader collective. It splits consent and intervention, minds and bodies, as if informed consent were not a mentally and physically mediated action leading to future mentally and physically mediated actions. It separates action from feeling, as if "to feel" were not "to act," as if actions were not taken by feeling subjects, both patient and physician, as if "to consent" were not *consentire*, to feel with, to feel together.

Informed consent as narrative action emplots feeling subjects, their actions in relation to one another, and the temporal order in which they interact. It engages these selves as another in open dialogue with each other and with a mutable collective action paradigm. It engages patient and physician, as they undertake their present action of generating together future actions, to feel with (oneself as another); to feel together (oneself and an other); to share rights and responsibilities for oneself, another, and others.

Informed Consent as Narrative History

While narrative history may seem to be redundant, Ricoeur uses the term to distinguish a narrative from an empiricist approach to the discipline of history, specifically historiography, the collective recounting of events in time. Unlike an empiricist approach, which pretends to an objective description of reality, a narrative approach recognizes its configuration of events in time and the power of this configuration to refigure the perception and interpretation of reality. Narrative history relies on the example of the transformative imaginative potential of literary narratives to transcend the impasses of rational thought and physical evidence in the description and redescription of human historicity. Narrative historiographic explication clarifies the confusion of the phenomenological experience of historicity and thus increases understanding. It integrates the time of the self and the other, the time of the subject's individual experience of historicity in relation to that of the intersubjective, collective experience. Like other narratives, narrative history has mimetic (descriptive), referential (creative), and ontologic (truth-making) functions. However fictitious it may be, as an explicitly historical rather than fictive enterprise, historical narrative overtly bears the *cachet of truth* (my term). In addition, every culture elevates certain "grand narratives" to broader truth paradigms that give meaning and structure interpretation.

What is true for the history of communities, groups, peoples, is true for individual life histories. They are narratively structured configurations of actions temporally refigured in the recounting. They explicate the confusion of experience and integrate it into individual and collective interpretive paradigms. Mimetic, referential, and ontologic, biographies and autobiographies have the cachet of truth about oneself.

Narrative history, whether individual or collective, answers the question: Who is recounting oneself? To recognize oneself as a character in a story, whether that story is narrated by oneself or another, is to recognize one's capacity to configure and refigure one's story and oneself. The choices made in the narration, in the configurations, and in the refigurations are ethical (at the collective level) and moral (at the individual level).

Contemporary informed consent is a collective narrative history, a refiguring of narratively configured events told and retold as a major paradigm of what constitutes moral medical action since World War II. Although at least one of the roots of contemporary informed consent, the Nuremberg Code, derives from a seemingly universally (internationally) agreed-upon need to protect persons from becoming uninformed and unwilling subjects of experimentation, the current dominant model of informed consent is highly influenced by particular currents in post–World War II culture in the United States. The evidence not only of the Nuremberg trials but of the Tuskegee experiment and a host of other historical and legal events[15] has been temporally configured and imaginatively conjoined to the growth of consumerism, litigation, individualism, and an ideological shift away from hierarchical to egalitarian relationships, away from physician paternalism in the name of beneficence to respect for persons in the name of patient autonomy. The individual and collective phenomenological experiences of these events have been clarified from a number of perspectives through bioethical explications—particularly principlism, but also rights-based ethics, virtue theory, deontology—themselves historical, occurring in time, making history, narratively configured and reconfigured in time, temporal. These explications reconfigure the events into a narrative history of informed consent that describes the past, creates a moral imperative, and has the *cachet* of truth.

The claim to *universal* truth of this particular "grand narrative" that valorizes informed consent as a fundamental element of bioethics and configures informed consent in a very specific way (one primarily based on a principlism, which usually denies narrativity) facilitates the expectation of universal meaningfulness to all within and without the North American mainstream culture. However, the expectation and the experience do not necessarily fit together well.

The explanation of the illness experience, the role of medicine, and the nature of the ethical physician-patient relationship offered by this grand narrative do not necessarily fit with the individual patient and physician experience of a specific instance of informed consent in North American culture or in other cultures. These stories of inadequacy, of meaninglessness, of increased confusion and negative feelings, have also become part of the collective history of informed consent, and have contributed to the generation of alternate approaches to principle-based bioethics, including narrative bioethics itself.

While the collective history of informed consent serves as a "grand narrative" for the interpretation, explication, and configuration of specific instances of informed consent, each specific instance of informed consent is also a narrative history. Taken together, the narratively configured speech acts in the communication of informed consent are refigured into an oral history composed of the interconnected discourses of each subject as person and role. This history provides a description of events over time—the informed consent process—and an interpretation of their meaning, the consent act which generates new actions. The oral recounting has the *cachet* of truth and is refigured into a written narrative history in the shape of the completed and signed written consent form. In both oral and written modes, informed consent has autonomous mimetic, referential, and ontologic functions recognized by the collective institutions of a culture (professional disciplinary bodies, health legislation, bioethics literature) as well as by the individuals involved in the particular instance of informed consent. Particular instances of informed consent refigure the collective narrative and individually and collectively configure future instances of informed consent.

The narrative history of a particular instance of informed consent is one of the narratively configured events in an individual's life-narrative. In the narrative history of one's life as a cohesive whole, in which one resembles oneself over time while not remaining atemporally identical to oneself, the experience of an informed consent, the events leading up to it, and the events leading out of it, are explicated and integrated into one's individual narrative paradigms about oneself and interpreted through the collective paradigms that shape one's recognitions of oneself as another. The narrative history of a particular informed consent and its related events will have descriptive, referential, and ontologic functions within the narrative life history. However fictitious it may or may not be, an informed consent and its biopsychosocial concomitants will have the cachet of truth about oneself.

This truth about oneself has meaning also for "others as oneself" (my term), for biological and nonbiological family members whose narrative identities include beliefs about themselves based on themselves as another and an other in relation to familial narrative paradigms. These narratives, constantly configured and refigured, and their open, dynamic meanings extend generationally and intergenerationally. The narrative histories and narrative identities of generationally contemporary family members, attentive to the present, are transformed by the illness, medical, and bioethical narratives of another family member. At the same time, the present memories of living and nonliving ancestors are narratively refigured, just as the future expectations for descendants, born and to be born, are narratively configured in the explicative light of this new information and comprehension (of heritable illness, for example, whether "inherited" through biology, learned behavior, or psychological repetition; or of response to illness, to medical authority, to the ethical norms of one's day, and so on). Individual and familial "grand narratives" of informed consent and its concomitants have the potential to figure, configure, and refigure the broader human collective narrative history of illness, medicine, and medical ethics.[16]

Informed Consent as Narrative Identity, Action, and History

The answer to the question "who?" in the fourth modality: Who is the moral subject? comprises the answers to the other three, Who speaks? Who acts? Who recounts oneself? Ricoeur's speaking subject, who acts, suffers, and recounts him or her self through the recognition that his or her autonomous self is self as another, solicits another and, taking moral responsibility, requires justice for the other. Narrative identity, action, and history form a dialectical link between linguistics and ethics.

In this study of a Ricoeurian poststructuralist narrative hermeneutic approach to the specific ethical paradigm of informed consent, narrative identity, action, and history have overlapped and intertwined to create a model where patient and physician are interconnected persons and roles with shared values of autonomy, solicitude, and justice that allow for sensitivity to cultural difference. They are engaged in a speech action that integrates individual expression and the demands of a collectively agreed-upon set of paradigms for that expression, includes the emotional experience of both patient and physician, and weds the mental and the physical. Together patient and physician create a narrative history of a specific instance of informed consent with individual, familial, and collective, mimetic, referential, and ontologic resonance through the past and the present—without determinism or hegemony.

As a Ricoeurian poststructuralist narrative hermeneutic, informed consent is an experiential, expressive, and interpretive action with sensitivity to the individual, relational, and cultural factors at play in the process and the outcome. The paradigms within a specific instance of informed consent are simultaneously integrated with the broader collective narrative of informed consent in this society. Moreover, each instance is an interpretation of the collective narrative and reinterprets and refigures it, just as each refiguration of the collective narrative affects the interpretation of future and past instances. Because the individual and collective narrative histories of informed consent are open works, and because of their triple present (past memory, present attentiveness, future expectation), they escape the determinism of past narration characteristic of substantive narrative ethics. The specific instances and the broader collective narrative of informed consent have the cachet of truth, but one that can be transformed mimetically, referentially, and ontologically. Indeed, this poststructuralist narrative hermeneutic approach is in itself a configuration to be refigured.

Through the primacy of narrative as figuring all identifications, all actions, all "real" and "fictive" stories, and all interpretations, this approach to informed consent accords with and can be adapted to Hilde Lindemann Nelson's three categories of narrative approaches to bioethics—the casuistic classification of clinical stories, the close reading of literary stories, and the particularized telling of life stories.[17] It is particularly compatible with the essence of any potential fourth: the use of narrative as creating meaning, not just showing it.[18] Moreover, rather than a narrative approach that can be optionally applied to moral questions from outside human experience, expression, and interpretation, in a poststructuralist view narrative is an omnipresent structure of identity, action, and history, an inescapable structuring of human (phenomenological) experience, (linguistic) expression, and (cultural) interpretation, whether one chooses to focus upon it or not, whether one adopts it as a point of worldview or not. A poststructuralist narrative hermeneutic approach does not see narrative creating meaning so much as meaning being narratively created. Narrative, then, cannot be merely optional, even if one can choose to make it a greater or lesser focus of attention.

The advantages of other narrative approaches as outlined by Nelson still obtain: giving moral theory a "personal turn"; working "up close" to construct ethical accounts that honor the particular and the personal but do so in a nonarbitrary way; constructing the moral ground projects that constitute the agent's core identity and give life its meaning.[19] Also, the poststructuralist narrative hermeneutic approach to informed consent described here, grounded in and illuminating individual and collective moral terms, resists the Scylla and Charybdis of a loss of moral weight and a divorce from the detail of the particular story, the two dangers Nelson identifies for narrative ethics.[20] While this has been but a preliminary study, it justifies increased attention to the transformative potential of a Ricoeurian poststructuralist narrative hermeneutic approach, not only for informed consent, but for our contemporary bioethics as it looks forward to the twenty-first century.

Notes

1. The standard medicolegal model of informed consent is not explicitly referred to in professional codes of ethics, but the tenets of these codes implicitly reprise its five components. See, for example, the American Medical Association's 1980 *Principles of Medical Ethics*, the American Psychiatric Association's 1981 *Principles of Medical Ethics with Annotations Especially Applicable to Psychiatry*, the Canadian Medical Association's 1986 "Policy Summary: Informed Decision-Making," and the Royal College of Physicians and Surgeons of Canada Bioethics Committee's 1987 *Informed Consent: Ethical Considerations for Physicians and Surgeons*.

2. This model and definition are derived from Ruth Faden's and Tom Beauchamp's *A History and Theory of Informed Consent* (New York: Oxford University Press, 1986) and represent the authors' synthesis of the dominant model from the historical, legal, philosophical, and clinical literature on informed consent. Although we are now in the mid-nineties the medicolegal disclosure model they describe prior to developing their own model still dominates.

3. See, for example, Alan W. Cross and Larry R. Churchill, "Ethical and Cultural Dimensions of Informed Consent," *Annals of Internal Medicine* (1982):96:110–113; Afaf Ibrahim Meleis and Albert Jonson, "Ethical Crises and Cultural Differences," *The Western Journal of Medicine* (June 1983):889–893; Joseph M. Kaufert and John D. O'Neil, "Biomedical Rituals and Informed Consent: Native Canadians and the Negotiation of Clinical Trust," in *Social Science Perspectives on Medical Ethics*, George Weisz, ed. (Boston: Kluwer Academic Publications, 1990), pp. 41–63.

4. See, for example, Howard Brody, "A Transparency Model of Informed Consent," *Hastings Center Report* (September/October 1989):5–9.

5. This paper is part of a larger work in progress on a narrative approach to informed consent and the integration of this approach with poststructuralist linguistic and psychoanalytic approaches into a new interdisciplinary model of informed consent.

6. The approach would allow for the difficulties of the less common situations where these criteria are not met (through incompetency or nonvoluntariness), but elaboration of this approach to such situations is beyond the scope of the current study.

7. "Consent" includes its opposite, "refusal," these terms being retained as opposed to "choice" in order to address the current dominant model, the traditionally constructed "informed consent."

8. The primary texts for this study are:

Paul Ricoeur, "Ce qui me préoccupe depuis trente ans," *Esprit, numéro spécial, La passion des idées* 8–9 (août-septembre 1986):227–243.

———"Le discours de l'action," *La sémantique de l'action* (Paris: Centre National de la Recherche Scientifique, 1977), pp. 3–63.

———*Du texte à l'action: Essais d'herméneutique, II* (Paris: Éditions du Seuil, 1986), available in English as *From Text to Action*, trans. Kathleen Blamey and John B. Thompson (Evanston, IL: Northwestern University Press, 1991).

———"Entretien," *Éthique et responsabilité: Paul Ricoeur*, ed. Jean-Christophe Aeschlimann (Neuchâtel: Éditions de la Baconnière, 1994), pp. 11–34.

———"Expliquer et comprendre: sur quelques connexions remarquables entre la théorie du texte, la théorie de l'action et la théorie de l'histoire," *Revue philosophique de Louvain* 75 (Autumn 1975):126–147, available in English as "Explanation and Understanding: On Some Remarkable Connections among the Theory of the Text, Theory, Theory of Action, and Theory of History," in *The Philosophy of Paul Ricoeur: An Anthology of His Work*, eds. Charles E. Reagan and David Stewart (Boston: Beacon Press, 1978), pp. 149–166.

———"L'identité narrative," *Esprit, numéro spécial, Paul Ricoeur* 7–8 (juillet-août 1988):295–304, suivi d'un Débat, 305–314. Ricoeur's text is available in English as "Narrative Identity," trans. David Wood, in *On Paul Ricoeur: Narrative and Interpretation*, ed. David Wood (London: Routledge, 1991), pp. 188–199.

————"Individu et identité personnelle," *Sur l'individu*, Actes du Colloque de Royaumount (Paris: Éditions du Seuil, 1987):54–72.

————"The Model of the Text: Meaningful Action Considered as Text," *New Literary History* V(1) (1973):91–117.

————"Pour une théorie du discours narratif," *La narrativité*, ed. Dorian Tiffeneau (Paris: Editions du CNRS, 1980), pp. 1–68.

————"Récit fictif-récit historique," *La narrativité*, ed. Dorian Tiffeneau (Paris: Éditions du CNRS, 1980), pp. 251–271.

————*Soi-même comme un autre* (Paris: Éditions du Seuil, 1990), available in English as *Oneself as Another*, trans. Kathleen Blamey (Chicago: Chicago University Press, 1992).

————*Temps et récit*, 3 vols. (Paris: Éditions du Seuil, 1983–1985), available in English as *Time and Narrative*, trans. Kathleen McLaughlin and David Pellauer, 3 vols. (Chicago: University of Chicago Press, 1984–1988).

9. Hilde Lindemann Nelson, "What's Narrative Ethics?" *Center View* 4 (2) (October 1995):1–2.

10. For a complementary view of the persons in informed consent, see Jan Marta, "Whose Consent Is It Anyway? A Poststructuralist Framing of the Person in Medical Decision-Making," *Theoretical Medicine*, forthcomng.

11. See Alasdair MacIntyre, *After Virtue* (South Bend, IN: Notre Dame University Press, 1981).

12. As proposed by John L. Coulehan in "The Word Is an Instrument of Healing," *Literature and Medicine* 10 (1989):111–129.

13. I have discussed a number of the issues raised in this section in a complementary manner in "A Linguistic Model of Informed Consent," *The Journal of Philosophy and Medicine* 21:41–60.

14. The basic structure of the metaphor in George Lakoff's and Mark Johnson's *Metaphors We Live By* (Chicago: University of Chicago Press, 1980), moving from physical experience to representation of the more abstract, is particularly apt here.

15. See Faden and Beauchamp, *op. cit.*

16. Concretely, this does occur through the importance of "the family history" in medical genetic research, for example, even though the narrative structure is usually suppressed or underplayed in the presentation of "scientific" results; and through the individual and societal concerns for the ethical impact of genomics on future generations possessed of, and possessed by, the resulting transformative new technologies.

17. Nelson, *op.cit.*, pp. 1–2.

18. *Ibid.*, p. 2.

19. *Ibid.*, p. 1.

20. *Ibid.*, p. 2.

FOUR

Narratives Invoked

14

Aphorisms, Maxims, and Old Saws
Narrative Rationality and the
Negotiation of Clinical Choice

Kathryn Montgomery Hunter

> Every physician is a different kind of gambler.
> ———*Ernest W. Saward, MD*

Although medicine draws much of its knowledge from the biological sciences, its practice relies on moral knowing. Like bioethics, which it comprises, clinical medicine requires the use of narrative, interpretive reason. A physician's practical know-how arises from experience with particular cases, both directly, in the care of patients, and vicariously, through oral and written reports. Transmitted and refined as diagnostic and therapeutic plots, this practical reason is summarized and expressed in aphorisms, old saws, and rules of thumb. These habits can be traced to the Hippocratic corpus, which includes not only the first case studies but also a collection entitled *Aphorisms*. Twenty-four hundred years later, such apparently unscientific wisdom still informs clinical education and the care of patients, and the parallel between this exercise of narrative rationality and the process of working out the best course of action in bioethics is instructive.

Clinical medicine's old saws and rules of thumb are frequently uttered but seldom argued—or argued with. Yet almost every one of them can be contradicted by a maxim or an aphorism of equal weight and counterforce. Far from being truly paradoxical, however, these contradictory maxims express the complex relation of knowledge and action in a field where information changes, its application to particular situations is radically uncertain, and every general rule seems to have its exception. Although the existence of clinical aphorisms has been noted[1] and their value asserted,[2] they have not been much studied. Like the moral at the end of a Victorian children's story, they are the summation of experience, what "everybody" knows—or ought to. Taken alone, they can be understood as mini-narratives, allusions to exemplary stories that could be told if there were time or pedagogical need. As reminders of life's practical lessons, aphorisms and maxims differ in status from test results and statistical studies. Far more *ad hoc* and personal, they can be challenged but are not precisely testable. Individual clinical teachers may polish their favorites or consider whether they have repeated them too often, even whether they should use them at all. But no one in academic medicine convenes a teaching conference on the better use of maxims or aphorisms; nor does anyone—teacher or learner—pay much attention to the fact that one may conflict with another. As part of the currency of medical discourse they pass all but unnoticed, their importance to clinical knowledge sensed but not well understood.

Despite their lowly status, clinical aphorisms play a role in clinical reasoning, the case-based process that characterizes rationality in clinical medicine.[3] Especially in academic medical centers, an ongoing practical inquiry into the relation of knowledge and action in the care of particular patients takes place daily, almost hourly, on every specialty service. These discussions of individual cases—narrative accounts of medical attention beginning with the patient's presentation of symptoms—model the clinical reasoning that is the goal of medical education. Whether undertaken silently to monitor a thought process or in public to communicate with colleagues and students, the construction of the case is the rational procedure followed by every physician, in and out of academic medicine. As conversation, these cases constitute much of the profession's communal knowledge and collegiality. As part of a clinical conference, their formal presentation is the occasion for scrutinizing the rational steps in diagnosis and treatment choice and thereby is a means of educating students and residents and maintaining the skills of the experienced. There, in the discussion of interesting or troublesome cases, physicians invoke the familiar maxims. "The diagnosis is usually made from the history," they'll say. Or, "Keep in mind Occam's razor." The sayings have the ring of collective wisdom. They counsel the young and trump the opposition. They are collegial reminders of the weight of accumulated experience and an effective means of closing off discussion. These are clinical medicine's summary guidelines, its operational rules.

This essay examines aphorisms concerned with history-taking, the physical examination, diagnostic reasoning, and therapeutic choice—activities at the core of clinical judgment and vital to the quality of medical care.[4] These sayings fall into a complex and fundamentally skeptical pattern of paradoxical pairs. In this, they resemble aphorisms more generally: "a penny saved is a penny earned," but "you can't take it with you"; "silence is golden" although "honesty is the best policy." Such contradictory wisdom is possible, even inevitable, because proverbs embody practical, experiential rules rather than invariant or generalizable principles or axioms. In medicine, each half of a contradictory pair has as its aim the judiciously balanced application of scientific knowledge to an individual patient. But the clinician must choose; it is impossible to follow both at once. This structure suggests that in the care of patients there is often no invariably right answer (although there clearly may be wrong ones). As a consequence, the practical education intended to inculcate clinical judgment is not a deductive, scientific undertaking but a tug-of-war between worthy but competing admonitions about how a clinician is to know the wiser, better course of action. Medicine might be practiced and learned without these old standbys, of course. But their wide and constant use underlines the contingent, time-dependent, contextual nature of clinical knowledge. Aphorisms are part of medicine's counterweighted, often paradoxical method of teaching and reminding in an uncertain, case-based domain of knowledge.

History-Taking

The diagnosis is usually made from the history.

. . . the patient denies alcohol use . . .

One of the most venerable pieces of clinical wisdom concerns the patient's account of the illness. "Listen to your patient," young physicians are counseled. "He [or she] is telling you the diagnosis." This is often stated as a statistical rule, one that is noteworthy for its assertion of approximate probability: "Eighty percent [in some versions 90%, but always at least three-quarters] of your patients can be diagnosed from the history." But this wisdom, however strongly stated, however well confirmed by thinkers in medical informatics,[5] has uphill work to do against medicine's ingrained skepticism about the history, history-taking, and, especially, the patient as a historian.

This clinical skepticism is clearest in accounts (written and oral) of the patient's presenting history. "The patient denies any history of alcohol use, IV drug use, or risk factors for HIV" a medical resident will intone in presenting a case—even when the patient is an 82-year-old great-grandmother with no symptom or life circumstance suggestive of such a history. The social history reveals she's the widow of a clergyman? It makes no difference. Everyone has had a case like *that*—or has heard of one. Textbooks of physical diagnosis and interviewing reinforce the skepticism.

Other history-writers have similar doubts about their sources of information, but physicians are especially dependent on the personal report of events by the individual most affected. They are aware that the information they acquire is always partial and, even with a well-intentioned, honest informant, potentially flawed. Like biographers and political and social historians, physicians must be as sure as possible of their data even as they inevitably exercise creativity in putting together the information they elicit.[6] For this reason they label the patient's account "subjective," although critics point out that it is no more subjective than their own observation of the clinical signs.[7] Oddly enough, this habitual suspicion does not necessarily contradict the high regard in which the patient's history is held. The oft-alleged claim that the patient "knows" the diagnosis or its pathognomonic clues and is thus the most important source of diagnostic information is not inconsistent with a generic skepticism, the belief that truth is less "out there" to be discovered than constructed by the perceiver in collaboration with the patient or in a community of discourse. Yet, over time, in the community of discourse that is clinical medicine, a physician's sense of that larger skepticism can slip away, replaced by a persistent, commonsensical suspicion of the patient's reliability and an unwillingness to waste time, look foolish, be misled—or, worst of all, be duped.

The value of the history remains, even as head CTs are ordered before the most routine lumbar punctures are permitted on fevered patients with flexible necks and no hint of headache. In the care of patients, a potential exception, especially one with an irreversibly bad outcome, trumps even the most reassuring statistics. After all, 5 percent or 15 percent or perhaps even 25 percent of patients *cannot* be diagnosed from their history, and this patient may be one of them. Two or three emergency room patients with no symptoms of increased intracranial pressure have died from lumbar punctures; better get a head CT on this one. Thus contradictory beliefs about the reliability of the patient's history have come to coexist almost side by side. So long as the risk to the patient is minimal, each serves as a corrective to the other.

> Always record the chief complaint in the patient's own words.
>
> If he says he has "gallbladder trouble" . . . ignore it.[8]

The fate of the chief complaint is an epitome of the tension in which the reliability of the history is held. At least as early as the creation of the Atchley-Loeb interview form in the 1920s, students were asked to record the patient's answer to "What brings you here today?" in the patient's own words.[9] But in this medically sophisticated time, the chief complaint (in British usage the "presenting" complaint) is often viewed as all but useless. William L. Morgan and George L. Engel leave it out of their classic introduction to patient care, and others have followed suit.[10]

Despised, undercut, the chief complaint nevertheless can be found in the case write-ups in almost every academic medical institution, although seldom now in the patient's own words. "CC:" the chart will read, "s.o.b." Shortness of breath is resolutely *not* a diagnosis; good clinical procedure forbids jumping to a diagnostic conclusion no matter how obvious—even if the patient literally reports it.[11] "S.o.b." is an intermediate construction, a medicalized symptom, an interpretation by the physician as history-writer. Few people come in saying: "I'm short of breath." They say instead: "I've been having a lot of trouble breathing lately," or "I can hardly draw a breath," or "I just can't pull the stairs like I used to," perhaps accompanied by a dominant hand high and flat on the chest. And is "shortness of breath" always an accurate medical translation? How many of those who actually say the words are short of breath in just the way the physician understands it as he or she writes, a little too easily, "s.o.b."? Engel has described the clinical peril in interpreting the patient's approximation as fact: a patient whose complete workup for hemoptysis, including bronchoscopy, had revealed nothing that could explain his coughing up blood turned out to have come to the doctor because he was "spitting blood," an entirely different matter.[12] In *Talking with Patients*, Eric J. Cassell defends the inclusion of the chief complaint in the case history and argues for recording it in the patient's words. He believes it must be addressed—trouble sleeping in a sitting position? help with daily activities? those stairs?—before the clinical encounter is over, even if it turns out not to be the actual problem, especially if there is no medical problem at all.[13] Unlike the history as a whole, which is both unanimously revered and universally suspect, there is no consensus on the value of the chief complaint. The patient's words may mislead or they may provide an important clue. Learners will hear advice on either side of the question.

Clinical Intuition

> Always do a review of systems.
>
> A good clinician will have an index of suspicion. . . .

In the initial interview with a patient, is the physician's mind to be a blank slate? Or is it an intuitive steel trap ready to close upon the first good hint? Students are traditionally cautioned against a premature narrowing of the diagnostic focus. To reinforce this, they are taught always to do a review of systems in which—no matter how specific the patient's chief complaint or how well it is supported by the patient's medical history—they ask questions about the other organ systems of the body. Like the custom of recording the chief complaint and other symptoms as subjectively reported observations rather than according them a diagnostic label, the review of systems is part of a suspension of diagnosis that is held to be essential to clinical objectivity. The survey of the rest of the body is a pledge of the physician's refusal to jump to conclusions, a hallmark of clinical thoroughness, the antidote for premature (and thus often inadequate) diagnostic closure. "Any chest pain? Any change in bowel habits?"

Yet experienced physicians are likely to omit the review of systems, even when their schedules are relatively unhurried. Most can tell stories of diagnoses that they or their illustrious professors have made "at forty feet": "I walked into the room and I could tell right away . . . ," one will say. Whether from the history or the patient's appearance, "every good clinician has an index of suspicion, a clinical intuition . . . ," another explains. A chief of dermatology, six months after the event he describes, still sounds amazed: "I hadn't seen a case since I was in the Air Force in Biloxi twenty years ago, fresh out of residency. But the minute she walked in, the signs were unmistakable. I did a history, of course, but I knew what it was the whole time."

Only recently has there begun to be a serious consideration of clinical intuition. Leaps of diagnostic insight involve the skillful reading of signs, many of which—like clubbing of the finger ends—are well established in clinical lore. Some skillful reading by an expert clinician becomes so rapid or "compiled" as to be all but undetectable.[14] Some leaps, however, rely on subtler (or less often taught) social signs. Faith T. Fitzgerald has enumerated many of these: the evidence of clothing, body habitus, possessions.[15] This clinical semiotics brings to consciousness the often-unacknowledged details that inform the experienced observer: lopsidedly worn shoes, asymmetric holes in a recently let-out belt, chipped fingernail polish. Patricia Benner, a pioneer in describing the relation of intuition to the development of clinical expertise, has argued that experts actually forget the rules of diagnostic procedure and orient themselves situationally with each new patient.[16] Faced with the characteristic inability of experts to formulate general rules to which there are no exceptions, Edward Feigenbaum, an originator of artificial intelligence (AI), once remarked: "At this point, knowledge threatens to become ten thousand special cases." Herbert L. Dreyfus, a philosopher who has long criticized AI as insufficiently contextual, and Stuart E. Dreyfus, a psychologist whose work on expertise inspired Benner, concur with Feigenbaum. They maintain that experts reason not by inference but "holographically," and therefore Feigenbaum's frustration is an accurate description of the difficulties faced by those who would model clinical expertise.[17]

With research into clinical reasoning and the diagnostic process, the relation between clinical intuition and the review of systems has begun to be clarified. Arthur S. Elstein and his colleagues established in 1978 that diagnostic skill is not separable from knowledge. It does not exist without the relevant clinical information that education provides.[18] Thus the review of systems is a useful fallback strategy for those who are either not yet (or not in this situation) experts. When Jerome Kassirer and G. Anthony Gorry looked at the self-reported reasoning process of experienced clinicians presented with the case of a patient suffering from kidney failure, they discovered that nephrologists, the appropriate specialists, asked relatively few questions in order to reach the diagnosis, while equally expert cardiologists, here out of their field, resorted to a review of systems. "Headaches?" the cardiologists asked, turning to a review. "What did you take for them?" "How much aspirin?" "Every day?" " For how long?" Although they asked many more questions than the nephrologists, the nonexperts were able to reach an accurate diagnosis: aspirin-induced kidney failure.[19] Given a good stock of general clinical knowledge, a physician's survey of symptoms in apparently unrelated organ systems proves invaluable in the absence of the specific, detailed, specialized information and experience that constitute expertise. The duty to conduct a review of systems with every patient, inculcated early, remains the default mode for clinicians who are not in the grip of overriding certainty.

Progress in understanding diagnostic reasoning has recently led some clinical teachers to modify their instruction to medical students. Rather than being given a procedural rule that will be contradicted by the practice of experienced clinicians, students may now be advised to proceed as those elders do, by forming a general idea of the malady—a "working diagnosis"—early in the clinical encounter, then testing and refining it as the interview proceeds. It will be interesting to see whether this practical acknowledgment of the way diagnostic reasoning really works will be as successful a teaching device as the old paradox. Will these new physicians be as thorough? Or will they be too confident of their first impressions? Will they resort to a review of systems at the right moment? Or, lacking the early injunction to "always do a review of systems," will they stick with a narrowed vision far too long or miss comorbidity, a second disease? This new pedagogy discards the old paradox that enjoined physicians both to suspend judgment and to form an initial impression of the diagnosis. This reduction of the tension between competing expectations reduces the student's anxiety, but it risks eliminating what was valuable in the old paradox: the maintenance, in beginner and routinized practitioner alike, of a certain balance, a consciousness, no matter which way they work through a diagnosis, of another way of proceeding.

Physical Examination

> Fit clinical observations to known patterns.
>
> Take account of every detail and weigh them all carefully.

Like the patient's history, the physical examination poses the question of whether the physician's proper clinical focus is the particular or the general, the immediately apparent malady or the full spectrum of bodily signs and symptoms. The answer is "both." Students learning the physical examination are advised to pursue their clinical suspicions. On the other hand, they are warned not to ignore or fail to give proper weight to any single finding. It boils down to "Focus!" and "Notice everything!" Each, of course, is good advice. The first maxim, to work by means of well-established patterns—that heart disease, for example, may also involve impaired lung function—is a practical help in threading the thickets of clinical signs. After all, as Perri Klass observed in a moment of witty despair, "all written descriptions of all clinical presentations of all diseases are similar: if you list every possible presenting symptom, eventually they all overlap."[20] But what if, in the process of fitting shortness of breath to the pattern of congestive heart failure, the clinical student fails to notice lung disease? The second rule applies: notice everything, take it all into account.

What do judicious physicians do with what they have noticed if one of the details does not fit a standard pattern? And what happens when a thorough investigation turns up an anomalous sign? Often it is just that ill-fitting detail—an inspiratory rub that does not sound like a splinter hemorrhage in a fingernail or an "ordinary" pleural rub—that can lead to a more precise diagnosis of the patient's malady or to a more efficacious treatment.[21] But that ill-fitting detail is just as likely to be a red herring. Here, as so often in his explication of The Method, Sherlock Holmes's handling of anomalous bits of information epitomizes medicine's practical reasoning. Two well-known examples point in opposite, apparently contradictory directions. In "The Six Napoleons," Inspector Lestrade puzzles over the villain's habit of breaking the valuable busts of Napoleon he has gone to great effort to steal: "Well, Mr. Holmes," he inquires, "what are we to do with that fact?" Holmes answers promptly, "To remember it—to docket it. We may come upon something later which will bear upon it."[22] But in *A Study in Scarlet* he responds quite differently to the discovery of an unexpectedly inert pill, hand-rolled by the man he believes to be the murderer:

"Surely my whole chain of reasoning cannot have been false. It is impossible! And yet this wretched dog is none the worse. Ah, I have it! I have it!" With a perfect shriek of delight he rushed to the box, cut the other pill in two, dissolved it, and presented it to the terrier. The unfortunate creature's tongue seemed hardly to have been moistened in it before it gave a convulsive shiver in every limb, and lay as rigid and lifeless as if it had been struck by lightning.

Sherlock Holmes drew a long breath, and wiped the perspiration from his forehead. "I should have more faith," he said; "I ought to know by this time that when a fact appears to be opposed to a long train of deductions, it invariably proves to be capable of bearing some other interpretation." (pp. 51–52)

Far from merely remembering or recording the anomaly, waiting for its significance to emerge, Holmes reinterprets it according to the account of the crimes he has retrospectively constructed: this is no ordinary villain; relying on divine providence he has offered his victims a choice of two pills, only one of which is poison.

Is this a contradiction in The Method? Only when the two rules are taken out of the context of their narratives. The situations in which the anomalous detail appears are in fact quite different. The refusal to interpret that is practical early in an investigation makes no sense near the end of a diagnostic process. Thus, when a younger physician, puzzling over an ominous but ill-fitting test result, stands poised on the brink of the "cascade of uncertainty,"[23] about to order more complicated and expensive, perhaps more invasive tests to determine the cause of an unexpected lab value, wise clinicians—the very people who earlier may have urged careful weighing of all the data—have been known to adopt Sherlock Holmes's insight. "Stick to your guns," they will advise. "The lab may have made a mistake. Do the test again."

Diagnostic Tests

The delivery of medical care is to do as much nothing as possible.[24]

Sutton's Law

Maxims about testing, like those about choice of treatment, participate in the clinical tension between watchful waiting and the "full court press." Because the testing options are so numerous as to constitute whole layers, new algorithms, in the process of clinical reasoning, physicians must be as knowledgeable about the options and the dangers, benefits, and limitations of available tests as they are about the therapy entailed by the results. Good clinical practice nowadays includes the ability to choose tests wisely and in the most efficient order so as to minimize pain, blood draws, financial costs, and time elapsed until diagnosis. Often these goals conflict, and so also does the received wisdom about testing strategy. The ideal, of course, is the diagnosis that can be made with certainty from a pathognomonic sign or symptom: a pain like an elephant sitting on a middle-aged man's chest, yellow eyeballs, or a tender, swollen temporal artery. Next best is a single, sensitive, specific, wholly reliable test.

But many diagnoses are not so easily made. The thirteenth law in Samuel Shem's underground classic, *The House of God*, is: "The best medicine is to do as much nothing as possible." This maxim is customarily associated with therapeutic nihilism, the belief that medicine's role is to assist the body to heal itself, but the law applies equally well to testing. Students and residents are admonished to test sparingly, but what is to be spared? The patient's pain and inconvenience? Money? Time? Fearful suspense? The staff's time and inconvenience? The hospital's or an HMO's money? The best critical path from differential diagnosis to diagnostic conclusion is not necessarily the shortest, and attempts to be expeditious risk premature closure. The goal is to avoid until necessary the invasive (and expensive) tests like CT scans and angiograms. Such technological advances not only have eliminated most "exploratory surgery" but also have made obsolete some of internal medicine's subtle diagnostic strategies. Still, in the intellectual exercise that is internal medicine, a physician who lacks tact and judgment in testing strategy is not only wasteful and inconsiderate but almost unsporting.[25] Those who resort to CT scans when simpler tests or a good history and physical would do as well risk their colleagues' scorn.

Yet, when the diagnostic stakes are high or there is some likelihood that an invasive test will ultimately be necessary, the usual prohibitions and cautionary advice may be set aside. In these circumstances, the neglect of finer points of test-choice strategy in the single-minded pursuit of a diagnosis is often justified by an appeal to Sutton's Law. The eponym does not derive from an honored researcher or clinical teacher but from an infamous outlaw. Asked why he robbed banks, Willie Sutton is said to have replied: "Because that's where the money is." The law is parenthetically interesting as unintended evidence of the continued fiscal innocence of academic physicians, who can invoke Sutton's Law even these days without hearing the double meaning that a critic of medical expenditure would surely hear. More important for pedagogical purposes, the reference to an outlaw (rather than to the similar Sufi tale of Nasrudin or the "little moron" joke about searching for a lost object under a lamppost) acknowledges the violation of a clinical maxim, and the countermaxim has been elevated to a "law," however tongue-in-cheek. Like Sutton, physicians in this particular instance are outside the rules; like Sutton, they have their reasons. Sutton's name reminds physicians that a decision to opt for the quick diagnostic payoff may be justified, but it ignores the beneficent canons of technological restraint.

Diagnosis

> Look for a single diagnosis that can explain all the findings.
>
> It's parsimonious, but it may be wrong.

Reaching a diagnosis engages in a practical way the tension between the welter of the phenomenal world and the patterns imposed on it by biological science and medical culture.[26] As the problem of the anomalous detail suggests, when a physician considers what a patient's history and physical exam add up to, the number and complexity of signs and symptoms occasionally raise the possibility of two disease processes at work instead of one. "Entities should not be multiplied unnecessarily," William of Occam declared, and Occam's razor, as this rule is called, is the surgical instrument most favored in internal medicine. Beginning diagnosticians are cautioned to resist the allure of comorbidity, a double diagnosis that will account for all the details. The principle of parsimony is invoked: if there is an anomalous detail, there is probably a better explanation for the whole. Physicians are urged to look for something that can account for all the signs and symptoms, all the test results. But the quest for the elegant single solution is contradicted by the very real possibility, especially among the elderly and the poor, that one patient really does have two diseases. Like the possibility of a "zebra," a statistically improbable disease,[27] a small but measurable chance of comorbidity must be kept in the physician's store of clinical wisdom to be used only in cases of demonstrated logical need, when efforts to find a single, simple solution have failed. Not to remember that misfortunes are sometimes multiple can be a source of embarrassment or, worse, diagnostic (and thus therapeutic) delay.

Treatment

> Relieve the symptoms.
>
> Make the diagnosis.

Treatment often resolves the tension that pervades questions of diagnosis, but it can pose a paradox of its own. The physician's task is to relieve suffering. But just as medicine's traditional maxim, "First do no harm," seems to be contradicted by the pain of testing and treatment, so the immediate therapeutic imperative is often constrained by larger considerations of obtaining a diagnosis. Good treatment begins with a good diagnosis. The tension between these two duties can be seen in the case of serious infection. The symptoms are distressing—fever, chills, rigors, with the possibility of seizures—but if antibiotics are given immediately the chance to determine which organism is causing the trouble may be lost. Cure may be delayed and other people put at risk. Broad-spectrum antibiotics provide some escape from this dilemma: What does its precise identity matter as long as the unknown agent of infection is eliminated? But here, as elsewhere in medicine, there is a trade-off. What is broad may be poorly targeted: those antibiotics may not work as soon or as well as others that might have been chosen had adequate tests been done before the treatment began, and the consequences for others exposed to the disease must be put into the equation. In philosophy the word "empirical" designates the experience-based practicality characteristic of science, but in medicine it labels treatment given without proof of diagnosis, the epitome of "unscientific" though sometimes well-reasoned practice.

A fairly common, more troubling example of this tension between the alleviation of suffering and the diagnosis of the disease is created by the detection of widespread cancer with an unknown primary site. A biopsy is necessary to make the diagnosis, and therapy, "real" therapy targeted at the source of the spread as distinguished from palliation of the symptoms from the secondary site, is impossible without a diagnosis. The gomer-language puts it simply, if crudely: "no meat, no treat." But will the therapy make enough difference in the course of the disease to be worth the pain of obtaining the tissue sample? Careful analysis is called for, and a decision not to pursue the diagnosis almost always has an edgy, defiant feel to it. Geriatricians are far more comfortable than other physicians with forgoing diagnosis. In the past fifteen years they have come to a consensus that an elderly patient's functional status is more important than a test that may have only a marginal value.[28] Such tests include quite routine ones that may nevertheless disorient elderly patients or upset the social network that supports them.[29]

Clinical education can exacerbate this tension between diagnosis and the care of the patient, and the pedagogical version of the problem replicates, farther along in the clinical process, the paradox of advice and example that teachers employ with the review of systems. For example, the diagnosis of chronic arthritis separates patients into two categories: those with degenerative and those with inflammatory disease. The two forms of arthritis are distinct, and discriminating between them is essential for rheumatology fellows, who are subspecializing after an internal medicine residency. Yet, while clinical hunches are strong, a definitive test may be expensive, time-consuming, or painful, and,

at least in the initial states of therapy, the difference is immaterial for many cases
and not immediately important for any. No matter which form of the disease the
patient has, the treatment proceeds in slow stages from low doses of a relatively
mild agent to higher doses, then to graduated doses of a stronger drug—and so
on in ascending steps. The drugs prescribed for the two forms of the disease are
initially the same. Not until fairly far along in the treatment of a recalcitrant case
does it matter whether the arthritis is established with certainty as degenerative
or inflammatory. Should teachers teach diagnosis of the disease or treatment of
the patient? The answer, as with much else in medicine, is "both." This balancing
act can be maintained over a practice full of patients, or even an afternoonful.
But when "both" is a logical impossibility—in the care of an individual patient—
physicians habitually remind one another (and themselves) of the other,
unchosen half of the paradoxical pair. "You really need a diagnosis," they will say
if the patient has been treated "empirically." Or if the diagnosis has been
pursued, "It's also important to treat the patient's discomfort." Whichever rule is
followed, the other is likely to be invoked.

Practicing Medicine

The therapeutic imperative

Primum non nocere

Every clinical decision takes place within a tug-of-war between the physician's
pride of craft and a knowledge of its dangers. For this reason and because the
knowledge of those dangers is imperfect, medicine's therapeutic imperative is
countered by one of the oldest clinical maxims: Above all, do no harm. Although
both physicians and patients continue to speak as if the "side-effects" of drugs
were separable from their power, pharmacology is taught to medical students
with almost as much emphasis on risks as on therapeutics. A mutual suspicion
is encouraged between residents in internal medicine and the surgical special-
ties. They are *prima facie* representatives of medicine's opposite poles: dillydal-
lying versus the quick fix. The tension between doing everything and doing
nothing, particularly for people nearing the end of a terminal illness, has been
the object of scrutiny in medical ethics over the last twenty-five years. *The House
of God* caught the conflict as technology brought it to crisis in the 1970s: the
hospital of the title, font of healing miracles, is headed by men who were trained
to do their utmost to preserve life. But clean water, good nutrition, and a century
without war on the continent combined with medical science and technology to

yield a cohort of old people whose selfhood dies well before their bodies fail entirely. At the heart of Shem's satire is the Chief of Medicine's once-noble slogan: "Always do everything for every patient forever." Since the 1970s medicine and the society that holds it in such regard have had to learn that its limits are not the impossible but the absurd. The therapeutic imperative rightly remains central to medical practice. But against a narrow, purely technological under-standing of the need to act, clinical teachers now occasionally intone a new maxim, itself a paradoxical inversion, that could well be the motto of geriatri-cians and hospice physicians: "Don't just *do* something, stand there."

Maxims, Casuistry, and Clinical Rationality

Aphorisms and maxims are the summary formulations of the not-quite-invariant truths of clinical practice. They are the intermediate rules of medi-cine's clinical casuistry. Noting the similarity between case-based moral reasoning and medical diagnostics, Albert Jonsen and Stephen Toulmin defined casuistry as:

> the analysis of moral issues, using procedures of reasoning based on para-digms and analogies, leading to the formulation of expert opinions about the existence and stringency of particular moral obligations, framed in terms of rules or maxims that are general but not universal or invariable, since they hold good with certainty only in the typical conditions of the agent and circumstances of action.[30]

In their definition, maxims are the "formulas drawn from traditional discussions and phrased aphoristically which served as fulcra and warrants for argument" (pp. 252–253) in moral discourse. As part of the process of considering what in good conscience can be done in troubling situations, maxims serve to fit prevailing wisdom—traditional, authoritative,[31] experience-based but often unstudied—to the circumstances of the particular case under consideration. Jonsen and Toulmin might have been describing the discussion of a medical case, the discursive reasoning about what ought best to be done for a particular patient. In that clinical casuistry, physicians call upon a paradigm or "classic" case, on cases known to them that, like the present one, depart in similar ways from the paradigm, and on aphoristic rules of thumb that summarize accept-able, customary practice in similar circumstances.

Because clinical knowing is inescapably uncertain, the effective means devised for rational practice are embodied not just in clinical aphorisms, them-selves dogmatic enough, but in their paradoxical pairings. Through their contra-diction, learners faced with difficult clinical questions are reminded to balance the alternatives. The goal is not to find a middle way or a compromise between them, but to choose the better—or less bad—course of action in the circumstances. Nevertheless, each of these contradictory rules may be uttered as if it were the singular truth, and the physicians who invoke them by and large behave and teach as if there were no contradiction. By this means, teachers of clinical medicine may lay claim to science, but they hedge like racetrack touts.

How can a rational science-using enterprise tolerate such apparent contradictions? And how can physicians seem to ignore them? The explanation lies in the interpretive nature of clinical reasoning and its focus on one patient at a time. Diseases are not diagnosed and treated in petri dishes or test tubes but in human beings, where they complicate and develop over time; both disease and the patient are best understood in light of their history. Nor is an aphorism intended for general application. It is a situational maxim that has arisen out of (and proved useful in) circumstances very like those in this case. Thus when one half of an aphoristic pair suggests itself, the other not only may seem irrelevant but may not even present itself to memory. A maxim is always contextual and interpretive. Its context is the history of illness and medical attention as well as the medical narrative of diagnosis and treatment. Other observers may interpret events differently, and in that case, the clinician who invoked the aphorism is very likely to hear someone of equal or higher rank invoke its opposite.

If clinical rationality has this casuistical character and if it is what Aristotle in the *Nicomachean Ethics* described as phronesis— a case-based, experiential, hermeneutical reasoning—then it is not surprising that, as a part of the care of patients, clinical ethics must be described in much the same way. Like the rest of medicine's thinking about patients, its ethics is worked out between widely accepted general principles, which must be applied (from the top down) to particular situations, and the lived experience of those situations, which (from the bottom up) extend and challenge our understanding of the principles. Practical reasoning—whether in history, literary criticism, law, anthropology, or clinical medicine—circles between the general rules and the particular circumstance: hermeneutically, retroductively, narratively.[32] For the most part, our culture has given its attention in medicine and biomedical ethics to the top-down, science-like half, ignoring or despising or sentimentalizing what has escaped strict definition. In both fields this leads to a falsely objectifying, scientistic attitude toward the objects of knowledge. Knowledge needs to be as rigorous as possible, of course. But no more so. Pierre Bourdieu has written that "the progress of knowledge presupposes progress in our knowledge of the *conditions* of knowledge,"[33] and that seems to me to be the challenge both in the care of patients and in bioethics. The practice of medicine and its clinical apprenticeship are more complex and interesting, richer human activities than they are now understood to be. I suspect this is also true of bioethics as it is taught and practiced.

Acknowledgments

Thanks to Tod S. Chambers, Rowland W. Chang, Julia E. Connelly, Mary Mahowald, Michael Morgan, Douglas R. Reifler, William Tock, and the members of two groups that heard earlier versions: the Chicago Narrative and Medicine Study Group, particularly Bill Donnelly, Patrick Staunton, and Suzanne Poirier, and the case-based reasoning group in the University of Chicago Department of Computer Science, especially Jeff Berger.

Notes

1. Clifton K. Meador, *A Little Book of Doctors' Rules* (Philadelphia: Hanley & Belfus, 1992); I am indebted to Ann Folwell Stanford for bringing this book to my attention.

2. Frank Davidoff, "'Principles are Powerful': Aphorisms and Maxims Put a 'Racing Stripe' on Learning," *ACP Observer* (September 1994): 17. I owe this reference to Raymond W. Curry.

3. Kathryn Montgomery Hunter, *Doctors' Stories: The Narrative Structure of Medical Knowledge* (Princeton: Princeton University Press, 1991).

4. Throughout this paper I quote without attribution commonly heard aphorisms and maxims and the representative comments of clinical colleagues in several medical schools, primarily but not exclusively in departments of internal medicine.

5. Marsden S. Blois, *Information and Medicine: The Nature of Medical Descriptions* (Berkeley: University of California Press, 1984), p. 165.

6. As Leon Edel observed, "The biographer may be as imaginative as he pleases—the more imaginative the better—in the way in which he brings together his materials, but he must not imagine the materials." Cited by James Atlas, "When Fact Is Treated as Fiction," *New York Times*, 24 July 1994.

7. William J. Donnelly and Daniel J. Brauner, "Why SOAP Is Bad for the Medical Record," *Archives of Internal Medicine* 152 (1992): 481–484.

8. Simon S. Leopold, *The Principles and Methods of Physical Diagnosis: Correlation of Physical Signs with Certain Physiological and Pathological Changes in Disease*, 2d ed. (Philadelphia: Saunders, 1957), p. 9.

9. The Atchley-Loeb Form—still so labeled—continues in use at Columbia University; Rita Charon, personal communication.

10. William L. Morgan and George L. Engel, *The Clinical Approach to the Patient* (Philadelphia: W. B. Saunders, 1969).

11. The exacerbations of chronic disease are the exception. Such a case is written up as "carries a diagnosis of COPD" or "with a history of breast cancer," promoting this detail from the "past medical history" to an aspect of today's presentation.

12. George L. Engel, "Physician-Scientists and Scientific Physicians: Resolving the Humanism-Science Dichotomy," *American Journal of Medicine* 82 (1987): 109.

13. Eric J. Cassell, *Talking with Patients*, vol. 2: *Clinical Technique* (Cambridge: MIT Press, 1985).

14. Sherlock Holmes gives several similar explanations to Watson. In "The Blue Carbuncle," he hesitates to unpack the compressed chain of reasoning because, he says, explanation will make the feat seem quite ordinary. "Compiled" is the term used in cognitive studies, see Patricia Benner, below, note 16, and Georges Bordage and Madeleine Lemieux, "Semantic Structures and Diagnostic Thinking of Experts and Novices," *Academic Medicine* 66 (1990): S70–S72.

15. Faith T. Fitzgerald and Lawrence M Tierney, Jr., "The Bed-Side Sherlock Holmes," *Western Journal of Medicine* 137 (1982): 169–175.

16. Patricia Benner, *From Novice to Expert: Excellence and Power in Clinical Nursing Practice* (Reading, MA: Addison-Wesley, 1984).

17. Herbert L. Dreyfus and Stuart E. Dreyfus, "From Socrates to Expert Systems: The Limits of Calculative Rationality," in *Interpretive Social Sciences: A Second Look*, eds. Paul Rabinow and William M. Sullivan (Berkeley: University of California Press, 1987), pp. 327–350. They quote Edward Feigenbaum and Pamela McCorduck, *The Fifth Generation: Artificial Intelligence and Japan's Computer Challenge* (Reading, MA: 1983), p. 82.

18. Arthur S. Elstein, Lee S. Shulman, and Sarah A. Sprafka, *Medical Problem Solving: An Analysis of Clinical Reasoning* (Cambridge: Harvard University Press, 1978).

19. Jerome Kassirer and G. Anthony Gorry, "Clinical Problem Solving: A Behavioral Analysis," *Annals of Internal Medicine* 89 (1978): 245–255.

20. Perri Klass, "Classroom Ethics on the Job," *Harvard Medical Alumni Bulletin* 60 (1986): 36.

21. W. Scott Richardson and Douglas R. Reifler supplied these examples.

22. Arthur Conan Doyle, "The Six Napoleons," in *The Complete Sherlock Holmes* (New York: Doubleday, n.d.), p. 813. Subsequent page numbers are from this edition.

23. J. W. Mold and Howard F. Stein, "The Cascade Effect in the Clinical Care of Patients," *New England Journal of Medicine* 314 (1986): 512.

24. Samuel Shem, *The House of God* (New York: Richard Marek, 1978), p. 376. The thirteenth law itself comes close to being a self-contained paradox since its escape clause, "as much . . . as possible," is open to widely differing interpretations, some of which could countermand the nihilistic ideal. The Fat Man's "laws" are, of course, satiric maxims invented to counter the attendings', especially the Chief of Medicine's rule, "Always do everything for every patient forever."

25. David L. Sackett, W. Scott Richardson, W.M.C. Rosenberg, and R. B. Haynes, eds., *Evidence-Based Medicine: How to Practice and Teach EBM* (London: Churchill Livingstone, 1996).

26. Lynn Payer, *Medicine and Culture: Varieties of Treatment in the United States, England, West Germany, and France* (New York: Holt, 1988).

27. Kathryn Montgomery Hunter, "'Don't Think Zebras': Uncertainty, Interpretation, and the Place of Paradox in Clinical Education," *Theoretical Medicine* 17 (1996): 225–241.

28. Mark E. Williams and Nortin M. Hadler, "The Illness as the Focus of Geriatric Medicine," *New England Journal of Medicine* 308 (1983):1357–1360.

29. Jill A. Rhymes, Cheryl Woodson, Christine K. Cassell, et al., "Nonmedical Complications of Diagnostic Workup for Dementia," *Journal of the American Geriatric Society* 37 (1989): 1157ff.

30. Albert Jonsen and Stephen Toulmin, *The Abuses of Casuistry: A History of Moral Reasoning* (Berkeley: University of California, 1988), p. 257.

31. Tom Tomlinson, "Casuistry in Medical Ethics: Rehabilitated or Repeat Offender?" *Theoretical Medicine* 15 (1994): 5–20, points out that casuistry is also likely to be conservative; Mark G. Kuczewski argues that it remains capable of social criticism: "Casuistry and Its Communitarian Critics," *Kennedy Institute of Ethics Journal* 4 (1994): 99–116.

32. "Narrative, Literature, and the Clinical Exercise of Practical Reason," *Journal of Medicine and Philosophy* 21 (1996): 303–320.

33. Pierre Bourdieu, *The Logic of Practice*, trans. Richard Nice (Stanford: Stanford University Press, 1990), p. 1.

15

The Moral of the Story

Ronald A. Carson

The debate now well underway in contemporary medical ethics between proponents of philosophical and interpretive approaches to moral reasoning about the
relative merits and limits of these approaches recalls an exchange between David
Burrell and Stanley Hauerwas, and Edmund Pellegrino that occurred twenty
years ago. In a 1977 article[1] Burrell and Hauerwas made a case for narrative as a
form of rationality particularly well suited to ethical reflection. They argued that
the (then, and arguably, still now) prevailing pattern of moral rationality,
whether in a Kantian or utilitarian mode, distorts the moral life and ethical
reflection by providing no account of the way in which moral selves are formed,
by insisting on the separation of moral selves and their interests, and by limiting
ethical considerations to decisional aspects of morality. "We are given the
impression that moral principles offer actual grounds for conduct, while in fact
they represent abstractions whose significance continues to depend on original
narrative contexts."[2]

Narrative, Burrell and Hauerwas claimed, is "a form of rationality especially
appropriate to ethics."[3] In particular, it is the capacity of narrative to connect
contingencies that recommends it as a vehicle for ethical reflection. Narrative
aims not at explanation but at understanding. It moves us to ask: What
happened then, and then what. . . ? And whatever happens next in a narrative
will follow intelligibly, though not by entailment, from what occurred before as
the story unfolds. Moreover, according to Burrell and Hauerwas, narratives are

normative in that they shape our perceptions and mold our moral sensibilities and practices. We relate to each other along the lines of stories we adopt and are adopted by. Stories that speak to us transform us and our ways with the world.

Narrative may be able to accomplish many of these things, Pellegrino countered, but in order to decide which stories we *should* adopt, we must look beyond narrative. To decide among the stories competing for our attention those worthy of our allegiance requires that we "resort to more explicit reason and more general principles" than those internal to the stories themselves. "Without insistence on some elements of objectivism, we easily confuse coherence and plausibility with something very different, namely, moral truth."[4]

Echoes of this exchange of twenty years ago, I have said, are reverberating in contemporary discussions between applied ethicists and those of an interpretive bent. I want to say why I think Burrell and Hauerwas got the better part of the 1977 exchange and why in my view interpretive approaches—approaches that locate the moral of the story in the dynamic rhetorical space between its telling and its reception—are particularly well suited to moral inquiry and moral reasoning.

To make sense of ourselves and our world to ourselves and to others, we tell tales—tales of truth, tall tales, tales of wisdom and woe—and listen to tales told by others. Stories, with their beginnings, middles, and ends, redeem life from contingency and make it something other than a meaningless succession of events. We wouldn't tell stories if we didn't believe that "life is susceptible of comprehension and thus of management."[5] Storytelling presupposes faith in the followability of experience—not only the connectedness of events but their truthfulness as well.

By truthful, I do not mean veracious but true to life, and that not in the sense of meeting preexisting criteria or corresponding to a predetermined pattern, but rather plausibly hanging together and imaginatively disclosing to us something about ourselves or about the human condition that we need to know, something that both "figures" in the light of our understanding of what life is generally like *and* throws light on the road we've traveled and the path ahead. Take James Dickey's poem, "The Celebration."[6]

The Celebration

All wheels; a man breathed fire,
Exhaling like a blowtorch down the road
And burnt the stripper's gown
Above her moving-barely feet.
A condemned train climbed from the earth
Up stilted nightlights zooming in a track.
I ambled along in that crowd

Between the gambling wheels
At carnival time with the others
Where the dodgem cars shuddered, sparking
On grillwire, each in his vehicle half
In control, half helplessly power-mad
As he was in the traffic that brought him.
No one blazed at me; then I saw

My mother and my father, he leaning
On a dog-chewed cane, she wrapped to the nose
In the fur of exhausted weasels.
I believed them buried miles back
In the country, in the faint sleep
Of the old, and had not thought to be
On this of all nights compelled

To follow where they led, not losing
Sight, with my heart enlarging whenever
I saw his crippled Stetson bob, saw her
With the teddy bear won on the waning
Whip of his right arm. They laughed;
She clung to him; then suddenly
The Wheel of wheels was turning

The colored night around.
They climbed aboard. My God, they rose
Above me, stopped themselves and swayed
Fifty feet up; he pointed
With his toothed cane, and took in
The whole Midway till they dropped,
Came down, went from me, came and went

Faster and faster, going up backward,
Cresting, out-topping, falling roundly.
From the crowd I watched them,
Their gold teeth flashing,
Until my eyes blurred with their riding
Lights, and I turned from the standing
To the moving mob, and went on:
Stepped upon sparking shocks

Of recognition when I saw my feet
Among the others, knowing them given,
Understanding the whirling impulse
From which I had been born,
The great gift of shaken lights,
The being wholly lifted with another,

All this having all and nothing
To do with me. Believers, I have seen
The wheel in the middle of the air
Where old age rises and laughs,
And on Lakewood Midway became
In five strides a kind of loving,
A mortal, a dutiful son.

In the flash of a few lines we are transported to a garish and gaudy midway. Everything is lit up and in motion—all except the narrator, who ambles anonymously and aimlessly among whirling wheels of risk (gambling wheels) and havoc (dodgem cars). Until, that is, his attention is caught by an unlikely vision of his aging parents weaving happily through the throng. Their movements draw him after them. He struggles to keep them in sight and feels his spirit surge with each glimpse of them, arm in arm and laughing.

Then suddenly he experiences a dizzying reversal of emotion. "The wheel of wheels was turning the colored night around." He stands still and watches, almost incredulous, as they get into a seat on the ferris wheel and ride up and down "faster and faster, going up backward, cresting, out-topping, falling roundly." He watches until his eyes blur, as he tells us, from the speeding up of the lights on the spinning wheel. But also perhaps from tears that well up as something comes to him, dawns on him. As he merges once more with the moving mass of humanity, he looks down to see his feet among the others and understands as never before from whence he came. He recognizes that he is the issue of a "whirling impulse . . . the great gift of shaken lights, the being wholly lifted with another, all this having all and nothing to do with me." "All" because he is the issue of his parents' passion, "nothing" because when his parents were suspended in ecstasy at the moment of his conception it was just the two of them alone, together.

This is what the poet sees in the vision of his parents joyously suspended from the wheel above the midway. But there is more. "*Believers, I have seen the wheel in the middle of the air.*" Are we to recall Ezekiel's vision among the captives in Babylon? "As if a wheel had been in the midst of a wheel . . . and the spirit of the living creature was in the wheels"—a vision of liberation and renewal. Self-renewal, surely, as the poet senses himself transformed (his heart enlarged) in the five strides that take him away from his singular experience of his parents in the rapture back into the surging crowd. Renewed, too, by the recognition that his life is a gift (he sees his feet "Among the others, knowing them given"). But beyond this, there is a renewal of the covenant between the child and his parents in that the recognition that his life is a gift transforms the poet into "a kind of loving, a mortal, a dutiful son"—loving because his mother and father loved each other and him, dutiful in that but for them he would not be, and mortal because what goes up on the wheel of life must come down. *All* wheels.

Hans-Georg Gadamer describes hermeneutics as "coming into conversation with the text." If we think about my reading of the story in this verse on the model of a conversation, we can see how I was taken in by the text. Not taken in in the sense of "duped," but captivated and prompted to ask: And then what happened? The interpreter who is thus drawn in no longer stands in an assertorical position over against the text but rather engages it in dialogue. Hermeneutics transforms the habit of making statements about a text into the practice of having a conversation with it. "Conversation," as Gadamer reminds us, "is a process of coming to an understanding."[7]

> We say that we "conduct" a conversation, but the more genuine a conversation is, the less its conduct lies within the will of either partner. . . . [I]t is generally more correct to say that we fall into conversation. The way one word follows another, the conversation taking its own twists and reaching its own conclusions, may well be conducted in some way, but the partners conversing are far less the leaders of it than the led. No one knows in advance what will come out of a conversation. Understanding or its failure is like an event that happens to us. . . . [A] conversation has a spirit of its own, and . . . the language in which it is conducted bears its own truth within it.[8]

Such truth, the truth of understanding, is, I believe, what we ordinarily mean by the moral of the story. It means "I get it," but not in a sense that could be verified in a putatively higher court of correspondence and demonstration.

How then are we to handle disagreements? What if you were to say to me that my reading of "The Celebration" is off the mark? I would ask you what makes you think that, and we would be drawn into a three-way conversation with the poem. I would listen attentively, though not uncritically, to how you read the text, invested as I certainly am in my own interpretation but allowing that I may have missed something crucial, and acknowledging that we all need all the help we can get in coming to an understanding. But if I detected an attempt on your part to avail yourself of "objective" standards of interpretation, we would be drawn into a different sort of dialogue in which I would ask you to tell me the story of those standards and I would tell you why I think there is only the hermeneutic circle, why I think it's all wheels.

Notes

1. David Burrell and Stanley Hauerwas, "From System to Story: An Alternative Pattern for Rationality in Ethics," in *Knowledge, Value and Belief*, H. Tristram Engelhardt and Daniel Callahan, eds. (Hastings-on-Hudson, NY: The Hastings Center, 1977), pp. 111–152.

2. *Ibid.*, p. 126.

3. *Ibid.*, p. 130.

4. E. D. Pellegrino, "Rationality, the Normative and the Narrative in the Philosophy of Morals," in Engelhardt and Callahan, 1977, pp. 164, 163.

5. Lionel Trilling, *Sincerity and Authenticity* (Cambridge, MA: Harvard University Press), p. 135.

6. James Dickey, "The Celebration," in *The Whole Motion: Collected Poems, 1945–1992*, Wesleyan University Press by permission (Hanover and London: University Press of New England, 1992), pp. 209–210.

7. Hans-Georg Gadamer, *Truth and Method*, second revised ed. (New York: Continuum, 1995), p. 385.

8. *Ibid.*, p. 383.

16

Medical Humanities
Pyramids and Rhomboids
in the Rationalist World of Medicine

Lois LaCivita Nixon

Paradigm Shifts

> [G]eneralizations about patients without careful attention to their cultural
> background, their values, and norms could lead to a number of ethical crises.
> ——Afaf Ibrahim Meleis and Albert Jonsen

When medical students arrive on campus to begin training, they expect two
years of basic science classes (anatomy, physiology, biochemistry, and so on), the
first steps on a well-defined professional path. In recent years, however, humanities classes have become part of the curriculum in many medical schools, where
they provide other nonscientific materials and approaches for considering
diverse cultures and contexts of illness and care.

Students are caught off guard by my humanities class; some respond with
cries of disapproval ("what a waste!") or, alternatively, sighs of relief ("Boy, time
to breathe!"). For ten years I have directed a *required* introductory course in
humanities for all first-year students as well as a series of month-long *elective*
rotations during the fourth or final year. In each course, we search for understandings and interpretations of what humanness means by exploring literature,
art, poetry, and film with students accustomed to close scrutiny, precise measurement, and exaltation of facts in their basic science laboratories and classrooms.

Sometimes the interdisciplinary terrain mapped out in my classes is regarded as an abyss to be avoided but more often, it is hoped, as an unexpected vista.

Increasingly, I am concerned to find technologically wired medical students unimpressed and unmoved by discussions about cultural shifts and differences in our rapidly changing and barrierless world. Because first-year students are so bright and because their chosen profession centers on people, I assume that they are interested in an examination of currents shaping and reshaping systems of knowledge affecting all members of society. In addition, I assume that, with their privileged and more intimate relation to people when they are sick and vulnerable, medical students' interest in and exposure to cultural similarities and differences will be especially strong. After all, I reason, the so-called third wave or informational age shifts derive from scientific advancements close to their hearts: communication systems, the airplane, and medical technology. "Let's consider," I say, "how we got to this point, how these achievements improved and complicated not just our lives, but medicine as well. Isn't it fascinating to see how Eurocentricity gained its dominance and why it is currently in decline? And how do the changes in health care delivery systems correspond to broader cultural shifts sweeping across the entire world?"

My assumptions are wrong. The look on too many of their faces suggests that I am part of a fringe leftist group, or a proponent of some feminist plot, or possibly a dangerous pyschotic. Even though the front-row students generally beam approvingly, the majority are not interested or pleased by my enthusiastic commentary. I answer their disinterest with a suppressed scream: "You are rationalists! How can you not want to understand cultural relativism in a world comprised of previously unimagined behaviors, perspectives, and ecosystems?"

Recently, I received a flyer from Wayne State University announcing a conference entitled *World: Out of Order* that would address culture and the three-world theory. Wow, I thought, this looks pretty good: cultural identities, nationalist literatures, feminine art, power, and writing! It seemed so positive, almost celebratory, and, quite different in spirit to the urgings of speakers at the hospital meetings I frequently attend, who seem to be forcing wake-up calls for health care professionals. Typically, these programs include speakers who describe cultural inertia or an unwillingness by health care leaders to respond to major shifts associated with the decentering of Western civilization. Invariably, their remarks sound something like this:

> Paradigm shifts of unprecedented proportions are occurring in health care. Look around; everything has changed. The old rules for success no longer work. In fact, following old rules can cause failure in the new reality. Unfortunately, administrators and employees usually resist change and are, therefore, swept

along or over by changing forces and outcomes. Rarely are they positioned to influence, control, manage, or direct the changes that will dictate their future.

Although respectfully retired in the academic world, the phrase *paradigm shift* remains useful in other settings for describing complexities in a time when exclusion has been replaced by inclusion, when known organizational forms and information sources have been disrupted and restructured, and when socioeconomic and political disorientation and anxiety are commonplace and widespread.

If I am excited by a world *out of order*, to use Wayne State's phrasing, many students—and hospital colleagues—are anxious about the current *disorder* and want the world to be restored to *what used to be*. In fact, when members of the Society for Health and Human Values convene to explore ethical issues, we understand that many of the dilemmas or concerns are rooted in cultural dislocations—or paradigm shifts. Old stuff, we sniff; but if, as the hospital observations and warnings suggest, the topic is still in the introductory stage for health care leaders and our students, are we reading from different scripts?

When students are caught in and pressured by the inherited patriarchal model, they can be reactive and impatient with ways of seeing and interpreting that are beyond the controls of close scrutiny, careful measurement, and firm conclusion, a space where there is little room for ambiguity, nuance, and complexity; but the untidy texture of life is, in fact, the substance with which doctors must deal daily by mixing technology and human sensibility. The unwillingness to consider cultural distinctions and cross-cultural vectors demonstrates how they, like the health care leaders described above, are locked into industrial age familiarities such as bureaucracy, patriarchy, and institutionalism. Resistance to change is quite natural, especially when placed in historical context: this, after all, is not the first disruption in our Eurocentric framework.

Commenting on the decline of medieval theocracy and the currents of Italian Renaissance engulfing North European shores, John Donne insightfully observed: "the new philosophy calls all in doubt" (Donne 1973, p. 111). Indeed, an entirely new worldview was evolving, with more consequences than John Donne and his seventeenth-century metaphysician colleagues could possibly imagine: the eventual obliteration of one civilization for another. Secular humanism, its guiding impulse, provided the spirit for exploration and geographic discovery, scientific enlightenment, and invention that would enable the so-called industrial age to develop, take hold, and dominate—and with it, permit the eventual preeminence of medicine to its current status.

Now, as we stand at the precipice of change, sliding gracelessly from the industrial age into the informational age, descriptors such as "future shock" (used by the Tofflers) and "shock of the new" (used by art critic Robert Hughes) give John Donne's distant pronouncement new resonance; to a lesser and greater degree, we share his doubts and anxieties about a "new" unknown. Encrusted economies and obsolete institutions symbolized by the banking industry, General Motors, communications networks, and health care are being reshaped by a seemingly chaotic and frustrating kineticism that creates "an entirely new landscape of connections, of phenomena that cannot be reduced to simple cause and effect" (Wheatley 1992, p. 12).

Yet in spite of health care's tumultuous state and what I see as an opportunity to fix two flat tires on a bicycle rather than just one as we are inclined to do, medical education remains grounded in the rationalist culture: its commitment to analytical and logical cognition as the source and process for everything one needs to know about the patient. Kate Brown suggests a need for cultural rationality and an increased sensitivity for "teasing out solutions to the interpersonal and institutional challenges facing professionals who work in cross-cultural clinical settings" (Brown 1992, p. 86) but medicine's cultural relativism is derived from institutional constraints that have served those with authority and power and, quite logically, those with little incentive for initiating change.

In addition to the traditional skills, students preparing for the transformed environment need to understand more about the development, impact, benefit, and cost of the various factors contributing to profound changes in most institutions and bureaucracies. Previously focused on the curing dimensions of medicine within patriarchal hospital settings, physicians now must deal with a much wider picture of health care delivery, management, and patient involvement and decision-making. Complicated issues in health care, many deriving from technological advancements such as life support measures, neonatal interventions, genome determinations, and so forth, join with sociocultural and economic factors to create important areas of concern not just for medical professionals but for ethicists and humanists as well to consider and discuss.

If ethicists and humanists are using one text and health care leaders and students—by subjugation—another, how can we conduct meaningful explorations of issues that require a grasp of epistemological dynamics and, more specifically, how can humanities courses lead to discovery of the world as it has been—and is becoming? What does fiction offer students and leaders whose nineteenth-century orientations remain narrow and categorical with assumptions that say there is a single, unchanging cosmic realm out there to be found, that persons or groups of persons have intrinsic natures that are predictable and discoverable? How can we discuss physician-assisted suicide or death with dignity and the entire panoply of ethical issues with health care leaders and students, who, like Bartleby, Melville's tenacious scrivenor, prefer not to budge?

The Medical School Landscape

> The problem with medical schools is that in medical
> school, every medical problem has one best answer.
> —— *James Parsons, MD*

Tucked away on the back side of the college near the cafeteria, the bookstore, and the security station is an area reserved for the "gonnabes," the as-yet uninitiated Med I and II students who spill out of the large lecture halls every fifty minutes in a manner that reminds me of a playground at recess and a favorite Brueghel painting, *Children's Games*. Visually and verbally, the released students blink their way into sunlight to fill the large patio with their antics and sounds. It is breathtaking to see an otherwise uninhabited space transformed so completely by two hundred students intent on making the most of the ten-minute break between lectures, and I often time my entrances and exits so that I can witness up close the reversed baseball caps, the rush for coffee and cokes, the exuberance of ball-throwing, clots of animated students, few of whom by appearance and action seemed destined for medicine.

Later, when survival skills are established, the short white coat symbolizes the first of many mechanistic steps forward along the well-marked road toward full professional status. With the classroom left behind, the new third-year initiates move to the clinics, the hospitals, and into internship and residency. Most move forever into the white world of medicine to become, in the words of Molière, "le médicin malgré lui" (the doctor in spite of himself).

The patriarchal model, comprised of ladderlike, linear tasks, emphasizes that certain steps must be taken to achieve expected goals. The unruly students, as I see it, are set physically apart in their first two years, frustrated by their desire to care for patients *now*, counting the days until the short white coat is issued and a higher level of status is acquired. The first two years test their endurance; successful completion gains them access to the wider walkways and more patrician air. Baseball caps and baseballs are left behind for those who follow in their footsteps.

To someone who teaches required and elective humanities courses in a college of medicine at a major university, the following passage by Wallace Stevens easily describes the landscape and some first-year students who are stunned by the inclusion of literature and art in the medical school curriculum. "Give me a break," they moan. "I'm here to study science and medicine, not poetry." Seemingly undeterred, I pop two sonnets into my mouth while repeating in my most courageous voice, "Do not go gentle into that good night."

Rationalists, wearing square hats,
Think, in square rooms,
Looking at the floor,
Looking at the ceiling,
They confine themselves
To right-angled triangles. (Stevens 1972, p. 17)

I am grateful for Stevens's lines; they speak to my frustrations, becoming helpful descriptors for the challenges I face. In my Med I classroom, not unlike some other social academic settings, there is a strong inclination toward rigidity, toward absolutes, toward the confinement of thought described by Stevens. It's not a pretty sight, of course, especially in a profession that requires listening skills and an understanding of our *inability* to measure with any accuracy the most defining elements of the human condition: ambiguity, nuance, and complexity.

Psychic panic occurs when the following assignment is made:

> Here is a slide I want you to think about for a few minutes. It's a painting by Picasso or a drawing by Layton or a photograph by Eudora Welty. Write down your impressions, what occurs to you as you consider its content and style. In ten minutes I will collect your thoughtful comments.

Short writing assignments cause anxiety attacks; many are hyperventilating, visually distressed. Hands are raised to ask for clarifications: "Did you say how long this should be?" Do you want sentences or is a list okay?" "Can we think about it and hand it in tomorrow?" "Is there an answer you're looking for?" Their training and experiences have prepared them for objective examinations and the pouring out of memorized facts. That which is unexpected, unpredictable, and unmeasurable can be overwhelming for some students. If there is no absolute or accurate answer, the endeavor is dismissed; it is soft, unimportant, and unworthy of their attention.

Most students prefer, of course, to hear what senior physicians have to say, those who have reached the highest places on the medical ladder. In the patriarchal model, it is likely that I and my humanities class occupy the bottom rung on the figurative ladder, with basic science professors positioned only a few steps above. In spite of serious moaning by two dozen students in each first-year class, more than half of the students come back by choice in their fourth year, electing to read novels and plays (*A Thousand Acres, Joe, Cancer Ward, A Doll's House*) and to consider films subjectively (*Antonia's Line, Philadelphia, Boyz 'n the Hood, Passion Fish*). In addition, we visit with curators at different museums to determine what aspects of current exhibits provide commentary on social issues and concerns and how we feel personally about the subjective statements.

In year one, but more so in year four, the approach is relational or multifaceted rather than decisional or authoritarian, moving away from what Patti Lather called the "lust for absolutes, for certainty in our ways of knowing" (Lather 1991, p. 6) long dominant in patriarchal constructs. In year four there is a central theme, but the approach is postmodernist; we walk around the subject listening to several voices, perspectives, interpretations. The nonmedical materials move students away from textbook description and analysis, forcing them to discover connections, to re-vision ways of knowing what we know.

The class, like most humanities classes, is interdisciplinary, an alien concept in post-Flexnerian medical curriculums. The irony, of course, is that Flexner,[1] Osler, Welch, and other reform leaders at the turn of the century expected students to arrive at medical colleges with strong liberal arts training that would serve as a foundation for the standardized science courses, then in need of development. Medical humanities stirs class participants to deconstruct their own conclusions and preferences, to stretch beyond traditional boundaries, to raise new questions. To include such classes or to expect physicians to have solid background in the liberal arts is not a new idea at all, only one that was deemphasized when another need, scientific standardization, was indeed essential.

With Med IV students I am able to observe some measure of growth deriving from clinical experiences with life and death during the rigors of year three in a hospital setting. We debate, discuss, confess, and laugh; mostly we discover that different orientations and perspectives color interpretations. Usually, students come to value the importance of listening to voices with other pitches and intonations. Providing them with space for expressing their innermost thoughts is especially illuminating for me as I evaluate what I have been able to stimulate; the expression of contrary or difficult admissions serves to challenge my own expectations and sharpen my ability to deal constructively with consciousness-raising.

Pyramids

> We need the courage to let go of the old world, to relinquish most of what we have
> cherished, to abandon our interpretations about what does and does not work.
> ———Margaret J. Wheatley

In an effort to explain the appearance of disorder and the role of humanities in the medical school setting, it is helpful to think about the controversy surrounding a recent expansion project at the Louvre Museum. The project and its accompanying furor serve as an exemplar for cultural collisions and demonstrate how change and resistance to change disrupt a society's most fundamental assumptions. In 1988 when La Pyramide was under construction in the Louvre Museum's historic courtyard, Parisians gasped at the audacity and uncoventionality of I. M. Pei's appropriated icon. *Mon Dieu!* What had seemed culturally immutable—the undisputed monarch of museums—was radically transformed by the large geometric structure irreverently errected on the museum's doorstep, an in-your-face transgression! Gradually, visitors, even Parisians, have come to appreciate the multifaceted, multilensed installation that paradoxically blurs cultural distinctions while simultaneously enhancing our ability to see past, present, and future.

Precisely, I say, as I think about the norms at the the college of medicine, an industrial-age environment committed to disciplined observation of fact, the triumph of reason, and intense belief in cause and effect, determininism, objectivity, and patriarchal structures. I am, in fact, a pyramid, a phrase I enjoy repeating to myself. The materials I bring to students for another exploration of the human condition seem surpassing strange and at times controversial. Using unorthodox tools, primarily fiction, art, and film, I function like that pyramid, prompting students to listen for new sounds and to see with an untried lens. Mainly we are seeking stories that help to make connections. Whether the students like it or not, they are outwardly affected—they cannot ignore the pyramid on the steps . . . !

Literature's contribution to medical ethics "is not as a mirror but as a lamp," as Ann Hudson Jones reminds us (1994, p. 340), for illuminating ethical dilemmas with fictional materials that stretch the "intuitive and imaginative faculties of mind . . . [so that we] empathize with others, understand more fully what it means to be human, and develop moral wisdom." Jones's point can be illustrated by any number of "literary cases," including Hemingway's short story, "A Clean, Well-Lighted Place," Jane Smiley's novel, *A Thousand Acres,* Ariel Dorfman's novel, *Death and the Maiden,* or Edward Albee's play, *Three Tall Women,* all of which deal with uneven pathways followed by human beings on their separate journeys from birth to death.

"Let's Talk About It," for example, David Rinaldi's short poem, portrays how information is processed, ingested, examined, and felt. Here the physician narrator is caught between the professional world he has known and intrusive elements that bring palpable discomfort and an uneasiness that cannot be put aside; the poem invites thoughtful discussion and critical thinking. Furthermore, the poem's content and style reveal how intrusive popular culture is and how "the pyramid" cannot be discounted as irrelevant to medicine:

with all the talk
about Dr Death
news-bites sandwiched
between circus and tragedy
hesitantly I say
in my confusion
"I understand him"
but still . . .
as a physician
morally and ethically . . .
and yet . . .

and surreptitiously
remember
how very secretly
I thought
thought how
Dad's castrated body
lay crooked in
prostatic pain on
his sweaty Tennesssee cot
his wife's terminal phone voice
drawing out the daily news . . .
I calculated
how many of
those little pain-killers
it might take . . .
and silently remember
how I put it all
out of my Hippocratic mind
yet felt ashamed
for weakness . . .

and so I waited. . . .
(Rinaldi 1995, pp. 389–390)

The physician-narrator twists and turns to reveal contradictory feelings, competing philosophies, and situational discomforts leading to provocative and unsettling ethical quandaries. As he slips between reason and passion, the poem captures an essentially human impulse. The absence of an answer or conclusion is especially appealing: how refreshingly unmedical, how puzzling for students in restrictive settings where structure and content of the environment reinforce cultural stasis and rationalist resolve. It is the initial impact or the collision between old and new realities that makes us unable or unwilling to act. The role of education is to help students gain practice in experiencing unsettling ideas and events, so that when they become doctors, they can better respond to life's inherent complexities. This training, of course, is analogous to or corresponds with hands-on practice with technical procedures in medicine.

The Doctor in Spite of Himself

> Oh I suppose I should
> wash the walls of my office
> polish the rust from my
> instruments and keep them
> definitely in order. . . .
> ——*William Carlos Williams*

The contemplative narrator in the poem is a physician, like Williams, who poses questions to himself about what he "ought" to be doing or what is expected of him as a physician. Readers listen to a list of tasks that would establish order, routine, and cleanliness. The physician-speaker provides a catalogue of small actions designed to establish an image appropriate to his profession, one in which he might "never think anything/but a white thought" (p. 127). In my classes, both of them, we step out of bounds to look under, around, and through the white coat to consider the human being and the human condition. Just as Williams's narrator felt restrained by the white coat, the "white thought," and what he was "supposed" to do, so do my class and I. Like him, we transgress traditional boundaries to seek out broader explorations, meanings, and interpretations.

A few weeks ago, my elective cluster of students and I began our approach to aging, the central topic for our month-long rotation. During the first meeting, when I asked students to relate their impressions of the elderly, I immediately heard about sick, even dying patients on respirators, encountered by them during the third year. I had not asked about infirm or hospitalized patients; rather, my inquiry centered on people who might be described as elderly.

We began again, this time with questions. What does elderly mean? Name and describe elderly people you know. What characterizes elderly people? This time I learned mostly about their grandparents and neighbors, but still, the emphasis was on a grave or final illness. Assignments included films, novels, several poems, and short stories, including "A Clean, Well-Lighted Place," by informal meetings with other faculty and community figures, a museum visit, and a trip to the mall. In addition, students selected a specific visual artist so that they could seek out nonverbal representations of the elderly for presentation in the class meetings.

At the end of the month, students had completed all assignments, contributed to the scheduled discussions, and provided classmates with repro-duced images that included paintings, sculpture, and photographs. In general their comments about aging now focused on nonillness issues such as family, friendships, compassion, sensitivity, thoughtfulness, and intelligence. Indeed, many elderly men and women may be incapacitated by their illnesses, but others, they agreed, are living lives that should not be framed by medicine.

Toward the end of the rotation, on a morning when I had been scheduled to speak at Tampa General's pastoral care grand rounds, I asked the students to become copresenters. The unwarned pastoral group responded to the unex-pected format of student inclusion with genuine interest and enthusiasm, almost as if medical students were an unfamiliar breed. After I made opening comments to thirty fellows ranging in age from 35 to 65 about the rotation, its goals, and assignments, the prepared students managed the remaining time. They intro-duced themselves, then turned to the Hemingway story by way of providing an introduction, a shared oral reading, and an exchange of interpretative remarks. It was impressive to watch the well-prepared students move from the story to narrative threads that had been identified by them in two prep sessions. Issues relating to dignity, isolation, loneliness, cultural and generational differences, and mortality were identified as they surfaced in the story, but students easily referred to other assigned and unassigned fiction and films. What the old man needed, one said, was community; another compared the two waiters at the small but well-lighted and clean bar where the old man had come for brandy. The younger waiter was impatient, eager to go home, while the older waiter, more thoughtful of the transiencies of life and his own place in the aging process, was sympathetic and more respectful. Generational differences such as these were introduced and responded to by various students. They thought aloud about light and dark, about the old man's journey into the night, about dignity, cleanliness, and respect.

The students, skilled in close observation of detail, had, as it were, dissected the story in their customary way before gathering among themselves for discus-sion of those details in preparation for our meeting with the pastoral group. Medical students have little difficulty with facts, but the need to reconstruct those facts into a meaningful presentation forced them to explore subjective elements in the fiction as they prepared together for their assignment. Emphasis on subjectivity in the medical school environment is unusual but, when assigned, can produce worthwhile results. Students seldom have an opportunity to express their personal feelings and interpretations; as this exercise demonstrated, an opening of the floodgates revealed a normally suppressed and highly energetic capacity for opinion and storytelling. The lively discussion with the pastoral group extended forty-five minutes beyond the scheduled time, with requests from both groups that another session should be arranged. No single point of view dominated.

The separate but common experiences of pastors and students provided other perspectives, as did the comments from various members who were African-American, Indian, and Hispanic. Because pastoral care is hospital based, some of their remarks dealt with patients, but students by and large continued to emphasize situations in which the elderly enjoyed good health or situations in which illness was inappropriately stressed or pronounced.

Rhomboids

> The classroom represents a rare arena for reasoned, honest, controlled, and sage discussion. . . . But if we lack diversity in the classroom, if we lack a range of opinion and personal experience, little learning with occur.
> ——*Christopher MacGregor Scribner*

This, I thought, is an aspect of narrative ethics for developing leadership in an uneasy society; caring, well-read, and thoughtful persons gathering to define problems, gather data, and understand the legal parameters, delineate the options, and reach some consensus. My role is one of license, of providing materials not usually found in the medical curriculum and creating an environment for reflection and civil discourse, preparing the students for an engaged citizenry in a world that must go forward, must be borderless, and must be funded in both knowledge and responsibility.

When rationalists in square rooms are dismissed by the narrator in Wallace Stevens's poem, he goes on to offer an alternative suggestion that, like the pyramid structure in Paris, provides a description of humanities classes in the medical school setting:

> *If they tried rhomboids,*
> *cones, waving lines, ellipses,*
> *half moons*
> *Rationalists would wear sombreros.*
> (Stevens, "Six Significant Landscapes," p. 17)

In spite of students squawking about nonmedical materials, their impatience with nonphysician lecturers, their occasional display of unattractive arrogance, *fiction and art* do get under their skin: they are remembered and recalled unexpectedly and involuntarily. Students may be trained in square rooms, but the world they face is composed almost completely of "rhomboids, cones, waving lines, ellipses, half moons." According to Howard Brody, as students move into their residency programs they need "an appreciation for the particular narratives of individuals . . . [that] constitute a person's life in sickness and in health" (Brody 1987, p. xii). "Sombreros" serve metaphorically to suggest that the world is culturally complex—an idea embodied in fiction—and of paramount importance to a profession dealing with human realities. What better place for those about to practice medicine to grapple with complexity, nuance, and ambiguity than the safety of the classroom? Together as learners, teachers and students may come together to realize that in the end, artists and writers of fiction

> press upon our minds the deepest mysteries, so we may feel again their majesty and power . . . [which] seizes our lives, and which reveals us startlingly to ourselves as creatures set down here bewildered.
> (Dillard 1989, pp. 72–73)

Acknowledgment

The poem "Let's Talk About It" by David Rinaldi (copyright 1994 by the Association for the Behavioral Sciences and Medical Education) is reprinted with the permission of ABSAME as it appeared in *Annals of Behavioral Science and Medical Education* (volume 1, issue 2, page 118).

Note

1. In 1910 Abraham Flexner, a consultant for the Carnegie Institute, reported that American medical schools were in dire need of a standardized curriculum, one that emphasized science and research. Flexner and other reform leaders, however, assumed that medical students would have strong liberal arts training prior to medical training. Unfortunately, the needed emphasis on science displaced expectations about liberal arts, so that students entering medical schools increasingly concentrated on basic science courses.

References

Brody, Howard. (1987) *Stories of Sickness*. New Haven: Yale University Press.

Brown, Kate. (1992) "Death and Access: Ethics in Cross-Cultural Health Care." In E. Friedman, ed. *Choices and Conflicts: Explorations in Health Care Ethics*. Chicago: American Hospital Publishing, Inc., 85–93.

Dillard, Annie. (1989) *The Writing Life*. New York: Harper and Row.

Donne, John. (1973) "The First Anniversary." In Barbara Lewalski and Andrew J. Sabol, eds. *Major Poets of the Earlier Seventeenth Century*. New York: The Odyssey Press, 105–119.

Harrison, Laird. (1992) "Aging Grace." *The New Physician* 41, (6):18–22.

Hughes, Robert. (1981) *The Shock of the New*. New York: Knopf.

Jones, Ann Hudson. (1994) "Literature as Mirror or Lamp." *Journal of Clinical Ethics* 5 (Winter): 340.

Lather, Patti. (1991) *Getting Smart: Feminist Research and Pedagogy with/in the Postmodern.* New York: Routledge.

Meleis, Afaf Ibrahim, and Jonsen, Al. (1983) "Ethical Crises and Cultural Differences." *The Western Journal of Medicine.* (June): 138: 889–893.

Rinaldi, David. (1995) "Let's Talk About It." In Richard Reynolds and John Stone, eds. *On Doctoring* (2nd ed.). New York: Simon and Schuster.

Scribner, Christopher MacGregor. (1996) "Racial Diversity Matters Within the Classroom, Too." *The Chronicle of Higher Education.* May 24.

Stevens, Wallace. (1972) "Six Significant Landscapes." In Holly Stevens, ed., *The Palm at the End of the Mind.* New York: Vintage Books, 15–17.

Toffler, Alvin. (1971) *Future Shock.* New York: Bantam Books.

Wheatley, Margaret J. (1992) *Leadership and the New Science.* San Francisco: Berrett Koehler Publishers.

Williams, William Carlos. (1984) "Le Médecin Malgré Lui." In Robert Coles, ed. *The Doctor Stories.* New York: New Directions Books.

17

Narrative(s) Versus Norm(s)
A Misplaced Debate in Bioethics

James F. Childress

Writing on narrative ethics legitimates telling stories. And my interest in narrative ethics has its narrative contexts, both personal and professional.

First, on the personal level, my beloved wife of almost 36 years died in August 1994 following an eighteen-month battle with non-Hodgkin's lymphoma. Since we had started dating seriously when we were sixteen, we were actually together longer than 36 years. In effect, our individual life-stories were largely our joint story. Her illness and premature death thus forced me to consider how to weave her story—our joint story—into my ongoing story.

This project was further stimulated by wife's main request as she lay dying: that I not let our grandson, then only two and a half years old, forget her. They had a wonderful relationship even though he was so young. Not forgetting, not letting our grandson forget, requires stories. Thus, for myself and for our grandson, I have had to try to connect past, present, and future in a narrative context.

Second, my approach to bioethics reflects what many term "principlism," which, over the last several years, has received vigorous criticism from various kinds of narrativists. I have tried to attend carefully to these criticisms, because I believe we learn more from critics than from supporters and because shifts in intellectual paths often occur from boredom rather than from problems with a particular paradigm.[1]

My title in this essay modifies one used by my teacher, James M. Gustafson, about thirty years ago—"Context Versus Principles: A Misplaced Debate in

Christian Ethics."[2] In his influential essay, Gustafson argued that the debate over context versus principles is no longer "fruitful": "The umbrella named 'contextualism' has become so large that it now covers persons whose views are as significantly different from each other as they are different from some of the defenders of 'principles.' The defenders of the ethics of principles make their cases on different grounds, and use moral principles in different ways." Gustafson further argued that context and principles represent two of the four major base points in Christian moral discourse (the other two are theology and moral anthropology), and that, whatever a Christian ethicist's starting point, each of the other base points will appear, either implicitly or explicitly.

Even though I borrow from Gustafson's title, there are some important differences between our approaches. First, Gustafson concentrated on Christian ethics, while I will focus on ethics broadly conceived—philosophical, religious, and especially practical ethics, including bioethics.

Second, I will often use the broad term *moral norms* of action, rather than the more precise language of moral principles and rules. Moral norms (hereafter "norms" without a modifier) include both principles and rules as "general action guides specifying that some type of action is prohibited, required, or permitted in certain circumstances."[3] I will construe principles as more general norms, which often provide warrants for rules, and rules as more concrete and detailed specifications of the type of prohibited, required, or permitted action. Principles and rules differ in their degree of specificity, but both are norms of actions that are distinguishable from particular judgments in concrete situations.

Third, Gustafson noted that the term "context" marks off no particular position because it covers so many different possibilities, ranging from the Christian community to the actual political situation. Here I deal with narrative(s) as one type of contextual approach to ethics.

However, my topic is not "narrative ethics," at least not in its broadest sense: It is rather "narrative (and norms) *in* ethics." I put matters this way to emphasize that I do not conceive ethics to be exclusively norm-based or even norm-driven. Instead, I will focus on the relations between norms and narratives in ethics. Both, properly understood, are essential and indispensable to ethics—the difficult questions concern their relations. My approach is not as dramatic as some other ways of formulating the problem, but it is, I believe, the most accurate and fruitful way.

At the risk of serious oversimplification, I will distinguish the direction I take from some other possibilities by altering the prepositions connecting ethics and narrative as well as the location of the terms "ethics" and "narrative." Possibilities other than "narrative *in* ethics" include the "ethics *of* narrative," which might refer to the ethics of narration and, equally importantly, the ethics of listening. I will briefly discuss the ethics of narrating and listening in the context of interpreting the norm of respect for persons. I will also only mention in passing the "narrative *of* ethics" when I note the importance of tradition, community, and the like, without trying to resolve the larger question of the narrative *grounds of* ethics.[4]

I won't discuss at all "narrative *for* ethics," by which I mean the use of narrative, mainly but not exclusively fictional narrative, to engender such moral qualities as empathy. In at least some of its versions, such an approach includes "ethics *in* narrative" (with attention to form as well as content) as a way to use "narrative *for* ethics." Still another approach to "narrative *for* ethics" might focus on the "narrative *background of* ethics"—for example, the understanding of the moral self in terms of narrative, an understanding that usually invokes such themes as time, history, community, emotions, and virtues, among others that normist approaches sometimes appear to neglect.[5]

Such a schematic interpretation of narrative ethics, or narrative and ethics, clearly depends not only on the different prepositions and locations of the key terms (narrative and ethics), but also on the content given to those terms, since narrative includes, for instance, cases, traditions, and fiction.

My overall thesis, which echoes Gustafson's charge, is that the debate about narrative(s) versus moral norm(s) in ethics and bioethics is (largely) misplaced because too many different positions fall under each umbrella category, and many of the most vigorous "opponents" in the debate, whether narrativists or normists, actually share more with each other than they recognize and more than they have in common with some who are usually placed in the same camp. Hence, we have to reconsider the broad labels that have probably already outlived any usefulness they ever had.[6] I will focus first on the controversy about cases and case judgments in relation to norms, then I will turn to the role of narratives of different kinds in explicating requirements of the principle of respect for persons, and finally I will examine the tension between personal and communal narratives in the context of appeals to experience and appeals to traditional norms. The last two parts will proceed by reference to two controversial cases.

Cases and Case Judgments in Normative Ethics

I want to start with the largely misplaced debate between casuists, as one type of narrativist, and principlists, as one type of normist, who appear to dispute the relation between the particular and the general, that is, the particular case judgment and the general moral norm. Each side has contributed to misunderstanding. For instance, normists, such as Tom Beauchamp and myself, have contributed to misunderstanding by our language of theory, applied ethics, application, and so forth, as well as by charts that appear to involve only top-down justification.[7] And casuists such as Albert Jonsen and Steven Toulmin have over-stated their position by unfurling such banners as "the tyranny of principles," when, in fact, they oppose only certain conceptions of principles, that is, princi-ples that are viewed as absolute, invariant, and eternal.[8] Only such principles are tyrannical. In general, principlists who view general norms as *prima facie* binding, rather than absolute, and who consider application an oversimplification, have more in common with many casuists than with many of their coprinciplists.

Casuists have greatly illuminated contemporary moral discourse and deliber-ation by directing our attention to cases, which, after all, are mini-narratives. They are narratives because of "the presence of a story and a story teller,"[9] but they are appropriately construed as "mini-narratives" in order to distinguish them from much fuller stories. Casuists have further shown that our particular case judgments are often independent of and enter into the formulation of general norms rather than being derived from those norms.[10]

However, sometimes casuists who insist on paradigm cases and analogical reasoning are more formalistic and even legalistic than some principlists, espe-cially principlists who recognize only *prima facie* binding norms. In their effort to categorize cases, casuists sometimes neglect the narrative quality of the cases they examine by forcing cases into "boxes" by locating them under such categories as medical indications, patient preferences, quality of life, and external factors.[11]

Richard Miller wonders whether paradigms and stories are compatible and thus whether casuists and narrativists can have a "happy marriage." For him:

> narratives are not clear and uncontroversial, but murky and complicated. It is usually difficult to see through them until the end, and even then the interpre-tation of the narrative is often up for grabs. Such a device for practical reasoning would seem to make casuistry interminable. Paradigms boast the ability to enable casuists to proceed more efficiently, without interpretative complications. In contrast to narratives, paradigms are more or less self-evident or self-interpreting.[12]

However, Miller's argument neglects the ineliminable narrative structure of cases, even of fairly thin cases sometimes used in bioethics.

Miller further argues (against John Arras) that it is a mistake to bring casu-istry and narrative close together because casuistry is occasioned, in large measure, by the two experiences of doubt and perplexity, the former involving uncertainty about the meaning or applicability of a moral principle, and the latter stemming from the experience of moral conflict.[13] Miller contends that casuistry's sense of separation or alienation of self, even if momentarily, from the guiding principle(s) is "difficult to reconcile with the *dominant strand of narrative ethics*, which views narrative as the antidote to doubt and perplexity—indeed, to practical reasoning itself" (my emphasis). As presented by Alasdair MacIntyre and Stanley Hauerwas, among others with a strong interest in virtue, narrative is connected with the unity of the self and virtue, rather than with problems, dilemmas, and quandaries: "Narrative is a genre in the service of an *undivided, unconflicted character*, one which is not anxious about practical decisions or conflicts of duties." However, the MacIntyre-Hauerwas conception of narrative and ethics is only one, and it is not clearly dominant even though it is clearly very influential. No particular approach to narrative and ethics, such as the MacIntyre-Hauerwas approach, should be taken as definitive, for, as my earlier schema suggested, there are many different approaches to narrative and ethics.

Rather than focusing on the method of casuistry, perhaps we should focus on "particular cases" and "particular case judgments," with attention to the moral judgments made in the context of a particular case narrative. Particular case judgments are not always problematic or dilemmatic. Indeed, quite often—even usually—it is clear what we should do in particular circumstances, for example, to assist someone in need, without any appeal to general moral norms or paradigm cases (that is, same type cases).

However, many who focus on particular cases and particular case judgments argue not only for their independence but also for their primacy or priority. What does it mean to affirm, as Jonsen and Toulmin do, the primacy or priority of particular judgments, that is, judgments related to particular cases?[14]

First, it might mean that particular judgments chronologically come first. But then the question is: For whom? Each individual participates in communities, many of which involve traditions of moral reflection. These traditions include both general moral norms and judgments about particular cases. Even if the particular judgments came first historically (a claim that is difficult to establish), we do not encounter the moral traditions of our communities only through their particular judgments; they usually present general norms too. Indeed, it is hard to imagine moral education proceeding without general norms as well as paradigm cases. Hence, the Jonsen-Toulmin view of principles as "top down" holds only if we think in terms of theoretical derivation; it does not fit with a historical, communal interpretation of morality.

Second, the primacy of particular judgments could mean logical priority. However, it is not clear that either general norms or particular case judgments have logical priority. Their relation is better construed as dialectical, with neither fully and completely derived from the other, but with each potentially modifying the other.

Third, assigning primacy to particular judgments could indicate normative priority. Here again the language of dialectic is more appropriate. Where particular judgments appear to conflict with general norms, adjustments are required, but it is not plausible to say that either should always take priority over the other.

We should note further what is implied when we make a judgment that an action is wrong in a particular set of circumstances. R. M. Hare argues that "if we, as a result of reflection on something that has happened, have made a certain moral judgment, we have acquired a precept or principle which has application in all similar cases. We have, in some sense of that word, learnt something."[15] If we learn something useful from reflection on a particular case, Hare claims, the principle we gain must be *somewhat general;* it cannot have unlimited specificity. Since no two real cases are exactly alike, we have results of reflection that can be useful in the future only if we "have isolated certain broad features of the cases we were thinking about—features which may recur in other cases." Hare's argument presupposes the formal principle of universalizability, which he rightly identifies as a condition of moral judgments. Accepting the principle of universalizability does not distinguish normism or principlism from casuistry. Indeed, casuistry, as Jonsen and Toulmin conceive it, also presupposes this formal principle of universalizability—after all, casuistry depends on identifying relevant similarities and differences between cases in analogical reasoning. (The principle of universalizability also appears in the common law doctrine of precedent, which provides one major model for casuistry.)

Once generated, norms still require interpretation, and this interpretive process also involves narratives. A case may not clearly fall under a general norm; a single norm may point in two different directions in the same situation; and norms may come into apparent or real conflict—perhaps even dilemmas as well as interpersonal conflicts. Henry Richardson identifies three models of connection between principles and cases: (1) application, which involves the deductive application of principles and rules, (2) balancing, which depends on intuitive weighing, and (3) specification, which proceeds by "qualitatively tailoring our norms to cases."[16]

Even though Tom Beauchamp and I use the metaphors of both application and balancing, we most often balance principles, especially if application is construed as deduction. A balancing approach is the most consistent with a conception of principles as *prima facie* binding. However, we have attempted to reduce the reliance on intuition by developing a rough decision procedure that attends to such matters as the necessity of breaching one principle in order to protect another, the effectiveness of doing so, minimization of the extent of the breach, and so forth.[17]

What Richardson calls "specification" is also prominently featured in our work, because, as Hare notes, "any attempt to give content to a principle involves specifying the cases that are to fall under it. . . . Any principle, then, which has content goes *some way down the path of specificity*" (my emphasis).[18] We have always used specification (though without the label, which was added only in the fourth edition) in determining the meaning, range, and scope of principles such as respect for autonomy, and in indicating how principles can take shape in rules, such as rules requiring voluntary informed consent. It appears in our discussion of the meaning of lying.[19] Specification also overlaps with casuistical categories—who, when, why, and so on—which themselves involve narratives, such as A is doing X to Y for Z reasons.

Instead of viewing application, balancing, and specification as three alternative models, it is better, I believe, to recognize that all three are important in parts of morality and for different situations or aspects of situations. Sometimes, however infrequently, we apply norms, sometimes we specify norms, but sometimes we can resolve conflicts only by balancing norms.

Perhaps *interpretation* is the most adequate general category, as long as interpretation includes the meaning, scope, and range of different general norms, along with their weight or strength, as well as attention to particular situations (narratives). If determinations of meaning and weight are not possible in total abstraction from situations (narratives), or at least types of situations, as I would argue, then the putative differences between casuistry and principlism may be less significant than is often supposed. These apparently different approaches may share more than many recognize. Beauchamp and I do not claim that appeals to norms are indispensable for every particular judgment and moral decision, but we do claim that norms play an important role in many moral judgments and decisions, in moral education, and in moral justification in a communal setting (for example, regarding public policy). At the very least, there is an important similarity in spirit between some casuistical approaches and our principlism.

Not all conceptions of norms are equally hospitable to narratives. In my view, a conception of norms as *prima facie* binding and thus subject to balancing—rather than subject merely to application or even specification—fits more closely with narrative approaches. Sometimes we have to balance general norms in the situation, the case, as appropriately described. While even application and specification need more attention to the narrative structure of cases than their proponents often recognize, balancing clearly requires thoughtful attention to the case narrative.

Many different kinds of cases appear in biomedical ethics—for example, real, hypothetical but realistic, hypothetical but fantastic. Writers in bioethics tend to use real cases drawn from practice and literature in health care and from legal decisions. However, as Hare suggests, the main contrast should be drawn between realistic cases, whether actual or hypothetical, and fantastic ones. Nevertheless, if we take ethical imagination seriously, fantastic cases may also play a significant if occasional role in stimulating our moral reflection, in testing the consistency of our judgments, and in challenging our formulation of norms and their applicability to certain cases. A great example is Judith Jarvis Thomson's famous case of the person who is kidnapped and plugged into an unconscious violinist with a fatal kidney ailment to save the latter's life.[20] This case has helped to reshape the way we ethically imagine or conceive the problem of abortion. Abortion does not merely concern agents' obligations not to harm or kill but also their obligations to assist others by providing bodily life support—what is the basis of the latter obligation, how far does it extend, and how much weight does it have? Thomson's fantastic case provided an imaginative reconstrual of the relationship between a pregnant woman and a fetus, which others then extended through analogy with organ donation to explore the basis and limits of moral obligations to provide bodily life support.[21] Much of the debate about fantastic cases concerns their analogical significance for real or realistic cases.

Real and realistic cases are not merely matters of accurate description, they also raise difficult questions of narration.[22] One question is how thick cases must be—narrativists are inclined to make them very thick to create a fuller picture, and this is often quite appropriate but not always necessary or unproblematic. There is also a place for thin cases. Much depends on what we hold about "moral relevance." If, according to the condition of universalizability, we are to treat (relevantly) similar cases in a (relevantly) similar way, then the criteria of relevance obviously become important—and these may stem from the narratives of the community(ies). According to Dena Davis, "we need thick descriptions [as in the case of Donald/Dax Cowart, to be discussed below] to allow cases to remain open to different interpretations over time, and also to enable cases to ground an ethics of care. The thicker the case, the more contextual the response."[23]

Even real cases, whether thick or thin, are not mere reports of objective reality. Tod Chambers and others have forcefully called our attention to unarticulated assumptions in bioethics cases. All narratives are constructed, even the mini-narratives of cases, however "true" to objective happenings they may be. These points drive another nail into the coffin of the fact/value distinction or separation that appears in some theories of the deductive application of norms to concrete cases. Application breaks down in part because so much evaluative work goes into the very construction of the case. Even real cases as narrated are, in Gustafson's phrase, "evaluative descriptions."

In moving from actual case to actual case, the ethicist (casuist) may be limited to mini-narratives that practitioners and others offer for analysis and assessment as their *felt* problems or dilemmas. General moral norms may help identify other cases that should be on the moral agenda, and they may direct our attention to *real* problems and dilemmas, which have not yet been experienced as such. But even general moral norms cannot be applied, specified, or balanced without narrative contexts, a point that I will develop in relation to the principle of respect for personal autonomy and the ongoing debate about the best way to interpret a particular case.

Norms and Narratives:
Respect for Personal Autonomy and the Case of Donald/Dax Cowart

The powerful case of Donald Cowart (later known as Dax Cowart), particularly as presented in the videotape *Please Let Me Die*, has become a focal point for some recent debates about the respective roles of narratives and norms. Recent commentators have sharply contrasted William May's "narrative approach" to this case with my (and Courtney Campbell's) principlist approach.[24] Even though the contrasts appear to be immediately instructive, they can be over-drawn, and in fact, the narrativist and principlist approaches to this case may be closer than many suppose. Despite their different starting points—narratives and norms respectively—there is considerable convergence between these positions, even though one analyst insists that they "could not be more different."[25]

Donald Cowart's case involves a very athletic man in his twenties who is severely burned in an accident that kills his father, and who over time indicates that he does not want to continue the treatment necessary to save his life.[26] Using a dramatic narrative approach to illuminate the burned person's shattered world, May argues that this case "challenges the conventional analysis of great moral issues in medical ethics," with its customary focus on conflicts between two rival values of life and quality of life and between two rival principles of paternalism and autonomy for selecting the right decision-maker. In his rich and powerful discussion, May contends that conventional frameworks fail in these world-shattering cases, mainly because the catastrophe is so devastating that the terms life/quality of life cannot adequately express it. The dramatic, narrative language of life/death/rebirth, May suggests, better expresses what is involved. However, May later returns to debates about paternalism and autonomy, observing that the image of rebirth, of the construction of a new identity, does not eliminate—and may even intensify—the problem of paternalism.[27]

By contrast, Campbell and I start with debates about the meaning and weights of the principles of beneficence and respect for autonomy in conflicts about paternalistic interventions; but we then attempt to show how difficult it is to respect persons in their concreteness, because they are temporal creatures (past, present, and future) and because they are social creatures (community). We cannot respect other persons' autonomy without listening to their narratives in order to determine what their wishes, choices, and actions really are. (Even though we did not use the language of narrative, it is consistent with and further explicates what we argued.)

So May begins with narratives but moves to norms; we begin with norms but move to narratives. And, substantively, we come to the same conclusion about what ought to have been done (or not done). Campbell and I concluded that "it was imperative to acknowledge Dax's right to decide for himself whether to accept or refuse treatment after enough time had elapsed to determine his prognosis, his competence, and his settled wishes. At some point paternalistic interventions were unjustified." And May concluded: "Whatever the team can do for the victim, it cannot bring him to new life without his consent. It cannot provide him with such parenting. The domestic analogy is wrong." Furthermore, just as May recognizes the dangers of both paternalism and antipaternalism—paternalists are tempted by the sins of the overbearing, and antipaternalists by the sins of the underbearing—so Campbell and I stressed both principles of respect for persons and of beneficence in order to avoid such temptations.[28]

The fact that May's rich, narrative discussion also concludes that Cowart should have been allowed to make his own decision about treatment is, according to some commentators, very important—a different conclusion would have called into question his narrative analysis. In short, norms can check narratives (experience), just as narratives can check principles.[29] Here again we can see a dialectical relation between norms and cases.

May reaches his conclusion by arguing that paternalistic interventions are wrong in cases such as Cowart's largely because they are ineffective for the end that is sought. He takes a proautonomy position, in the sense of prochoice as a resolute will to make good on a primary decision. Proautonomy is justified in such cases because it is a necessary condition for the constitution or reconstitution of moral identity following such a catastrophic loss. May thus offers a consequentialist justification for allowing Cowart to choose/refuse treatment: "Perhaps . . . leaving the door open to the possibility of his refusing treatment may make it easier for him to accept treatment and to persevere in the consequences of that acceptance and make good" on it. The health care team cannot bring Cowart to a new life "without his consent." If he chose to live, he could not simply "take up his old life. He must become a new man. Don Cowart becomes Dax. No parentalist can force him down that role." What is required is an "interior transformation . . . the reordering of one's identity from the ground up." While the community can assist this "heroic movement" in various ways, "without consent to transformation the patient cannot move from saying 'please let me die' to 'I am glad to be alive.' "[30]

In contrast to May's consequentialist argument, Campbell and I accept a nonabsolutist norm of respect for personal autonomy that justifies Cowart's and others' *prima facie* right to make decisions in both catastrophic and noncatastrophic cases—it is morally important to respect persons and their own stories. To respond otherwise would insult Cowart and treat him with disrespect. Why our position is more adequate as a baseline than May's, even though it too needs a narrative perspective, emerges more clearly in the light of some problems that May's approach encounters.

May appeals to some broad interpretive categories to "locate" and illuminate Cowart's experience, his ordeal, as a severely burned patient. Especially important are the categories of life/death/rebirth and Christian conversion as well as the hero in Greek tragedy. Such broad narrative categories can indeed be illuminating for certain purposes but confusing and even dangerous for others. In particular, they are confusing and even dangerous when used to illuminate others' particular narratives in order to determine how caregivers ought to respond to their refusal of (or request for) treatment. Archetypal narratives may obscure individual narratives and thus seriously distort what a particular patient is saying—for instance, May's use of religious, often Christian, narrative patterns may be quite out of context for a severely burned patient who is atheistic. Any interpretive categories must be sufficiently broad and neutral to encompass a wide range of conceptions of a good life and death.[31]

Physicians and other health care professionals should attend to the patient's own narrative, as required by the principle of respect for persons and their autonomy, rather than construing that narrative as a mere instance of a grand pattern of life/death/rebirth or even of a set of substantive beliefs, such as a religious community's core convictions. This point holds even if the individual explicitly identifies in some way with the larger narrative. The implications are significant: we have to respect, for instance, a particular Jehovah's Witness's position on blood transfusions, even if it is wholly rejected by his/her larger religious community—it is his or her own position that matters. Or, to take another example, caregivers should respect a particular Navajo's own views about negative information and treatment decisions, rather than simply inferring them from the traditional Navajo narrative or worldview, which holds that language creates rather than reflects reality. After all, a particular Navajo may largely reject that grand narrative or worldview.[32]

While May's narrative perspective can help us see what went wrong, from the standpoint of both care and respect, over the first ten months of treatment, that is, up to the time of *Please Let Me Die*, it may be unjustifiably paternalistic or imperialistic to interpret a particular patient's story through a larger narrative pattern that blurs his or her own identify and individuality.

That this is a serious risk in May's arguments is evident in his comments about Dax as a "new man," with a new identity. May bases his claim in part on the narrative patterns of life/death/rebirth and in part on the fact that Donald

Cowart changed his name to Dax Cowart. While conceding that Cowart had a manifest, functional reason for changing his name—he couldn't write his full name again (and he has also stated that he could hear Dax more clearly than Don)—May finds latent, symbolic meaning in this act: Cowart "knows that Donald Cowart has, if not biologically, existentially died; he must assume a new identity."[33] It is not clear, however, that Dax constituted a new identity for Donald—he still insists that he was wrongly treated against his will, even though he is happy to be alive now. At most, Sumner Twiss notes, Cowart "appears only to have deepened his original sense of willful independence and determination to live his life on the terms that he chooses. To interpret the forced changes in his life-plan as a reconstruction or even revision of identity may be to impose on Cowart a moral vision that he does not share and that misinterprets his existential response to his ordeal."[34]

What finally is the upshot of the proposed shift in perspective from norm to narrative, from quality of life to life/death/rebirth, or from a "'right-to-die' story" to a "'chronic illness' story"? What should Cowart's caregivers have done when deciding whether to allow him to choose to die at the point of the original videotape, that is, ten months after the accident? Should they have acquiesced to his stated desire to die, or should they have forcibly treated him against his stated preference? Focusing on narratives, as May does, may simply push the procedural question of decision authority to a different level—away from the patient's particular decision to the patient's own story—without fundamentally altering the question or even the appropriate answer. "On the face of things," Lonnie Kliever writes, "the Cowart story is a classic case of autonomy versus paternalism. Certainly that clash is the perceived message of the film *Dax's Case* and *represents Dax's own construal of his experience as a patient*" (my emphasis).[35] Even though Dax's own story is not incorrigible, and even though respect does not require others to accept it at face value, the shift to narrative simply rewrites the fundamental question so that it now becomes "whose story is it anyway?"[36] Problems of respect for persons and beneficence arise on the level of narrative, just as they do on the level of concrete decision-making.

The case of Donald/Dax Cowart thus raises some important issues about ethics in the narrative encounter—not only about narration, such as whose perspective and whose story, but also about listening, a term that I will use to encompass all forms of receiving narration. Without being able to develop the important points here, I will simply note that both narration and listening are *performative*. Analyses of narrative often draw, explicitly or implicitly, on J. L. Austin's analysis of performative speech and suggest that "narration" is the "performative function of story telling."[37] J. Hillis Miller writes that "storytelling, the putting together of data to make a coherent tale, is performative. *Oedipus the*

King is a story about the awful danger of storytelling. Storytelling in this case makes something happen with a vengeance. It leads the storyteller to condemn, blind, and exile himself, and it leads his mother-wife, Jocasta, to kill herself."[38]

As Miller's example suggests, listening is performative, just as narration is. At the very least, listening is active, not merely passive, because it involves interpretation. It is very important to ask exactly what constitutes ethical listening when the health care professional listens to the narrative of "the wounded storyteller."[39] To listen ethically means to listen with respect, but respectful listening does not entail that the listener merely accept at face value the narrative that he or she hears. Campbell and I suggested the difficulty of interpreting what is heard, especially when the temporal and communal dimensions of the self and his or her stories are recognized. Furthermore, when the patient is ambivalent, it may be very difficult to determine exactly where to put the interpretive weight.

Ethical listening is indispensable, whether we start with narratives or start with norms, such as beneficence and respect for persons and their autonomous choices. Within either approach, the listener cannot avoid interpretive frameworks but, nevertheless, must be as careful as possible to hear what this particular person is saying, what his or her story is, without acting under a larger story that putatively illuminates the patient's particular story.

Narrative Experience: Proximity and Distance

In the last section of this essay I want to consider the authority of particular narrative experiences, especially in setting and resolving moral problems and conflicts, over against general moral norms, often grounded in a tradition's story. This level of the debate about narratives versus norms often focuses on different construals of reality, on what, in an oversimplified formulation, constitutes "moral reality"—individual lived experience or communal moral norms?

Bioethicists at one point or another encounter resistance on the grounds that they are removed from practice, or that, even when they are also clinicians, they are still distant from the actual case for which other agents have primary responsibility. More broadly, this resistance sometimes denies that general norms fit or illuminate practical reality. The military metaphor enlivens some statements of resistance. Critics protest that only those who are in the trenches or who stand on the firing line can really understand and appreciate the moral problems in health care, which may even take the form of what narrators call "war stories." Although such encounters in health care regularly embody the conflict between narratives and norms, a closer look suggests a different question: Whose narrative experience and what kind of narrative experience authoritatively sets problems for ethical reflection and indicates directions for resolution?[40]

In order to sharpen this question, and identify a couple of major possible answers to it, I will move outside biomedical ethics altogether and consider a remarkable exchange about the authority of different narratives in evaluating the U.S. decision to drop the first atomic bomb on Hiroshima. Paul Fussell, a distinguished literary critic and author of a fine book on World War I, *The Great War and Modern Memory*,[41] wrote an article entitled "Hiroshima: A Soldier's View" for *The New Republic* near an anniversary of the dropping of the atomic bombs.[42] Echoing those who thanked God for the atomic bomb, Fussell charges that critics of the bombing betray their "remoteness from experience." By contrast, when the bombs were dropped, he was in the infantry in Europe, awaiting transfer to the Pacific to continue the war there. He wants to show how one's views about the first use of the bomb are influenced by "experience, sheer vulgar experience." The experience is evident, too, in his other writings—that is the experience "of having come to grips, face to face, with any enemy who designs your death," the experience of having your ass shot at, if not shot off, the experience of infantry and Marines and line Navy and all those who were told over and over again "to close with the enemy and destroy him."[43] In this discussion of Fussell's claims, I will view his appeal to experience as "a sort of storytelling," and view the forcefulness of his appeal to experience as a result of "the persuasive power of a coherent narrative."[44]

Presenting these narratives of experience is necessary, Fussell suggests, because "historical memory" tends unwittingly "to resolve ambiguity," but ambiguity can be restored by considering the way "testimonies emanating from experience complicate attitudes about the cruel ending of that cruel war." These frontline people would have had to carry the war in the Pacific, island by island, if the bomb had not been dropped. In the context of such experiences, he quotes the Naval officer who said of Hiroshima: "Those were the best burned women and children I ever saw." Fussell himself says that it is a pity not that the bomb was used to end the war with Japan, but that it wasn't ready earlier to end the war with Germany. That is the story from "down there"—in the trenches, particularly from one who has been seriously wounded, as Fussell was. "Down there" is "the place where coarse self-interest is the rule."[45]

By contrast, another remarkable book on war, *The Warriors*, by J. Glenn Gray, a philosopher, reports that the U.S. soldiers he was with in Europe were saddled with guilt and shame when they heard about our first use of the atomic bombs.[46] Fussell sarcastically observes that Gray was not in the infantry, but was only an interrogator, and that *The Warriors* "gives every sign of remoteness from experience. Division headquarters is miles behind the places where the soldiers experience terror and madness and relieve those pressures by sadism."[47] Fussell deflects several other criticisms of the dropping of the bombs because they too display "a similar remoteness from experience." For instance, he dismisses John Kenneth Galbraith's criticisms by noting that Galbraith served in administrative offices during the war.[48]

In contrast to Fussell's claims for the authority of particular narratives of lived experience, there are good arguments for the value of *distance* expressed in general moral norms embodied in a community's narrative traditions. One of the sharpest criticisms of the decision to drop the bomb comes from another thinker with a strong, but different, narrative orientation—Michael Walzer, whose superb book *Just and Unjust Wars* has the subtitle: *A Moral Argument with Historical Illustrations.*[49] When Walzer was preparing his book, which is, in my judgment, the best single twentieth-century work on just war theory and practice, he realized that his lack of experience in war put him at a disadvantage, and he thus read widely in memoirs of war in order understand and appreciate its experiences and its traditions. "It is important to my own sense of my enterprise that I am reporting on experiences that men and women have really had and on arguments that they have really made."[50] For example, when Walzer attempts to understand the norm of noncombatant immunity from direct attack as a matter of justice, he begins with the stories told by soldiers who were usually quite willing to fire at enemy soldiers but who refrained from doing so in some quite specific circumstances. In one narrative, George Orwell reported that he had refrained from shooting at an enemy soldier who was running along holding up his trousers: "I had come here to shoot at 'Fascists'. But a man who is holding up his trousers isn't a 'Fascist', he is visibly a fellow-creature, similar to your self, and you don't feel like shooting at him."[51]

Beyond particular memoirs, Walzer concentrates on what he calls "the moral reality of war," which involves moral norms, arguments, and judgments: "Reiterated over time, our arguments and judgments shape what I want to call *the moral reality of war*—that is, all those experiences of which moral language is descriptive and within which it is usually employed." Over against the claims for authority of certain particular narratives, Walzer insists "that the moral reality of war is not fixed by the actual activities of soldiers but by the opinions of mankind."[52] And yet this moral reality is expressed in arguments about particular narratives, that is, cases, and Walzer's approach is thoroughly casuistical: "The proper method of practical morality is casuistic in character."[53]

From this perspective, Walzer vigorously responds to Fussell's assertion that in war "there are no limits at all; anything goes, so long as it helps to bring the boys home." According to Walzer, there are some limits in war. The "bombing of Hiroshima was an act of terrorism; its purpose was political, not military." It was murder, as defined by general moral norms, which include the immunity of noncombatants from direct attack. Such norms should and often do shape military choices. Even if these norms, and the arguments associated with them, are "most often expounded by those professors far from the battlefield," for whom Fussell has "such contempt," the moral argument "is an argument as old as war itself and one that many soldiers have believed and struggled to live by." And it is one that should guide those who make decisions apart from the heat of battle itself about the use of weapons. We have responsibilities, Walzer argues, to the "huddled masses" of civilians on their side, as well as the soldiers on ours. Furthermore, he contends that, to be morally responsible, a decision such as the one to drop the atomic bomb must take account of "all the future victims of a politics and a warfare from which restraint has been banished."[54]

The norm Walzer articulates is not stripped from history, from a larger narrative—indeed, his argument draws on that narrative. His conception of "historical memory" has to do not only with individual or collective recollections of World War II, as in Fussell's approach, but also with the traditions of moral reflection conveyed in various ways, including individual narratives, such as memoirs, and debates about particular cases. Of course there is no single tradition of reflection on war, but rather, along the lines of Alasdair MacIntyre's argument, the tradition of war is an ongoing argument. However, some important norms receive widespread and virtually universal acceptance in that tradition, and judgments we make about particular incidents in war, including exceptional cases, further contribute to the tradition of reflection.

In response to Walzer's critique, Fussell doubts that he and Walzer can ever agree, because their dispute is really "one between sensibilities," between "two different emotional and moral styles." He designates his own style as "the ironic and ambiguous (or even the tragic, if you like)"—it is "the literary-artistic-historical" style—and Walzer's as "the certain" sensibility.[55] To continue the contrast, the one sensibility or style "complicates problems, leaving them messier than before and making you feel terrible. The other solves problems and cleans up the place, making you feel tidy and satisfied." His own aim in writing about Hiroshima "was to complicate, even mess up, the moral picture" in order to dispute the critics. "I observed," Fussell continues:

> that those who deplore the dropping of the bomb absolutely turn out to be largely too young to have been killed if it hadn't been used. I don't want to be needlessly offensive, nor to insist that no person whose life was not saved by the A-bomb can come to a clear—by which I mean a complicated—understanding of the moral balance-sheet. But I note that in 1945 Michael Walzer, for all the emotional warmth of his current argument, was ten years old.

Thus Walzer really couldn't appreciate what was involved: "understanding the past means feeling its pressure on your pulses." Furthermore, according to Fussell,

[t]hose who actually fought on the line in the war, especially if they were wounded, constitute an in-group forever separate from those who did not. Praise or blame does not attach: rather, there is the accidental possession of a special empirical knowledge, a feeling of a mysterious shared ironic awareness manifesting itself in an instinctive skepticism about pretension, publicly enunciated truths, the vanities of learning, and the pomp of authority.[56]

I have told the story of this debate in considerable detail because it captures so well tensions between claims of authority for particular experiences—which, as Paul Lauritzen notes, are "narrative experiences"—and the claims of authority for particular casuistical judgments and for general moral norms, which may also be grounded in and expressed in narratives. However, it is a mistake to try to settle the question of moral authority apart from complex arguments, which often include narratives in various forms. Once we recognize that narratives take many different forms, as do norms, then we can see that the interesting question is how they can and should relate. But in order to make progress on this debate we need much greater clarity, more than I have provided, about what is involved in both narrative(s) and norm(s), two complex areas of human discourse.

In conclusion, the debate about norm and narrative in ethics, especially practical ethics, including bioethics, is (largely) misplaced. The norm camp and the narrative camp encompass so many different positions as to be virtually meaningless. Some positions that emphasize norms are much closer to some positions that emphasize narrative than they are to other normists. If we start with either norms or narratives, we are driven to the other.[57] We need both in any adequate ethics. Each plays a corrective, enriching, enhancing role in relation to the other—one by moving to the more general, the other by moving to the more particular. However we conceive their relation—dialectic, conversation, dialogue, and so on—the important but difficult task is to determine how they function together in a rigorous and imaginative ethical perspective or framework, story or theory.

Notes

1. In light of such criticisms, as well as my own personal needs, I arranged with Larry Bouchard, a colleague who specializes in religion and literature, to coteach a new graduate seminar in the spring of 1995 on "Narrative in Theology and Ethics." This seminar helped me better understand the possibilities and limitations of narrative in ethics, and I am grateful to my coteacher and to the students in that seminar.

2. James M. Gustafson, "Context Versus Principles: A Misplaced Debate in Christian Ethics," *Harvard Theological Review* 58 (1965); reprinted in James M. Gustafson, *Christian Ethics and the Community* (Philadelphia: Pilgrim Press, 1971), pp. 101–126. All references will be to the latter.

3. William David Solomon, "Rules and Principles," in *Encyclopedia of Bioethics*, ed. Warren T. Reich (New York: Free Press, 1978), vol. I, pp. 407–413.

4. See various works by Alasdair MacIntyre and Stanley Hauerwas, among others. For more discussion, see the paper by John Arras elsewhere in this volume.

5. See, for example, various works by William F. May, including some referred to below.

6. I will often use the term "norms" and the label "normist" in order to avoid the associations triggered by the term "principles" and the label "principlist," particularly as the label was coined by critics. See K. Danner Clouser and Bernard Gert, "A Critique of Principlism," *Journal of Medicine and Philosophy* 15 (1990):219–236.

7. See Tom L. Beauchamp and James F. Childress, *Principles of Biomedical Ethics* (New York: Oxford University Press, ed. 1, 1979; ed. 2, 1983; ed. 3, 1989; ed. 4, 1994). These formulations and charts were more evident in the first three editions than in the fourth.

8. Albert R. Jonsen and Steven Toulmin, *The Abuse of Casuistry* (Berkeley, CA: University of California Press, 1988). See also Steven Toulmin, "The Tyranny of Principles," *Hastings Center Report* 11 (December 1981):31–39.

9. See Robert Scholes and Robert Kellogg, *The Nature of Narrative* (New York: Oxford University Press, 1968), p. 4, who offer these criteria for narrative literary works.

10. The contributions of casuists often overlap with those of other contemporary perspectives, such as feminist ethics.

11. See the approach taken in Albert R. Jonsen, Mark Siegler, and William J. Winslade, *Clinical Ethics*, 2nd. ed. (New York: Macmillan, 1986).

12. Richard B. Miller, "Narrative and Casuistry: A Response to John Arras," *Indiana Law Journal* 69 (Fall 1994):1015–1019, written in response to John Arras, "Principles and Particularity: The Roles of Case in Bioethics," *Indiana Law Journal* 69 (Fall 1994):983–1014. For one of the best analyses and assessments of casuistry, see John D. Arras, "Getting Down to Cases: The Revival of Casuistry in Bioethics," *Journal of Medicine and Philosophy* 16 (1991):29–51.

13. Miller, "Narrative and Casuistry," pp. 1015–1019, which is also the source of the quotations in the remainder of this paragraph. For Miller's fuller perspective, see *Casuistry and Modern Ethics: A Poetics of Practical Reasoning* (Chicago: University of Chicago Press, 1996).

14. The next several paragraphs draw freely from James F. Childress, "Ethical Theories, Principles, and Casuistry in Bioethics: An Interpretation and Defense of Principlism," in *Religious Methods and Resources in Bioethics*, ed. Paul Camenisch (Boston: Kluwer, 1994), pp. 181–201.

15. R. M. Hare, "Principles," *Essays in Ethical Theory* (Oxford: Clarendon Press, 1989), pp. 49–65.

16. Henry Richardson, "Specifying Norms as a Way to Resolve Concrete Ethical Problems," *Philosophy and Public Affairs* 19 (1990):279–320.

17. Beauchamp and Childress, *Principles of Biomedical Ethics*, 4th ed., pp. 33–37.

18. Hare, "Principles."

19. See Beauchamp and Childress, *Principles of Biomedical Ethics*, 4th ed., chap. 1.

20. Judith Jarvis Thomson, "A Defense of Abortion," *Philosophy and Public Affairs* 1 (1971):47–66.

21. See, for example, Susan Mattingly, "Viewing Abortion from the Perspective of Transplantation: The Ethics of the Gift of Life," *Soundings* 67 (1984):399–410; and Patricia Beattie Jung, "Abortion and Organ Donation: Christian Reflections on Bodily Life Support," *Journal of Religious Ethics* 16 (1988):273–305.

22. See the important work by Tod S. Chambers, including "The Bioethicist as Author: The Medical Ethics Case as Rhetorical Device," *Literature and Medicine* 13, no. 1 (Spring 1994):60–78. For a partial response, see James F. Childress, *Practical Reasoning in Bioethics* (Bloomington, IN: Indiana University Press, 1997), chap. 5.

23. Dena Davis, "Rich Cases: The Ethics of Thick Description," *Hastings Center Report* 21 (July/August 1991):12–17.

24. See William F. May, *The Patient's Ordeal* (Bloomington, IN: Indiana University Press, 1991),

chap. 1, which presents a revised version of his chapter "Dealing with Catastrophe," in *Dax's Case: Essays in Medical Ethics and Human Meaning*, ed. Lonnie D. Kliever (Dallas: Southern Methodist University Press, 1989), pp. 131–150. The essay by James F. Childress and Courtney Campbell entitled " 'Who is a Doctor to Decide Whether a Person Lives or Dies?' " also appeared in *Dax's Case*, and is reprinted in Childress, *Practical Reasoning in Bioethics*, chap. 7. For recent commentary, see Sumner B. Twiss, "Alternative Approaches to Patient and Family Medical Ethics: Review and Assessment," *Religious Studies Review* 21 (October 1995):263–276; and Paul Lauritzen, "Ethics and Experience: The Case of the Curious Response," *Hastings Center Report* 26 (January/February 1996):6–15.

25. Lauritzen, "Ethics and Experience."

26. The videotape *Please Let Me Die*, which consists mainly of psychiatrist Robert B. White's interview of Donald Cowart, is available for rental or pruchase from Robert B. White, MD, Department of Psychiatry, University of Texas Medical Branch, Galveston, Texas. A transcript of that videotape appears in Robert A. Burt, *Taking Care of Strangers: The Rule of Law in Doctor-Patient Relations* (New York: Free Press, 1979), pp. 174–180. The follow-up videotape, *Dax's Case* (1985), which includes interviews with many of the participants in the original case, is available for purchase or rental from Concern for Dying, 250 West 57th St., New York, NY 10016, or Filmmakers Library, 124 East 40th St., New York, NY 10107. The latter is also discussed in Kliever, ed., *Dax's Case*.

27. May, *The Patient's Ordeal*.

28. See also James F. Childress, *Who Should Decide? Paternalism in Health Care* (New York: Oxford University Press, 1982), p. ix.

29. See Lauritzen, "Ethics and Experience."

30. May, *The Patient's Ordeal*, pp. 34–35.

31. Sumner Twiss makes a similar argument in "Alternative Approaches," but he then uses categories that may be excessively rationalistic, such as "life plan."

32. See Joseph A. Carrese and Lorna A. Rhodes, "Western Bioethics on the Navajo Reservation: Benefit or Harm?" *Journal of the American Medical Association* 274 (September 13, 1995):820–825.

33. May, *The Patient's Ordeal*, p. 16.

34. See Twiss, "Alternative Approaches," p. 274. I have similar reservations about Lonnie Kliever's important and somewhat similar effort to reenvision "Dax's case" as a " 'chronic illness' story" rather than a " 'right-to-die' story." See Kliever, "Rage and Grief: Another Look at Dax's Case," in *Chronic Illness: From Experience to Policy*, ed. S. Kay Toombs, David Barnard, and Ronald A. Carson (Bloomington, IN: Indiana University Press, 1995), pp. 58–76.

35. Kliever, "Rage and Grief," p. 73.

36. I borrow this question from Sue E. Estroff, who uses it for a different prupose in "Whose Story Is It Anyway? Authority, Voice, and Responsbility in Narratives of Chronic Illness," in *Chronic Illness: From Experience to Policy*, ed. Toombs, Barnard, and Carson, chap. 5.

37. Adam Zachary Newton, *Narrative Ethics* (Cambridge: Harvard University Press, 1995), p. 58.

38. J. Hillis Miller, "Narrative," in *Critical Terms for Literary Study*, ed. Frank Lentricchia and Thomas McLaughlin (Chicago: University of Chicago Press, 1990), p. 74.

39. The phrase "wounded storyteller" comes from the title of Arthur W. Frank's book, *The Wounded Storyteller: Body, Illness, and Ethics* (Chicago: University of Chicago Press, 1995).

40. It is not critical to try to resolve whether experience is necessarily narrative or is only communicated narratively.

41. Paul Fussell, *The Great War and Modern Memory* (New York: Oxford University Press, 1975).

42. Paul Fussell, "Hiroshima: A Soldier's View," *The New Republic* (22 & 29, August 1981):26–30. This article is reprinted in Fussell, *Thank God for the Atom Bomb and Other Essays* (New York: Oxford University Press, 1988). See also Fussell, "My War: How I Got Irony in the Infantry," *Harper's* (January 1982):40–48, and, more recently, Fussell, *Doing Battle: The Making of a Skeptic* (Boston:

Little, Brown, 1996), which recycles part of the essay "My War" in the context of his memoir.

Another important expression of Fussell's perspective appears in his *Wartime: Understanding and Behavior in the Second World War* (New York: Oxford University Press, 198), which examines the immediate impact of the war on both soldiers and civilians.

43. Fussell, "Hiroshima: A Soldier's View," p. 27.

44. See Lauritzen, "Ethics and Experience," pp. 6–15, from which these quoted phrases are drawn.

45. Fussell, "Hiroshima: A Soldier's View," and "My War."

46. J. Glenn Gray, *The Warriors* (New York: Harper and Row, Torchbook edition, 1967), chap. 6, "The Ache of Guilt."

47. Fussell, "Hiroshima: A Soldier's View," p. 29.

48. *Ibid.*, p. 27.

49. Michael Walzer, *Just and Unjust Wars: A Moral Argument with Historical Illustrations* (New York: Basic Books, 1977; 2nd. ed., 1992).

50. *Ibid.*, 1st ed., p. xvi. This role of the memoirs Walzer read was particularly evident in his lectures on just war prior to the completion of his book. I had the pleasure of auditing these lectures in 1972 to 1973 while I was a postdoctoral Fellow in Law and Religion at the Harvard Law School.

51. Walzer, *Just and Unjust Wars*, 1st ed., p. 140.

52. *Ibid.*, p. 15.

53. *Ibid.*, p. xvii.

54. Walzer, "An Exchange on Hiroshima," *The New Republic* (September 23, 1981):13–14.

55. See Fussell, "An Exchange on Hiroshima," *The New Republic* (September 23, 1981):14. Elsewhere Fussell notes that World War II produced his sense of irony. See "My War," and *Doing Battle: The Making of a Skeptic.*

56. Fussell, "My War."

57. This was part of Gustafson's argument about principles and context in his classic essay.

Contributors

JOHN D. ARRAS is the Porterfield Professor of Biomedical Ethics at the University of Virginia, Charlotte, where he directs the Undergraduate Bioethics Program. Before coming to Virginia in 1995, he was for fourteen years a professor of bioethics at Montefiore Medical Center/Albert Einstein College of Medicine and Adjunct Professor of Philosophy at Barnard College, Columbia University. He is the editor (with Bonnie Steinbock) of *Ethical Issues in Modern Medicine*, 4th ed. (Mayfield, 1995) and *Bringing the Hospital Home: Ethical and Social Implications of High Technology Home Care* (Johns Hopkins, 1995).

HOWARD BRODY is Professor of Family Practice and Philosophy, and Director of the Center for Ethics and Humanities in the Life Sciences, at Michigan State University in East Lansing. He is a practicing physician and the author of *Stories of Sickness* (Yale University Press, 1987) and *The Healer's Power* (Yale University Press, 1992), as well as various papers on the application of narrative concepts to medicine and to medical ethics.

RONALD A. CARSON is Harris L. Kempner Professor and Director of the Institute for Medical Humanities at the University of Texas Medical Branch at Galveston. With Thomas Murray, he edits *Medical Humanities Review*. Most recently he also edited, with Chester R. Burns, *Philosophy of Medicine and Bioethics: A Twenty-Year Retrospective and Critical Appraisal* (Kluwer, 1997).

RITA CHARON is Associate Professor of Clinical Medicine at the College of Physicians and Surgeons of Columbia University, New York, and a doctoral candidate in the Department of English and Comparative Literature of Columbia University. She maintains an active practice as a general internist and directs medical student education in the medical humanities. She has published and lectured widely on topics of narrative theory, narrative ethics, patient-physician communication, empathy in medicine, and the narrative forms of Henry James.

TOD CHAMBERS is Assistant Professor of Medical Ethics and Humanities at Northwestern University Medical School. He has published in the *Hastings Center Report,* the *Journal of Medicine and Philosophy,* and *Literature and Medicine.* His research interests focus on the rhetoric of bioethics and cross-cultural issues in clinical medicine.

JAMES F. CHILDRESS is the Kyle Professor of Religious Studies and Professor of Medical Education at the University of Virginia, Charlottesville. Coauthor (with Tom Beauchamp) of *Principles of Biomedical Ethics,* 4th ed. (Oxford, 1994), he has also written *Priorities in Biomedical Ethics* (Westminister Press, 1981), *Who Should Decide? Paternalism in Health Care* (Oxford University Press, 1982), and *Practical Reasoning in Bioethics* (Indiana University Press, 1997). He has served on the national Task Force on Organ Transplantation, the board of directors of the United Network for Organ Sharing, the UNOS Ethics Committee, the Recombinant DNA Advisory Committee, and the Biomedical Ethics Advisory Committee. In July 1996 President Clinton appointed him to the newly formed National Bioethics Advisory Commission.

ARTHUR W. FRANK is Professor of Sociology at the University of Calgary, in Alberta, Canada. He is the author of *At the Will of the Body: Reflections on Illness* (Houghton Mifflin, 1991) and *The Wounded Storyteller: Body, Illness, and Ethics* (Chicago University Press, 1995). From 1994 to 1996 he edited the "Case Stories" series in the journals *Second Opinion* and *Making the Rounds in Health, Faith, and Ethics.* He is an associate editor and contributor to the journal *Body & Society* and writes frequently for *The Christian Century.*

JOHN HARDWIG is Professor of Philosophy at East Tennessee State University, Johnson City, where he also teaches in the medical school. He has published a number of essays in anthologies and such journals as *Ethics,* the *Journal of Philosophy,* and the *Hastings Center Report* on the ethics of personal relationships, social epistemology, and the role of families in medical treatment decisions.

ANNE HUNSAKER HAWKINS is Associate Professor of Humanities at Pennsylvania State University College of Medicine. A specialist in medieval English literature, she is the author of *Archetypes of Conversion* (Associated University Press, 1985), *Reconstructing Illness: Studies in Pathography* (Purdue University Press, 1993), and, with James O. Ballard, *Time to Go: Three Plays on Death and Dying* (University of Pennsylvania Press, 1995). She coedited, with K. Danner Clouser, an issue of the *Journal of Medicine and Philosophy* (June 1996) on the topic of literature and medical ethics. At present she is working with Marilyn Chandler McEntyre on *Teaching Literature and Medicine,* a volume in the Modern Language Association's Options for Teaching series.

KATHRYN MONTGOMERY HUNTER is Professor of Medical Ethics and Humanities and of Medicine at Northwestern University Medical School and Director of its Program in Medical Ethics and Humanities. Author of *Doctors' Stories: The Narrative Structure of Medical Knowledge* (Princeton University Press, 1991), she is interested in the curious process that turns science students into physicians.

MARK KUCZEWSKI is Assistant Professor of Bioethics at the Medical College of Wisconson in Milwakee, where he directs the Master of Arts in Bioethics programs. A philosopher by training, his main research interest has been the relationship between theory and practice. He is the author of *Fragmentation and Consensus: Communitarian and Casuist Bioethics* (Georgetown University Press, 1997).

JAN MARTA is Assistant Professor at the University of Toronto in the Department of Psychiatry and at the Joint Centre for Bioethics. A psychiatrist, she also holds a French doctorate in comparative literature and has published on literary theory and criticism, psychoanalytic thought, and medical ethics. She is writing a book on a poststructuralist psychoanalytic, linguistic, and literary model of informed consent.

MARTHA MONTELLO is an instructor of Social Medicine in the Division of Medical Ethics at Harvard Medical School. She teaches courses in narrative ethics and literature and medicine for both preclinical and clinical students, and also develops ethics curricula for the required patient-doctor course. Currently she is working on a book about the physician-writer Walker Percy.

THOMAS H. MURRAY is Professor of Biomedical Ethics and Director of the Center for Biomedical Ethics in the School of Medicine at Case Western Reserve University in Cleveland. He is a founding editor of *Medical Humanities Review*, a member of the U.S. Olympic Committee's Sports Medicine Committee, and a member of the ethics committee of HUGO (the Human Genome Organization). A founder of the Working Group on Ethical, Legal, and Social Issues to the NIH, he is also a presidential appointee to the National Bioethics Advisory Commission. His most recent book is *The Worth of a Child* (University of California Press, 1996).

HILDE LINDEMANN NELSON is Director of the Center for Applied and Professional Ethics at the University of Tennessee, Knoxville. An editor at the *Hastings Center Report* from 1990 to 1995, she writes on issues in bioethics and feminist theory, and is the author (with James Lindemann Nelson) of *The Patient in the Family* (Routledge, 1995) and *Alzheimer's: Answers to Hard Questions for Families* (Doubleday, 1996). She is also the editor of *Feminism and Families* (Routledge, 1997) and coedits the Reflective Bioethics series for Routledge.

LOIS LaCIVITA NIXON is Associate Professor in the Division of Medical Ethics and Humanities of the College of Medicine, University of South Florida. During her tenure as chair of the governing board for Tampa General Health Systems, she established the hospital ethics committee and was instrumental in developing the Tampa Bay Ethics consortium. She is coauthor of *Literary Anatomies: Women's Bodies and Health in Literature* (SUNY Press, 1994) and coeditor of *On Doctoring* (Simon and Schuster, 1995) and *Trials, Tribulations and Celebrations: African Perspectives on Health, Illness, Aging, and Loss* (Intercultural Press, 1992).

TOM TOMLINSON is Professor in the Department of Philosophy and the Center for Ethics and Humanities in the Life Sciences at Michigan State University, where he has taught health care ethics to medical, nursing, and veterinary students since 1981. In addition, he teaches graduate courses in the Department of Philosophy and in the Interdisciplinary Programs in Health and Humanities, which he directs. He is currently at work on a book about methodologies in bioethics.

CHARLES WEIJER, a physician, is a bioethicist at Mount Sinai Hospital/Joint Centre for Bioethics, University of Toronto. He is currently completing a Ph.D. in experimental medicine at McGill University and his research is supported by a fellowship from the Medical Research Council of Canada.

Index